Marlowe's Complaint

Peter B. Hodges

Published by New Generation Publishing in 2021

Copyright © Peter B. Hodges 2021

First Edition

The author asserts the moral right under the Copyright, Designs and Patents Act 1988 to be identified as the author of this work.

All Rights reserved. No part of this publication may be reproduced, stored in a retrieval system or transmitted, in any form or by any means without the prior consent of the author, nor be otherwise circulated in any form of binding or cover other than that which it is published and without a similar condition being imposed on the subsequent purchaser.

ISBN   978-1-80369-064-3

www.newgeneration-publishing.com

New Generation Publishing

For Fred,
    who doubted,

and Sharlene,
    who did not.

Contents

Chapter One: Christopher Marlowe's Dangerous Letter 3
Chapter Two: Immortall 17
Chapter Three: a Marriage Proposal 29
Chapter Four: The Essex Plot 47
Chapter Five: What Really Happened in Deptford and Why 61
Chapter Six: Christopher Marlowe's Motto 74
Chapter Seven: Philip Sidney's Device 88
Chapter Eight: Working for Walsingham 106
Chapter Nine: The Man Who Wasn't There 122
Chapter Ten: The Stylometric Fallacy 138
Chapter Eleven: Theatrical Agents 156
Chapter Twelve: Enchanted Summer 172
Chapter Thirteen: Strange Brew 189
Chapter Fourteen: Enter Shaxpere 203
Chapter Fifteen: The Unfortunate Traveler 218
Chapter Sixteen: Marlowe and Rape 235
Chapter Seventeen: The Night of Errors 254
Chapter Eighteen: Publish or Perish 276
Chapter Nineteen: Love on the Run 297
Chapter Twenty: Love's Wound 313
Chapter Twenty One: The Missing Person 331
Chapter Twenty Two: Mr. W.H 347
Epilogue 370
Acknowledgements 383
Notes 384

Chapter One

Christopher Marlowe's Dangerous Letter

Sometime late in 1598, Christopher Marlowe, the brilliant poet and playwright, wrote a scathing letter to his patron and protector, Sir Thomas Walsingham. Accusing him of having an "inconstant mind"[1], Marlowe threatened to "set down a story of faults concealed"[2] and challenged him to "hate me when thou wilt."[3] Sir Thomas, veteran of his "uncle's" anti-Catholic intelligence service, would immediately have recognized the danger. Marlowe, who most of the English-speaking world believed had notoriously been "stabd to death by a bawdy seruing man"[4] in a sleazy tavern brawl in mid-1593, was very much alive and threatening to reveal a secret that had kept them both safe for more than five years.

Not unlike a photograph of a kidnap victim forced to display the date on a copy of today's London Times, this fateful letter was proof of Marlowe's survival. It unmistakably identified a third celebrity, a rival poet, who Marlowe believed had been hired by Sir Thomas to replace him. Worse, if the letter had fallen into the wrong hands, it would inevitably come to the attention of the hot blooded and extremely ambitious Robert Deveraux, second Earl of Essex, the man who had attacked Marlowe forcing him to run for his life in the Spring of 1593. The letter would prove that Sir Thomas had helped Marlowe escape. While a handful on the Queen's Privy Council knew he had survived, and a few friends suspected, written proof of it in Marlowe's own hand addressed to Sir Thomas would be their ultimate death warrant. With that in his hands, Essex could finally destroy them both.

In all his previous correspondence, Marlowe had been careful to avoid making mention of any current events. Knowing that if anyone could link a message in one of his letters to the present, they might realize that he was not, in fact, dead, his earlier letters to Sir Thomas had never mentioned politics or policy. He ignored parades and proclamations, and never spoke of recent plays or poems, especially not his own. Instead, he emphasized either his continuing love and respect for the man who had risked everything to save his life or pleaded for his return from the exile that had been the result. Now, however, he had reason to believe that Thomas was turning on him, that he might even sacrifice him to Essex to protect his own family. In response, with fear and anger, he threatened to "tell all."

What could Marlowe have known that would cause Sir Thomas to think twice about turning on him? For one thing, long before he had become a renowned poet and playwright, Christopher Marlowe had been a "secret agent" for the crown. Known in their day as "intelligencers", they served as couriers, spies and occasionally as enforcers, men capable of violence for political ends. Marlowe may not have been violent himself, but he certainly knew such people and, more importantly, he knew where the bodies were buried.

He had been recruited while still a student at Cambridge, if not earlier, and had been protected in that role by the Queen's Privy Council. Proof of this appeared in 1587 when he was about to be denied his MA degree due to frequent absences. That June a clerk recorded the draft of a letter which conveyed the Council's request that Marlowe:

> "should be furthered in the degree he was to take this next Commencement: Because it was not her majestie's pleasure that anie one emploied as he had been in matters touching the benefit of his Countrie should be defamed by those that are ignorant in th'affaires he went about."[5]

The letter was signed by William Cecil, 1st Baron of Burghley and Elizabeth's Secretary of State and Treasurer, intelligence chief Sir Francis Walsingham, Sir Thomas' close relative, and

Arch-Bishop Whitgift, head of the Anglican church. With the support of three of the most powerful men in all of England, Marlowe's degree was awarded shortly thereafter in July.

Marlowe had been regularly engaged as a courier and intelligencer since 1583 when he first started writing for the Queen's Men, an acting troupe organized by Sir Francis Walsingham "in connection with the intelligence system". The company deployed "alert persons - writers for example - who could be employed for specific tasks"[6] such as recording attendance at performances and gathering other local information. He had also been installed "as Arbella Stuart's tutor"[7] to keep an eye on the great-great-granddaughter of King Henry VII of England who was favored in the line of succession by various Catholic sympathizers. And, when Fernando Stanley decided to celebrate his elevation to the title of Lord Strange by creating Lord Strange's Men to rival the Queen's Men onstage, Marlowe was installed as one of their leading playwrights while making frequent reports on Stanley's Catholic activities.

The young Essex, meanwhile, had been making his first attempts to take command of the intelligence service. He believed that would increase his influence at court and he pressed his challenge when Sir Francis died in late 1590. His ambition was bitterly disappointed when control of the intelligence network reverted instead to the firm hand of Lord Burghley, Walsingham's director. Essex was further displeased when Burghley passed the daily intelligence responsibilities to his son, Robert Cecil, even though the Earl had been stridently campaigning for the position and had been recruiting Walsingham's men into his own web. Inevitably, Marlowe, who had first worked for Walsingham and then for Burghley and Cecil, became a pawn in the middle of a power struggle between Essex and Burghley, one that would determine the fate of the English crown and define an era.

Marlowe had by then become one of Burghley's most valuable assets. Capable of charming the most elite society while simultaneously trafficking with the crudest thugs, he seemed to have infinite untapped potential. Burghley had plans to advance him and Essex believed that thwarting those plans would help him undermine Burghley's empire. For all his fame, Marlowe was vulnerable because of his identification with some of his most outrageous theatrical characters, including the atheist Faust and terrorist Tamburlaine. Seizing an opportunity created by religious unrest, Essex managed to back Marlowe into a corner by launching a "smear campaign"[8] which incriminated Marlowe. Accused of atheism and sedition, Marlowe was put under investigation by the same Privy Council that had previously defended him, a cabinet which by then included Essex as well as Burghley, Cecil and the Archbishop. In the upshot, Marlowe barely escaped interrogation and hanging by way of a staged dispute in a Deptford tavern with family connections to Lord Burghley. The following day, the poet and playwright had been officially declared dead by the Queen's Coroner.

The cover story of Marlowe's infamous demise had served to keep his secret so safe that it almost seemed as if he had been entirely forgotten. He repeatedly complained about this in his letters to Sir Thomas, second cousin to Sir Francis and himself a former intelligencer who had been instrumental in bringing down Mary Queen of Scots. Marlowe's career as a spy further fed the rumor, which that year had found its way into print, that his death had been the just result of his "Atheism and impiety."[9] But neither a damaged reputation nor personal safety mattered as much to him as the possibility, however remote, that he might someday return to London. That had been a promise that he believed Thomas had made to him before he had been forced to flee. For years Marlowe had survived with Walsingham's loyal support, but suddenly in 1598 he had powerful reasons to believe that Thomas was planning to drop him, cut off all sustenance and leave him stranded and anonymous in permanent exile.

Thomas Walsingham had been a cool and careful part of the Queen's intelligence service since October, 1580[10], longer than Marlowe. When they first met, Thomas had been working as a courier for Sir Francis' network for several years. By 1581 had become Sir Francis protégé, accompanying him to Paris during the unsuccessful attempt to negotiate Elizabeth's proposed marriage with the French king's brother, Francis, Duke of Anjou. These early adventures led to further responsibilities later in the decade, when he is believed to have become Marlowe's "case officer".[11] He also collected intelligence from Robert Poley[12], chief operative in exposing the Babington Plot which ultimately led to the execution of Mary, Queen of Scots. It was during this enterprise that he also met Nicholas Skeers and Ingram Frizer who, along with Poley, were all on the scene in Deptford when Marlowe made his hasty escape.

Thomas' career as an intelligencer took a sudden turn in November 1589 when his older brother, Edmund, passed away at the age of 32, still a bachelor. Although he was the youngest of four brothers, Thomas was thus the sole surviving son when, at the age of 26, he became eligible to inherit the Walsingham estate which "placed on par with the other great Elizabethan houses of Kent, such as Knole and Penshurst."[13] It could not have been surprising then that when his "uncle" Sir Francis died after prolonged illness in April, 1590, and Lord Burghley took over the intelligence operation, Thomas stepped away from the trade to concentrate on his new role as landed gentry.

This new status seems to have enhanced Thomas' friendship with Marlowe as he became both patron and confidant. Marlowe had been keeping at the Walsingham estate in Scadbury when the Privy Council issued its summons for him in May 1593 and the two had exchanged frequent correspondence throughout the following years of his exile. These letters were more than the formalistic exchanges between a patron and his servant, they were heartfelt, sincere avowals of an abiding devotion which, by themselves, were they discovered by unfriendly eyes, could call into question the nature of Walsingham's friendship with their author. To protect him they had always been written in a kind of code and they were so artful that Walsingham kept them as reminders of a connection that, no matter how strained by time and distance, remained powerful and undeniable. But, following the death of Burghley in 1598, it appeared that things had changed.

One of those things was the fact that Thomas had been knighted, most likely on a private visit by the Queen to his Scadbury estate in 1597[14]. No less significantly, he had in the interim married the beautiful and vivacious Audrey Shelton. Daughter of Sir Ralph Shelton of Shelton, Norfolk, Audrey served as Elizabeth's Lady of the Bedchamber. Perhaps in celebration of his elevation, Sir Thomas made his wife a gift of Marlowe's recently published but unfinished poem, Hero and Leander. To further enhance the offering, he engaged the services of the widely admired and rising young poet, George Chapman, to complete it and compose a dedication to Audrey.

It was news of this gift that made Christopher Marlowe not merely apoplectic, but terrified. While two other versions of Hero and Leander had been published earlier in that same year, this time it was published as a joint composition by Marlowe and Chapman as if it had been passed as a torch from one poet, officially confirmed dead, to another newly enshrined as Walsingham's favorite. To Marlowe, it must have seemed like the newly created peer was not only preparing to replace him with a newly favored poet, but in the process cut him loose entirely, leaving him permanently adrift and exposed to the dangers still alive in the person and long reach of the Earl of Essex.

Marlowe had been working on Hero and Leander when he'd been at Scadbury in the Spring of 1593. It was one of his last projects before the incident that forced him to bolt out of London. He apparently left the unfinished manuscript with Thomas. It was then entered with Marlowe's translation of The First Book of Lucan in the Stationer's Register by London's City Printer, John Wolfe, on 28 September 1593, barely three months after Marlowe disappeared from London. Wolfe did not print either poem, however, and the rights to both passed to Edward Blount, best known today as the publisher of The First Folio. In 1598, Blount published Marlowe's original "unfinished" version with Blount's own dedication of the volume to Thomas Walsingham. Lest anyone forget, Blount repeatedly made note of Marlowe's officially deceased status, observing that "that in his lifetime" Walsingham "bestowed many kind favors" on Marlowe, and that:

> "whatsoever issue of his brain should chance to come abroad, that the first breath of it should take might be the gentle air of your liking; for since his self had been accustomed thereunto, it would prove more agreeable and thriving to his right children than any other foster countenance whatsoever."[15]

Blount's publication was soon followed by a version with additions by Henry Petowe, the first to attempt to complete the original. Petowe dedicated his publication to Henrie Guilford Knight, H. P., who served as Henry VIII's Master of the Horse and died in 1532 without issue. The poem was published by Thomas Purfoot for Andrew Harris, neither of whom have any obvious connections to Walsingham, Blount or John Wolfe. Petowe's additions were shorter than Marlowe's original, only 682 lines as opposed Marlowe's 819, and undistinguished but included a tribute to Marlowe, whom Petowe obviously believed was dead:

> "Whose name in Fames immortall treasurie,
> Truth shall record to endless memorie,
> Marlo late mortall, now fram'd all divine."[16]

Of the three versions, Petowe's was the least successful; it never resulted in a reprint while the Blount and later Chapman versions were reprinted five times by 1609. Together, they established Hero and Leander as a contemporary best seller. Marlowe may or may not have been thinking of Petowe when he complained in his furious letter that "every alien pen hath got my use, and under thee their poesy disperse."[17] Regardless, he clearly held Walsingham responsible.

Publishing in the Elizabethan era was neither cheap nor without risk. Publishing pirated texts was the surest way to run afoul of the Stationers' Company and no one understood the consequences of printing piracy better than John Wolfe, whose entire career before becoming Beadle of the Stationers' Company in 1587 had been in printing unlicensed manuscripts and purloined copies of other publisher's work. As the company enforcer, however, he pursued violators aggressively and served as a legal assistant in several cases the Stationers' brought against other printers.[18] It seems remarkable therefore that a manuscript by an author of doubtful reputation thought long dead and which was registered by Wolfe himself only to languish unpublished for six years suddenly appeared under two separate imprints in two separate shops, only one of which should have had legitimate right to it.

For three separate publishers to produce three separate versions of the very same poem in the same year suggests that something unusual was happening behind the scenes. Of all the people involved in this multiple enterprise, Christopher Marlowe would have had the least idea why this poem was suddenly in such remarkable currency at the very moment when he would feel such personal uncertainty. Regardless, it was Chapman's version that upset him the most, particularly because it was dedicated to Lady Audrey, Sir Thomas' wife.

Chapman seems to have felt it incumbent upon him to explain why he decided to complete a poem already in print. In his dedication, he asserted that he had been "drawn by strange inspiration to employ some of my serious time in so trifling a subject, which yet made the first author, divine Musaeus, eternal." He then elaborated on this theme in what he called the Third Sestiad, the first in his continuation, explaining that a "most strangely-intellectual fire", presumably Marlowe's, "drunk to me half this Musaean story", specifically Marlowe's half, and inspired him to finish it so that "neither's draught be consecrate to sleep"[19].

Chapman's claim to Marlovian authority struck biographer John Bakeless as "obscure with more than Elizabethan obscurity"[20] but he nevertheless considered it "quite possible" that, before he died, Marlowe asked Chapman to finish the poem. Neither Bakeless nor any other holder of this opinion has explained when or how this request was transmitted and whether it occurred at Deptford, or Scadbury, or sometime before when Marlowe had no reason to suspect that the poem would be finished by anyone other than himself, if at all.[21]

If Petowe was an annoyance and Marlowe's reference to him glancing, Chapman was an actual threat and Marlowe cited him and his earlier work specifically in his letter. Clearly, he wanted Sir Thomas to know why he was upset and by whom. In fact, he proceeded to check off the list of Chapman's previously published work, leaving no doubt whatsoever about the target of his wrath.

In that same year Chapman had published his first translation of Homer, titled <u>Seven Books of The Illiad</u>, books I, II and VII through XI. This was then and is still considered one of the singular achievements in Elizabethan poetry and it easily eclipsed Marlowe's own translations of Ovid's <u>Amores</u> (1582?). That Chapman had dedicated this poem to the Earl of Essex could not have comforted Marlowe. If Thomas Walsingham had somehow not been aware of this dedication to their mutual enemy before he hired Chapman, he certainly would have discovered it immediately after Marlowe's letter.

Speaking sarcastically, Marlowe wrote:

> "O, how I faint when I of you do write,
> Knowing a better spirit doth use your name,
> And in the praise thereof spends all his might
> To make me tongue-tied speaking of your fame.
> But since your worth, wide as the ocean is,
> The humble as the proudest sail doth bear,
> My saucy bark, inferior far to his,
> On your broad main doth willfully appear."[22]

Marlowe's use of sea faring imagery, "ocean", "bark", "sail" and "main" recall Odysseus' epic journey as translated by

Chapman. His use of "spirit" would be repeated and would similarly aim at Chapman.

Chapman's first published work was <u>The Shadow of Night</u> (1594). It was composed of two hymns, one to Night and one to Cynthia (Passion), modeled on Greek hymns of Proclus, Callimachus, and the Orphic hymns with borrowings and echoes from contemporary literature. Marlowe fingered the poem with a sneer:

> "I think good thoughts whilst others write good words,
> And, like unlettered clerk, still cry 'Amen'
> To every hymn that able spirit affords
> In polished form of well-refined pen."[23]

Both of these poems were printed after Marlowe's flight from London. He appears not only aware of Chapman's reputation but seems to have read the work himself as his evaluation of it is personal. His identification of Chapman is so specific that, despite the careful omission of his name, the question of his identity is no longer held in doubt by the great majority of scholars familiar with the subject. Indeed, this would be no more obscure to Thomas Walsingham, the man who had this same poet dedicate a 1500-line poem to his wife than the phrase "I'll be back" would be to movie audiences today.

Marlowe then aimed his anger directly at Chapman's claim of "strange inspiration":

> "Was it his spirit, by spirits taught to write
> Above a mortal pitch, that struck me dead?
> No, neither he, nor his compeers by night
> Giving him aid, my verse astonishèd.
> He, nor that affable familiar ghost
> Which nightly gulls him with intelligence,
> As victors of my silence cannot boast;"[24]

With "spirit" and "ghost" Marlowe satirized Chapman's homage to "divine Musaeus", the author of the original legend, and with "compeers by night" and "nightly" he mocks Chapman's "sleep". Chapman could not silence him, Marlowe insisted, but Walsingham could:

> "When thou shalt be disposed to set me light
> And place my merit in the eye of scorn,
> Upon thy side against myself I'll fight
> And prove thee virtuous, though thou art foresworn.
> With my own weakness being best acquainted,
> Upon thy part I can set down a story
> Of faults concealed wherein I am attained,
> That thou in losing me shall attain much glory."[25]

By threatening to tell his own story, however, Marlowe knew he was contemplating a terrible risk. What he feared most was that Walsingham had already decided to cut him loose and that his patronage of Chapman and Chapman's appropriation of his work was confirmation of this intent. Despairing to the point of hopelessness, he concluded his letter thus:

> "If thou wilt leave me, do not leave me last,
> When other petty griefs have done their spite,
> But in the onset come; so shall I taste
> At first the very worst of Fortune's might,
>   And other strains of woe, which now seem woe,
>   Compared with loss of thee will not seem so."[26]

Marlowe's fateful letter was written in the form of a series of fifteen sonnets each including twelve lines with a rhyme scheme of abab cdcd efef and a two-line couplet. Mary Queen of Scots had had her head chopped off for signing a letter far less revealing. Sir Thomas had participated in the government plot that acquired that letter. If the Earl of Essex had ever laid hands on Marlowe's letter he would have had the very tool to put Walsingham and even Cecil in the Tower awaiting trial for their lives as protectors of a traitor. It was imperative that Thomas keep the letter secret.

A little more than ten years later, however, after Essex's plots had all failed and he himself had been hung for treason, Marlowe's letter was finally published, along with 139 other sonnets, as Shake-Speare's Sonnets and A Lover's Complaint in 1609. If the intent was to conceal Marlowe's hand either in the form of a cipher or by mingling it with sonnets from one or another's hand, it succeeded beyond anyone's imagining: the format has succeeded in confusing generations of scholars ever since. Remarkably, one of the major points of academic dispute has been the identity of the "Rival Poet" attacked in the letter. While the identity of this rival would not have escaped Essex, it is significantly problematic for modern scholars.

The first person to assert that Chapman was the leading candidate for the title of "The Rival Poet" was William Minto, Professor of Logic and English at The University of Aberdeen. In his 1874 volume, Characteristics of English Poets from Chaucer to Shirley, Professor Minto based his conclusion on a "probable connection with Southampton" and all of the internal evidence which he thought was "too pointed to be mistaken."[27] While this identification has since been disputed, John Kerrigan summed up the current consensus: "if an identification had to be made on the strength of Sonnet 86 alone, Chapman would seem a strong candidate."[28] This identification has been seconded by the majority of leading scholars, including Arthur Acheson[29], F. J. Furnival[30], and more recently Katherine Duncan-Jones[31].

The chief difficulty with Chapman, as it is with almost all the other possible "rivals", is that the scholarly community is at pains to explain why Shakespeare would have any reason to attack any of them, particularly Chapman. Arthur Acheson attempted to explain it as a feud prompted by Chapman's supposed jealousy of Southampton's patronage of Shakespeare:

> "We know that The Shadow of Night, issued in 1594, was the first published poem of Chapman's; and that Ovid's Banquet of Sense, The Amorous Zodiac, and A

> Coronet for his Mistress Philosophy, issued in 1595, were the second published efforts of his Muse; yet we find that he rages and fumes both in these poems and in their dedications, over his lack of patronage. It is reasonable to infer that he would not do this unless he had sought such patronage and been repulsed. The poems of both these years are dedicated to his friend Matthew Roydon, a poor scholar like himself; but the disgruntled tone of these dedications argues that Chapman had previously sought a more shining mark than his friend Roydon as sponsor for the children of his brain. There can be little doubt but that Chapman was numbered amongst the many suitors who were drawn at this time, by the fame of Shakespeare's success, to seek some share of Southampton's bounty."[32]

In this version, Chapman must have been jealous of Shakespeare, even if he never actually says that, and therefore he must have attacked him in print, even if no trace of this attack can be found. Shakespeare, therefore, able to read Chapman's intent with finer clarity than the most able modern scholar, responded in sonnets that weren't published for more than a decade after the fact but were distributed among mutual friends all of whom were in on the game and also understood clearly, although no one has since, what was going on.

The fact that Chapman never actually names or refers by way of poetic proxy to either Shakespeare or Southampton, apparently, is more of the "Elizabethan obscurity" which seems to pervade this affair. It is even more difficult to believe that there is anything substantive here when Chapman's unfocused ire is compared with Ben Jonson's all too direct attacks on Shakespeare which received no response whatsoever.

It never seems to occur to anyone that the reason these things are so obscure is because they aren't there at all. Instead, what has happened is that this very obscurity, this difficulty of locating what cannot be found has forced contemporary scholars to look away, to search for meaning in textual devices such as line endings and word repetitions and vowel counts, all of which leads to more uncertainty and equivocation, as if the words themselves could not be trusted to convey their own plain meaning. The scholars, it seems, have got the right rival, but the wrong writer.

Keep in mind that the universe of people who could possibly have written those sonnets of such high quality and specificity for the purpose of attacking George Chapman is extraordinarily small. It is a universe of one. George Chapman was commissioned for the explicit purpose of imitating Marlowe and had unlimited access to the very poem he was to mimic, and he could not come close. No writer of his generation was ever able to match Marlowe's mighty line. The very notion is preposterous.

No one knows for certain what Thomas Walsingham thought upon receipt of Marlowe's letter and its reckless threat to tell all. If he had intended to compliment Marlowe's genius with Chapman's additions, then the gesture had exploded on itself and put him in an even greater danger than when he'd helped stage manage the demise of Mary Queen of Scots in 1586. Marlowe had crossed a line that Thomas could not ignore. Officially on notice, he kept the letter and its threat to himself; it was not seen again until eleven years had passed.

That said, what seems abundantly clear from all of this is that Christopher Marlowe was alive and well in 1598, so furious and terrified that his best friend and protector had replaced him in the eyes of the world with the pretender, George Chapman, that he seemed prepared to say or do anything no matter how dangerous to himself or the Walsingham family. Sir Thomas could not know then whether or not Marlowe would make good on his threat, but he did know that Marlowe would continue to write, and that Essex was watching.

Chapter Two

Immortall

Anyone who doubts that Christopher Marlowe was alive in 1598 needs to take a closer look at sonnet 81:

> Or I shall live your Epitaph to make,
> Or you survive when I in earth am rotten,
> From hence your memory death cannot take,
> Although in me each part will be forgotten.
> Your name from hence immortall life shall have,
> Though I (once gone) to all the world must dye,
> The earth can yeeld me but a common grave,
> When you intombed in mens eyes shall lye,
> Your monument shall be my gentle verse,
> Which eyes not yet created shall ore-read,
> And toungs to be, your being shall rehearse,
> When all the breathers of this world are dead,
>   You still shall live (such virtue hath my pen)
>   Where breath most breaths, even in the mouths of men.

Traditional and non-traditional scholars have almost uniformly asserted that this sonnet "appears to diverge from the theme of the 'rival poets'"[33] and "interrupts the rival poet(s) sequence"[34]. They are no less certain that the sonnet is addressed to the hypothetical "fair youth" who is doubtless male even though "we never learn the young man's name."[35] All of that is wrong. The sonnet does not interrupt the sequence, it is not addressed to a male and, in fact, we already know the name of the person to whom it is addressed.

Audrey Walsingham was the person to whom George Chapman dedicated his version of Christopher Marlowe's <u>Hero and Leander</u> in 1598. When Marlowe wrote "Your monument shall be my gentle verse" it was true. It was true then in 1598, it was true when the Sonnets were first published in 1609 and it is still true today. Every single copy of Hero and Leander proves it.

It is important to recognize that this is a separate line of confirmation that Chapman was the Rival Poet. It runs not through Thomas Walsingham, who commissioned the extended poem as a gift, it runs through Audrey who received it. If all the other sonnets appear to be addressed to Thomas, this one is addressed specifically to Audrey alone. While sonnets 80, 85 and 86 each refers to Chapman's contemporaneous published poetry, this line of confirmation makes reference solely to the dedication of Hero and Leander itself which reads, in part:

> "This poor Dedication (in figure of the other unity betwixt Sir Thomas and yourself) hath rejoined you with him, my honoured best friend; whose continuance of ancient kindness to my still-obscured estate, though it cannot increase my love to him which hath been entirely circular; yet shall it encourage my deserts to their utmost requital, and make my hearty gratitude speak; to which the unhappiness of my life hath hitherto been uncomfortable and painful dumbness.
>
> By your Ladyship's vowed in
> most wished service,
> GEORGE CHAPMAN.

Chapman claimed that his additions to Hero and Leander were married to Marlowe's original in a fashion similar to Audrey's marriage to Thomas, which he considered a fitting parallel. Marlowe, on the other hand, asserted that it is his poem, not Chapman's, which will be her monument. Sonnet 81, therefore, is not an interruption in the sequence, it is central to the argument and to the attribution of the individuals identified in the sequence. None of which has anything to do with Shakespeare.

Audrey Walsingham was no mere matrimonial ornament. As a Lady of the Queen's Bedchamber she was "given a secret cipher to correspond with [Robert] Sidney"[36], Lady Pembroke and Philip's younger brother who had been English governor of Flushing when Marlowe was arrested there on charges of counterfeiting with Richard Baines in 1592. Marlowe was later cleared of all charges by Lord Burghley. Audrey also had business dealings with Thomas' "business agent", Ingram Frizer who took the blame in the Coroner's Inquest for stabbing Marlowe. Later, when King James took the throne, Audrey gave Frizer authority as her agent over several valuable leases of Crown lands granted her by the King. Audrey's marriage to Thomas can be seen, therefore, as a partnership of intelligence agents. It would not be surprising then that her life at court led her to a close relationship with Robert Cecil, head of the intelligence service originally established by Walsingham's "uncle" and later maintained by his father, Lord Burghley.

The youngest of six children born to Sir Ralph Shelton and Mary Wodehouse, Audrey Ethelred Shelton was related by blood with the Queen. Her grandfather, Sir John Shelton, married Anne Boleyn, an aunt of Henry VIII's second wife, the more famous Anne Boleyn and mother of Elizabeth. An old Norfolk family with large estates in Suffolk, the Sheltons "had sheltered Elizabeth during the time of her persecution by her half sister Mary."[37] A. D. Wraight reports that Audrey "was evidently a fascinating woman who, like Arbella Stuart, retained her youthful looks and charm so as to belie her years."

Audrey was known to have a strong interest in theater: her first appearance in Queen Elizabeth's court record memorializes her presence in the Queen's 1599 summer progress and their stopover at the Countess of Derby's mansion, Harefield. A drenching rain gave Audrey the opportunity for an impromptu staging of an entertainment in which she played "a guileless lady" who presented the Queen with "a robe of rainbows"[38] speaking verse "which may have been composed by Audrey herself."[39] Later, in the court of King James, Audrey performed in the masques organized by Anne of Denmark, playing the role of Astraea in Samuel Daniel's The Vision of the Twelve Goddesses, (1604), and Periphere in Ben Jonson's Masque of Blackness (1605). Her first participation in one of Anne's masques may have been in 1603 when, according to Arbella Stuart, "The Queen intendeth to make a mafk this Chriftmas, to which end my Lady Suffolk and my Lady Walfingham hath warrant to take of the late Queen's belt apparrell out of the Tower of theyr difcretion."[40]

Perhaps more significantly, she became a close confidant of Robert Cecil and "some suspected she was his political tool as well as his mistress."[41] While Thomas appears to have been largely content to enjoy the life of a landed Knight at Scadbury and absentee M.P. for Rochester, Audrey was busy making a name for herself as Lady of the Bedchamber to Elizabeth and Mistress of the Robes to Anne with significant influence in both courts.

No biography of Christopher Marlowe has ever made mention of any relationship between him and Lady Walsingham. So far as anyone has ever reported, they never met. It is not known when or under what circumstances Thomas met her or exactly when they married. And yet, here she is, in the middle of the sonnets in the middle of the "Rival Poet" sequence, the person without whom the sequence itself might never have been written. The question then is how did these fifteen particular sonnets come to be included in the middle of a collection attributed to Shakespeare?

The original publication of Shake-speare's Sonnets and A Lover's Complaint appears to have gathered little interest. By comparison, Hero and Leander had already gone through six printings by the time the Sonnets appeared and would be published three times more before an abridged version of the Sonnets emerged in 1640. A fully restored, critical edition of the Sonnets was not available until 1780. It was in this edition, prepared by Edmund Malone, that attention was first drawn the attack on a "better spirit" in a note to Sonnet 80:

> ""Knowing a better spirit doth use your name" Spirit is here, as in many other places, used as a monosyllable. Curiosity will naturally endeavour to find out who this better spirit was, to whom even Shakspeare acknowledges himself inferior. There was certainly no poet in his own time with whom he needed to have feared a comparison; but these Sonnets being probably written when his name was but little known, and at a time when Spenser was the zenith of his reputation, I imagine he was the person here alluded to."[42]

Malone made his observation based on the notion that Shakespeare felt inferior to another poet and then picked the best poet he could think of in the period who was not Shakespeare, in this case Edmund Spenser, author of Faerie Queene (1590). The difficulty with Spenser, however, is that of the specific references in the letter to the works of the "better spirit", the hymns, the allusions to the Illiad by way of sailing imagery, the repeated mention of spirits and ghosts, none of which match any of the poems written by Spenser.

Over the following decades at least a dozen poets suspected of being the "rival" have been rounded up, including Ben Jonson, Michael Drayton, Gervase Markham, Richard Barnfield and even, of all people, Christopher Marlowe. All of them, however, have presented the same problem recognized by Sir Sidney Lee: "none of these shared Southampton's bounty, nor are the terms which Shakespeare applies to his rival's verse specially applicable to the productions of any of them."[43]

When the Sonneteer says that "every alien pen hath got my use", he's not saying that every alien poet is printing their own poems under his name; that's not an insult and it's not piracy; if anything, it would be a compliment. After all, it's not an altogether uncommon name; in his experience there must be many others similarly christened. What he's saying is that his work is being printed under alien names. That is why he feels used. His name, once written, can be rewritten by a hundred different people and still be the same; only he can write a poem to which a hundred others can attach their name.

In order to fit the text to a person, there needs to be a person who, rather than printing his work under Shakespeare's name, printed Shakespeare's work under his name. So far as anyone has ever been able to determine however, that never happened. In fact, the opposite happened so frequently, Shakespeare's name being used as a trademark for the work of a dozen or more others, that it almost precludes the possibility of the opposite.

More than any other Elizabethan writer, Shakespeare has been credited as collaborative author with at least a dozen of his fellow poets. The New Oxford Shakespeare Authorship Companion, the most conservative of scholarly publications, has identified and documented a long list of writers who are believed to have co-written plays with Shakespeare, many of whose contributions are collected under his name in The First Folio, including George Peele (Titus Andronicus, 1589), Christopher Marlowe (Henry VI Parts Two and Three, 1590), Thomas Nashe (Henry VI Part One, 1595), Thomas Kyd (Spanish Tragedy, 1599), Ben Jonson (Sejanus, 1603), Anthony Munday, Henry Chettle, Thomas Heywood and Thomas Dekker (Sir Thomas Moor, 1603-04), Thomas Middleton (Measure for Measure, 1604, All's Well that Ends Well, 1605, Timon of Athens, 1606, and Macbeth, 1606), George Wilkins (Pericles, 1609), and John Fletcher (Cardenio, 1612, Henry VIII, 1613, and Two Noble Kinsmen, 1613)[44]. Shakespeare was additionally credited as author in the original publication of several plays, including Locrine (1595), The First Part of Sir John Oldcastle (1600), The London Prodigal (1605), and The Yorkshire Tragedy (1608) that are not now accepted as being from his pen. An earlier collection of poems, The Passionate Pilgrim (1599), contained twenty poems in all, all of which were credited on the title page to Shakespeare only four of which are now considered appropriately assigned.

And then there is A Lover's Complaint (1609). First included with the Sonnets, its legitimacy was disputed by

William Hazlitt in his Characters of Shakespeare's Plays (1817) where he compared Passionate Pilgrim and A Lover's Complaint and reported that "it has been doubted whether the latter poem is Shakespear's."[45] This doubt was echoed by J.W. Mackail, who made a detailed study of the poem and proposed the "provisional working hypothesis" that "A Lover's Complaint is a composition by the unknown rival poet of the Sonnets."[46] This conclusion was seconded by J.M. Robertson, another scholar known for his in depth textual analysis, who called it "a singularly happy hypothesis."[47] While many others, including Kenneth Miur and Katherine Duncan-Jones believe the poem is genuine, the debate continues unresolved.

Finally, there remains a controversy over whether or not the Sonnets were pirated, a charge made by Sir Sidney Lee who characterized Thorpe's acquisition of the poems as the result of "the predatory work of procuring, no matter how, unpublished and neglected 'copy.'"[48] Katherine Duncan-Jones argued persuasively against this view: "Thorpe was a publisher of some deserved status and prestige, handling work of some close associates of Shakespeare and producing, in many cases, highly authoritative texts"[49]. Arthur Marotti revived these doubts, however, concluding that Thorpe may have "followed a quite ordinary practice of printers in publishing a valuable and interesting manuscript without seeking authorial permission."[50]

In fact, Venus and Adonis (1593), the first publication to bear Shakespeare's name, borrowed heavily from Hero and Leander[51]. John Bakeless argued that "Hero and Leander influenced Shakespeare directly and powerfully when he was writing Venus and Adonis[52]. . . . Shakespeare had read Hero and Leander since he quotes from it, since his scheme and treatment are essentially similar in Venus and Adonis."[53] This is not a contrarian point of view.

Based on this history, it is no stretch to say that Shakespeare's literary career was heavily defined by collaboration and appropriation which included being credited for other writers' work. It is therefore not at all impossible, nor would it be extraordinary for Marlowe's letters to Thomas and Audrey Walsingham, written as a series of sonnets, to have been included in the volume published under the heading Shake-Speare's Sonnets.

It is simply not necessary to assert that William Shakespeare wrote all of the sonnets printed under the title Shake-speare's Sonnets. It is certainly not necessary to assert that he wrote what are now called "the rival poet sonnets."

The question is not who is the "rival poet"? The answer to that question is obvious: George Chapman. The question is who wrote the "rival poet" sonnets? The answer is: Christopher Marlowe.

Was Marlowe thinking of Petowe or Shakespeare when he complained of "alien pens"? After all, both of them appropriated parts of Hero and Leander. Perhaps he thought of them, perhaps not. He was certainly thinking of Chapman; his identification of him is crystal clear. When Henry David Gray asserts that "it is impossible to take seriously Acheson's suggestion that Chapman sought Southampton's patronage but was repulsed, for according to Shakespeare's Sonnets, the rival poet has all the patron's favor"[54] he innocently proves the point. Southampton wasn't Chapman's patron, Thomas Walsingham was. Shakespeare didn't complain about Chapman trying to court favor with Walsingham, Christopher Marlowe did.

Marlowe was writing at a particularly hazardous time. The danger to him was real. Lord Burghley had just passed away[55] leaving his son, Robert Cecil, in charge of his spy network while his chief opponent, the Earl of Essex, was scaling up his challenge to his influence over the crown. Burghley's adversary for the better part of the 1590s, Essex had engaged in a long running battle opposing his moderate diplomacy with Spain and had established his rival intelligence network with the aim of replacing him.

Burghley had been in frail health even when he had approved Walsingham's dangerous gamble for the life Marlowe. He had not only helped Marlowe escape his enemies, he had helped keep his supply line intact even when under attack by Essex or other mutual adversaries such as Archbishop Whitgift, still head of the Anglican church.

Although Cecil was by then the Queen's Secretary of State, he was not as close to Marlowe as his father had been, he had not been instrumental to Walsingham's scheme, had not been part of its execution and could not be expected to honor it as thoroughly as his father had if Essex renewed his attacks. He and Lord Burghley had already had to sacrifice one highly placed agent, Rodrigo Lopez. The Queen's physician and an intelligencer for Burghley, Lopez' fortunes turned when Essex suddenly accused him of being a Spanish spy and possible assassin.

The story goes that Lopez "fell foul of Essex by revealing details of the earl's medical treatments."[56] Essex, it seems, had a case of the pox. The doctor's indiscretion became a mortal allegation in the hands of the furiously ambitious Essex. Played down, even ridiculed at first, Essex persisted and soon exposed evidence of Lopez' Spanish connections which had long been known by and useful to both Burghley and Cecil. Rather than defend their agent, however, they instead covered their flank, advocating the prosecution of and ultimate death sentence for Lopez, who was convicted of treason and hung in June, 1594.

Essex had tried similar tactics against Marlowe using Richard Baines, an informer of uncertain loyalties. In 1582, Baines had been imprisoned and tortured for his role in the so-called Lennox Plot to raise a Catholic army in the north of England. A decade later, Baines was with Marlowe in Flushing in the spring of 1592 attempting to entrap Lord Stanley's agents with a clumsy counterfeiting scam. Lord Burghley, however, did not let Baines off as easily as he treated Marlowe and Baines grew resentful. Soon recruited by Essex, he became one of Marlowe's chief accusers before the Privy Council in 1593. While Essex's scheme against Marlowe had failed to take his head, the poet's exile served his purposes well enough so long as Marlowe kept himself silent and invisible. In 1598, with Burghley out of the picture, Essex would be watchful for any advantage against Cecil and the possibility that Marlowe might be teased into exposing himself would give him special leverage in a contest that had been as personal as it was political since they were boys.

Was Marlowe attempting to simultaneously communicate with his protectors while confusing other readers who might chance to come across his letter, say for instance George Chapman who had dedicated his Illiad to the same Earl of Essex who had chased him out of London and might still pursue him if news of his exile got out? Is that why he consistently chose to write in sonnets what could have been more easily understood in prose? Marlowe was not merely a poet, he was a practiced member of Lord Burghley's intelligence network; he'd been trained by Sir Francis Walsingham and isn't one of the oldest tricks in the intelligencer's toolbox that so long as the investigator keeps asking the wrong question, the suspect never has to answer the right one? And isn't it a maxim of tradecraft that the best place to hide a secret is in plain sight?

The answer to those questions would explain not only why his dangerous letter was written the way it was but also why it has been so difficult to decipher ever since. Why generations of scholars who have focused reflexively on Shake-speare have rarely, if ever, considered even the possibility that not all the sonnets in Shake-speare's Sonnets were written by the man known today as William Shakespeare.

That possibility leads, of course, to the next question: if Christopher Marlowe was alive and wrote a dangerous, highly compromising letter to Thomas Walsingham in late 1598, what happened to him? The answer to that question is the subject of this book.

For now, it is enough to say that Christopher Marlowe did write that dangerous letter in the form of fifteen sonnets where he threatened to tell all in 1598 and that, thankfully, it did not result in a permanent rift between him and his protectors, Sir Thomas and Lady Audrey Walsingham. We know this because he later wrote a second letter, one of reconciliation, which confirms that he survived even that moment of doubt and fear.

It is not certain how or under what circumstances this was accomplished but their renewed friendship was memorialized in this second, shorter letter, which ends:

> "O that our night of woe might have remembered
> My deepest sense how hard true sorrow hits,
> And soon to you, as to me then, tendered
> The humble salve which wounded bosom hits!
>   But that your trespass now becomes a fee;
>   Mine ransoms yours, and yours must ransom me."[57]

The context is highly suggestive, and it is difficult to imagine what Marlowe might think was a worse "night of woe" for them than the night when he ran for his life with the desperate help of Sir Thomas and his agents, Poley, Frizer and Skeers. Clearly, he made his peace with his protector and friend by recalling how much had been risked saving his life.

Many years later, when the danger had passed, after Essex had made his final blundering attempt on the crown and paid for it with his head in 1601, after Queen Elizabeth herself had passed away in 1603 and King James was safely installed, and after Archbishop Whitgift had been laid to rest in 1604, the Sonnets were at last published by Thomas Thorpe, who had begun his publishing career in 1600 with Lucan's First Book, Translated Line for Line by Chr. Marlowe. In his dedication to Lucan, Thorpe claimed that Marlowe's "ghost or genius is to be seen walk the Churchyard, in, at the least, three or four sheets"[58], an apparent reference to the fact that Hero and Leander was in its third printing (or fourth if Petowe is included) that same year. Thorpe, it so happens, had previously been a member of Essex's intelligence syndicate,[59] rival to Cecil, Burghley and Walsingham, but in the manner of many such spies appears to have switched sides. Did Thorpe know then that Marlowe was still alive? Was his reversed allegiance the result of the realization that Essex had hounded Marlowe unfairly? Did he knowingly include Marlowe's fifteen Rival Poet sonnets with other poems by several hands, including A

Lover's Complaint? Thorpe never says. He, after all, was the author of the mysterious dedication of the collection to "Mr.W.H." and obviously knew as well as anyone how to misdirect the curious by crafting the wrong question.

Chapter Three

A Marriage Proposal

If Christopher Marlowe was really alive and writing sonnets in 1598, why then did everyone other than a select few believe that he died in a tavern brawl in May, 1593? Was this belief a mass delusion or was it something more deliberate? Was it all an accident or was it part of a plan?

The answer to these questions and more are at the heart of one of the most notorious political struggles in the last decade of Queen Elizabeth's rule. It involves many of the plots and schemes of the Earl of Essex and is tied directly to his all consuming ambition to surpass the Cecils, Lord Burghley and his youngest son Robert, as the Queen's leading minister and possible heir to the throne of England. Despite all the partisan stakes, however, it all started with the rather prosaic question of how to best accomplish an arranged marriage.

The groom in this case was to have been the young Earl of Southampton. The bride was to be Elizabeth deVere, daughter of Edward deVere, the Earl of Oxford and son-in-law of Lord Burghley, the Queen's Secretary of State.

Even at the age of sixteen, Southampton's personal history was much more interesting than the handsome and charming patron of the arts that is typically portrayed in Shakespearean biographies. His remarkable fortune was the result of his grandfather's tireless campaign against the Catholic monasteries in England on behalf of Henry VIII. The first Earl amassed an enormous legacy by leveling abbeys, chapels and rectories and carting off not only their contents but the stonework, tiles and masonry itself, all sold off on behalf of the crown while the lands were confiscated with the larger holdings in townships and counties across the realm converted to Anglican use. All of this devotion was well rewarded and upon his death at the age of fifty Thomas Wriothsley possessed "the manors of Upton and Ipley, Micheldever, East Stratton, West Meon, North Stoneham and Abbot's Worthy, Popham Grange and lands in the parish of St. Pancras Middlesex."[60]

Loyal service and asset acquisition on behalf of the crown do not guarantee a peerage, however. As Henry had not elevated him prior to his own death in 1547, it fell to Secretary of State Paget to declare the King's deathbed wish promoting Wriosthley to Earl of Southampton, an honor "nobody had the hardihood to question."[61]

The first Earl did not long enjoy his estate, falling ill not three years later and, when he died in 1550, his only son, Henry, became the second Earl at the age of five. Henry immediately became a ward of John Dudley, who had been created Earl of Warwick by the same agency as Southampton and who by that time was Master of Wards and de facto regent for Edward VI. During the subsequent Restoration under Queen Mary, Henry's mother was able to instill her devotion to Roman Catholicism in the young Earl, a faith that was to create complications when Elizabeth succeeded Mary in 1558.

If the first Earl was known for his ardent pursuit of property and position, the second Earl, with nowhere left to climb, was better known for his profligacy and piety, the one in pursuit of the other. From 1568, the time he turned twenty-one and settled his estate until the birth of his son and heir in 1573, he engaged in the dangerous hobby of rebellion, hosting a variety of plots against the Queen and ultimately found himself locked in the Tower of London. It took eighteen months of steady pleading to secure his release, whereupon he again faced imprisonment for the crime of not paying the bill for his first visit. It wasn't until the Countess gave birth to his namesake that he managed to settle down and forego further political adventure.

For the remainder of the decade the Earl enjoyed an extravagant, apolitical lifestyle that came to an abrupt end in 1580 when he accused the Countess of infidelity. The estrangement lasted the rest of his life and strongly affected his son who kept his distance from his mother ever after. The second Earl died in 1581, two days before his son turned eight.

As with his father, the third Earl's care passed to the then Secretary of State, William Cecil, Lord Burghley, the second most powerful person in England, who thereby held the right to determine his eventual marriage. Young Henry moved to Cecil House in London and there met a fifteen year old Robert Deveraux, the Earl of Essex, also a ward of Lord Burghley. Like Essex before him and Roger Manners, the Earl of Rutland after him, Henry took lessons at Cecil House and later proceeded to Cambridge where the three of them formed a friendship that would last into the turn of the century when Essex's ambitions brought them all to grief.

Lord Burghley's long term interest in Southampton's domestic arrangements was memorably noted in his diary where he recorded his ward's age as 16 on his birthdate, October 6, 1589. His next recorded notice of Southampton came on July 15, 1590 in correspondence with Sir Thomas Stanhope, MP for Nottinghamshire, who was apparently upset that Burghley had got the impression he was trying to propose a match between his daughter and the young Earl and wanted to go in writing to assure the Secretary that he never had any such intention but, in fact, supported Burghley's own plan to marry Southampton to his granddaughter, Elizabeth deVere:

> "I apele [appeal] yf she [Lady Southampton, the Earl's mother] can apeche [impeach] me of suche symplisety, or presumption so to Intrude my self, or of the meaning of so trecherous a part towards yor honor having evermore fond [found] my self so bound unto you as I have donne, I name it trechery because I herd before then, you Intended a matche yt way wth [with] the Lady Vayer to whom you know also I am ackyn [kin] And my L[ord] I confesse that talking wth the Countes of Southe hampton thearof she told me you had spoken to her in that behalf, I replyed she should doo well to take hold of it, for I knew not whear my L[ord] her sonne should be better bestowed her self could tell what a stay you would be to hym (& his), and for profit

> experiens did teache her how benefituall you had ben
> unto yr Lady's father (though by him littell deserved)"

Stanhope went on to say that the Earl's mother approved of the plan as well, but that Southampton himself did not:

> "She answered I sayd well & so she thought & would
> in good faythe doo her best in the cause, but saythe she
> I doo not fynd a disposision in my sonne to be tyed as
> yett, what wilbe hereafter tyme shall trye & no want
> shalbe found on my behalf"

Burghley was not to be discouraged by the whims of his young ward, and spreading his net further, put out feelers to others in Southampton's family. As a result, the plan was further addressed on September 10th, 1590 by Viscount Montague, Henry's grandfather, who explained after meeting with Henry that:

> "Ffirst my dawghter [Lady Southampton, the Earl's
> mother] assi upon her faith and honor, thatt she is not
> aquaynt wth any alteration of her sonnes mynd from
> this yor grandechild And we have layd abrode u[nto]
> him bothe the comodityes & hinderances like to […]
> unto him by chaunge And in deede receave to or [our]
> [par]ticuler speaches This generall answere thatt yor
> […] was this last winter well pleased to yeld unto […]
> a further respitt [respite ie delay] of one yere, to
> answere resolute in respectt of his yonge yeeres I
> answered thatt this yere wche he speaketh of, is now
> almost dep[arted] . . . wherunto my L[ord] gave me this
> answere & we […] I showlde imparte the same to yor
> L[ordship] thatt if you wold [would] requier att his
> owne hand, his sone [soon] answ.. he wold deliver itt to
> yor L[ordship] And this is so m[uch] as towchinge the
> matter I can now aquaintt yor L[ordship] the care of his
> personne & the circumstancyes [circumstances] of his

> can butt most effectuallye recom[m]end to yor L[ordship]

[ellipsis added]

Clearly, the young Earl was not inclined to marry and was being rather impolite in his persistent refusal, which his mother and grandfather did their best to modulate in their communication with Burghley. According to the Viscount, if left to his own devices, Southampton would have been pleased to give his answer, but it would not have been pleasing to his guardian. With the date of Henry's independence on the horizon, it appeared that Burghley's hopes for his granddaughter might go unrequited.

Burghley had other tools at his disposal, however, and if the Earl could not be persuaded by his elders, he might be more amenable to an appeal to his vanity. Shortly before his eighteenth birthday, Southampton received the gift of a poem that appeared to encourage him to marry. Titled <u>Narcissus</u> (1591) and written by John Clapham, a clerk in Burghley's employ, it was the first poem publicly dedicated to Southampton and was based on Ovid's version of the tale Echo and Narcissus in his <u>Metamorphoses</u>.

G. P. V. Akrig in his biography of Southampton argues unconvincingly that this none too obscure warning against the dangers of pride and dying without issue was composed without Burghley's involvement. Instead, he asserts that "the bright young secretary who as a household jest, knowing it would do no harm with his chief, writes a poem on Narcissus and then dedicates this 'Short and Moral Description of Youthful Love and Especially Self-Love' to Southampton."[62] Putting aside the issues of how this secretary of less than one year's employ could afford to have the "elegantly printed little book"[63] produced, or who would have printed such a thing touching simultaneously on matters concerning the richest youth in England and the most powerful man in the same country who happened to be the dedicatee's guardian and who also not by accident happened to have considerable influence among the Stationers with whom any disapproval could be literally fatal, who can imagine that a mere secretary for a head of state, any secretary of any head of any state anywhere ever, would ever dare to take such a step without specific authorization? Not Katherine Duncan-Jones who concludes that "it is likely that Burghley himself encouraged Clapham both to write and publish Narcissus as a pro-marriage poem dedicated and presented to his ward Southampton."[64]

Narcissus appears to have had little effect as Southampton did not take the hint and accept Burghley's proposal. In fact, his resistance increased and in 1594 after he reached legal maturity, he paid a £5,000 fine to his former guardian against his defiance. When he finally did marry in 1598, it was to Essex's niece, Elizabeth Vernon.

This often reported story leaves out several details, however, the principal one being Burghley's motive for the marriage itself. While the rationale that he was concerned for the well being of both his granddaughter and his ward seems acceptable on its face, it does not take into account the fact that Burghley could have married Elizabeth earlier but "tenacious to the last, Burghley had kept his granddaughter unmarried and available as long as Southampton was his ward."[65] More important was Burghley's need for increased capital with the death of Sir Francis Walsingham in 1590 and the assumption of full responsibility for the Queen's intelligence network.

In fact, intelligence work was an expensive business for which the Crown did not allocate funds. Instead, courtiers and counselors were expected to finance their own agents and Walsingham, for all his success, never managed to come close to covering his expenses. When he died the government owed him over £5,000 primarily from his intelligence expenses.[66] Not much later, Robert Cecil, who took over the service after his father's death in 1598 and who had help from a revived secret treasury, nevertheless ran expenses of up to £13,000 a year.[67]

Having assumed control of the spy network after his colleague's death, Burghley appears to have been heavily invested in securing outside support for that part of his overhead. Since the Queen was generally unsympathetic, he had to look elsewhere and inevitably his gaze fell on his ward, Henry Wriothsley, the Earl of Southampton, heir to one of the greatest fortunes in England.

With this motive, it should not be surprising that Burghley did not limit his effort to the advice of elders or the insinuations of a pointed poem written by a secretary. In fact, he had better tools than any of those. One, of course, was the threat of financial harm, which appears to have been on Southampton's mind when he complained to Burghley's confidential servant, Michael Hicks, that his guardian was letting his estate decay through indifferent management. Burghley, of course, could not afford to allow the estate to be ruined, but he could send the warning. If that was his stick, he could also reassert his carrot by way of literary enticement.

Of all the 154 Sonnets collected and printed by Thomas Thorpe in 1609, only the first seventeen are generally agreed to have been commissioned. Specifically, they are judged to have been written to convince a recalcitrant young man to marry. Katherine Duncan Jones finds Dover Wilson's assertion that the young man in question was William Herbert, son of Mary Pembroke, "attractive".[68] The more widely held theory, the one that is endorsed by G. P. V. Akrigg, Southampton's chief biographer, is that the target was indeed Henry Wriothesley.[69] Akrigg, however, dates the sonnets from 1593-94, conveniently after Venus and Adonis (1593). This seems a curious argument for a commissioned set of poems that few dispute are limited to the first seventeen.[70] Southampton was not seventeen in 1593, he was twenty. He turned seventeen in October, 1590, the same year that Burghley made his correspondence with Stanhope and continued with Viscount Montague on the subject of his ward's marriage to his granddaughter. It would not seem unlikely that the seventeen commissioned sonnets were written at a time when they would make an appropriate gift for a seventeen year old Earl.

As to the question of why anyone would think that a package of perfumed sonnets, however charming, could convince a hot-headed seventeen year old to marry before he had been able to at least partially enjoy being the most eligible bachelor in the English speaking world, what is important is not the poems but what they signify in terms of patronage and influence. It is a sign of success to have a poet dedicate his work to a worthy patron, it demonstrates status and power. By bestowing such a gift upon his ward even as he made his entry into society, Burghley signaled that there was plenty more where that came from if his ward would simply fall in line.

This begs the further question of who then accepted the commission; who wrote the seventeen sonnets in an attempt to convince Southampton to marry the granddaughter of Lord Burghley? Orthodox scholars automatically identify Shakespeare. His name, or something like it, was on them when they were published after all. These same scholars assert that the sonnets were written no earlier than 1593 because Venus and Adonis, which was dedicated to Southampton claims to be the "first heir" of the author's invention, presumably making it impossible for the seventeen sonnets to have preceded it if the same author wrote both. If that were so, why not then write twenty sonnets when Southampton was himself twenty and not yet old enough to declare himself free of Lord Burghley's guardianship? Would twenty be so much harder to write than seventeen? The author had just completed Venus and Adonis, so was he too tired to go past seventeen sonnets? Moreover, if these sonnets were commissioned specifically, what then is the significance of the number seventeen? It would make sense if that was the recipient's age at the time of the gift, but if he was in fact twenty, what then?

Shakespeare, however, is not recorded as "present", in school or otherwise, in 1590 making it difficult for him to have come to the attention of Lord Burghley, much less anyone else offering a commission for seventeen sonnets. That commission would not be something just anyone could do, not as a gift arguing marriage for the young, freewheeling Earl. For scholars who believe the dedication attached to Venus and Adonis it is therefore necessary to believe that the seventeen sonnets were written after it when Shakespeare was more visible and thereby credible as their author.

Christopher Marlowe, on the other hand, was not just visible in 1590, he was riding high; a rising star on the London stage and in Lord Burghley's secret service. Author of the wildly successful Tamburlaine Parts One and Two (1587-88) and the stunning Doctor Faustus (ca 1589)[71], Marlowe was already the leading dramatist in England. He had also been promoted from courier to a more vital role in Burghley's service, tutor to the teenaged beauty, Arbella Stuart, second cousin to Queen Elizabeth with a strong claim to the succession. Her grandmother, Bess of Hardwick, recorded in a letter to Lord Burghley that "one Morley ... attended on Arbell and read to her" over "the space of three years and a half".[72] Of all the people available to him, which certainly included all of the poets in England, all of whom would have gladly accepted his patronage, the most significant, the one most likely to impress Southampton as a member of his own generation, the most trusted and the one most certain to satisfy his commission in that moment was none other than Christopher Marlowe.

Stephen Greenblatt, who also thought it was "more likely"[73] that Clapham was commissioned to write Narcissus rather than advance it unapproved, argues that "someone, either in the circle of Burghley or in the circle of Southampton's mother"[74] commissioned the 17 sonnets. Ever so careful not to say that this was done without Burghley's knowledge, Greenblatt nevertheless leaves open the possibility, thus dodging the issue of the potential for Burghley's displeasure should the gambit fail, as it clearly did. The Stanhope correspondence makes it clear how careful even the best intended were of being suspected of interfering in Burghley's designs. It is highly unlikely, therefore, that anyone other than Burghley was proposing to send literary inducements to his unwilling ward.

Moreover, if Southampton's age is any guide in the matter, then the first seventeen sonnets preceded Narcissus altogether since it was presented on the Earl's eighteenth birthday. This would make Narcissus more of a rebuke than an appeal, which it certainly appears to be. The question then remains, who would Burghley be most likely to commission to make his initial appeal? A complete unknown? Or would he turn to a more highly regarded, significantly more successful poet who also happened to be in his employ?

If Chapter One proves that Shakespeare could not have written the "Rival Poet" sequence of sonnets, then there is no reason to assert that he was the author of the first seventeen. If the number of sonnets is in itself significant, and it obviously is, then there is no point in trying to square it with an arbitrary timeline made necessary by a single "first heir" quip in a subsequent dedication. Lord Burghley, meanwhile, may or may not have known or cared much about contemporary poetry, but he certainly knew that having his case argued by an unknown scribbler with no traceable credentials would be inevitably less effective than having it advanced by a more accomplished, better-known poet.

Who then should he have asked? He could easily have asked the Earl of Oxford to dash off some sonnets on behalf of his daughter. Assuming he was up to it, he certainly had an interest in the matter. That, however, may well have argued against him in this case. If asked for a recommendation, Oxford might have volunteered Tom Watson, the same man who had dedicated to him his Passionate Centurie of Love (1586), one of the first collections of sonnets, 100 in all, including some written in English. Or, Oxford might have proposed John Lily, the leading playwright in the early '80s and another of his protégés. If Burghley had wanted to look outside Oxford's orbit, he might have asked Edmund Spenser, whose Faerie Queene (1590) was all the rage. But Spenser had irritated him with Mother Hubberd's Tale (1589), a satiric poem about a fox and an ape which had mocked him and his son, Robert Cecil.

Marlowe then. And if Burghley, not famed for his knowledge of poetry, asked around, Tom Watson could have easily suggested the playwright who was even then experimenting with sonnets and had inserted one or two into a romance about a star-crossed pair of Italian teenagers the two of them had been adapting for the Queen's Men. Burghley could not help but also know that Marlowe had written "the most popular lyric of the age"[75]. Known commonly as "The Passionate Shepherd to his Love", the "disarmingly simple"[76] poem, set to music, seemed to be on everyone's tongue:

> "Come live with me and be my love,
> And we will all the pleasures prove
> That valleys, groves, fields and hills
> Woods or steepy mountain yields.
>
> "And we will sit upon the Rocks,
> Seeing the Shepherds feed their flocks,
> By shallow Rivers to whose falls
> Melodious birds sing Madrigals.
>
> "And I will make thee beds of Roses
> And a thousand fragrant posies,
> A cap of flowers, and a kirtle
> Embroidered all with leaves of Myrtle;
>
> "A gown made of the finest wool
> Which from our pretty Lambs we pull;
> Fair lined slippers for the cold,
> With buckles of the purest gold;
>
> "A belt of straw and Ivy buds,
> With Coral clasps and Amber studs:
> And if these pleasures may thee move,
> Come live with me, and be my love.
>
> "The Shepherds' Swains shall dance and sing

> For thy delight each May-morning:
> If these delights thy mind may move,
> Then live with me, and be my love."

This was a poem even Burghley could appreciate. He could hum it, literally, or he could if he could hum. Raliegh had even written a sequel, not as good, but itself a high compliment. If any poet could give his reluctant ward reasons to marry that his elders or political persuasion could not, then perhaps the most remarkable poet of his generation, celebrated author of epic theatre and popular pastorals could. Among the almost unlimited range of candidates available to him, the very best of all of them would have to have been Christopher Marlowe.

The result, of course, was brilliant and perfectly encapsulated Burghley's argument:

> "From fairest creatures we desire increase,
> That thereby beauty's rose might never die,
> But as the riper should by time decrease,
> His tender heir might bear his memory;
> But thou, contracted to thine own bright eyes,
> Feed'st thy light's flame with self-substantial fuel,
> Making a famine where abundance lies,
> thyself thy foe, to thy sweet self too cruel."
> Sonnet 1: 1 - 8

Mixing heady praise with pleasant duty, Marlowe produced seventeen variations on a single theme which have inspired generations of admirers ever after. Never was the cause of marriage and family better pled. And yet, somehow, the sonnets failed to move Southampton. He was, after all, a headstrong boy all of seventeen and, as his grandfather admitted, "resolute in respectt of his yonge yeeres". This stubborness, reflected in the subsequent <u>Narcissus,</u> was a harbinger of problems to come when his reckless allegiance to Essex would get him sentenced to the Tower following Essex's own execution for treason.

There is a deeper meaning in all this maneuvering around a marriage proposal: from the Queen's point of view, Southampton's fortune was the direct result of her father's largesse to Southampton's grandfather in pursuit of his anti-Catholic campaign, the very campaign that had resulted in her own birth. Southampton's unfortunate Catholic sympathies, inherited from his grandmother by way of his father, were well known but tolerated so long as he toed the line. Lord Burghley, on the other hand, was Elizabeth's staunchest Anglican supporter and his role in crushing prior and continuing Catholic plots against her person made him an extension of her identity. The marriage being proposed was not merely a convenience, it was intended to be confirmation of Southampton's loyalty and recompense of a bond encompassing generations of royal patronage and statecraft. The last thing the Queen could tolerate would be to have Southampton's fortune used to support Catholic causes. More than any possible gain for her own finances, marriage with Burghley's granddaughter would remove that possibility.

Southampton was fortunate that his refusal appears to have been interpreted at first as that of a headstrong, unsophisticated youth. Indeed, he appears to have been welcomed at court and he pursued a life of privilege that befit his stature, including attendance upon the Queen's progress at Tichfield and at court, time spent at Cambridge, hunting and habitué of the theatres as patron of players and playwrights. He was then not yet twenty and was making his way in the world as the most eligible of young men.

Burghley, meanwhile, had his eye ever on the calendar. Southampton would turn twenty on October 6, 1593. At twenty one he would be able to declare his independence from Burghley and while Southampton proved himself adept at holding off his guardian one year at a time, by the Spring of 1593, Burghley revived his efforts in singular style, calling upon his intelligencer poet once again. As fate would have it, with the theaters closed due to plague, Christopher Marlowe was at that moment half way through composing his first long poem, Hero and Leander.

One of the most remarkable claims made on behalf of Marlowe's Hero and Leander is that, even though he never finished it, the poem somehow was "circulating in manuscript"[77] before May, 1593. Anyone reading it who was also familiar with the first seventeen "sugred"[78] Sonnets would inevitably have noticed some remarkable coincidences of subject and phrasing. For instance, when Hero begins to attempt to seduce Leander, she argues against self-love:

> "Leander, thou art made for amorous play;
> Why art thou not in love, and lov'd of all?
> Though thou be fair, yet be not thine own thrall."
> Hero and Leander, 88 – 90.

> "But thou contracted to thine owne bright eyes,
> Feed'st thy lights flame with selfe substantiall fewell,
> Making a famine where aboundance lies,
> Thy selfe thy foe, to thy sweet selfe too cruell:"
> Sonnet 1: 5 - 8

Further on, Hero echoes the first Sonnet's first two lines:

> "The richest corn dies, if it be not reaped;
> Beauty alone is lost, too warily kept."
> Hero and Leander: 328 - 329

> "From fairest creatures we desire increase,
> That thereby beauties Rose might never die,"
> Sonnet 1: 1 – 2

In a similar fashion, both of the following excerpts compare selfish beauty to a bequest withheld:

> "Unthrifty lovelinesse why dost thou spend,
> Upon thy selfe thy beauties legacy?"

Sonnet 4: 1 - 2

"But this fair gem, sweet in the loss alone,
When you fleet hence, can be bequeathed to none."
Hero and Leander: 247 - 248

A further pair of similarities encourages investment of beauty in beauty to create more beauty:

"Make sweet some viall; treasure thou some place,
With beauties treasure ere it be selfe kil'd:
That use is not forbidden usery,
Which happies those that pay the willing lone;"
Sonnet 6: 3 - 6

"Then treasure is abused
When misers keep it; being put to loan,
In time it will return us two for one."
Hero and Leander: 234 - 6

All of these echoes and more are consistent with "Marlowe's habitual repetition of his own lines,"[79] a signature that would be self-evident to those familiar with his plays. It would not have surprised anyone then that, if Burghley had asked him to quickly produce a poem certain to impress his ward's vanity, Marlowe would repurpose a poem already begun, recasting his pair of youthful lovers, borrowing themes and imagery from the former to serve the latter's deadline. The question of whether or not the suspended Hero and Leander would be eventually completed would have to wait until after the new poem, Venus and Adonis, was finished and presented to Southampton in accordance with Burghley's commission.

As if on cue on April 18th, Richard Field, a printer supported by Burghley[80], registered for publication a new poem titled Venus and Adonis (1593), author unnamed. Anyone who could get an advance look at this poem would almost immediately notice, if they were at all familiar with the manuscript for Hero and Leander, the striking similarities between the two. Starting with the fact that, like lines 328 and 329 of Hero and Leander quoted above, it too echoed the very first lines from the first of the seventeen Southampton Sonnets:

> "From fairest creatures we desire increase,
> That thereby beauties Rose might neuer die,"
>   Sonnet 1: 1 – 2

> "Beautie within it selfe should not be wasted,
> Faire flowers that are not gathred in their prime,
> Rot, and consume them selues in litle time."
>   Venus and Adonis: 130 - 132

Further on, the new poem echoes both the Sonnets and Hero and Leander (lines 234 - 6 above) a second time when it encourages investment of beauty in beauty to create more beauty:

> "Make sweet some viall; treasure thou some place,
> With beauties treasure ere it be selfe kil'd:
> That use is not forbidden usery,
> Which happies those that pay the willing lone;"
>   Sonnet 6: 3 - 6

> "Foule cankring rust, the hidden treasure frets,
> But gold that's put to use more gold begets."
>   Venus and Adonis: 767 - 8

Comparisons are frequently drawn between the Sonnets and Venus and Adonis as both are presumed to have been written for the purpose of convincing Southampton to marry. Altogether, A. V. K. Akrig lists half a dozen specific comparative excerpts to illustrate the similarity of their style and to suggest that the author borrowed from one to feed the other. Other scholars, such as Maurice Charney, freely admit the debt owed by Venus and Adonis to Hero and Leander calling the latter a "model" for the former and, downplaying the verbal parallels, points out that "the two works are related by other literary criteria such as genre, conception, tone and handling."[81] Douglas Bush meanwhile declared that "there are a few bits of Venus and Adonis that could be mistaken for quotations from Hero and Leander."[82] In fact, there are eight "quotations" in all (see note 51 in Chapter Two).

What is much less, if ever, observed are the degree to which all three, the seventeen Southampton Sonnets, Hero and Leander and Venus and Adonis complement each other. While the Sonnets are premised on the appeal of marriage and children, Hero and Leander and Venus and Adonis are premised on an act of seduction which leads to the same result. A distinction without difference, the language of all three has a remarkable resemblance that argues for them all being by the same hand. If that were true, then there would be no need for the unconfirmed notion that the unfinished Hero and Leander had circulated in manuscript in order to influence Venus and Adonis. This could also explain the following pair of allusions to Narcissus:

>"Those orient cheeks and lips, exceeding his
>That leapt into the water for a kiss
>Of his own shadow, and, despising many,
>Died ere he could enjoy the love of any."
>   Hero and Leander: I: 73 - 76

>"Narcissus so him selfe him selfe forsooke,
>And died to kisse his shadow in the brooke."
>   Venus and Adonis: 161 - 162

There are no references to Narcissus in the seventeen Southampton Sonnets even though it makes an extended argument against self-love, of which he is the eponymous example. Not only does this argue, as does the specific number of sonnets, that the seventeen Southampton Sonnets came first, but the fact that both Venus and Adonis and Hero and Leander mention Narcissus suggests not only a sequence of composition, but also a single author for all three, Christopher Marlowe.

Although <u>Venus and Adonis</u> was registered without authorial attribution, no one who had the opportunity to get a look at an advance copy would have been faulted for immediately concluding that it was the work of England's most famous playwright and poet. The person most likely to make this connection and act on it, the person who would have had the most to lose if Southampton could be convinced, by means of this poem or by any other method, to marry Elizabeth deVere, was Robert Deveraux, the second Earl of Essex and Lord Burghley's fiercest political rival. Southampton's intimate friend and thereby familiar with the seventeen sonnets and <u>Narcissus</u>, with no reason to doubt that Burghley would persist in his matchmaking and therefore on the lookout for and with the resources to discover just such a text, Essex would suspect <u>Venus and Adonis</u> immediately. What scholars have the luxury of debating today would not, in the heat of the moment, have seemed at all uncertain to the ever hasty and suspicious Earl of Essex.

If the seventeen sonnets, <u>Hero and Leander</u> and <u>Venus and Adonis</u> were all apparently connected and with no other poet visible, then Essex would inevitably conclude that Christopher Marlowe was the source for all three. What he would do next in his effort to prevent that text from helping Lord Burghley consummate a proposal of marriage between his granddaughter and the richest heir in England and thus increase his already vast power, would forever shape the history of English literature.

Chapter Four

The Essex Plot

The rivalry between Robert Deveraux, the Earl of Essex, and Robert Cecil, Lord Burghley's son, was personal, intense, and started when they were very young. Essex had been a ward in Burghley's house from the age of eleven when his father, Walter, 1st Earl of Essex, died in 1576. There he met the thirteen-year-old Robert Cecil, the youngest of Burghley's sons but already his favorite. On the face of it, Essex would seem to have had all the advantages, he was handsome and athletic, his mother was soon married to his godfather, the Earl of Leicester, the Queen's favorite courtier, and in 1590 he married Frances Walsingham, daughter of Sir Francis, the Queen's principal Secretary and head of her intelligence network. Cecil, on the other hand, was undersized and hunchbacked, son of a "base-born nobleman"[83] and not well liked by the court or the public. Yet, while Essex made progress at court, becoming a favorite of the queen and succeeding his stepfather as Master of the Horse, it was Cecil who became her trusted adviser and who was appointed to the Privy Council ahead of him in 1591.

Essex, meanwhile, attempted to distinguish himself with military pursuits, often in the face of the Queen's displeasure. Notably, he ignored her order in 1589 to refrain from joining Drake's largely unsuccessful reprisal against Spain's Armada. He managed to avoid arrest only by the intercession of his father-in-law. Later, in 1591, while Southampton continued to withstand Burghley's siege in London, Essex was given command of a force sent to the assist King Henry IV of France during the no more effective siege of Rouen, an exploit that may have enhanced Essex's public reputation, but diminished his standing with the Queen.

Characteristically, Essex took political stands which put him in opposition to Burghley and Cecil, chief of which was his advocacy of increased antagonism toward Spain. Burghley's position was essentially more diplomatic, believing that the cost of such conflict was best avoided which further expressed his concern about the cost of intelligence in general.

In pursuit of his ambition, Essex organized a challenge to Burghley's intelligence network which had originally been developed by Sir Francis Walsingham, Essex's father-in-law. In making the match, Sir Francis and Essex may have had hopes of establishing a political dynasty, but this had been complicated by Sir Francis' early death in April, 1590. Worse for Essex was the fact that Walsingham's state papers had passed to Burghley and Cecil. There were and continue to be rumors that Walsingham's private papers might contain valuable information[84], but Burghley never allowed Essex to see or make use of what remained.

Despite this and the disadvantage of trying to compete with an established network, by 1592 Essex had set up a rival syndicate and was actively recruiting talent, such as Thomas Phelippes, famed as a code breaker and as Walsingham's lead counter-agent in the Babington Plot, and William Sterrell, "a one-time Oxford philosophy lecturer who for nearly 50 years was an intelligencer."[85] The team was not without its early mistakes, however, and had suffered a recent and embarrassing failure on behalf of Essex in an attempt to impress the Queen with details of a Spanish plot against the crown. Essex, who had primed the Queen to anticipate revelations that would surpass the Babington intrigue, went to great expense in the summer and fall of 1592 only to discover that his agents had been misled into pursuing agents of Lord Buckhurst, another of Elizabeth's privy councilors. Angry and humiliated, Essex was still looking for ways to restore his reputation in early 1593.

Setbacks notwithstanding, Essex had been able to set up a credible challenge to Burghley's network. By exposing Lord Buckhurst's operation, he had managed to make his own group appear more formidable. The fact that his company included former and sometime members of the opposition force was nothing unusual, spies were less tied to the ideals of their employers then; they tended to follow the money. Finance was one resource in which Essex had an advantage; he could better afford the expense of his faction. Moreover, he knew that if he could cripple Burghley's funding, he could quickly gain strength at his rival's expense. All he needed was an opportunity. This was exactly what he saw in the continued frustration of Burghley's enticements to Southampton; the possibility of depriving his older rival and his rival's son of the funds they lacked. Essex viewed Southampton as a natural ally with Catholic sympathies who he could use to starve Burghley simply by helping to prevent the proposed marriage to his grand-daughter.

London, meanwhile, was not quiet. For several years Archbishop Whitgift's Court of High Commissions on Ecclesiastical Causes had been jailing alleged pro-Catholic Separatists, in particular anyone suspected of being involved in the Martin Marprelate pamphlets that targeted and satirized corruption in the Anglican clergy. On February 17th, 1593, a group of protesters got hold of a coffin containing the remains of Roger Rippon, a noted Separatist, and carried it from Newgate prison to the house of Justice Richard Young in Cheapside. A legend attached to the coffin declared that Rippon was "the last of 16 or 17 which that great enemy of God, the Archbishop of Canterbury, with the High Commissioners, have murdered within Newgate within these five years for the testimony of Jesus Christ."[86] The Commissioners retaliated, arresting more than two dozen suspects, interrogating and deposing them at length and then, in March, arresting John Penry on suspicion of being involved in the Marprelate protests. The investigation widened further and on March 26th the Queen established a new Royal Commission to hunt out any and all who "secretlie adhere to our moste capitall Enemy the Bishoppe of Rome or otherwise do willfullie deprave contemne or ympugne the Devine Service and Sacraments."[87] The result was "the first all-out heresy hunt since the reign of Elizabeth's sister Mary."[88]

Drifting toward the middle of this turmoil, Christopher Marlowe seemed to be well aware that he could be suddenly threatened by it but was somehow unable to avoid it. He had already been accused of atheism in Greene's Groatsworth of Wit, a pamphlet written by fellow playwright Robert Greene and published in September, 1592 by Henry Chettle after Greene died. Marlowe had protested and Chettle printed a vague apology, but the allegation stuck. Meanwhile, several of Marlowe's closest friends and supporters, including Tom Watson and Sir Francis Walsingham, had recently died.

Then had come Burghley's desire for a new poem to further twist the arm of Southampton, a request that, if Marlowe had received it, he could hardly refuse. Despite doing his best to keep his head down, camping out at Thomas Walsingham's Scadbury estate and trying to revive his spirits with the unfinished Hero and Leander, he was being dragged back into Burghley's personal intrigue and matters of state well above his station.

Venus and Adonis appeared in the Stationer's Register very soon after, thanks no doubt to the head start provided by the suspended work on Hero and Leander. If Marlowe hoped that he could quickly move on and leave the intelligence world behind, he could not have been more off the mark.

Venus and Adonis was entered on April 18, 1593 into the Stationers' Register by Richard Field (entered as "ffeild"), a printer from Stratford-upon-Avon. No author was named in the entry, but Field was well known to be in the employ of Lord Burghley, as had Field's predecessor in the shop, Thomas Vautrollier. Did Burghley think that just because the poem had been registered without attribution that Essex wouldn't notice? Field was just the type of person that Essex would want his agents to watch. Printer of anti-Catholic propaganda and in touch with the Huguenot immigrant population, he would be a likely source for information on Burghley's intelligence operation. The thought that Field, not known for publishing poetry, would have in his hands an Ovidian poem by an unnamed author would have to concern Essex. With this poem registered, publication would be likely to result.

It would not be any stretch for someone like Essex, keeping an eye on the publishing world, to link the title of a poem based on an Ovidian source to one of England's leading Ovidian poets who was known to be working on just such a poem and conclude that the poem had been commissioned by Burghley for a purpose. Essex knew perfectly well that Marlowe lived the double life of an intelligencer; if he could have he would have converted him to serve his interests, but as he could not, and as the poem, which was itself a phenomenal work that would certainly impress Southampton, could not be suppressed once it was registered, he decided to ruin its author. The idea would be to single him out as a potential threat to the crown and the machine of the state would do the rest. All Essex required was a simple scenario based on the fevered mood of the time with an already smeared target needing very few extra hands to execute. Make the author appear a pariah and his work would be instantly untouchable. Not even Burghley could make a gift of a poem written by an atheist. Very few would ever dare wonder aloud why such a thing could happen, much less that it could in any way be connected to the jealousy of Robert Deveraux for the success of Robert Cecil.

In those days, England was a hot bed of plots, real and imagined and Essex was as adept as anyone in the game. No sooner had <u>Venus and Adonis</u> been registered for publication than he and his proxies devised a three part plan. First would come public denunciations intended to defame Marlowe, connect him to religious agitation and suggest a connection to the Marprelate pamphlets which had driven the Anglicans and Whitgift in particular to distraction. The second step would be to encourage an investigation which would lead to planted anti-Marlowe accusations from Essex's pawns. The third step would be a trial, public or private, which would, even if it cleared Marlowe of sedition, would ruin his name and value to Burghley. Essex could control all three steps, either as the head of the conspiracy for the first two parts, or as a member of the Privy Council for the third.

The plan was instantly put into motion by the mysterious appearance of the "Dutch Church Libel". For several months anonymous incitements had been scrawled on and pasted to walls and fences all over London. Then, late on the Saturday night of May 5th an infamous page of verse was "set upon the wall of the Dutch Churchyard"[89] in Broad Street ward. In fifty-three lines of rude doggerel, it accused Jews and immigrants of Machiavellian duplicity in practicing foreign religions and usury while supposedly driving up rents and stealing jobs:

> "Ye strangers y^t doe inhabite in this lande
> Note this same writing doe it understand
> Conceit it well for savegard of your lyves
> Your goods, your children, & your dearest wives
>   Your Machiavellian Marchant spoyles the state,
> Your usery doth leave us all for deade
> Your Artifex, & craftesman works our fate,
> And like the Jewes, you eate us up as bread"

Further on, it threatened terror and violence on them and those who did business with them:

> "Then you doe us; then death shall be your lotte
> Noe prize comes in but you make claime therto
>   And every merchant hath three trades at least,
> And Cutthrote like in selling you undoe"

It also made a point of referencing Marlowe's latest stage spectacle, <u>The Massacre at Paris</u>:

> "Not paris massacre so much blood did spill
> As we will doe just vengeance on you all"

If the Marlovian references in "Machiavellian", "Jewes"[90] and "paris massacre" weren't clear enough, it was signed "Tamburlaine".

Regardless of whether or not anyone actually thought Christopher Marlowe had indeed written the thing, investigators were quickly assembled to search for incriminating evidence and on May 12th Marlowe's former roommate and fellow playwright, Thomas Kyd, was arrested. A search of Kyd's room uncovered a batch of papers which were subsequently labeled "vile, hereticall Conceipts, denyinge the diety of Jhesus Christe our Savio'" to which was added in a different ink, apparently after Kyd had been tortured, "w/ch he affirmeth that he had from Marlowe".[91] These pages have been identified as extracts from John Proctor's Fall of the Late Arian (1549)[92] which refutes Arian denials of Christ's divinity but which, unfortunately, in order to dispute them, includes large quotations of the denials themselves.

Meanwhile, backstage, part two of Essex's plan was steadily progressing with the able assistance of Richard Chomeley. A part-time "cony catcher" and con-man with a March 19th warrant for his arrest hanging over his head, Chomley was obligingly making confession to an unnamed correspondent in what has since come to be known as "The Remembrances of Richard Chomley", including claims that he:

> "had a certen booke (as hee saith) delivered him by Sir Robert Cecil of whom he giveth very scandalous reportes

> "That he saith & verily beleveth that one Marlowe is able to shewe more sounde reasons for Atheisme then any devine in Englande is able to geve to prove devinitie & that Marloe tolde him that hee hath read the Atheist lecture to Sir Walter Raliegh & others.

> "That being imployed by some of her Majesties privy
> Counsaile for the apprehenson of Papists & other
> dangerous men hee used as he saith to take money of
> them & would lett them passe in spight of the
> Counsell."[93]

There, combined in one report, were all of Essex's targets, Cecil, Marlowe and Raleigh, as implicated by an underworld denizen who claimed to have already written several "libellious verses" of his own. In a following interview shortly after, Chomeley claimed that "Jhesus Christe was a bastarde & St. Mary a whore" and that "Moyses was a jugler"[94], claims that would be repeated by another informer, Richard Baines, who put them in Marlowe's mouth.

Chomeley's connection to Essex was later substantiated by Essex himself, writing that Chomeley was his "servant"[95] in a letter thanking Robert Bagot for interceding on Chomeley's behalf after his arrest that June on charges of atheism connected to the "Remembrances". For this reason and because "in Essex's eyes - powerful and well-informed eyes - it ['The Remembrances'] is a lie", Charles Nicholl concluded that "Chomeley was working for him [Essex] all along" and that "the evidence against him [Marlowe], in this aspect at least, has been manufactured".[96]

Then there is Thomas Drury, whose role in these events can perhaps best be described as open to interpretation. Drury, whose "main occupation was loan sharking[97]" and sometime partner-in-misconduct with Chomeley who subsequently sold him out, had been imprisoned thanks to Chomeley at Marshalsea since mid-1591 until he was recruited there in late 1592 by Lord Buckhurst and Sir Puckering. Acting independently of Essex, Puckering and Buckhurst hired Drury "to perform certain unspecified services"[98] which, in the minds of many, including Marlowe biographers Riggs and Nicholl, makes him "a likely candidate for the informer who compiled the 'Remembrances'"[99] on the notion that he was repaying Chomeley's earlier favor by trying to implicate Chomeley in the Atheist underground. More probably, Chomeley, still working for Essex, was using the gullible Drury and his dictated "Remembrances" to spread the same suspicions about Marlowe that were echoed by the Dutch Church Libel.[100] Essex would thus be repaying Buckhurst for the earlier embarrassment of having mistaken Buckhurst's agent for a Catholic seditionist the previous spring.

Regardless of whether or not Drury was in fact the ghost writer for Chomeley's memoir, it made its way to the Privy Council where it, along with the statements tortured out of Thomas Kyd and the infamous Libel, resulted in a warrant for Marlowe's arrest on May 18. Meanwhile, others accused of heresy and sedition, such as Marlowe's Cambridge friend John Greenwood and Henry Barrow, both of whom had written Marprelate related tracts against the Anglican Church, had been hanged together on April 6th. Shortly after that on May 21st, the previously arrested John Penry, a Greenwood associate who Archbishop Whitgift "believed to be the author of the Marprelate tracts",[101] was convicted and awaited a similar fate. As for Kyd, he was still in jail, a circumstance that could not have reassured Marlowe, his former roommate.

Stage three of Essex's plot was initiated when Marlowe was required to appear before the Privy Council on May 20th and told to give his "daily attendance", an instruction which various biographers and historians, including Bakeless, Tucker Brooke and Kuriyama have asserted was "a routine procedure"[102], portraying the event as "nothing extraordinary,"[103] as if Marlowe would have no reason to concern himself at a moment when all of London was being turned upside down in a search for atheists, something he was even then being accused of in Greene's Groatsworth which was still on sale in St. Pauls Churchyard. These scholars also ignore the fact that the arresting officer, Henry Maunder, was explicitly instructed to "repair to the house of Mr. Tho. Walsingham in Kent, or to anie other place where he shall understand xopher Marloe to be remayning. . . ."[104] Walsingham's connections to the intelligence service and the Privy Council have been extensively documented. While some may think it unlikely that he would have been concerned about the reasons for or the seriousness of the Council's interest in his houseguest and protégé, he certainly had the means of finding out about it. If Marlowe really didn't know what was going on before May 20th, then he could easily have asked Walsingham if he should have any concerns afterward.

Matters reached a climax with the delivery of the notorious Baines Note, a letter written by Richard Baines, a former priest and part time intelligence operative who had had several prior run-ins with Marlowe, including an assignment with him in the winter of 1592 in Vlissingen when, to throw suspicion off of his own activities, he accused Marlowe of counterfeiting, a scrape that ultimately required separate interviews with Burghley to sort out. "Probably submitted on May 26th"[105], the Baines Note lists a series of heretical, seditious and scurrilous statements attributed to Marlowe, including among many others:

> "That Moses was but a jugler."
> "That the first beginning of Religion was only to keep men in awe."
> "That Christ was a bastard and his mother dishonest."
> "That all they that love not Tobacco and boies are fooles."

To this, Baines added an even more damning charge:

> "almost into every Company he Cometh he persuades men to Atheism . . ."[106]

In conclusion, Baines declared: "I think that all men in Christianity ought to indevor that the mouth of so dangerous a member may be stopped . . . ."

Baines, however, did not actually deliver the note, that task was performed by none other than Thomas Drury, the same man who recorded "The Remembrances". This fact became known with the discovery in 1974 by S. E. Sprott of Drury's letter of August 1st, 1593 to Anthony Bacon, then head of Essex's intelligence network, in which Drury claims to have been commanded "to stay one mr Bayns which did use to resort unto me" after which:

> "ther was by my only means set doun unto the Lord Keper and the Lord of Bucurst the notablyst and vyldist artickeles of Athemysme that I suppose the lyke wer never known or red of in eny age all which I can show unto you they wer delyvered to her hynes . . ."[107]

Drury, who likely took dictation from Chomeley, claims to be Baines' scribe and courier as well and rather credulous at that. Either he was playing a subtle game with his betters, offering them obviously manufactured "evidence", or he really thought he was performing good intelligence on their behalf. The results suggest the latter.

Conspiracy theories are often derided merely by title, but Essex was a chief dabbler in this indulgence, as the later Lopez affair demonstrated, and he went out of his way to hire disaffected informants from the Cecils who trafficked in them as a profession. It was a core group of these people, Chomley, Baines and Drury, who were all connected in putting Marlowe in the cross hairs. Essex might not have anticipated that the investigation into the atheist menace would result in a threat of real harm to Marlowe, but he certainly intended to cripple his reputation.

Why else would Essex decide to attack Marlowe if not for <u>Venus and Adonis</u>? Charles Nicholl documented his belief in <u>The Reckoning</u> that Essex's intended target was Walter Raliegh, who he planned to discredit by libeling Marlowe.[108] But Raliegh was already in disgrace himself by virtue of daring to marry one of the Queen's Maids of Honor, Bess Throckmorten. Having spent the last half of 1592 in the Tower and exiled from Court upon his December release, Raliegh had fallen from favor never to return. Essex, meanwhile, despite his botched Buckhurst intrigue, had been made a full member of the Privy Council on February 25th and had little need to attack, directly or indirectly, a rival who had proven quite capable of ruining himself. As Constance Kuriyama noted, "that he was targeting Raleigh seems especially unlikely since Raliegh was already in eclipse."[109]

Closer to the mark, but still wide, is her observation that "if he could conjure up an atheist menace, Essex could not only aggrandize himself, but also discredit the Cecils and other members of the council for ignoring it."[110] Essex, however, did not have to conjure anything, the menace was already perceived to be in full flood and the Privy Council was violently confronting it. Essex did not need to create a menace, he just decided to take advantage of it.

While "it seems highly unlikely that Essex would target anyone for religious reasons"[111], Whitgift and his agents were not so mild and other members of the Privy Council, including Puckering and Lord Buckhurst, "wanted to be given evidence of an atheist threat."[112] As a result, Essex's struggle with Burghley for control of the intelligence network had put Marlowe in mortal danger.

Essex had a perfectly sensible reason to attack Marlowe directly because Marlowe was under Burghley's control and Marlowe was known to be writing Hero and Leander, a poem that might become a gift from Burghley to his ward Southampton as part of Burghley's ongoing effort to persuade him to marry Burghley's grand-daughter and thereby put Southampton's fortune under Burghley's control, giving him the means make Essex's rival intelligence service irrelevant.

Essex's aim therefore was not to attack Raleigh or Cecil by way of Marlowe, but to attack Marlowe directly, to humiliate and isolate him in order to discredit any favor his poem might have had in the eyes of Southampton. If he could slander Marlowe by tying him to the religious and immigrant unrest, he could disrupt Lord Burghley's control of the government itself by depriving him of the means to operate his most crucial network.

This then was the culmination of the plan put into motion because Essex believed that Marlowe was the unnamed author of Venus and Adonis. No other credible reason has been proposed for Essex to want to attack Marlowe, but attack him he did. Barely two weeks after Venus and Adonis had been anonymously registered, the Libel penned by Essex's "servant" Richard Chomeley was slapped to the Dutch Churchyard wall. Barely three weeks after that, during which Thomas Kyd had been arrested, interrogated and forced to name Marlowe as the owner of papers containing "vile, hereticall Conceipts", the Baines Note was delivered to Lord Buckhurst.

It is rather absurd to think that Lord Burghley and Robert Cecil, the two most experienced and least gullible members of the Privy Council, would be hoodwinked by the obvious falsehoods of the "Baines Note" and "The Remembrances". If anything, they could quickly point to the connection between them both and Thomas Drury, not to mention their resemblance to "The Libel", all three cut from very similar cloth by the same pair of hands. Although the Baines Note came to the council by way of Lord Buckhurst, it, the Libel and "The Remembrances" could all be tied directly back to Essex. Burghley himself had debriefed both Baines and Marlowe after the Flushing business and could judge for himself the character of the two men. Well attuned to Essex's antagonism, it would not be difficult for him to see his influence in all of this and, in defense of Marlowe, he could easily have pointed to The Massacre at Paris, as powerful a piece of anti-Catholic propaganda yet conceived by a playwright who had made a career out of promoting Tudor legitimacy with Henry VI, The First Part of the Contention and The True Tragedy of Richard, Duke of York. How could anyone believe he was seditious?

In the days preceding the Baines Note's delivery they would have had no difficulty conferring with Walsingham and Marlowe himself and made demonstrations of his innocence. The delivery of the note must have shifted the balance, however. The charge of atheism was far more serious than that of Catholicism for while both challenged the Queen, atheism challenged her Divine right to the throne and therefore the government itself. Whitgift was by then out for blood, Hundston and Buckhurst supported him. Puckering was perhaps on the fence while Essex, new to the club but no less influential, manipulated the evidence.

No doubt the Cecils did what they could to alter and delay the course of events, but they had their own problem; Marlowe was Burghley's protégé, this was an attack on them both and many scholars now believe that in order to preserve his position, Burghley was willing to sacrifice the poet just as he later sacrificed the physician Dr. Lopez. But that would mean letting Essex have his coup. Whatever Marlowe's value as a poet and intelligencer, it simply would be weakness to allow Essex to so easily target one of their own. But, if Marlowe was to be saved, they would have to act quickly and they would have to improvise.

Chapter Five

What Really Happened in Deptford and Why

No history of Marlowe is complete without a recounting of the incident at Deptford where he is reputed to have met his end.

The details of the incident were laid out for the record two days after the fact by Richard Danby, the Queen's Coroner, an unusual participant in the inquest, made necessary by the fact that it occurred while the Queen was "on the verge", ie: within twelve miles of the event, thus placing it under his rather than local jurisdiction.[113]

> "a certain Ingram ffrysar, late of London, Gentleman, and the aforesaid Christopher Morley and one Nicholas Skeres, late of London, Gentleman, and Robert Poley of London aforesaid, Gentleman, on the thirtieth day of May . . . at Detford Strand . . . , met together in a room in the house of a certain Eleanor Bull, widow; . . . & after supper the said Ingram & Christopher Morley were in speech & uttered one to the other divers malicious words for the reason that they could not be at one nor agree about the payment of the sum of pence, that is, le recknynge, ... it so befell that the said Christopher Morley on a sudden & of his malice towards the said Ingram aforethought, then & there maliciously drew the dagger of the said Ingram which was at his back, and with the same dagger the said Christopher Morley then & there maliciously gave the aforesaid Ingram two wounds on his head of the length of two inches & of the depth of a quarter of an inch; where-upon the said Ingram, in fear of being slain, . . . gave the said Christopher then & there a mortal wound over his right eye . . . of which mortal wound the

aforesaid Christopher Morley then & there instantly died;"[114]

[ellipses added]

The Coroner's Report was filed and did not become known to the public until Harvard scholar Leslie Hotson[115] discovered it in the Calendar of Close Rolls and published it in 1925, 332 years after the fact. Although several names had been associated with the tale of Marlowe's tragedy, Hotson, who had been researching Chaucer's Nun's Priest's Tale in the archives of the English Public Records Office, discovered the official report when he decided to pursue a listing for Ingram Frizer. The name struck him as significant because it combined two names which before had been mentioned separately as being involved in Marlowe's demise.

Almost inevitably, everyone in attendance not only had some connection to the spy network reporting to Lord Burghley, they also had close dealings with Thomas Walsingham, Marlowe's chief patron and the man who had looked after him and let him stay at his Scadbury home during the months leading up to May 30, in particular during the last week of May when Marlowe was ordered to make daily attendance before the Privy Council.

Walsingham's relationship to Ingram Frizer, the man credited with the fatal stabbing, was not altogether above board. In fact, Frizer was a "business agent"[116] for Thomas Walsingham. In addition to his discovery of the Coroner's Report, Leslie Hotson revealed that Walsingham was the recipient of a bond for 200 Pounds made out by Drew Woodleff as the final stage of a scam engineered against him by Frizer and his associate, Nicholas Skeers.[117] Skeres was the second of the three men present for the event at Deptford. The third was Robert Poley, a long-time agent of Francis Walsingham, Thomas' "uncle", who had made good use of Poley in the Babington Plot. It was Poley who secured the confession that ultimately led to Mary Stuart's execution and Thomas had been one of Poley's contacts during the unravelling of the plot.[118] Even Eleanor Bull, the hostess, had a connection to Lord Burghley by way of her family relation to Blanch Parry, Chief Gentlewoman of the Privy Chamber who left Mistress Bull a legacy of £100 in 1589. As Park Honan noted, "Mrs. Bull was a widow of good family lineage, whose likely discretion would have suited secret agents."[119]

Those were the people in the room when Marlowe's fate was decided. They were all connected to the intelligence service and they all reported ultimately to Lord Burghley by way of Thomas Walsingham. Rather than assassinate him quietly and disappear into the night, they all remained in the vicinity and two days later made an appearance before and gave testimony to the Queen's Coroner, Richard Danby, even as the Queen resided at Nonesuch palace.

While Hotson's remarkable discovery put to rest certain disputed facts, rumors regarding Christopher Marlowe's death had been circulating in print for many years before the publication of the Sonnets. George Peele paid tribute to Marlowe on June 26 in The Honor of the Garter, calling him "The Muses' darling." Similarly, Thomas Nashe included an elegy (now lost) to Marlowe in the preface to his 1594 publication of Dido, Queen of Carthage. In the second edition of Christ's Tears Over Jerusalem (1594) Nashe also referred to "poor deceased Kit Marlow".

Others took a much less charitable view, in particular Dr. Thomas Beard who in his book The Theatre of God's Judgements (1597) accused Marlowe of "Atheisme and impiety" and reporting: "so it fell out, that as he purposed to stab one whom he ought a grudge unto, with his dagger, the other party perceiving, so avoyded the stroke, that withall catching hold of his wrist, he stabbed his owne dagger into his own head; in such sort, that notwithstanding all the means of surgery that could be wrought, he shortly after died thereof."[120]

Francis Meres cited Beard in Palladis Tamia (1598) and added that Marlowe was "stabbed to death by a bawdy Servingman, a rival of his in his lewde love."[121]

The most remarkable report, and the nearest to the statements made by witnesses in Danby's official report, was published by William Vaughan in his book The Golden Grove (1600). Commenting on the deaths of famous poets, he included Marlowe:

> "by profession a playmaker, who, as it is reported, about 7 years ago wrote a book against the Trinity: but see the effects of God's justice; it so happened, that at Detford, a little village about three miles from London, as he meant to stab with his poniard one named Ingram, that had invited him to a feast, and was then playing at tables, he quickly perceiving it, so avoided the thrust, that withal drawing out his dagger for his defence, he stabbed this Marlowe into the eye, in such sort, that his brains coming out at the dagger's point, he shortly after died."[122]

A reasonable question must be, what was Marlowe doing there? With those people? One answer is that Poley, Frizer and Skeres were the very kind of people who could be counted on to commit murder on behalf of the Queen. Not that any of them had ever been known to have done anything like that before, but there are those today who want to believe that such a thing is possible, even likely. This would mean that Marlowe was betrayed by Thomas Walsingham, his friend of ten years or more, a man who later allowed George Chapman to complete Marlowe's Hero and Leander and have it dedicated to his wife, Audrey. A man who Blount claimed in print was a friend to Marlowe. The level of cynicism necessary to behave this way strains credulity.

On the other hand, Pooley, Frizer and Skeres could also be the very type of men who could be relied upon to pull off a scheme, fake a death and connive to convince a roomful of credulous witnesses that the body brought in for display was the man they claimed to have killed in self-defense. In fact, there was a body nearby, freshly hung.

John Penry, accused of participating in the Martin Malprelate tracts, had been convicted by the Queen's Bench on May 21st, 1593, on charges of having "feloniously devised and written certain words with intent to excite rebellion and insurrection in England"[123]. The charges were based upon excerpts taken from manuscript notes found in his house at the time of his arrest, a method that had been similarly employed to implicate Marlowe by way of papers found in Thomas Kyd's room on May 14th. Penry was then held but was not hanged until May 29th at the unusual hour of 4 p.m. at St. Thomas-a-Watering, less than three miles from Deptford. One of his biographers commented that "it was strange that it was now the fourth evening since he left the Court, under condemnation to be hanged without delay."[124]

In 1996, David More suggested that Penry's corpse could "have served well for Marlowe's."

> "Modern coroners claim that the body would be well preserved in England's cool weather, though Coroner Danby would not have performed a complete autopsy. The body would be clothed and the head wound clearly visible. There would be no reason to doubt the witnesses' story, or suspect a switch. John Penry was an exact contemporary of Marlowe's at Cambridge and also a 'Gentlemen.'"[125]

There is a gruesome irony in the idea that Penry's body could have been used as a substitute for Marlowe's. This might seem outrageous to some, but to make the Coroner's report valid, a dead body would have to have been swapped for a live one. Regardless, it is a fact that to this day "the place of [Penry's] burial is unknown".[126]

A significant feature of Mistress Bull's house was that it was adjacent to the Deptford dockyards on the Thames. As such, it was also in the vicinity of the home of the Muscovy Company, the first company incorporated in London to lead shipping with Russia. Walsingham had been a company director since 1569 and Burghley had been an investor since its founding in 1555. Anyone needing swift transportation out of England could hardly do better than secure passage on a Muscovy vessel.

All of which goes to show that the tools were readily available for people with experience in clandestine action to stage manage the swift, secret departure of an agent in mortal danger. Whether or not this was entirely the work of a small, rogue enterprise or one that had tacit approval from above is a question explored by Peter Farey, in his Hoffman Prize winning essay:

> "The most likely situation would therefore seem to be that the Archbishop of Canterbury, John Whitgift, wanted Marlowe tried and executed, and that the Queen agreed with him. The Cecils, however, managed to persuade her that faking his death could be just as effective - that he could be forced to refrain from ever again propagating his atheistic views, and would be seen by her subjects to have suffered God's punishment for his blasphemy and heresy. She therefore agreed to this as a compromise, but to appease Whitgift also insisted that the records would show beyond any doubt that he was dead, he would be banished the country (albeit under some sort of control?), and must never under any circumstances, of course, write another word as Christopher Marlowe."[127]

The possibility that this was indeed agreed upon at the Privy Council level and blessed by the Queen receives confirming evidence from, of all people, Thomas Drury, the man who connects the Earl of Essex to The Dutch Church Libel and the Baines Note.

In his August 1st letter to Anthony Bacon, Drury claims that he can "bring you to the man that doeth know who did wryght the bocke, and thay to howe it was delyvered as allso who red the lecture and wher and when with dyverse other such other secrytes as the state would pay a thousand poundes to know."[128] Nichols believes Drury is presumably referring to "the text of the 'atheist lecture' which Marlowe supposedly read to Raliegh", and further asserts:

> "He claims he can find the man 'who did write the book' - since Marlowe was universally said to be the author of it, *and is now dead*, Drury must be referring to a copyist who prepared it for distribution."
>
> [Italics added]

One would think that Bacon, by then working as the head of Essex's intelligence network, would be very interested in this information. Instead, Drury was promptly arrested on the order of Henry Carey, Lord Hunsdon, the Lord Chamberlain and Essex's Great Uncle, son of William Carey and Mary Boleyn. From jail, Drury wrote to Robert Cecil trying to explain that the charges, that he had slandered Lord Hundson by way of "The Remembrances", were all a misunderstanding, that "it was other's lies and practices, not my own".[129] Remarkably, Drury was released on August 17 with money sent by Cecil for which he thanks him in a second letter.[130] Still more striking is the fact that he later shows up in 1595 being paid £16 under authorization "signed by Lord Burghley"[131] for services as a confidential courier.

There would be no need to arrest Drury or subsequently reward his services, much less bring him into the Burghley network, if his information merely related to accusations against Marlowe or Raliegh when the former was supposedly dead and the latter disgraced and politically irrelevant. The atheist frenzy was more or less over by August, Penry, Greenwood, et al. had been hanged and the libels and other disturbances had been put down. Although plague still kept the public theaters closed, plans were being laid to reopen them and the city was returning to normal.

Drury's information would only be valuable if he actually knew where Marlowe was, if Marlowe was not dead as Nicholl asserts but was "flown beyond the Alps" as Machevill says his soul has done in his speech from The Jew of Malta.[132] When Drury writes about "the man that doth know who did write the book" he is not talking about "a copyist", he himself was a copyist for both Chomeley and Baines, he knows the difference between that and an informer. He's talking about "dyverse other such other secrytes as the state would pay a thousand poundes to know." What would such a secret be? Not who wrote the book, that was already assumed to be Marlowe as Chomeley in his reference to "The Atheist Lecture" and Baines in his reference to his having "quoted a number of contraieties out of Scripture which he hath given to some great men" testified to Drury. There is no reason then why Drury would think this was new information worth a thousand pounds.

When Drury wrote of "the man that doeth know who did wryght the bocke" he could just as easily be thinking of Thomas Kyd, another person writing to members of the Privy Council for mercy, in this case Lord Puckering. Another person who got roughed up in the investigation and subsequently released. Fortunate for Drury that he ended up better than Kyd.

In August of 1593, Drury would be well aware that Marlowe was reported to have been killed in a tavern brawl. It was his business to know things like that and he had been investigating Marlowe for members of the Privy Council. Only if he had information contrary to popular belief would it be worth "a thousand poundes."

Drury appears to believe that Anthony Bacon does not know what he has heard about Marlowe. He claims that he has information in addition to the source of "the bocke" and that it is important. Bacon's reaction, however, having Drury arrested, suggests that the last thing he wanted was to have that information repeated.

Drury then writes from jail to Cecil and he is subsequently paid and released. Rather than being paid for his information, Drury was paid for his silence. There wasn't anything Drury could tell Bacon, Cecil or anyone else that could possibly be worth a fortune to them, including the possibility that Marlowe might still be alive. As the link between Chomely and Baines, the one person who could not only put all the players together, but also foolish enough to risk talking about it, Drury had to be silenced. It speaks to Burghley's innately careful weighing of costs and benefits that Drury was patted on the head and enlisted into discreet service rather than being disposed of by crueler means.

That result would only have been possible if Bacon and Burghley were working together to keep the business secret. If either suspected the other, then Drury would have to be eliminated. Together, however, they could agree to buy him out, as that was what he wanted, and keep him close. That would be one death less to explain.

What then did Marlowe think of all this? Given that he complained vociferously about Chapman's appropriation of <u>Hero and Leander</u>, it would be surprising indeed if he managed to survive the incident at Deptford without making note of it. The answer to the question can be found in sonnet 74, which matches point for point the particulars of the Coroner's report:

> "But be contented when that fell arrest
> Without all bail shall carry me away;
> My life hath in this line some interest
> Which for memorial still with thee shall stay.
> When thou reviewest this, thou dost review
> The very part was consecrate to thee.
> The earth can have but earth, which is his due;
> My spirit is thine, the better part of me.
> So then thou hast but lost the dregs of life,
> The prey of worms, my body being dead,
> The coward conquest of a wretch's knife,
> Too base of thee to be rememberèd.
>> The worth of that is that which it contains,
>> And this is this, and this with thee remains."

Modern scholars are generally loathe to treat the Sonnets as autobiographical, instead favoring "techniques of 'close reading' which [are] on principle decontextualized, thus prohibiting biographical reference."[133] According to Katherine Duncan-Jones, this approach "has been the dominant mode of criticism up to the present day." The modern emphasis is on style, methodology, metaphor and lexical measures rather than on content.

Sonnet 74 frequently receives this treatment. Brandin Cormack summarizes the standard reading: "[the reader] need not despair at the idea of poet's death, but instead should be 'contented' insofar as the poem will pass on the poet's spirit. . . ."[134] Focusing on the "wretch's knife" which appears to be the proximate cause of this "death", Colin Burrow asserts that "wretch" refers to "any worthless person"[135], an identification which is broad enough to include almost anyone in the right, or wrong, circumstances. John Kerrigan, on the other hand, believes that "the most plausible identification [of the wretch] is with Mortality."[136] Thomas Tyler is still more specific:

> "There is no reason whatever for supposing from this line that Shakespeare had encountered highwaymen or assassins to whose violence he had succumbed, and who had left him half-dead. The meaning is, that what of him had not been treasured up in his verse was mean and base, liable to succumb to the assassin's knife."[137]

It is only with MacD. P. Jackson's tantalizing suggestion that line eleven might reflect Shakespeare's similar preoccupation in As You Like It (1598) with Marlowe's death[138] do the critics approach a reason why the poet would focus on death as a topic for sonnet 74 or would choose the particular objects, scenes and metaphors described in it to illustrate and detail his theme. Otherwise, the best that most of these commentators will allow is that the sonnet is on the subject of death. This can be reliably reported because that word, and others like it, appear many times. Beyond this their agreement hesitates.

MacD. Jackson notwithstanding, most academic commentators have been reluctant to even suggest that Sonnet 74 might in any way be alluding to Christopher Marlowe, never mind that he might have actually written it. Regardless, the sonnet follows very closely the descriptions of Marlowe's death offered by Beard, Meres and Vaughn.

There are some divergences, however. "That fell arrest without all bail" suggests a sudden, unanticipated event without recourse, something that trumped expectations of a scheduled, regular interview perhaps before the Privy Council. This line would not then be a metaphor, it would be a reference to a very real event.

This gives lines 3 and 4 a particular significance:

"My life hath in these lines some interest,
Which for memorial still with thee shall stay."

Interest refers not only to significance, but also to payment of a debt which would be owed to anyone who assisted in Marlowe's escape. Line four, meanwhile, asserts that the reader will be the only one who will both understand the poem and be able to respond to it. The reader most likely to understand all this would be the same person who would have stage managed Marlowe's escape with the assistance of Poley, Frizer and Skeres.

The third quatrain makes the very odd reference to the writer's body "being dead". This is asserted in the present tense by the phrase "thou hast but lost", but the writer is clearly not dead. Marlowe, of course, was declared officially dead by the Queen's Coroner[139].

The writer then refers to his body as a "coward conquest". Kerrigan claims that this is a reference to "the wretch with the knife" and that he "makes a coward (acting as an adjective) conquest when it stealthily assassinates the body"[140].

The word "coward", however, clearly refers to "my body" and suggests that the poet considers his behavior in the midst of the arrest was cowardly because he did not resist. Again, the writer is alive when he says this and when he speaks of a "wretch's knife" which, in the context of the Coroner's Report, would be Ingram Frizer, the man named as the killer. The poem is not speaking of some metaphorical wretch, it is speaking of a real person and a real event.

The person most likely to understand these references would be the same person to whom the "Rival Poet" sonnets were addressed, the person by whom the other participants at the scene at Deptford were employed, the person who provided shelter for Marlowe during the weeks that preceded it, Thomas Walsingham.

Viewed from Walsingham's perspective, Sonnet 74 carries that much more impact. No longer is it a vague, curious metaphorical consideration of the inevitability of death, it is instead a direct reminder to the one person who understands the specific situation of the writer. Neither would this have escaped the comprehension of Lord Burghley or Robert Cecil.

Of course, the sonnet includes all of the textual, metaphoric, lexical and poetic content agreed upon and debated by modern scholars. Even their inability to credit it with autobiographical references is intentional as sonnet 74 was, as were the "Rival Poet" sonnets, written as a coded message intended to maintain the fiction of Marlowe's death. Just as with the Southampton sonnets, none of these need to have been written by Shake-Speare to have been included in the collection.

Shortly after the incident, <u>Venus and Adonis</u> was printed and dedicated to the Earl of Southampton. The earliest purchase of a first edition was on June 12, 1593, by Richard Stonley, a Teller of the Exchequer of Receipt and therefore employed by Burghley, who was sent to Fleet prison in 1597 after being convicted of embezzling more than £12,000 from the Exchequer. Stonley's estate was seized in order to pay his debts and his copy of the poem does not survive. His diary does, however, and records that he paid twelve shillings for the poem and a copy of John Eliot's <u>The Survey, or Topographical Description of France</u> (1592).

Meanwhile, tensions within the Privy Council did not go unnoticed. In a letter of late June, 1593, Richard Verstegan, a Dutch Catholic reporting on English anti Catholic intrigue, states:

> "The Lord Treasurer and the Earl of Essex are at unkindness, so that it is thought they will fall to open enmity. In the meanwhile the Treasurer, with his son Sir Robert, have left the court and are gone to Tybolles [ie: Theobalds]"[141].

Charles Nicholl further notes that "this information is based on a letter sent from England on 10 June" and then wonders "does this 'unkindness' between them perhaps relate to the event at Deptford a few days previously?"[142] If so, then perhaps not everyone agreed with the result.

Regardless, Southampton did not marry Burghley's granddaughter. Instead, he continued to hold out until he reached his majority at the age of twenty-one in 1594. At that point, Burghley fell back on plan "B" and assessed a £5,000 fine, which he was entitled to do as his guardian, for "refusing the Lady Veere."[143] Burghley required immediate payment which forced Southampton to sell a major part of his inheritance and left him more or less strapped for years to come.

When Southampton finally did marry, in 1598, it was secretly to a lady in waiting to the Queen, Essex's first cousin, Elizabeth Vernon, who Southampton had got pregnant. The scandal so incensed the Queen that she sent them both to Fleet prison until after the baby was born.

Marlowe meanwhile was apparently laying low in Flushing, scene of his counterfeiting debacle the year before. Alone, desperate to return, he would have plenty of time to review the odd turns his life had taken along the way.

Chapter Six

Christopher Marlowe's Motto

Near the end of the 1991 revision of his oft quoted text, <u>Shakespeare's Lives</u>, Samuel Schoenbaum considers Shakespeare's apparent silence on the subject of his own life and lamented: "What we would not give for a single personal letter, one page of diary?" and then quoted Thomas Hardy on the same subject:

> "Bright baffling Soul, least capturable of themes,
> Thou, who display'dst a life of commonplace,
> Leaving no intimate word or personal trace,
> Of high design outside the artistry
>   Of thy penned dreams,
> Still shall remain at heart unread eternally."

Schoenbaum concluded that "A kind of literary biography, rich in detail about (in Yeats' phrase) the momentary self, is clearly impossible."[144]

The odd thing about this statement is that, until very recently, <u>Shake-speare's Sonnets</u> had been considered exactly that document of the author's "momentary self."

For centuries, the <u>Sonnets</u> have been regarded as primarily autobiographical. Scores of noted critics, artists and scholars, from W.H. Auden to Stephen Spender, have recognized and even celebrated their deeply personal nature, a perception that was perhaps first noted by A. W. Schlegel:

> "These Sonnets paint most unequivocally the actual situation and sentiments of the poet; they make us acquainted with the passions of the man; they even contain remarkable confessions of his youthful errors."[145]

More recently, however, the general trend of modern scholarship has been to make a virtue out of a refusal to recognize the slightest hint of biographical content. In his introduction to the Penguin edition of the Sonnets, John Kerrigan summarizes the attempts by dozens of noted scholars to analyze them on biographic or formalistic terms and then confidently asserts "The Sonnets are not autobiographical in a psychological mode."[146] This statement entirely reverses the perspective of the volume's previous editor, G.B. Harrison, who asserted that "they are personal and intimate poems written to individuals, which could tell much about Shakespeare's life if only some facts about them could be indisputably established."[147]

Perhaps to make his repudiation of Harrison and the autobiographic school absolutely clear, Kerrigan adds in the section devoted to Commentary, "a premise of this edition [is] that, in the reading of Shakespeare's Sonnets, biography need not impinge."[148]

Katherine Duncan-Jones speculated that this aversion might have something to do with a "fear that a personal interpretation of the "young man" sonnets might link Shakespeare, or even the Love of Shakespeare - as in the case of Wilde - with criminalized activity . . ."[149] and quotes several scholars who appear to be uncomfortable with the issue. For her own part, Duncan-Jones confides that reading the Sonnets "as a continuum" is "a demanding, perplexing, painful experience."[150]

Indeed, the anti-biographical position has become so absolute that the 2018 version of The New Oxford Shakespeare Authorship Companion refuses even to consider biographic detail gleaned from the Sonnets to guide its proposed chronology of their composition and then declares that: "more recent work identifying patterns within Shakespeare's lexical and stylistic preferences establishes that it is unhelpful and misleading to produce results based on the Sonnets as a whole."[151]

While the tender feelings of nineteenth century scholars might explain why they would avoid any view of the Sonnets that would suggest their author was homosexual, this concern cannot adequately explain the disinclination of modern critics to view the Sonnets as autobiographical. The more likely reason for the persistence and codification of this perspective is that the more closely scholars study the Sonnets the less they match up with any of the known facts about the life of Willim Shakspere. Modern scholars therefore have apparently chosen to avoid any examination of the Sonnets in autobiographical terms.

Despite this trend in scholarship, it is clear from the preceding chapters outlining the origins of the "Rival Poet" sonnets, the seventeen Southampton sonnets and sonnet 74, that many of the Sonnets are, in fact, autobiographical and that they are made up of facts, references and links to individuals who, like dots on a map, connect, interlock and reinforce each other in ways that clearly describe the life of Christopher Marlowe. This set of facts includes not only the personal, private history that is the inspiration for the poems, but also the people who knew him, who patronized and helped publish his work and who were present for these events at the times and places they all knew about and experienced together. Taken alone these facts are curious and seemingly inexplicable, but together they form a web of repeated statements and connections to individuals and events that tell a very remarkable story.

With this framework in mind, it is well worth taking a close look at sonnet 73, which is generally considered a companion to sonnet 74 and, sitting coincidentally at the start of the second half of the full 154 sonnet sequence, includes more compressed biographical detail than any other, starting near the beginning of the writer's life and ending at the moment of its composition after including an eerie echo of the source of all his inspiration.

Sonnet 73

That time of year thou mayst in me behold
When yellow leaves, or none, or few, do hang
Upon those boughs which shake against the cold,
Bare ruin'd choirs, where late the sweet birds sang.
In me thou see'st the twilight of such day
As after sunset fadeth in the west,
Which by and by black night doth take away,
Death's second self, that seals up all in rest.
In me thou see'st the glowing of such fire
That on the ashes of his youth doth lie,
As the death-bed whereon it must expire,
Consum'd with that which it was nourish'd by.
   This thou perceiv'st, which makes thy love more strong,
   To love that well which thou must leave ere long.

When attempting to interpret this sonnet, most contemporary commentators appear to limit themselves either to surface readings or to paraphrases that do not venture far from the literal, offering formalistic, textually restrained accountings. Richard B. Hovey, for instance, proposes that "in Sonnet 73 the poet-narrator compares his state with three things: autumn, the passing of day, and the burning out of a fire."[152] More grandly, Barbara Estermann observes that the poet is comparing himself to the universe through his transition from "the physical act of aging to his final act of dying, and then to his death."[153] John Prince, on the other hand, argues an alternative interpretation in which the author does not intend to address death, but rather the passage of youth which shifts the focus "from the speaker's life to the addressee's life."[154] In a similar vein, Amanda Mabillard suggests that "the poet is preparing his young friend, not for the approaching literal death of his body, but the metaphorical death of his youth and passion."[155]

   Despite the abstraction of modern critical tradition, there is a surprising amount of autobiographical information readily recognizable in this sonnet. The first would be the reference to "bare ruin'd choirs" in line four. Many scholars have noted that the line "inevitably evokes visual recollections of chancels of abbeys left desolate by Henry VIII's dissolution of the monasteries."[156] These would be the same monasteries that were destroyed in the creation of the Southampton fortune that Burghley and Queen Elizabeth wanted so much to secure via the young Earl's marriage with Elizabeth deVere, Lord Burghley's grand-daughter, the same marriage that Burghley attempted to promote with the commission of the seventeen "Southampton Sonnets" which, as shown in Chapter Three, were written by Christopher Marlowe.

What is rarely mentioned in this context, however, is that while there are no monasteries, ruined or otherwise in the neighborhood of Stratford, there is a very famous ruined choir in Canterbury, Marlowe's home. Founded in 598, St. Augustine's Abbey had been surrendered to Henry on 30 July 1538 as part of his Reformation of the Church. During the rest of Henry's reign, it was held by the Crown with some of its buildings converted into a royal residence while the remainder of the abbey's buildings were wrecked. Everything of value was seized. The shrines of St Augustine and the abbey's other saints were destroyed, as were the tombs of the Anglo-Saxon kings of Kent who were buried in the church. The abbey's magnificent library was dispersed and its chapel and other structures were dismantled. The ruins of the chapel and its grounds are a tourist attraction to this day.

Thomas Walsingham, Marlowe's patron and protector, was from Kent where the abbey is located. He would have been very familiar with the image of "bare, ruin'd choirs." He would also have known that the "Southampton Sonnets" failed to sway the young Earl, that the Earl eventually married the Earl of Essex's sister, much to the Queen's dismay, and was following Essex in his challenge to Lord Burghley and what would ultimately lead to the rash rebellion that resulted in Essex's ruin and Southampton's disgrace. He would know too that Marlowe was raised in Canterbury in the shadow of those same "ruin'd choirs" and that Essex drove him into hiding where sonnet 73 was written. The following lines would compound that image of ruin for him with less concrete, but no less indelible significance:

> In me thou see'st the twilight of such day
> As after sunset fadeth in the west,
> Which by and by black night doth take away,
> Death's second self, that seals up all in rest.

While a considerable number of scholars have been employed in the attempt to decipher this Sonnet, one thing that does not appear to have drawn comment is the likely geographical position of the poet as suggested by these lines. Very simply, a person in twilight is to the east of the setting sun. Moreover, the position of the reader is similarly fixed to the west of the poet because a person cannot simultaneously see the eastern twilight and be in twilight. Therefore, if the person to whom the poem is addressed is in London, or more broadly, England, then the author is to the east of that.[157]

Among the many observations that can be made about this is that on top of everything else it is a contemporary reference. Although the poet is writing about death, he is very much alive and, if his spatial references are to be given credit, he is not in England.

What then does the poet mean when he speaks of "Death's second self?" Most commentators who venture a guess at this phrase suggest that it means "sleep" by which the twilit day is sealed up "all in rest." Rest, or sleep, however, does not necessarily suggest the finality of death. Rest in this instance would mean the imitation of death.

This would seem to contradict most commentators who appear to believe that the poet is obsessed with actual death, not sleep. What the commentators also overlook is that the phrase itself implies a sequence; in order for death to have a second self, there must be a first. What then is the first death if sleep is the second when sleep cannot follow actual death?

If this is viewed from the geographical perspective, the poet from his location East of England appears to view his position as a form of death, a life separate and apart from actual life, asleep or, possibly, life in exile.

Is it reasonable to think that the author would view mere exile as a form of death? Romeo appears to think so:

> There is no world without Verona walls,
> But purgatory, torture, hell itself.
> Hence banished is banished from the world,
> And world's exile is death. Then 'banished'
> Is death mistermed. Calling death 'banished,'
> Thou cuttest my head off with a golden axe
> And smilest upon the stroke that murders me.
>
> Romeo and Juliet, Act III, Scene 3, 17 - 23

All of this follows from taking a literal reading of the author standing in twilight while the sun sets over the bare ruined choirs of England.

Read this way, the sonnet emerges as an intensely personal statement. No longer is it some brooding rumination on death and death's imagery, it is instead a direct appeal to an individual well aware of the poet's despair and the proximate cause of it.

All of this is a prelude, however, to the most important and personal lines in the poem:

> In me thou see'st the glowing of such fire
> That on the ashes of his youth doth lie,
> As the death-bed whereon it must expire,
> Consum'd with that which it was nourish'd by.

Most modern commentators regard these lines as a continuation of the sunset metaphor, with youth being extinguished. Carl D. Atkins suggests that the final quatrain depicts the final stage in which youth disappears forever. "As the fire goes out when the wood which has been feeding it is consumed, so is life extinguished when the strength of youth is past".[158]

This particular idea, however, is echoed more directly by the preceding lines: "In me thou see'st the glowing of such fire / That on the ashes of his youth doth lie". Line 12, on the other hand, takes the thought further, from a dying flame which consumes its source to a glowing flame that is consumed by its source. This is a peculiar metaphor, a devouring flame that is itself devoured by its own fuel, and it has baffled many of the scholars who have attempted to discover its inspiration. It turns out that this line holds one of the keys to the entire sonnet sequence, one that reveals the source of Marlowe's original muse.

Duncan-Jones suggests that the line mirrors Ovid's line from Metamorphoses 15.234-6:

"tempus edax rerum, tuque, invidiosa vetustas"
(Eaten up by that which it ate up)[159]

J. B. Leishman translates the line differently and gives the complete extract:

tempus edax rerum, tuque, invidiosa vetustas,
omnia destruitis vitiataque dentibus aevi
paulatim lenta consumitis omnia morte!

(Time, devourer of things, and you, Jealous Age,
You destroy all, and, when they have once been impaired by the teeth of transience,
Gradually consume all with lingering death!)

Leishman concludes that this passage was very much in the poet's "memory and imagination when he was writing those sonnets about poetry as the defier of time."[160] Defying time, however, does not destroy it, nor does time consume itself.

While Ovid inspired much of Marlowe's work and life, this passage falls short as a possible basis for line 12 of sonnet 73.

Some scholars, including Philip Edwards, have noted the resemblance of line twelve of Sonnet 73 to the motto declared by the Fourth Knight in Act II, Scene 2 of Pericles: *Qui me alit me extinguit* [Who feeds me extinguishes me].[161] Interestingly, Pericles was published in 1609, the same year that the Sonnets were published, so there is some question as to which of these phrases came first. The issue is complicated by the fact that current scholarship attributes the first two acts of Pericles, including the scene where the motto is displayed, to George Wilkins who published a novelized version of the play in 1608 and, according to Suzanne Gossett, "was probably Shakespeare's collaborator on the play".[162] The New Oxford Shakespeare Authorship Companion re-enforces this position, giving Wilkins sole credit for scenes 1 through 11 of the first quarto[163], or Acts I through II of the third folio version. This contradicts the verdict of Geoffrey Bullock in his 1966 Narrative and Dramatic Sources of Shakespeare, vol VI where he observed that "Wilken's novel is largely founded on [Lawrence] Twine's recently republished Pattern of Painful Adventures (1607)"[164] and went on to cast doubt on any collaboration with the playwright:

> "We are driven to conclude that, having seen a Pericles play performed (perhaps more than once), Wilkens remembered what he could of it (maybe with the help of notes) and turned dramatic materials into prose as he interwove it with matter from Twine."[165]

Regardless of Wilken's possible contributions, none of these authorities speculates on the possible derivation of the *"Qui me alit"* motto, probably because Henry Green, in his famous work Shakespeare and the Emblem Writers (1870) which traces linkages and similarities between the play's and poem's themes and symbolism and the thought and expression of a considerable number of emblematist writers, confused the matter considerably by offering three potential sources for the Pericles motto: Gabriel Symeoni's Tetrastichi Morali (1561), Claude Paradin's Devises Heroïques, first published in 1551, translated into English in 1591, and Geffrey Whitney's Emblemes (1586). Based on the time line indicated by these sources, the relative resemblance of the Pericles motto to the individual sources and on the assumption that Pericles was a very early play, Green concluded that there is "a closer resemblance, both of thought and expression, to Whitney than to the other two."[166] This, despite the fact that Symeoni includes the exact motto *"QVI ME ALIT, ME EXTINGVIT"* in his 1561 edition while Whitney and Paradin do not and, in an addition to the 1574 edition, details the use of the motto in "the battle of the Swiss, routed near Milan by King Francis, M. de Saint Valier" and then paraphrases the motto in Italian, which Green then translates as:

> "the beauty of a lady whom he loved nourished all his thoughts, so she put him in peril of his life."[167]

Whitney's version, offered by Greene in comparison, is more elaborate and even less exact:

> "Even as the waxe doth feede, and quench the flame,
> So, love gives life; and love, dispaire doth give:
> The golie love, doth lovers croune with fame:
> the wicked love, in shame dothe make them live.
>   Then leave to love, or love as reason will,
>   For, lovers lewde doe vainlie languishe still."[168]

Green evidently credits the earliest English version over the earlier Italian as being the most likely source for the motto in Pericles despite the fact that it is King Simonides in Pericles, an obvious stand-in for Symeoni, who provides the clearest translation of the motto:

> "Which shows, that beauty hath this power and will,
> Which can as well inflame as it can kill".
> <u>Pericles</u> II, 2, 34-5

It is here that modern scholarship almost purposefully runs aground. While it is possible that King Simonides line could have been modelled after Green's translation of Symeoni, it does not seem at all possible that it could be restored to the exact Latin original by someone unaware of it, much less by someone relying, as Green supposes, on Whitney's version of Symeoni's Italian translation. Regardless, modern scholarship does not pursue the issue further, evidently satisfied that an English derivative has been found, even though it is no more authoritative than any other translation lacking reference to its actual source.

There is, however, another possible source for both the <u>Pericles</u> motto and line 12 of sonnet 73, one that is never mentioned by Greene or most other scholars but which mimics it more precisely than Symeoni's Latin: "Consumed by that which nourished me" bears a striking resemblance to the motto inscribed on Christopher Marlowe's famed Cambridge portrait: *"Quod me Nutrit me Destruit"* which translates as: What nourishes me destroys me.

Dated 1585 and preceding both the sonnet and <u>Pericles</u> by a quarter century, the portrait has a remarkable history. Discovered in 1952 in a garbage bin by an undergraduate during preparations for the 600th Anniversary of Cambridge's founding, it was in two wooden pieces that were covered in soot and grime, had been nailed through and, after spending untold decades as the flooring beneath a gas fired stove, had been discarded not far from rooms once assigned to Christopher Marlowe. The painting was subsequently cleaned, restored and authenticated. In addition to the date and motto, it bears an inscription that declares the model to be 21 years old, the same age as Marlowe in that year. Further research confirmed that Marlowe had the funds at the time to commission the portrait and that out of all the other students then at Cambridge, he was most likely its original. It has since become one of the most familiar of all Elizabethan portraits.

As for the motto, no one could explain its source. Neither F. S. Boas or John Bakeless, two Marlowe biographers, had ever heard of it. Rosemary Freeman of the University of London compared it to the motto in Pericles, but also admitted that she had never seen the combination of "Nutrit & Destruit".[169] Noel Purdon concluded:

> "This is a most unusual motto; it belongs to no crest of arms, has no heraldic significance. It is rather a personal emblem, one chosen by the sitter himself as an indication less of his public symbolism than of his private drama."[170]

Tarnya Cooper, on the other hand, discounts its significance:

> "The Latin inscription . . . is a version of a reasonably well-known Latin tag or impressa that appeared in various forms in emblem books of the period. Versions of this expression appear in the works of Marlowe and Shakespeare. As with the portrait of John Donne, the motto must have had some personal significance that is lost to us. The statement can probably be read as a plea from the sitter to a lover (or patron)."[171]

Cooper, however, offers no other examples of the expression, only another's gloss of the extinguit motto already discussed, and can offer no other examples in either Shakespeare or Marlowe except for the ones already noted which post-date it. Unwilling to even grant that the portrait depicts Marlowe, Cooper undermines her own argument by repeating evidence already submitted as evidence of additional evidence.

Regardless, when Henry Green translates Symeoni's *"QVI ME ALIT, ME EXTINGUIT"* motto, the same motto that appears in Pericles, he writes: "Who nourishes me, extinguishes me".[172] This clearly resembles the "What nourishes me, destroys me" of Marlowe, but Green had no access to Marlowe because he was writing in 1870 while Marlowe's painting was not discovered until 1952.

A simple timeline suggests Symeoni, then the portrait, then the Sonnet with <u>Pericles</u> either before or after it. This, of course, puts Marlowe smack in the middle. If, on the other hand, Whitney is substituted for Symeoni, then Marlowe's motto, which was painted a year before Whitney was published, precedes all the rest.

Line 12, which restates the motto from Marlowe's portrait, is followed immediately by "This thou perceiv'st", which is to say, "I know you understand me." It is a directly personal assertion that would only be made to a person the author knows and who he believes knows everything implied by the motto; not just the connection with the portrait, but also the link to <u>Pericles</u>. And how much more poignant is this when it is understood that the author was himself alive, still alive, in the East, in twilight, anticipating nightfall while the reader saw the sun still above him? Marlowe would not expect everyone to grasp this, but he knew that Thomas Walsingham would perceive it clearly because the sonnet would have called forth the extensive web of relationships, professional, personal and artistic, that composed a very significant part of Thomas' own life.

The motto is a single line that connects multiple threads in a life filled with great achievement and greater disappointment. It is a kind of prophecy that shortly after it was composed had to feel like the hand of fate. Sonnet 73 summarizes all of this and then concludes with a statement of resignation to a love that must be left "ere long". Positioned before 1598 and the "Rival Poet" sonnets, "Consum'd with that which it was nourish'd by" foreshadows the subsequent calamity of those sonnets which can be read in the context of a person who has journeyed far from home only to discover that his patron is suddenly replacing him with another closer to hand. Thomas Walsingham would not be able to deny his part in both nourishing and consuming Marlowe.

And yet, despite his involvement from the earliest days of Marlowe's work as an intelligencer and his knowledge of him from his days at Cambridge, even Thomas might not have known the motto's actual source. On the other hand, if he had known that Symeoni's motto was the prophetic source for Marlowe's motto, if Marlowe had explained it to him when he showed him the portrait, if he ever did, then he would also have known that sonnet 73's echo of it and the Fourth Knight's motto in <u>Pericles</u> were all connected, as the next chapter will show, to Marlowe's own origins and to the man who fired Marlowe's boyhood imagination, the man who is memorialized in <u>Pericles</u>, Marlowe's pole star, Philip Sidney.

Chapter Seven

Philip Sidney's Device

Well before his untimely death in October 1586 not far from the Netherlands battlefield at Zutphen and the eastern bank of the river Ijssel, Sir Philip Sidney was considered the leading poet of his or of any previous English generation. This, despite never having been published during his lifetime. Widely read in manuscript, his <u>Arcadia,</u> <u>Defense of Poesy</u> and <u>Astrophel and Stella</u> influenced both his own and following generations of poets, playwrights and novelists, to say nothing of critics, scholars and screenwriters. It was left to his beloved sister Mary, later the Countess of Pembroke and mother to William Henry, the third Earl of Pembroke, and his brother Philip, to whom together the First Folio is dedicated, to edit and publish his major works even while making a substantial name for herself as a poet, playwright and patron. Christopher Marlowe's connection to the Sidney family was substantially enhanced when he started writing for Pembroke's Men, the company established in 1592 in honor of William, but his attachment to them appears to have been initiated long before that.

In addition to his poetic accomplishments and his less fortunate exploits in battle, Philip Sidney was a notable participant in festival tournaments and "tilts" of the mid 1570s and early 1580s, in particular the Callophisus challenge and the "Four Foster Children of Desire" tournament in May, 1581. Edmund Molyneux described his special talent:

> "at jousts, triumphs, and other such royal pastimes (for all such disports he commonly made one) he would bring in such a lively gallant show, so agreeable to every point which is required for the expressing of a perfect device,

(so rich was he in those inventions) as, if he surpassed not all, he would equal or at least second the best."[173]

If the parade of knights and their devices in Act II of Pericles is any indication, then the author of the play and sonnet 73 had an interest in heraldic mottos that echoed Sidney's. According to Henry Green, there are hundreds of references in the plays and poems to these emblems and mottos.[174] The parade, which has no known source and compares only to the testing of suitors in The Merchant of Venice, appears to be a very literal memorial to Philip Sidney.

The mottos displayed by the knights in Pericles are:

1. Knight of Sparta: *"Lux tua vita mihi"*: YOUR LIGHT IS MY LIFE,

2. Prince of Macedon: *"Piu por dulzura que por fuerza"*: MORE BY GENTLENESS THAN BY FORCE,

3. Knight of Antioch: *"Me pompae provexit apex"*: THE DESIRE OF RENOWN HAS CARRIED ME FORWARD,

4. Knight (not named): *"Quod me alit, me extinguit"*: THAT WHICH NOURISHES ME, DESTROYS ME

5. Knight (not named): *"Sic spectanda fides"*: SO IS FIDELITY TO BE PROVED,

6. The Stranger Knight (Pericles in rusty armor): *"In hac spe vivo"*: I LIVE IN THIS HOPE

While Green was able to establish sources for the first five of the mottos displayed in the parade of emblems in Pericles, he stated that "at present we must be content to say that the source of the motto and device of the sixth knight has not been discovered."[175]

What Green apparently did not know is that the Strange Knight's motto bears a strong resemblance to the original motto of Sir Philip Sidney, Spero [Hope], attributed to him by George Whetstone in his commemorative poem Sir Phillip Sidney, His Honorable Life, His Valiant Death.[176] William Camden revealed that this motto has a poignant history:

> "Sir Philip Sidney, who was a long time heir apparent to the Earl of Leicester, after the said earl had a son born to him, used at the next tilt-day following SPERAVI, thus dashed through, to show his hope therin was dashed."[177]

Camden's summary leaves out a significant part of the story. It was Robert Deveraux's mother, Lettice Deveraux, wife of the second Earl of Essex, who married Leicester and dashed Sidney's hopes. On his deathbed in 1576, the Earl had recommended Sidney as a husband for his daughter, Penelope Deveraux, but Sidney had been slow to act and when Sidney's fortunes declined Penelope eventually married Robert Rich in 1581 about the same time that Liecester's son is believed to have been born. Sidney may well have regretted his hesitation and Penelope is "traditionally thought to have inspired Sidney's Astrophil and Stella."[178] Sidney finally married Frances Walsingham, Sir Francis' daughter in 1583. Upon Sidney's death, Frances married Robert Deveraux, by then the third Earl of Essex and soon to become Marlowe's nemesis. The intertwining of these family histories by way of marriage and dashed hopes of inheritance would soon yield a political storm that would engulf Marlowe. It should be no surprise that he chose to allude to it in a play about a famous knight whose hopes for family and fortune were repeatedly thwarted by outside forces beyond his control.

Sidney used other mottos, depending on the occasion. To have SPERO repeated in Pericles inevitably recalls the misfortune to which it once applied. In the opening scene, Pericles is challenged to resolve Thalia's riddle:

> "Hee's Father, Sonne, and Husband milde;
> I, Mother, Wife; and yet his child;
> How that may be, and yet in two,
> As you will live resolve it you."

In the play, Pericles realizes this Mother/Wife/child has been sexually abused by her father. In life, Sidney had failed to marry the daughter of the woman whose child deprived him of an inheritance. The situations are not perfectly parallel, but they come close and the play certainly intends to underscore the incestuous nature of so much of royalty.

Whetstone's commemorative poem includes many of the images and metaphors found in the parade of emblems. For instance, the first and second mottos, YOUR LIGHT IS MY LIFE, and MORE BY GENTLENESS THAN BY FORCE, appear to echo:

> "In peace he liu'd, admired of the best,
> In peace he liu'd, beloued of the worste:
> In peace he liu'd, and neuer man oppreste,
> In peace he liu'd, and euer, with the first.
> Layde helpe on those, whom fortune had accurste,
> And to be short, the rising sonne he was:
> That comforted and shinde in eu'ry place."

Similarly, the Third Knight's motto, THE DESIRE OF RENOWN HAS CARRIED ME FORWARD, appears to echo the following lines from Whetstone's poem:

> "Honour to gaine, by many a worthie deede,
> On Hope, truth, zeale Learning, and the Launce:
> He built his fame and had no foe but Chaunce."

The device, "a withered branch, that's only green at top" remains obscure, but Whetstone provides some tantalizing possibilities as the imagery of foliage is woven throughout his poem:

> For why as yet, my seruice is but greene,
> My yeres are young, and brought forth Leaues of late:
> The blomes were faire, but yet no fruit is seene,
> I studied haue, to benefit the state.
> To execute I am forbid by fate,

This argues that this part of Pericles was written after Sidney's death with an awareness of Whetstone's memorial. The choice of the SPERO motto, and the implied meanings, could not be accidental. Although Green reported that the source of the motto was unknown, William Camden, familiar with Whetstone and Sidney, could have known about it. Moreover, it would not be merely a literary reference, but would rather be a personal reference in the same spirit as Whetstone's memorial.

The parade of knights, by which means Pericles first appears before Thasia, the King's daughter, appears to be entirely the playwright's invention. None of the recognized sources for the play, not Gower's Confessio Amantis (1554), Twine's The Pattern of Painful Adventures, nor Sidney's Arcadia (1591), include such a parade which crosses the stage almost like a personal appeal.

One unrecognized source for this effect would have to be the powerful influence of The Queen's Men on the English stage of the 1580s. The "largest professional company England had ever known"[179] employed a performance style that was objective and literal in which "the unmistakable sign is crucial". "It consists of the figures and costumes of the actors, the objects they handle, and the properties and structures which frame their acting space."[180] In this theatrical world, emblems are more than decoration, they convey power, place and personality without reliance on poetic text. This was a tradition that had been developed over decades, that was re-enforced in pageants and festivals and could be seen everywhere in the form of heraldic images decorating houses great and small. It would be inevitable for the same imagery to be on display in Pericles and other plays of the period.

Another source for the pageantry of Pericles would have to be Philip Sidney. Sidney's use of emblems combined with his poetic skill to create highly theatrical events which included his attention to staging and spoken tributes composed specifically for the occasion. One of his most notable jousts was the "Four Foster Children of Desire" staged in celebration of the state visit by the Duc d'Alençon, heir to the French crown and then Queen Elizabeth's suitor. Katherine Duncan-Jones asserts that Sidney was the likely author of the tournament because "much of the language and imagery of the piece connects so closely with other writings by Sidney that his hand and brain seem to dominate."[181]

The "Foster Children" tournament was played before the French legation and featured Sidney cast in the role of "Anjou's Desire" tilting on behalf of Elizabeth's French suitor. He memorialized this double role, serving the Queen by representing a marriage proposal he opposed, in sonnet 41 of Astrophel and Stella:

> "Having this day my horse, my hand, my lance,
>   Guided so well, that I obtained the prize,
>   Both by the judgement of English eyes
> And of some sent by that sweet enemy, France;
> Horsemen my skill in horsemanship advance;
>   Town-folks my strength; a daintier judge applies
>   His praise to slight, which from good use doth rise;
> Some lucky wits impute it but to chance;
>   Others, because of both sides I do take
> My blood from them, who did excel in this,
> Think *Nature* me a man of arms did make.
> How far they shoot away! the true cause is,
>   *Stella* look'd on, and from her heav'nly face

Sent forth the beams, which made so fair my race."

A recent Sidney biographer, Alan Stewart, echoes the opinion of many when he asserts that "in May 1581 he was already writing the sequence of 108 sonnets, irregularly interspersed with eleven 'songs' which was posthumously published as Astrophel and Stella."[182]

If that is true, then Sonnet 42 of Astrophel and Stella would appear to be even more significant as it incorporates the idea behind *"Qui me alit, me extinguit"* and *"Quod Me Nutrit Me Destriut"* (What Nourishes Me, Destroys Me) by casting Stella's eyes as the nourishment that feeds death:

> "Oh eyes, which do the spheres of beauty move,
> Whose beams be joys, whose joys all virtues be,
> Who while they make Love conquer, conquer Love,
> The schools where Venus hath learned chastity;
> Oh eyes, whose humble looks most glorious prove,
> Only lov'd tyrants, just in cruelty,
> Do not, oh do not from poor me remove,
> Keep still my zenith, ever shine on me.
> For though I never see them, but straight ways
> My life forgets to nourish languished sprites;
> Yet still on me, oh eyes, dart down your rays
> And from the majesty of sacred lights,
> Oppressing mortal sense, my death doth proceed
> Wracks triumph be, which Love (highset) doth breed.

[emphasis added]

In this sonnet, Sidney has taken Symeoni's gloss of the *Qui Alit* motto: "the beauty of a lady whom he loved nourished all his thoughts, so she put him in peril of his life" and expanded it for his poetic purpose. With this sonnet and Marlowe's motto the two poets are clearly sharing the same contemporary inspiration, which is then echoed in both Pericles and Sonnet 73's "Consumed by that which it was nourished by". Indeed,

Pericles does this twice. When Helicanus swears his loyalty to Pericles after being challenged by him he clearly echoes Sidney's sonnet 42:

> Pericles: How durst thy tongue move anger in our face?
>
> Helicanus: How dares the plants look up to heaven,
> From whence they have their nourishment?
>
> Pericles: Thou knowest I have power to take thy life from thee.
>
> Helicanus: I have ground the axe myself.

Here the metaphor of nourishment capable of taking life more closely echoes lines from Astrophil and Stella than from Symeoni, re-enforcing the presence of Sidney in the text.

The repetition does not end there. This reverberation is further felt, with a caution against narcissism, in Sonnet 1, lines 5 to 8:

> "But then thou, contracted to thine own bright eyes,
> Feed'st thy light's flame with self-substantial fuel,
> Making a famine where abundance lies,
> thyself thy foe, to thy sweet self too cruel."

Written for Southampton's 17th birthday in 1590, this sonnet is positioned before Sonnet 73 which is generally agreed to have been written after the Deptford incident in May, 1593. Marlowe has, in short, taken his own motto which echoes Sidney's to frame the argument for his commission from Lord Burghley for the Earl of Southampton and then repeated it in sonnet 73.

The sequence of inspiration first outlined in Chapter Six then becomes: Symeoni (1574), Sidney (circa 1581, published 1591), Marlowe's Motto (1585), Sonnet 1, (circa 1590, published 1609), Pericles Acts I and II (circa 1591, published 1609), Sonnet 73 (after 1593, published 1609).

Katherine Duncan-Jones asserts that "Astrophel and Stella does not appear to have been circulated during Sidney's lifetime in the way that we know the 'Old' Arcadia was."[183] While it is possible that Marlowe and Sidney came to Symeoni's influence separately, the similarity between the use they made of it argue against this. Marlowe's repetition seems especially significant, as if the return to the idea recalls its first restating by Sidney so that, for Marlowe, Sidney is more the inspiration than Symeoni. What all of this suggests is that Marlowe's interest in Sidney was not simply literary, as extensive as that was, it was deeply personal. For the author of Pericles, Sidney was a hero.

Another "favorite"[184] Sydney motto: "Vix ea nostro voco", meaning "I scarcely call our ancestor's deeds our own" is taken from Ovid's Metamorphosis, 13:141 and was intended to credit his family for the honors he received. This motto is engraved on Sidney's battlefield memorial at Zutphen where he fell. Symeoni dedicated his 1559 "Vita et Metamorfoseo D'Ovido" to Signora Duchessa di Valentinos, the daughter of King Francis, M. de Saint Valier, to whom Symeoni credited the standard with an upside down torch and the motto "Qui me alit, me extinguit"[185]. Sidney would have been well aware of these connections, Symeoni with Ovid and the two mottos with each other when he chose them, one for his own emblem and the other for his sonnet. If Marlowe was not also aware of these connections either by way of reading Symeoni directly or under Sidney's influence, then he mirrored them by way of one of the most incredible accidents in literature. Ovid, of course, is a perpetual presence in Marlowe's writing, in particular his unfinished Hero and Leander.

A handful of commentators, in particular Sidney Blumenthal, have suggested that "there is good reason to believe that when Christopher was eight he was recruited as a page to serve one of the young noblemen about to embark on a tour of the Continent."[186] Blumenthal believes that the nobleman in question was Philip Sidney and bases this surmise on the fact that Marlowe's whereabouts from the age of eight to fourteen when he entered the King's School are undocumented, that this period overlaps Sidney's 1572 to 74 tour of Europe, that Sidney embarked by way of Dover not far from Marlowe's Canterbury home, that Marlowe wrote The Massacre of Paris which "is virtually a straightforward but compressed retelling of the horrible events that took place in Paris, to which Sir Francis Walsingham and the 17-year-old Philip Sidney were witnesses."[187] It is striking that in Scene vii of The Massacre Marlowe includes the murder of Petrus Ramus, the philosopher whose friendship with Sidney was so notable that several of the logician's books were dedicated to him by their translators.

Robert Ayers, Professor Emeritus, of Insead, Fontainbleau, France, believes that "it is doubtful that the details which finally appeared in his play Massacre at Paris (1593) could have come from anywhere but the official report based on Tomasso Sassetti's original, sent from Walsingham to Lord Burghley."[188] That said, he does not explain how Marlowe might have been permitted to read that report or why, if he was not particularly fascinated by the event, have any interest in reading about it. Ayers further suggests that "it is fairly likely that the boy encountered French Huguenot refugees near John Marley's home in Canterbury"[189], but none of that explains his interest in Petrus Ramis. The simplest explanation is that Marlowe witnessed the event first hand as a boy in the company of Philip Sidney who was definitely there.

The notion that the young Marlowe was scooped up by Sidney and taken with him on a three year tour of Europe, including an extended stay in Italy, where he would witness the ruling class first hand and benefit directly from Sidney's own interest in literature is tantalizing. The difficulty is that, for all the close associations, there is no direct evidence to support it. Other than the dozens of common associates, including Walsingham, Essex, and Burghley to name but a few of the most significant, and the multiple literary links, the closest report of an actual sighting is Dominicus Baudius remark that when Sidney, dying in September, 1586 from his musket wound in Arnheim, proposed to respond to a communique from Leicester, "he immediately orders that young man to be sent in (whom I remember to have seen with you, very witty and well-educated) and tells him to prepare a letter of personal commendation to the earl."[190] Marlowe, in fact, was absent from Cambridge at exactly that time. The rumor was that he had "gone beyond the seas to Reames"[191] and was therefore in danger of forfeiting his degree. Whatever else he might have been doing, the Queen's Privy Council denied the rumor in their June 29, 1587 record advocating his degree and further declared that "it was not her Majesties pleasure that anie one emploied as he had been in matters touching the benefit of his countrie should be defamed by those that are ignorant in th'affaires he went about."[192] Which is to say that, since he was not at Reims, he could have been at Arnheim in the field of battle with Leicester and Sidney employed in matters benefitting his country. On the other hand, Sidney does not include him in his will and Fulke Greville, Sidney's close friend and biographer makes no mention of him whatsoever.

Still, it is odd that someone entering an elite institution like the King's School, on a scholarship no less, did not leave more of a record of his prior education, and there are good reasons to believe that Marlowe began his playwrighting career working for Leicester's Men and that the staging of the parade of emblems echoes similar parades staged by Sidney himself. Regardless of whether or not there was ever a direct connection between them, Philip Sidney was very influential in Marlowe's work as evidenced in the <u>Sonnets</u> and in <u>Pericles</u>.

The observation is often made that Pericles appears to have been written by more than one playwright and that George Wilkens, who also wrote and published a novelized version of the story in 1608, was responsible for the first two acts, which are considered less skillful. Amateurish style does not, however, explain how or why Wilkens, or any other writer, would have incorporated the Sidney references into the parade of emblems, which itself is original to the play.

An earlier generation of poet/critics saw the play as the work of a single, less mature author. John Dryden asserted that Pericles was an early work in his Prologue to William Davenant's Circe: "'Tis a miracle to see a good first play / All Hawthorne's do not bloom on Christmas-day."[193] Edmund Malone also thought it was the work of a young playwright, observing that "[t]he wildness and irregularity of the fable, the artless conduct of the piece, and the inequalities of the poetry, may, I think, be all accounted for, by supposing it either his first or one of his earliest essays in dramatick composition".[194]

The dramaturgy of the play, particularly the first two acts, is notably archaic with an emphasis on the visual and the literal. This was the theatre of The Queen's Men of 1582/3, a style focused on "objects, costumes, the gestures of actors and patterns of stage movement" to which "spoken language tend[ed] to be subordinate."[195] This style has been dubbed "Theatrical Literalism" by Scott McMillan and Sarah-Beth MacLean "in order to set it apart from the plays of . . . Marlowe . . . which selected some elements of literalism, transformed them by means of an astonishing advance in dramatic poetry, and eventually marginalized the older style. . . ."[196]

The modern consensus, however, is that the play is the first of the "late" plays, which includes The Winter's Tale, Cymbeline, and The Tempest. This assessment is complicated by the fact that "while the boundaries between what is early and what is late may appear fixed, Pericles's reception at the hands of critics, editors and producers also exhibits a series of seemingly contradictory moments at which binary oppositions between early and late, young and old, are put under strain."[197] Most editors have attempted to resolve these contradictions by proposing a co-author, such as Wilkens (see above), for the less accomplished parts of the play, in particular Acts I and II.

Some support for this idea can be found in the fact that the play splits very neatly into two parts, the first being the struggles of Pericles from his deciphering of Antiochus' incestuous riddle through his rescue of Cleon's city and finally the joust which features the parade of emblems and his marriage to the daughter of Symonides, Thaisa. The second part of the play begins in Act III with a new series of trials which first separates Pericles, Thaisa and their daughter Marina by way of shipwreck and then follows each of them through personal trials to their final reunion. In fact, the title page of the first quarto proclaims the dual nature of the play:

> "THE LATE and much admired Play, Called Pericles, Prince of Tyre. With the true Relation of the whole Historie, adventures and fortunes of the said Prince; As also, The no less strange, and worthy accidents, in the Birth and Life of his Daughter MARIANA"

The general perception that the first two acts are less accomplished than the final three is disrupted only by an equally strong agreement that major parts of Act IV, which depict Marina's ordeal in a brothel, are also awkwardly realized. As usual, whenever deficiencies in the text occur, they are attributed to the collaborator, whoever he may be.

Complicating the theory of collaboration, however, is the fact that a number or editors and directors have utilized sections of the brothel scenes in Wilken's novel in order to "smooth out their problems of tone and characterization."[198] Indeed, <u>The Oxford Shakespeare: The Complete Works</u> goes so far as to present "A Reconstructed Text", including major contributions from Wilken's <u>The Painful Adventures of Pericles, Prince of Tyre</u> based on the premise that the novel appears to have reported parts of the play as performed "both more accurately and more fully than the quarto."[199]

A major problem with this notion is that it begs the question: if Wilkens is reporting unprinted parts the play's performance in his novel, parts which resolve textual issues that Taylor felt were left incomplete in the play's original quarto, why then would Wilkens, who appears to anticipate Taylor's concerns, omit those same speeches from the printed text of a play he supposedly co-authored? It would be one thing if the play were adapted from the novel, but this is clearly not the case because the novel mimics the play in performance.

Considering that Wilkens is an unlikely source for the parade of emblems, with all of its references to Philip Sidney, and that, according to Bullough, he appears to have been pirating a play in performance in order to get his version into print before the authorized version, he makes an unlikely contributor at any remove. If Wilkens had the ability to perceive the need for the additional material in the brothel scene, and then added it to the novel, was it ever onstage in the first place? Or, if it did get onstage, why wasn't it included it in the published play?

One reason may be that the added material taken from Wilken's novel is not very good. The following, for instance, sandwiches the quarto's text with the Oxford additions by way of Wilkins, which are underlined for clarity:

> Marina: <u>Let not authority, which teaches you
> To govern others, be the means to make you
> Misgovern much yourself.</u>
> If you were born to honor, show it now;
> If put upon you, make the judgement good
> That thought you worthy of it. <u>What reason's in
> Your justice, who hath power over all,
> To undo any? If you take from me
> Mine honor, you're like him that makes a gap
> Into forbidden ground, whom after
> Too many enter, and of all their evils
> Yourself are guilty. My life is yet unspotted;
> My chastity unstained ev'nn in thought.
> Then if your violence deface this building
>> The workmanship of heav'n, you do kill your
>> honor
> Abuse your justice, and impoverish me.</u>

Ultimately, Marina's extended pleadings are not very satisfactory and the mixed metaphor of a gap in the ground of a house of ill repute is just crude and about as tasteless as the title joke in the film comedy "American Pie". The fact that in the printed text Lisymachus is disarmed by Marina's purity and innocence is more significant than any argument reported by Wilkins. So often the quartos are declared corrupted by faulty reporting, but the "gap into forbidden ground", as well as most of the other additions included by Wilkins, if not his own inventions, were those of an actor, something that goes on all the time, as Hamlet complained, and which in this case was reported literally by Wilkins. All of this argues against Wilkins as a collaborator. As F. D. Hoeniger concluded, "it would be odd if a habitual plagiarist were to follow his own composition so very much less than someone else's."[200]

Other candidates have been proposed as co-authors for Pericles, including John Day, Thomas Heywood and William Rowley, but none of the assertions in their favor have been convincing. Rejecting all such speculation, Geoffrey Bullough, after detailing the scene by scene application of the source material, offers the simplest assessment: "Q represents an earlier play that was even more sprawling than it is now, . . . and that it was mainly written in a style which still predominates in Acts I and II, though with flashes of genuine poetic feeling."[201]

Current scholarship presupposes that the play could not have been written before 1592 because the presumed author is not known to have been active in the English theatre before that time. Marlowe, however, is known to have been active as Dido, Queen of Carthage is believed to have been written while he was still at Cambridge in 1586. If Marlowe, whose affinity for Sidney appears to be fairly well established at this point, was the author of the original Pericles, then there is no reason why its original composition cannot be dated as early as 1586, even before the time of Sidney's death.

There is no record of any performance of Pericles in the 1580s or 90s which, given its subsequent popularity in 1608, strongly suggests that it was not in production before then. Which then begs the question, if it was an early play, as Dryden and Bullough believe and the evidence seems to show, and it is clearly stage-worthy, why wasn't it staged?

The answer may well be that in the wake of Sidney's death the novice author, faced with a "sprawling play" and lacking the heart or skill to revise it, simply put it aside. Sidney's presence permeates the play, especially the first two acts. His death at Arnheim hit the nation very hard and was very publicly observed:

> "his body made its slow way from the Low Countries where he had died at Arnheim, to lie in state at the Minories Church just outside Aldgate, thence to be carried through the streets of London to St. Paul's Cathedral, where he was buried on 16 February, 1586."[202]

Thomas Lant commented at the time that the city streets "were so thronged with people that the mourners had scarcely room to pass; the houses likewise were as full as they might be, of which great multitude there were few or not that shed not some tears as the corpse passed by them."[203] His funeral was staged by the combined power of the Earl of Leicester and Sir Francis Walsingham and was intended to enshrine his memory as "a great national hero, courtier, soldier and poet, who epitomised the ideals of Elizabethan chivalry."[204]

Sydney died on the field of battle, defending England shortly after his parents died that same year. Sidney's 42nd Sonnet, echoed by Marlowe's motto from 1585, had become a kind of bitter prophecy as Sidney was consumed by the fire of patriotism that nourished him in the siege of Arnheim. If Marlowe had intended <u>Pericles,</u> with its multiple references to this fraught motto, to be an ironic tribute to the fiery poet and courtier, it could not have been an attractive subject for him in the wake of a national and possibly personal tragedy.

The question then is not why was Pericles never staged before 1608, but why did its author return to it after more than twenty years? If, as Suzanne Gosset complained:

> "Almost all readers of Pericles note a striking change in the quality of the poetry at the beginning of the third act. The persistent question has been how to account for the evident differences, in verse and imaginative density, between the first two acts and the remaining three."[205]

The answer to this question can be found in the same Sonnet that includes the echo of *Quod mi Alit, mi extinguit*. Line 12 of Sonnet 73 is that echo and what comes after reminds the reader, "This thou perceiv'st," which is to say, "I know you understand". The writer is speaking to a specific person, not just anyone, and that person is the same person to whom the "Rival Poet" sonnets were addressed, Thomas Walsingham.

All the evidence suggests that Pericles was left unfinished after Philip Sidney's death for a multitude of reasons, chief among which was the traumatic effect of that death on the author himself. Twenty years later, Marlowe resurrected the play and repurposed it, infusing it with a revived spirit of hope (Spero), Sidney's own motto and the motto concluding the parade of emblems.

In addition to the improvement in poetic skill in the second part of Pericles there is a change in the theme. No longer the progress of a champion through adversity to reward, now it becomes a trial of innocence against cynicism with an ultimate reward of reunion where, as Gossett observes, "all members of the family are reunited after undergoing suffering, purification . . . and miraculous renewal."[206] This has nothing to do with Sidney. The first two acts echo Sidney's progress from marriage interrupted to marriage hopes (Spero) achieved. In the final three acts, Marina and Thaisa are finally reunited with Pericles.

The reunion scenes in the final act are especially strong, particularly Pericles and Marina, Thaisa less so because hers repeats the stronger scene, but both redeem the awkwardness of first part of the play. It is the hope of reunion, reflected in many of the sonnets, that would have been enough to motivate Marlowe to revisit one of his earliest plays twenty years later. When viewed in this context, the first part of the play testifies to Marlowe's youthful aspirations, his hero worship of Sidney and desire to follow his lead. Revising those first two acts would only betray that innocence. Better to leave them intact to recall that innocence and have it be honored by the stronger completion of the long journey home.

If sonnets 73 and 74 encapsulate an entire autobiographical narrative up to the moment before the publication of Hero and Leander, then Pericles recaptures and reframes that narrative in the aftermath of despair and the revival of hope. A series of sonnets, in particular sonnets 50 and 51 which describe a journey on horseback, and 56, 60 and 65 which speak of separation as if by a body of water, imply a voyage away from the reader foreshadowing the twilight of lines 5 - 8 of sonnet 73. The "Rival Poet" sonnets should thus be read in the context of a person who has traveled far from home, not unlike Pericles, only to discover that his patron is suddenly replacing him with another closer to hand. It would take years for the shock to wear off and understanding replace outrage.

Meanwhile, Marlowe had a two-track career to pursue, as intelligencer and playwright. Each would be enabled by his apprenticeship with Sir Francis Walsingham's pet propaganda project, the Queen's Men theatre company.

Chapter Eight

Working for Walsingham

Almost all biographies of Christopher Marlowe have him starting his theatrical career with the explosion of Tamburlaine. John Bakeless expresses the conventional view thus:

> "the young scholar, after six years at least theoretically withdrawn from the world at Cambridge, supported by the archbishop's scholarship, came up to London - probably with Tamburlaine and a few translations in his pocket, perhaps with other plays we can only guess at - and cast about for a means of livelihood."[207]

While it is no small compliment to credit a cloistered divinity scholar possessing no training in any public venue other than mock court, boys choir and the occasional holiday theatrical with blowing the lid off of the established professional theater with a play so revolutionary that no one saw him or it coming, there is plenty of evidence to support the view that Marlowe spent years in preparation for a career in the professional theater even as he studied for his M.A. degree. For one thing, Marlowe was absent from Cambridge for extended periods, including "most of autumn 1584"[208], three weeks in January 1585, then from mid-April to June, 1585, and leaving again in mid-July before the end of the Summer term. He was absent for Spring of 1586 and half of Winter 1587 when his scholarship expired. It was at that point that the Cambridge Dons were apparently unwilling to award him his graduate degree, whereupon the Privy Council intervened to secure it. Two other things about this period are notable. First, Marlowe went home to nearby Canterbury and witnessed Katherine Benchkin's will on August 19, 1585. The document is the only record of his movements during his absence from the fourth (summer) trimester at Cambridge and includes the only known specimen of his signature. Second, according town records of the time, The Queen's Men theatre troupe was performing in the neighborhood of Cambridge from February to July, 1585 having previously visited the town and university in early July, 1584.

The Queen's Men was then the leading theatrical company in England, having been created at Francis Walsingham's instigation in March, 1583. It was an all-star troupe assembled by the Master of Revels, Lord Edmund Tilney, with the leading players from the principal acting companies then separately sponsored by the Earls of Leicester, Sussex, Oxford and Derby. It included the talents of Richard Tarlton, then the most famous comedian in England, and John Adams, a star player with Tarlton from Sussex's Men. From Leicester's Men came Robert Wilson, like Tarlton also an occasional playwright, John Lanham and William Johnson as well as seven other top talents from rival companies who together, in accordance with design, swiftly became the dominant company at court and in the provinces.

The purpose of the company was immediately twofold: not only was it to provide reliable entertainment of the highest quality for the court, it also had a political component, as Scott McMillin and Sally-Beth MacLean have pointed out:

> "The formation of the Queen's Men in 1583 should be regarded particularly in connection with the intelligence system - not because the Queen's Men were spies, but because Walsingham used licensed travelers of various kinds to give the impression of an extensive court influence within which the actual size and constitution of the spy system could not be detected."[209]

As the pre-eminent theatrical company, the Queen's Men helped regulate and standardize the plays that the court preferred, promoting a pro-Tudor political message with historical dramas like The Famous Victories of Henry V (1598) and The Troublesome Reigne of King John (1591). At the same time, their presence as a touring company tended to discourage anti-Protestant activities among the common neighborhoods. It would "not only carry the name and influence of the monarch through the country but would also give the impression of a watchful monarch, one whose 'men' ranged over the land."210

While the names of several actors in the company, including Robert Wilson, John Dutton, John Garland and William Smith, have been connected with courier services, Walsingham appears to have a decided preference for writers such as Anthony Munday, Thomas Watson, Thomas Kyd and, of course, Christopher Marlowe. All things considered, it would be quite remarkable indeed for someone with the talent and ambition of Marlowe, frequently absent from his studies with employment by the crown and proximity to the creator of the most significant theatrical company in England, familiar with other writers of less talent similarly employed, to have somehow avoided contact with anyone in the theatrical profession before he sauntered into London and presented Tamburlaine, without so much as an introduction, to Philip Henslowe.

In fact, Marlowe has been reliably credited by a wide range of noted scholars, supported by documentary evidence and textual analysis, with the origination, inspiration or revision of several of the Queen's Men's most important surviving scripts, many of which were not only independently published, but which were subsequently rewritten for the Lord Chamberlain's Men and eventually incorporated in the First Folio. The list includes not only The Famous Victories and The Tragical Reign, but also King Leir (1605) and The True Tragedy of Richard III (1594). Before any of that, however, came the unpublished comedy Timon, which appears to have been written in 1580-81, about the same time as the first draft of Pericles.

Based on the Timon story in Lucian's Misanthropos, a manuscript copy of Timon, now at the Victoria and Albert Museum in London, is apparently a copy of an earlier, student work that can be traced by means of internal evidence to the King's School in Canterbury from about the time of the completion of Kentish native Francis Drake's circumnavigation of the globe. Drake returned to England in the fall of 1580. As Park Honan observed, "exactly when Timon was completed is unclear, but its humor depends on people's having Drake's voyage freshly in mind."[211]

For instance, in scene ii a "lying traveller" named Pseudocheus boasts that he has circled the world by riding a flying wooden Pegasus for three and a half years. Drake's own journey on the Pelican ended on September 26, 1580, three and a half years after he left Deptford in March, 1577 and two months before Christopher Marlowe entered at Cambridge in December of 1580. Further satirizing Drake's circumnavigation, Pseudocheus measures his trip in the air-mileage of "ducks and drakes" and claims to have seen the Antipodes, Africa, Arabia and the Ganges, all places that Drake visited.

Honan goes on to add that the play "includes expressions soon to appear in Marlowe's own works-fairly unusual words, such as *brabbling*, *insinuate*, *ruinate*, *strategm*, *adamantine*, or *invocate*, which are unlikely to have been used by other young playwrights, as well as phrases such as "cruel Scythians", and other proper names which Marlowe uses and favors such as these, to mention a dozen: Lybia, Boreas, Hecuba, Antarctic, Caucasus, Zodiac, Pylades, Tantalus, Amazons, Proserpina, Ganges, or Antipodes."[212]

Timon, like Timon of Athens, "is built on the kinds of allegorical narrative inherited from the late medieval morality play"[213] but is no less stage-worthy for its time than its better known rewrite. In fact, William Warner, an Oxford educated London attorney, author of Albion's England (1586) and a poet celebrated by Francis Meres in Paladis Tamia as "the best of wits of both our universities, our English Homer"[214], appears to have made note of a stage version of the Timon story in the Note to the Reader of his Pan his Syrinx, or Pipe, Compact of Seven Reedes (1584):

"And yet, let his coy Prophetise presage harde euentes in her Cell, <u>let the Athenian</u> ⟨ in non-Latin alphabet ⟩ , or <u>Man-hater bite on the Stage</u>, or the Sinopien Cynic barke with the Stationer, yet, in Pan his Syrinx, wil I pype, at the least to my self."[215]

[Emphasis added]

While the reference to the man hating Athenian, a.k.a. Timon, is clear enough, it is not possible to tell from this whether or not it is Marlowe's <u>Timon</u> or who staged it, but the timing would work well enough as Marlowe was absent from Cambridge for most of the fall of 1584 and the Queen's Men would have been a more than viable producer and worthy of note. There are no other Timon scripts extant, no other recorded performances of a Timon play from that period and the only other company associated with Walsingham and Marlowe would be Leicester's Men, which was by then in steep decline and no longer performing at court.

Although <u>Timon</u> is generally recognized as the chief source for <u>Timon of Athens</u>, primarily because it includes several scenes found in the later play which are not found in any other source, the 1580 dating is much disputed by orthodox scholars because <u>Timon</u> is also believed by some to be a source for <u>King Lear</u> (1605) due to the similarity between the character of Laches in <u>Timon</u> and Kent in <u>Lear</u>. In addition, Laches dupes another character, Hermongenes, into believing he is suddenly blind and leads him around the stage just as Edgar leads Gloucester in <u>Lear</u>. This similarity led Robert Goldsmith to suggest that <u>Timon</u> was used as a source for <u>King Lear</u>.[216] Geoffrey Bullough, however, objected to this observation, arguing that the Kent character is instead based on Perillus from the older <u>King Leir</u> (1594) (which itself was taken from Book II of *De gestis Britonum* (On the Deeds of the Britons) (1136) by Geoffrey of Monmouth) and that the Edgar/Gloucester scene is separately based on the story of the blind king of Paphlagonia in Philip Sidney's Arcadia (1590). "It is much more likely," Bullough concluded, "that the academic Timon drew on Shakespeare's King Lear than that it independently combined material from the old Leir play and Sidney's romance."[217] For this reason, Bullough and others date Timon from 1607-8, sometime after King Lear would have been performed.

The later date, while supportive of the orthodox position, ignores both the Drake material, which would have been twenty years out of date by 1600, but also the fact that Marlowe, as evidenced by Pericles, would have had no difficulty combining a scene from Arcadia with material from his college days. John Baker argued exactly this based on the internal evidence of style, vocabulary and allusions, and added that other elements, including the character of a drunken 80-year old woman, look like comic drafts for Dido, Queen of Carthage.[218] No one other than Marlowe has ever been nominated as author of the Timon comedy and resistance to this conclusion, rather than evidence based, appears to be largely the effect of a predisposition to look elsewhere.

Regardless of whether or not Timon was ever performed, by the Queen's Men, Leicester's Men, Sussex's Men or by a group of Cambridge scholars, there is ample confirmation that Christopher Marlowe spent some part of his time away from Corpus Christi college working for Walsingham's newly formed enterprise.

As long ago as 1783, Edmond Malone, the first critic to establish a chronology for the plays in the Folio, which is still largely accepted, credited Christopher Marlowe with the authorship of The Troublesome Reign of King John. That credit has more recently been somewhat disputed (typically, The New Oxford Shakespeare Authorship Companion refuses to even mention Marlowe in this context, much less offer counter arguments), but never fully overturned. Meanwhile, J. M. Robertson, M.P. for Tyneside 1906-18, elected to the Privy Council in 1915, author of The Shakespeare Canon (1922-32), echoes Malone's assessment that "Marlowe was the 'chief plotter' of The Reigne, with Lodge, Peele, and Greene as collaborators."[219] Not published until 1592, the play is typically dated from 1587-8 because "it represents popular opinion at about the year of the Armada."[220]

The inference is often made that because The Troublesome Reign was printed one year after Tamburlaine (1590) and because its preface deliberately complains about "the Sycthian Tamburlaine", it must therefore have followed Tamburlaine in composition. Prefaces are not plays, however, and the fact that the publisher broke the single script of The Troublesome Reign into two parts in order to mimic the two parts of Tamburlaine, suggests that the preface itself may be more part of someone's marketing strategy than a clear indicator of the chronological sequence of a trio of plays written and performed several years before. Regardless, the plays were written for, owned by and produced by completely separate companies. Either Marlowe was working for both companies, or he worked first for one and then for the other in sequence.

In the case of King Leir, which has been variously attributed individually or in some combination to Thomas Kyd, Robert Greene, George Peele, Thomas Lodge and Anthony Munday, all of whom are believed to have written plays for the Queen's Men, John Munro pointed out the numerous similarities between it and The Troublesome Reign and came to the conclusion that they were written by the same person:

> "Both plays exhibit the same admixture of religion and ribaldry. Both possess singular verbs in plural cases. The verse in each case has the same characteristics of flat pedestrianism and classical allusions in tragic circumstances. The murderer in each play is provided with a letter which he shows to his victims, and the victims prevail upon the murderer with arguments on "everlasting torments" in "grisly hell." The Bastard-Limoges wrangle is equivalent to the Mumford-Cambria wrangle; and the same interludes of farce in prose are provided. Ragan, like Constance, is desirous "with these

nails" to "scratch out her [enemy's] hateful eyes." A perusal of the plays is very persuasive that the same author wrote them."[221]

This series of mutual and interlinked sources and scripts puts Marlowe as the author of Timon (attributed conditionally by Honan and entirely by Baker), author (Malone) or at least chief plotter (Robertson) of The Troublesome Reign of King John and likely, by inference, contributor to King Leir (Munro) in the very middle of three major Queen's Men productions while he was still at Cambridge in the mid 1580s. No other single author has been credited with sole or contributory authorship of all three plays and Timon survived in manuscript to later influence the rewrite of not only itself into Timon of Athens, but of Leir into King Lear, which is quite a journey for a Drake era, collegiate satire.

It is also interesting to consider that both Timon and King Leir are comedies with happy endings. After scorning Athens and cursing mankind for its faithlessness and cowardice, Timon relents at the very end and, in the epilogue, offers to forgive the faults of men if the audience will simply applaud the play. Leir, meanwhile, learns the folly of his selfishness and reconciles with Cordelia who forgives him and then helps him defeat his two ungrateful daughters, Goneril and Regan.

The purpose of The Troublesome Reign of King John, on the other hand, was largely political. This was also true of John Bale's earlier King John which depicted him as a precursor of Henry VIII: "Strongly nationalistic, the play [Bale's King John] glories in the good king, who is fighting the Catholic church."[222] During the Elizabethan period, however, "the propaganda value of John's reign had shifted: rebellion was wrong, even if the king, like John, was not perfect."[223] At a time when Francis Walsingham was more and more concerned with plots against the Queen, it would be a practical use of his traveling theatre company to present a play advocating support for the crown against Catholic sedition and it would be in keeping with the purpose of a company "formed to spread

Protestant and royalist propaganda through a divided realm"[224] to employ a literate, skilled poet and intelligencer to contribute to or even compose such a play based on a familiar, proven original. Christopher Marlowe would certainly fit that practical need.

King Lear was entered into the Stationer's Register on November 26, 1607 as "A booke called Master William Shakespeare his historye of Kinge Lear as yt was played before the Kings Majestie at Whitehall uppon Sainct Stephens night at Christmas Last, by his majesties servantes playing usually at the Globe on the Bancksyde."[225] For most scholars, and readers in general, this is pretty conclusive proof that the play was written by William Shakespeare. The play is believed to have been completed sometime after October 12, 1605 (October 2, Old Style) because it makes reference to the "late eclipses in the sun and moon" (Act I, sc. 2, 108) with the sun on the 12th and the moon on September 27th of that year. It is, of course, interesting to note that according to NASA[226] the path of the eclipse passed directly over Sicily while England remained always in a partial view.

The debate doesn't end there, however, because a number of scholars have had to recognize the fact that King Lear appears to have relied upon the manuscript of the otherwise unknown Timon as a source for the Kent/Gloucester scenes. Robert Hills Goldsmith has already been noted, but Geoffrey Bullough, who disputed this attribution also admits that "the faithful servant Laches (whose name was taken from that of one of the syncophants in Lucian [inf. 277] reminds one of Kent in King Lear, who is driven out for reproving his master, but returns in disguise and stays with Lear to the end."[227] As previously noted, Bullough asserts that King Leir's Perillus is the source for this character, not imagining that the same playwright might have written both, but even he has to admit that there is another significant resemblance between Timon and King Lear in the scene where Timon proposes that the unhappy Gelasimus kill himself:

> "What, art thou wretched, and desir'st to die?
> Ile tell thee where are wild beasts, where's the sea,
> Where's a steepe place upon a stony rock
> That scytuated on a Mountaine high,
> And underneath the roaring sea doth swell:
> Wilt thou go thither? drowne thyself from thence?
> Ile be thy guide, and helpe thee at a push,
> And when thou fall'st into the lowest hell,
> I will rejoyce. What say'st thou, wilt thou die?"
>
> Timon, V. 3.

"This passage with its likeness to King Lear IV.1.74ff. and IV.6 has no parallel in the old Leir."[228] Regardless, Bullough then claims that the source for this scene is "the story of the blind King of Paphlagonia in Sidney's Arcadia" and then asserts that the author of Timon drew on King Lear rather than combining the old Leir and Sidney's Arcadia while adding its own original touch with Timon's murderous proposal which was then echoed less extremely by Kent in King Lear. Bullough and most scholars therefore see the sequence of influences as Arcadia, Leir, King Lear, Timon of Athens and then Timon being last and influencing nothing.

In fact, however, Bullough is flatly wrong about Arcadia being the supposed source for Kent bidding Gloucester "farewell" prior to letting him make his imagined leap from the cliffs of Dover. There, the King of Paphlagonia instead praises his son for refusing to do exactly what Timon and Kent both said they would do:

> "Till this sonne of mine (God knowes, worthie of a
> more vertuous, and more fortunate father) forgetting
> my abominable wrongs, not reckning danger, and
> neglecting the present good way he was doing himself
> good, came hither to doo this kind office. . . . And for
> this cause I craved of him to leade me to the toppe of
> this rocke, indeed I must confesse, with meaning to free

him from so Serpentine a companion as I am. But he finding what I purposed, onely therein since he was borne, shewed himselfe disobedient unto me."

Arcadia, Book II, Chapter 10

Bullough's claim notwithstanding, there is no way that this can be interpreted to mean that the King of Paphlagonia's loyal son encouraged him to commit suicide; quite the opposite. This is not at all the way that Timon very pointedly encouraged Gelasimus or anything else that could be interpreted as a source for Kent's "farewell" to Lear.

It is upon this misreading of the source material that the fragile case against the reliability of Timon as a source for King Lear rests. This is the entire case for dating Timon after King Lear and for claiming that it is an academic "spoof"[229] written in 1606 rather than an original student work written at Cambridge in 1580-2. Without that misreading, often quoted, never questioned, Timon and King Lear are linked as are King Leir and Timon of Athens, all four of them being linked together, all four of them being tied back to Philip Sidney and Arcadia, unpublished at the time of Timon and King Leir.

And, of course, Bullough admits: "it is unlikely that Shakespeare could ever have known the academic Timon . . ."[230] a sentiment that Park Honan echoes: "as a borrower, Shakespeare could be a magpie, of course; but how and when he would have been able to see the Timon manuscript is not clear to me, at least."[231] But Marlowe knew it very well, he saw it when he wrote it.

The sequence then is Arcadia, Timon, Leir, King Lear and finally Timon of Athens with the comedy Timon providing source material for the two later plays, some of which is drawn from Arcadia, some of which is drawn from *De gestis Britonum,* and some of which is drawn from the language of Cambridge.

King Lear and Timon of Athens are infused with links that are thematic, poetic, personal, historic, mythological, political, cultural and religious all tying back to Marlowe. Moreover, they extend from one end of Marlowe's life story to the other and touch all of the people involved. It is well worth remembering that it was Geoffrey of Monmouth who identified Leir as the founder of the house of Leicester, whose earl in the 1580s, Robert Dudley, had been the favorite of Queen Elizabeth and uncle to Philip Sidney and who had upset Sidney's hopes for inheritance when he married the earl of Essex's widow, Lettice Knollys, mother of Robert Deveraux, Marlowe's nemesis. Leir connects to Timon which connects to the Queen's Men which connects to Walsingham who connects to Leicester who connects to Sidney who connects to Essex who connects to Marlowe who connects to them all. Note too that Kent leads the blind Gloucester, whose namesake once opposed Leicester's ancestor, to the cliffs of Dover. Marlowe was from Canterbury which is adjacent to Dover which is in Kent.

When Marlowe went to work for Walsingham he was barely twenty, still at Cambridge, and just starting up his playwrighting career. When King Lear was published, at least five years had passed between Marlowe's falling out with Thomas and Audrey Walsingham. The other plays from this period, including Hamlet, MacBeth, and Othello, are typically considered consistent with the mood of someone who felt abandoned and betrayed and was expressing his disillusionment by using the tools of his art.

The record shows that King Lear was performed once, Timon of Athens not at all. There is even some doubt that it was ever intended for publication as the pagination of the Folio suggests that it was a late addition. Dating for the play rests largely on traditional assumptions of its relationship to Lear which have now been shown to be flawed. But for anyone as aware of Marlowe's history as Thomas and Audrey Walsingham, reading the manuscript of a story about a man who is foolishly generous and then unfairly cheated, the message would have been especially poignant. Shakespeare's name may be on them, but his fingerprints are not.

Most modern scholars, on the other hand, display a curious blindness, a refusal to read the plain text and even to skew textual evidence against any inference that might lead them away from the person traditionally credited with the work. It is true that for centuries most scholars had no idea what happened at Deptford because the Coroner's report was sealed. They had no idea how it tied into sonnet 74. They had never heard of Marlowe's portrait, which wasn't discovered until 1952, or its motto or how it tied into sonnet 73 or Philip Sidney's sonnet 43 and how all of them tied together with Pericles. They did suspect that George Chapman was the "rival poet" but they also knew, have always known, that Willim Shakspere had no reason to complain about him. They also have known that sonnet 86 referred directly to Chapman's version of Hero and Leander and that the person most likely to complain about that, if he was still alive to do so, would be Christopher Marlowe.

The pattern repeats with Timon, The Troublesome Reign of King John and King Leir which separately and together establish Marlowe's apprenticeship with the Queen's Men. Evidence is glossed over or mischaracterized with the result that history is further obscured instead of fully explored. Whether or not this is intentional or habitual is anyone's guess.

Marlowe's tenure with the Queen's Men would have to have been limited and brief. Although his absences from Cambridge were not insignificant, the Privy Council asserted responsibility for his employment, which if true would have left him little time for separate theatrical activity. On top of which, if the inference made by Frederick Boas and others that "it can scarcely be questioned"[232] that Tamburlaine was first staged in 1587 because Philip Gawdy's November 16, 1587 report of witnessing a play describes the Act V, scene 5 shooting of the Governor of Babylon in II Tamburlaine, then Marlowe would have been in London by the fall of 1587 at the latest.

In The Queen's Men, Scott McMillan and Sally-Beth MacLean assert that Marlowe launched a "cultural contest"[233] against the Queen's Men and their style of theatre. Without directly disputing Malone, they appear to believe that Marlowe never worked for the company and that when the Prologue in Tamburlaine speaks of "jiggling veins of rhyming mother wits, and such conceits as clownage keeps in pay"[234], it is "a fair guess" that "Marlowe had Queen's Men in mind."[235] In their view, the reference to Tamburlaine in the Preface to The Troublesome Reign of King John was part of an "anti-Marlowe" reaction that viewed the enemy as blank verse itself and Marlowe as "that infidel".[236] The fact that the debut of Tamburlaine preceded the publication of The Troublesome Reign by four years and that the Queen's Men would be unlikely to benefit by the over the counter sales of an outdated play they had already sold to the publisher Richard Jones seems less important than the opportunity to cast further aspersions at Marlowe who is forever branded as "unmistakably the genius of disturbing ventures."[237]

This is part of what has become a tradition in Marlovian criticism, the salacious attacks on his character layered on the shabby foundation of lies promoted by Essex, his cronies, like Chomely, and their dupes, like Baines and Drury. According to Charles Nichol, "he is remembered not just as a writer, but as an atheist and blasphemer, a dissolute homosexual, an Elizabethan 'roaring boy' who lived fast and died young."[238] All by way of marginalizing Marlowe's life and work. It is a tiresome shorthand lacking reliable testimony, a caricature based on smears, a game of three card monte and a warning to others not to look too closely at the historical record which might not only call the libel into question but would undermine the carefully constructed mythology that implicitly promotes the man who wasn't there.

It is almost a truism that, apart from his recognition as first perfecter of staged blank verse, Marlowe is considered the Elizabethan playwright most closely identified with bad behaving men. The list includes all of his chief accepted plays, Tamburlaine, Faust, Barabas in The Jew of Malta, and Edward II. This is an artificially assembled group which excludes epic heroes and comedians, never mind women, in favor of anti-heroes who, by implication, represent the dark side of Marlowe's character which, as an intelligencer and all around shadowy figure, dominates his portrayal in the mind of even his most sympathetic biographers. So it is ironic that these same scholars hesitate to credit Marlowe with King John or Timon who are certainly examples, and early ones at that, of bad behaving men.

And so the misperceptions of the past continue to play out today. As if the scholars and academics most familiar with the issues prefer the notion that Marlowe was a "bad" boy who got what one should expect, as if they endorsed the judgements of biased boors like Thomas Beared, Francis Meres, and William Vaughan. As if it never occurred to them that Chomeley might be a liar, Drury a mark and Baines a dupe. None of this, of course, would come as a surprise to Christopher Marlowe.

What the record shows is that Christopher Marlowe had the connections to both Walsingham and Leicester that would have secured him an introduction to the Queen's Men, that he was writing plays while still at Cambridge, that he has been identified as the likely author of <u>Timon</u>, that a play on the subject of <u>Timon</u> was performed at the same time that the Queen's Men were touring Cambridge, that Marlowe has been identified very early on as a contributor to and possibly principal author of <u>The Troublesome Reign of King John</u>, that the publisher of <u>The Troublesome Reign</u> thought that it ought to be compared to and sold beside <u>Tamburlaine</u> as if he wanted readers to believe that they were somehow connected and finally that <u>King Leir</u> was directly influenced by <u>Timon</u> and that <u>Leir</u> in turn influenced <u>The Troublesome Reign</u>. The only person who fits all of these measures is Marlowe.

As for any challenge aimed at the Queen's Men, there is no reason to think that Marlowe's departure was in any way a personal rejection of Walsingham's company. If anything, it was straightforwardly opportunistic. Marlowe found an ally in Edward Allen, an actor of unsurpassed talent, and he chose to work with the one man who could embody the powerful roles he was beginning to write. It would have been very difficult for the Queen's Men, made up of the supposedly best and most experienced actors and writers from all the other companies in England, to allow Marlowe, a young, academic poet, and Alleyn, two years younger and less known even than Marlowe, to suddenly take over their company, which is basically what they did with the then otherwise undistinguished Admiral's Men when Alleyn debuted in Marlowe's Tamburlaine.

There is one other event that had to have hit Marlowe hard and inevitably played a part in his decision to leave the Queen's Men: the death of Philip Sidney after the Battle of Zutphen in October, 1586. The earl of Leicester, Sidney's uncle, staged a funeral procession the following March that mesmerized England, raising his memory to heroic heights. For Marlowe, this would have been a deeply personal loss that was soon expressed in his work; from that moment forward his plays and poetry became more internalized and more expressive of the inner life of his characters and thought. As early as The Troublesome Reign it was clear that Marlowe's approach to theatrical production was outside the Queen's Men's medley style. Marlowe depicted worlds complete to themselves which very much ran counter to the "multigeneric mixture always deployed in roughly similar proportions"[239] by the Queen's Men. Following the death of Sidney, Marlowe clearly lost interest in the tumblers and clowns featured by the Queen's Men and in Edward Alleyn he found a powerful partner to express the revolutionary "theater of introspection and implication"[240] that he set out to create.

Chapter Nine

The Man Who Wasn't There

Of all the thousands of words he ever wrote, Robert Greene would probably not be terribly pleased to know that the lines of his most often quoted are these:

> "Yes trust them not: for there is an upstart Crow, beautified with our feathers, that with his *Tygers hart wrapt in a Players hyde*, supposes he is as well able to bombast out a blanke verse as the best of you: and beeing an absolute *Johannes factotum*, is in his owne conceit the only Shake-scene in a countrey."[241]

Worse still, he would probably have been apoplectic to learn that for over four hundred years this pointed insult would be completely misunderstood.

Tradition holds that this excerpt, a one-line mention in the introduction to Greenes Groats-Worth of Wit (1592) is a specific reference to Shakespeare (i.e.: "Shake-scene") and that Greene was warning his fellow poets, in particular Marlowe, Nashe and Peele, to be wary of this interloper from Stratford. Academic scholars are so keen for any historical reference that might fill in the enormous gap in the record of Shakespeare's life prior to April, 1595 that they continuously grasp at this statement. Even The New Oxford Authorship Companion repeats this assertion, claiming that it is a "jibe at Shakespeare as a country bumpkin."[242] The trouble is that Greene wasn't talking about Shakespeare. He never met Shakespeare. He was talking about England's most famous actor and target of Greene's deepest envy, Ned Alleyn.

Before his untimely death in September, 1592 at the age of 34, Robert Greene wrote and published over 25 books, plays and pamphlets, becoming one of the first English poets to make his living as a professional author. Educated at Cambridge, he took his MA from Claire College in the Spring of 1583 and moved to London where he shortly become "England's first celebrity author."[243] Many of Greene's pamphlets focused on his personal life and the lives of his circle of friends, associates and perceived enemies. In this way, Greene was something of a self-made celebrity and he and those who came after, such as Thomas Nashe and Gabriel Harvey, created a body of work that highlighted and fed on personal encounters and animosities. Chief among Greene's targets was Edward Alleyn and he attacked him several times in print before the Groats-Worth.

Based on Alleyn's known association with Worcester's Men and their travels and Greene's earlier book, Francescos Fortunes (1590), A. D. Wraight estimated that Greene first met Edward Alleyn in the late summer of 1586.[244] In Groats-Worth, Greene describes meeting a boastful actor who, after also claiming to be able to write heroic monologues, offered to pay Greene to write for him:

> "I am as famous for *Delphrigus*, and the King of the *Faries*, as ever was any of my time. The twelve Labors of *Hercules* have I thundered on the Stage, and plaied three scenes of the Devill in the Highway to heaven. Have ye so (saide *Roberto*?) [ie: Greene] then I pray you pardon me. Nay more (quoth the Player) I can serve to make a pretie speech, for I was a countrey Author, passing at a Morrall, for twas I that pende the Morrall of mans witte, the Dialogue of Dives, and for seven yeers space was absolute Interpreter to the puppets. But now my Almanacke is out of date:
>
> "The people make no estimation,
>
> Or Morrals teaching education.
>
> "Was not this prettie for a plaine rime extempore? if you will ye shall have more. Nay its enough, said *Roberto*, but how meane you to use me? Why sir, in

making Playes, said the other, for which you shall be
well paid, if you will take the paines."[245]

To be clear, this player who "thundered on the Stage" was not a young Shakespeare claiming to be an "Interpreter to the puppets", a leader of other actors, or to have been "a contrey Author"; this bold actor proposed to hire Greene to write speeches and scripts for him, something not even Shakespeare's most devoted acolytes would ever imagine necessary or possible. This is Edward Alleyn, star player for the Admiral's Men, formerly of Worcester's Men, a country touring company, a man to whom Greene sold half a dozen scripts.

In his earlier title, <u>Francescos Fortunes</u> (1590), Greene reports that he, alias Francesco, accepted the offer:

> "In this humor he fell in amongst a companie of
> Players, who perswaded him to trie his wit in writing of
> Comedies, Tragedies, or Pastorals, and if he could
> performe anything worth the stage, then they would
> larglie reward him for his paines. . . [Francesco] getting
> him home to his chamber writ a Comedie, which so
> generally pleased all the audience, that happie were
> those Actors in short time that could get any of his
> workes, he grewe so exquisite in that facultie."[246]

Despite his success, Greene could not avoid finding fault with one actor in particular:

> "It chanced that *Roscius* & he [Francesco/Greene] met
> at a dinner, both guests unto *Archias* the Poet, where
> the prowd Comedian dared to make comparison with
> *Tully*: which insolencie made the learned Orator to
> growe into these termes: why *Roscius*, art proud with
> *Esops* Crow, being pranct with the glorie of others
> feathers? of thyself thou canst say nothing, and if the
> Cobler hath taught thee to say *Ave Caesar*, disdain not

thy tutor because thou pratest in a Kings Chamber: what sentence or conceipte of the invention the people applaud for excellent, that comes from the secrets of our knowledge."[247]

The similarities between the player in Groats-Worth and Franciscos Fortunes are fairly obvious, including their boastfulness, claims to literary skill and employment of professional writers and the reference to a crow wearing others feathers. Ned Alleyn was known so much for his powerful acting style that he was frequently compared to Rocius, the Roman actor of legend, most notably by Thomas Nashe:

> "Not Roscius or Aesope, those admired tragedians that have lived ever since before Christ was borne, could ever performe more in action than famous *Ned Allen*"[248]

Ben Jonson made a similar comparison in his Epigram 89. No other actor in the period was ever praised in this way.

The reference to "the cobler" is clearly intended to be Marlowe, whose father was a shoe maker in Canterbury, and the argument that developed over Tully's defense of Archais[249] is highly suggestive of Marlowe's encounter in Hogg Lane with William Bradley, a local tough who attacked him on September 18, 1589 at knife point only to be killed in self-defense by Thomas Watson, himself a playwright and poet who fought Bradley to protect Marlowe. Bradley had a financial dispute with John Alleyn, Ned's brother, and apparently attacked Marlowe as the result of his association with Ned who rose to fame playing Marlowe's Tamburlaine. Greene, therefore, is accusing Alleyn of claiming that he would have defended Marlowe just as Tully/Watson defended Archais/Marlowe, a boastful claim that Greene could not endure unopposed.

The assertion that the "Cobler" had taught Alleyn how to say "Ave Caesar" is clear a reference to Edward III's Prince

Edward, speaking to his father in "A Room of State In the Palace" (ie: "in a King's Chamber") at the end of Act I, Scene 1:

> "As cheerful sounding to my youthful spleen
> This tummult is of war's increasing broils,
> As, at the Coronation of a king,
> The joyful clamours of the people are,
> When Ave, Casear! they pronounce abroad."

Alleyn, the star of the Admiral's men, would inevitably have played the title role and therefore spoke those very lines. Just as he played the title role in Tamburlaine and said "Is it not passing brave to be a King / And ride in triumph through Persepolis?" as many times as the play was performed. Even as he is mocking Alleyn, Greene is unmistakably identifying Marlowe as the author of Edward III. This is the very same thing he did in Groats-worth when he quoted the "Tyger's Heart" line which, spoken by the title character, would necessarily have been played by Ned Alleyn.

With Marlowe now being credited as "co-author" of 3 Henry VI by Gary Taylor and Rory Loughnane, co-editors of The New Oxford Shakespeare Authorship Companion[250], the parallels between these excerpts from Francesco's Fortunes and Groats-Worth are striking, both involving Marlowe as an author of lines quoted by a boastful actor described as a "crow" adorned in the "feathers" of others, and both pointing at Alleyn in the guise of "Rocius". These passages echo each other and are entirely consistent with Greene's long standing, well known enmity toward Alleyn.

Greene complained so much about Alleyn that he even got Thomas Nashe to toss a tomato can at him for inspiring a horde of cheap imitations in his preface to Greene's Menaphon (1589):

> "But Tolosa hath forgotten that it was sometime
> sacked, and beggars that ever they carried their fardels

on footback, and in truth no marvel, whenas the
deserved reputation of one *Roscius* is of force to enrich
a rabble of counterfeits. Yet let subjects for all their
insolence dedicate a *De profundis* every morning to the
preservation of their *Caesar*, lest their increasing
indignities return them ere long to their juggling and
mediocrity, and they bewail in weeping blanks the
wane of their monarchy."[251]

Greene does not go so far as to call Alleyn a writer, he won't give him that credit; instead he warns that Alleyn claims to be a writer, which he disputes. In fact, however, Alleyn appears to have been paid as a writer by his father-in-law, Philip Henslowe, for the play Tamburcame, since lost. Henslowe recorded the transaction in his diary:

"pd unto my sonne E Alleyn at the A poynt
ment of the company ~~of the~~ for his Booke
of tambercam the 2 of octobr 1602 the somme of
XXXX[75]"

The notation "for his Booke" is consistent with a notation on the same page for the payment to Thomas Heywood for his play "oserecke". J. P. Collier concluded:

"Hence we see, that Alleyn was separately paid for whatever he did for the company by way of authorship, if it may be so called. It is supposed that Tamar Cam (like Tarlton's "Plott" of the "Seven Deadly Sins", & etc.) was an entertainment made up of a dumb show, action and extempore performance. Alleyn was the principall actor in Tamar Cam, as well as the contriver of the whole representation . . ."[252]

Collier's estimation of the quality of Tamburcame doesn't quite square with a play that resulted in a sequel, never mind one that could be compared with Tamburlane, which Ben

Jonson, who clearly saw it in performance, did in his Timber: or, Discoveries. Not caring much for either, he complained that "the Tamerlanes, and Tamer-Chains of the late Age, . . . had nothing in them but the scenicall strutting, and furious vociferation, to warrant them to the ignorant gapers."[253] Regardless, the play was real enough and both Henslowe and Collier confirm that Alleyn was its author.

That said, it is less important that Alleyn was actually a playwright on par with Greene, Marlowe or Nashe than that he was accused of claiming he was. Greene was consistent about that and one of the plays he had the most reason to complain about appears to have been Orlando Furioso (1591), which Alleyn bought from Greene sometime in 1588-89. An original play script of part of this play is among Alleyn's personal papers at Dulwich College. W. W. Greg made a close study of this rare text, a transcript of the actor's part of Orlando with its cues, including fifteen separate annotations in Alleyn's hand. Greg concluded:

> "From the fact that Alleyn corrected the part, the inference that he studied it and therefore, since his company is known to have performed a play of the name, that he actually acted Orlando, is irresistible."[254]

A. D. Wraight took this observation one step further:

> "The extant playscript of the part of Orlando shows Alleyn as a critic deftly touching up and improving a playscript for performance, adding a line or word discriminatingly."[255]

For all his faults, Greene could be counted upon to recognize when his words had been altered, especially by Alleyn who he eyed with deep suspicion. There was apparently no small amount of projection in this because, as Greene himself boasted, he had doubled his income from the script for Orlando by selling it twice:

> "Aske the Queens Players, if you sold them not *Orlando Furioso* for twenty Nobles, and when they were in the country, sold the same Play to the Lord Admirals men [Alleyn's company] for as much more. Was not this plaine *Cony-Catching* Master R. G.?"[256]

Being hoist on his own petard could not sit well with the man who authored five pamphlets on the art of swindling. Never mind that Alleyn owned the script and could do what he wanted with it, Greene clearly thought re-writes by an untutored actor, no matter how famous, were unthinkable.

All of which goes to show that Greene was attacking Alleyn in the Groats-worth, not Shakespeare. When Greene talked about a "Shake-scene" he was talking about a type of actor, someone who indulged in bombast, who was "well able to bombast out a blanke verse" and whose style emphasized "scenicall strutting, and furious vociferation," someone who in modern terms chewed the scenery, while making the further pun on bumbast which is stitching, which is to say that this person imagined that because he could shout out a playwright's lines he therefore imagined that he could stitch together better lines. And the person he was pointing to was Alleyn.

Traditional Scholars argue that Greene is complaining about Shakespeare in the Groats-worth, but this would mean that Greene's identical complaint against Alleyn in Francescos Fortunes has been transposed to the letter from Alleyn to Shakespeare and the scholars have no other evidence of that. Meanwhile Greene's disputes with Alleyn/Roscius are simultaneously expressed in Groats-worth against the player who offered to buy plays from him, which is what Alleyn actually did when be bought Orlando Furioso.

No one ever identified Shakespeare as a bombastic actor. If they had, he would have been more noticeable. To say Greene identified him as such is to make a circular argument. "Gentle", "honey tongued"[257] Shakespeare was not and has never even been confused with an actor of Ned Alleyn's caliber.

Alleyn was, by all reports, and as Jonson and Nashe confirm, a bombastic actor who commanded the center of the stage and blasted out his lines in a fury. In this regard, he was very well matched for the roles that Marlowe wrote for him, characters who were larger than life, given to prolonged proclamations and violent action. Greene's pun on "Tyger's heart" is taken from a line, spoken by the Duke of York, in Henry VI, Part 3 (originally published as The True Tragedy of Richard Duke of York) and since Henslowe recorded its performance on March 3, 1592 it is very likely that Greene heard Alleyn blast out the title character's line.

Edward Alleyn was the most important actor on the London stage in 1592. He played the lead role in Greene's Orlando Furioso and had extraordinary success in Marlowe's Tamburlaine, Faustus and The Jew of Malta, not to mention as Heronimo in Thomas Kyd's Spanish Tragedy. His memory for roles was prodigious; Bernard Beckerman estimated that from 1594 to 1597, the period recorded in Henslowe's diary, Alleyn would have "had to secure and retain command of about seventy-one different roles, of which number fifty-two or fifty-three were newly learned."[258] With so many lines and speeches to choose from, it is not hard to imagine that he may have inserted a favorite excerpt from one play into another when it suited him. On the other hand, Shakespeare, whose sole player credits are from two plays of Jonson's, the first of which was produced in 1598, is nowhere in sight.

Robert Greene died in 1592 at the age of 34, reportedly of drink and dissipation, shortly before the publication of Groatsworth. Alleyn, meanwhile, married Joan Woodward, stepdaughter of Philip Henslowe, in October 1592, and lived to the age of sixty, becoming so wealthy that he was able to found the College of God's Gift at Dulwich which exists to this day.

The story, however, does not end there.

Henry Chettle, a playwright, novelist and friend to Robert Greene, much like Thomas Nashe who Greene had encouraged to attack Alleyn in print, arranged for the posthumous publication of the Groats-worth in late September, 1592. Apparently, he hadn't anticipated the response he got from two of the individuals mentioned in the pamphlet, both of whom complained angrily against what Greene had written about them. Three months later he published a following pamphlet, Kinde Hart's Dream (1592) and included a preface wherein he attempted to set the record straight:

> "With neither of them that take offence was I acquainted, and with one of them I care not if I neuer be: the other, whome at that time I did not so much spare, as since I wish I had, for that as I haue moderated the heate of liuing writers, and might haue vsde my owne discretion (especially in such a case) the author being dead, that I did not, I am as sory, as if the originall fault had beene my fault, because myselfe haue scene his demeanor no lesse ciuill than he exclent in the qualitie he professes: besides, diners of worship haue reported his vprightness of dealing, which argues his honesty, and his facetious grace in writting, that aprooues his art. For the first, whose learning I reuerence, and, at the perusing of Greenes booke, stroke out what then, in conscience I thought, he in some displeasure writ: or had it beene true, yet to publish it was intollerable: him I would wish to vse me no worse than I deserue."[259]

The identity of the two men who took offence has been debated for centuries. Orthodox scholars have avidly promoted the notion that the person Chettle described as having "a demeanor no less civil", "excellent in the qualitie he professes" and who has "diverse of worship" must necessarily be Shakespeare. However, since this claim is based on the "Shake-scene" reference, which has been shown above to refer to Ned Alleyn there is no evidence that Greene was referring to Shakespeare in the Groats-Worth and so no reason for Shakespeare to take offence or complain about it to Chettle.

Christopher Marlowe, on the other hand, had plenty of reasons. Not only did Greene refer to him directly as Machiavel but, as David Riggs noted, he also accused him of atheism:

> "Greene's public address to Marlowe levels an extraordinary accusation of atheism, made by one 'who hath said, with thee (like the fool in his heart), There is no God.'"[260]

In Elizabethan England, to be accused of atheism is worse than being accused of blasphemy since it attacks the foundation of the state: The Queen cannot rule by Divine right if there is no Divinity to grant that right. Atheism, for all its intellectual interest, was tantamount to treason.

In his defense, Chettle claims not to have known either author, which does seem a bit odd, given that he was close friends with Greene. Chettle's career as a dramatist, however, does not appear to begin in force until 1597, so it is possible that he was not close to the theaters until then.

What is clear is that he was very apologetic to one of them, saying that he wished he had used better judgment in printing Greene's full text: "that I did not I am as sorry as if the original fault had been my fault."

He was less charitable to the other, saying that while he respected his scholarship, he cared not if they ever should be acquainted, but added that he, "at the perusing of Greene's book, struck out what then in conscience I thought he in some displeasure writ, or had it been true, yet to publish it was intolerable, him I would wish to use me no worse than I deserve."

Shakespearean scholars assert that Chettle made his polite apology to Shakespeare and that his other, dismissive apology was to Marlowe. Not only is this contrary to the fact that Greene was warning Marlowe because he was his friend, Chettle printed the warning because he was Greene's friend. Alleyn, on the other hand, was the subject of Greene's attack. If Chettle was going to print this attack, he might or might not afterward have reason to withdraw it, but he would inevitably regret the accidental attack on Marlowe because Greene had not intended to attack him; Marlowe had "diverse of worship"; he had friends in high places, such as Lord Burghley, Sir Francis Walsingham and Lady Pembroke, to name but a few, and Greene considered him a friend. To say that Chettle did not care for Marlowe is to impute motives to him that are only shared by current scholars, not by his contemporaries.

Marlowe is the innocent party in all of this. He was the author of the "Tyger's heart" and "Ave Caesar" lines, but he has offended no one. Alleyn may be equally blameless, but he was Greene's target and Chettle got caught in the crosshairs of someone else's dispute much like Marlowe who, to a more significant degree, had been caught up in the antagonism between William Bradley and John Alleyn, brother of Ned.

Some recent scholars, such as Harold Jenkins[261], John Jowett[262], and Warren B. Austin[263] have pursued the notion that the Groats-Worth was itself a forgery by Chettle. While this might in itself be an interesting sidebar to the larger issue, it hardly matters from the perspective of the two authors who objected to it in real time. If Chettle did forge the Groats-Worth, then he merely mimicked the accusations against Alleyn which were originally voiced by Greene in Francescos Fortunes and seconded by Nashe in his preface to Greene's Menaphon. If, on the other hand, Greene is the true author, then he is simply being consistent in ridiculing Ned Alleyn's boast that he can write a good play. In either case, Shakespeare is not Greene's target; Shakespeare is not being accused of anything by anyone, not by Greene, not by Nashe and not by anyone else because no one thinks that whatever he might be doing it is worth mentioning in print in 1592. As Peter Bull concluded, "On purely historical grounds, the balance of evidence arising from the critical sentence at the heart of Greene's Groats-Worth of Witte clearly supports the identification of Edward Alleyn far better than it does William Shakespeare."[264]

The reason why all of this is so very important is that without the "Shake-scene" reference, scholars have no evidence at all that Shakespeare was on the theatrical scene prior to his being listed as a member of the Lord Chamberlain's Men in April 1595. For all that it may seem reasonable to assume that Shakespeare *must* have been an active actor/playwright before that date, there is no actual evidence of it. Without the "Shake-scene" aspersion, it is not possible to credit him with authoring the "Tyger's heart" line, which is what Gary Taylor and Rory Loughnane have done in The New Oxford Shakespeare Authorship Companion, asserting that a stylometric analysis of Henry VI Part 3 which assigns Act I scenes 1 to 4 to Shakespeare "makes sense, because 1.4 must be by Shakespeare (because of the allusion by Greene)"[265] even though Greene was alluding to Alleyn, not Shakespeare, and was not claiming that Alleyn or Shakespeare, who he does not mention at all, anywhere, ever, wrote that line.

Consider that Greene very clearly attributed Edward III to Marlowe when he scolded Alleyn for prating *"Ave Caesar"*, but for Taylor and Loughnane and The New Oxford Shakespeare the attribution of that play remains in doubt. Without the "Tyger's heart" allusion, however, Shakespeare is pushed off the stage altogether.

As for Ned Alleyn, who never left a stage until he was good and ready to make a furious exit, support for his claims to authorship has received some entirely unexpected and largely unrecognized assistance from the orthodox academy. In their series of authorship tests for Henry VI Part 3, Hugh Craig and John Burrows attempted to confirm the reliability of what they called computer based "Zeta Tests" by comparing two groups of plays, one attributed to Marlowe and the other attributed to Shakespeare. They chose seven pre-1600 plays for Shakespeare, including Henry IV Part 1, Comedy of Errors, Merchant of Venice, Love's Labour's Lost, King John, Richard III and Taming of the Shrew. In all 667 lexical and "function word" tests were performed on the plays of which 666 "reliably" produced the attribution of Shakespeare. The same series of tests were performed on the seven academically accepted plays of Marlowe, including Tamburlaine Parts 1 and

2, Dr. Faustus, The Jew of Malta, Edward II, Dido Queen of Carthage and The Massacre at Paris. A total of 474 tests were performed, but only 394 segments were attributed to Marlowe. The problem, they determined, was the "spectacular failure"[266] of The Jew of Malta which scored only 29 positive segments against a total of 81 tested, accounting for 52 of the total 80 misses.

Scholars have always been a little suspicious of The Jew of Malta. It's first performance was recorded in 1592 and it was entered in the Stationer's Register in 1594, but the earliest surviving printed version is from 1633. The play was owned by Henslowe but the title role was played by his son-in-law, Ned Alleyn and no one else played it during his lifetime. Howard S. Babb summarized what he considered the traditional view of critics such as E. K. Chambers, W. W. Greg, F. G. Fleay, Tucker Brooke and H. S. Bennett when he observed:

> "For all critics, from Charles Lamb on, who require some sort of verisimilitude in dramatic action, Marlowe's The Jew of Malta has proven a troublesome hurdle. The difficulty arises from the tonal change that follows two acts of apparently conventional seriousness. What are we to think when the heroic Barabas is suddenly transformed into a plotter? Why the crudities of Bellamira and Phila-Borza? how should we react to the Horrors of the Jew's revenge, which seem absurd if only because they pile up so quickly? Most commentators seek a way around such questions by ascribing the third, fourth, and parts of the fifth act - though without agreeing precisely on the limits of Marlowe's authorship - to the hand of another, usually Thomas Heywood, who was responsible for the play's first printing in 1633"[267]

Thomas Heywood was a prolific author and wrote both a prologue and an epilogue for the published text, but he is probably not responsible for the scholarly confusion over authorship of the play. That distinction should be more likely be awarded to Robert Greene's bête noire, Edward Alleyn who had control of the script, either directly or by means of his father-in-law throughout his lifetime. No one could have amended the script without his approval and the person most likely to have done that was himself, responding to his audience in a role that became his signature, even more than Tamburlaine.

Written at about the same time that Greene was complaining about his behavior in Henry VI Part 1, it appears to have come in for the same treatment, if not more so presuming Craig and Burrow's test results can be trusted. A huge hit when it debuted, Alleyn would have had many temptations to update it in order to keep it fresh for an audience that saw it repeatedly over the years, much as producers and directors freshen old plays with new stagings today. Unfortunately, there's no way to confirm that because there are no plays attributed to Alleyn in the surviving canon. The Fortune, Henslowe's theater, burned down on December 9, 1623, taking with it any manuscripts that might have resolved dozens of questions, authorship and otherwise.

What can be observed is that of the 20 plus "parallelisms" of The Jew of Malta that Calvin Hoffman found in the Folio plays,[268] only one of them is from the middle acts, III and IV and those from Act V are concentrated at the very end of the play. Marlowe, who frequently quoted the classics and habitually borrowed from himself but never from any contemporary, would have been very unlikely to steal lines from Ned Alleyn. Alleyn, on the other hand, with his encyclopedic memory and access to all of the best scripts, could be counted upon, if Greene is any authority, to stitch together his favorite lines whenever the mood suited him. He had over thirty years to meddle with his favorite role; it is almost surprising that so much of it survived intact.

It is impossible now to know when or whether Alleyn introduced his improvements to the script of The Jew of Malta or what Marlowe might have made of it, whether he objected à la Greene or made the best of it or even worked with Alleyn, hand in glove, to tweak the script to suit his star actor as best he could. But the play, with all of its faults, confirms once again, if such confirmation is still necessary, that when Greene attacked "an upstart crow" who thought himself a "Johannes Factotum" as capable of bombasting "out a blanke verse as the best of you" and deliver "a plaine rime extempore", a fact which cannot help but pop out of both modern and classic textual analysis of <u>The Jew of Malta</u>, he was not attacking Shakespeare, the-man-who-wasn't-there, Greene was attacking Ned Alleyn, the "Shake-scene" who most definitely was.

Chapter Ten

The Stylometric Fallacy

The centuries old search for confirmation of Shakspere's presence in the Elizabethan theatre before April, 1595 has led orthodox scholars to resort to computer aided stylometric studies which, by way of various word and usage based tests, purport to assist in clearing away the difficulty of separating the alleged multiple participants in Elizabethan texts, in particular the plays of Shakespeare, Marlowe and any possible collaborators. The methodology is not new, but the power of computers in assisting the research is and has given some researchers the hope of advancing the question of Shakespeare's authority once and for all.

One of the earliest versions of these tests was devised in 1880 by Dr. Thomas Mendenhall which involved the deceptively simple method of counting the number of multisyllabic words, from two syllables to twelve, used by an individual author.[269] With the aid of dozens of human "computers" hand counting each syllable in a given text, he slowly and methodically charted the raw numbers of two, three, four, etc. syllable words in each author's canon, in all several million words. When charted on a graph, this revealed a distinctive curve that was unique for each of the twenty writers he and his team examined, including Francis Bacon, Ben Jonson, Francis Beaumont, William Shakespeare and Christopher Marlowe. The original purpose of the test had been to prove that Bacon and Shakespeare were the same author. It turned out, however, that Bacon consistently used many more long words than Shakespeare. As Calvin Hoffman explained it:

> "The graphs of other writers were entirely different from each other. From Jonson to Beaumont to Addison to

Lord Lytton - each writer disclosed his own peculiarity of style in composition."[270]

It was only when Mendenhall compared Marlowe to Shakespeare that he found a surprise: "In the characteristic curve of his plays Christopher Marlowe agrees with Shakespeare as well as Shakespeare agrees with himself."[271]

The elegant simplicity of Mendenhall's tests, to say nothing of their conclusions, did not satisfy most orthodox scholars. As a result his conclusions, which were reprinted in Calvin Hoffman's book The Murder of the Man Who Was "Shakespeare" (1955), were completely ignored. The issue rested quietly until modern computers with their brute force calculation and rapid modeling capabilities revived the topic. The resulting application of various computer aided stylometric tests, championed notably by Hugh Craig, working with John Burrows and Arthur F. Kinney, has enabled traditional scholars to renovate and in some cases even extend Shakespearean claims of authorship to texts dated prior to 1593, including some as early as 1588. These tests, considered more sophisticated than Mendenhall's simple and all but forgotten syllable counts, were developed by John Burrows in the 1980s and have been given names such as "Delta", "Zeta" and "Iota" tests. Delta tests measure the frequency of "function words" which are frequently used words that operate grammar, such as "and", "with", and pronouns, such as "she". Zeta tests measure mid-frequency combinations of function and lexical words which carry meaning, such as nouns, verbs, adjectives and adverbs. Iota tests measure the use of rare words which are typically lexical and are sometimes called "marker words" because they are deemed more exclusive to a particular author when compared to others in tests based on batch sifting of multiple texts. There are multiple variations of these basic tests, including word adjacency networks which attempt to codify word usage relationships, all of which involve computer aided counting (not unlike Mendenhall, only faster) to create visual models in the form of charts and graphs which are believed to describe the more or less unique signature of an individual writer (also not unlike Mendenhall who rendered his results in easily understood graphs). As Craig and Kinney explained in their introduction to their influential Shakespeare, Computers, and the Mystery of Authorship: "Computational stylistics offers abundant evidence that writers leave subtle and persistent traces of a distinctive style through all levels of their syntax and lexis."[272] While the general observation of the hypothesis and the tools are very similar to Mendenhall, the reported results were not.

The most celebrated consequence of these tests is that Christopher Marlowe has recently been given certified credit by the New Oxford Authorship Companion for "co-authorship" of Henry VI Parts 1, 2 and 3. Craig and Kinney subjected all three of the plays to a series of extensive tests and came to the conclusion that they all showed evidence of extensive collaboration with Shakespeare. This, of course is false. Shakspere was never involved and contributed nothing.

Nevertheless, focusing first on Henry VI, Part 1, after eliminating all other playwrights of the period, Craig and Kinney concluded that "there is, therefore, a strong case on our measures for seeing Marlowe as the author of one part at least of the play,"[273] specifically, "the middle part of the strand of the play involving Joan of Arc."[274] Turning their attention to the next play in the series, and following a similar series of tests, they reported that "it seems that in 2 Henry VI another powerful episode, the Cade rebellion, derives from Marlowe."[275] Finally, when it came to Part Three, Craig and Burrows weighed in separately with assertions of greater accuracy, according to Marlowe specific scenes, including I.1, I.2, II.3. III.3, IV.2, IV.3, IV.4, IV.5, IV.6, IV.7, IV.8, IV.9 and V.2.[276] In this fashion, the academy has finally been able to allow shared recognition for what Robert Greene alleged four hundred years before was Marlowe's sole enterprise.

All is not uniform agreement in the world of stylometrics, however. Brian Vickers, champion of "*N*-grams" (ie:

idiosyncratic 3 and 4 word strings) has long challenged Craig and Burrows reliance on function words:

> "Hugh Craig's use of both function and lexical words to question Shakespeare's sole authorship of 2 Henry VI is a failure on every count. Despite the diligence with which he carried out his tests, and the care with which he explained the statistical procedures, only one conclusion is possible: this atomistic approach to language, using only function words, ignoring the difference between authors and their characters, is wholly unsuitable for drama."[277]

Vicker's *N*-gram study comparing Henry VI Part 2 with Henry VI Part 3 directly contests the collaboration hypothesis of Craig, Kinney and Burrows, not to mention Taylor and Loughrane and most scholars past and present, by identifying "every collocation of three words or more" which reveals that "a general match between the two plays occurs once every five lines, and a uniquely Shakespearian match every 24 lines." These matches, which were compared with a database of all the plays performed in the public theatre between 1579 and 1596, represented a "score far higher than anything" he had found in the eight years he'd been using the *N*-gram method. On this basis, he concluded that Craig and Burrows' "authorship division is self-evidently false."[278]

Vickers, who believes that Shakespeare wrote all of Henry VI Parts 2 and 3, denies that Marlowe had any collaborative hand in them, but his broad rejection of "authorship division" is equally true if that same sole author is Christopher Marlowe.

David Hoover, supporting Craig and Burrows, fired back on *N*-grams: "As attractive as Vickers's rare Ngram method initially seems, and in spite of its apparent effectiveness for some authors, it cannot offer the conclusive proof of authorship that Vickers claims."[279]

The basis of these tests ultimately are the words themselves. The proponents of applying this methodology to Elizabethan playwrights typically proceed to assemble test segments of generally 2,000 word blocks taken from the plays under examination, some of disputed authorship, some for which there is general, historical and scholarly agreement. Blocks of texts can thus be boiled down to component parts that can be charted or graphed and then compared to determine whether or not and by how much one resembles another which then can become the basis for attempted attribution of authorship for disputed or unattributed texts. In theory, these test are neutral data mining tools that provide clear, simple and verifiable results. In practice, however, they suffer from several, potentially irreparable deficiencies, the most significant of which is sample size. Many specialists in the field of language studies have doubts about the efficacy of such small samples. Maciej Eder, Director of the Institute of Polish Language at the Polish Academy of Sciences, and head of the Computational Stylistics Group, a cross-institutional research team focused on computer-assisted text analysis, stylometry, and authorship attribution, recently observed that:

> "It seems that for corpora of modern novels, irrespective of the language tested, the minimal sample size is some 5,000 words (tokens). Latin prose required only 2,500 words, and Ancient Greek prose just a little more to display their optimal performance. The results for the three poetic corpora (Greek, Latin, English) proved ambiguous, suggesting that some 3,000 words or so would be usually enough, but significant misclassification would also occur occasionally."[280]

In the same study, Eder further concluded that: "using 2,000-word samples will hardly provide a reliable result, to say nothing of shorter texts."

It is one thing, therefore, to attempt attribution when the subject play text is greater than 3,000 words (as for instance, Vickers has done by comparing whole plays), but when plays are broken up into scenes, some of which can be little more than a few hundred words, such as many of the scenes in the Henry VI plays, the attribution is inevitably suspect. The New Oxford Shakespeare Authorship Companion, for instance, divides the twenty seven scenes of Henry VI Part 2 by assigning Act I, scene 2, II:1, III:1, III:2, III:3, III:4, IV:2, IV:4, IV:6, IV:8, IV:9, and V:1 to V:5 to Shakespeare while allotting I:1, I:3, I:4II:2, II:3, II:4, IV:1, IV:3, IV:5 and IV:7 to Marlowe, a division which objective sample sizes would not be expected to support because objective sample sizes simply cannot be supplied by the individual scenes in the text.

Beyond the limitations of sample size, Rosalind Barber, in her 2019 article, "Marlowe and Overreaching, A Misuse of Stylometry"[281], castigates Hartmut Ilsemann's application of the Delta method, which measures the frequency of "function words" such as "and", "with" or "but", in disputing Marlowe's authorship of Dr. Faustus and Edward II by pointing out the flaws in his analysis, such as "a poorly designed test environment" marked by the lack of independent, verifiable controls which exclude bias; "ignoring the effect on style of a play's date and genre, failing to consider the effect of different-length comparison texts, and dismissing external evidence of authorship that conflicts with the test outcomes." While her critique in the article is limited to the specific case, it seems fair to say that her summary could be considered quite useful in evaluating much of the pseudo-science claimed by many stylometric advocates.

With regard to the effect of style, consistency of style has been shown to be variable over time for writers as diverse as Ben Jonson, Jane Austin and Henry James. Surveying Jonson, Hugh Craig observed:

> "the most important axis of differentiation, proves in each case to be a spectrum from elaborate, authoritative pronouncements to a dialogue style of reaction and interchange. . . . In Jonson it has a chronological aspect -- there is a shift over his career from one end to the other

-- and there is often significant change within the idiolects of his characters as well."[282]

[Emphasis added]

David Hoover, meanwhile, applied cluster analysis, Delta, and Delta Prime techniques to nineteen novels by Henry James and was able to show that "the early (1871-81) and late styles (1897-1904) are very distinct indeed, and that an 'intermediate' style (1886-1904) can also be distinguished", observing that:

> "These results paint a remarkable picture of an author whose style was constantly and consistently developing, a picture that is congruent with James's reputation as a meticulous craftsman who self-consciously transformed his style over his long career."[283]

Building on that and other studies, Hoover has concluded that "many analysts assume that change in an author's style over time is either universal or the norm, given a career of significant length."[284]

Given these empirical observations by leaders in the field, including those who are closest to the question of Shakespeare's authorship, it seems fair to ask why the assumption that "The Marlowe and Shakespeare canons are discrete and separate" has not been properly challenged with double-blind, randomly controlled data tests. Except, of course, it has been challenged and proved utterly false by Mendenhall. It is therefore absurd for these scholars to claim that they can separate Shakespeare from Marlowe on the basis of lexical tests when they cannot prove that they are not simply comparing the same author to himself who, in this case, is and always will be Marlowe.

Not that they haven't tried. One of the most extraordinary claims put forth by Craig and Kinney is that Shakespeare authored part of Arden of Faversham (1592). Based on a notorious 1551 murder reported locally in Faversham and memorialized by Hollingshed, the play is a striking, almost unique blend of documentary realism, poetic intensity and comic slapstick all wound around a tale of infidelity, crooked business dealings and murderous plots which careen wildly toward a burst of violence followed by swift, implacable justice. Published anonymously, it has long been thought to bear a striking relationship to the hand of Christopher Marlowe but attribution has been withheld largely due to the fact that, according to John Bakeless, "its style and theme are entirely different from his."[285] This remarkable assessment is made despite the immediately prior observation that:

> "The verse is often much like Marlowe's and much better than Kyd could write. The wording, especially of ejaculations and epithets, suggests Marlowe. The play shows an intimate knowledge of Kent, and Marlowe was (except for Lyly, who is out of the question here) the only Kentishman among the early dramatists."[286]

Bakeless details more than a dozen parallels and borrowings between Arden and Edward II, The Jew of Malta, Leir, and The Contention[287] and adds:

> "Marlowe's favorite exclamation, "tush", appears ten times. "Seeing" is used for "since" seventeen times in Arden and nine times in Edward the Second. "Peasant," "slave," "groom," and "ungentile," are more frequent than in the dialogue of other dramatists."[288]

As Brian Vickers has noted: "Self-repetition is a phenomenon found in literary language of all periods and cultures, between (at least) Homer and Samuel Beckett.[289] Marlowe is very much known for repeating himself from play to play, it is one of his "wholly habitual"[290] signatures.

No less notable is the fact that the play references Ovid's "Dawn Song", Elegy 13 from Book One of the Amores twice.

In Act I, Scene 1 Arden says to his wife, Alice, the opening lines:

> "Sweet love, thou knowest that we two, Ovid-like,
> Have oft chid the morning when it 'gan to peep,
> And often wished that dark knight's purblind steeds
> Would pull her by the purple mantle back,
> And cast her in the ocean to her love."
>   I:1, 59-63

Later, in Act V, Scene 1, with Arden murdered by her hirelings, Alice alone speaks the closing lines of the same Elegy:

> "Had chaste Diana kissed him, she like me
> Would grow love-sick, and from her watery bower
> Fling down Endymion and snatch him up:
> Then blame not me that slay a silly man
> Not half so lovely as Endymion."
>   V:1, 155-9

These excerpts serve as poetic bookends to the action; they have no dramatic purpose, but they are typical of Marlowe in that they show him tinkering with simultaneous projects, frequently letting one pop up in another as another kind of signature. During the period of the play's composition, Marlowe was working on his translation of Ovid's Amores, a first-person sequence of 48 poems that details an adulterous relationship with, Corinna, a rich and unhappily married woman who is stupendously unfaithful to her husband with the poet and many others. While the collection was not published until 1594, they must have been in private circulation in 1593 because Thomas Nashe quoted two lines from Marlowe's translation of Book II, E iii, "To a Eunuch who had the Keeping of his Mistress", lines 3-4 in his Unfortunate Traveller, dated June 27, 1593:

> Who first depriude yong boies of their best part,

> With selfe same wounds he gaue he ought to smart.[291]

M. L. Stapleton observed that the best explanation for Marlowe's interest in the Amores was that: "it could be said to have informed the concept of the sonnet sequence itself, since it served as an important influence on lyric poetry in the west from the earliest troubadours onward to Dante's *La vita nuova* and Petrarch's *Rime sparse*, which both revise and Christianize Ovid's foundational work."[292] Marlowe, meanwhile, had already written the Southampton sonnets and, of course, he was soon to begin work on Hero and Leander, sparked by his fascination with Ovid which also found its way into Arden of Faversham.

Rev. Ronald Bayne, in his "Preface" to the 1897 J. M. Dent reprint of the play, lavished praise on "the special excellencies of the play" and in particular noted that:

> "the picturesque ferocity and grim humor of Black Will and Shakebag are described with a firmness and ease and restraint of style which critics have not sufficiently noted. I can compare it only with the Jack Cade scenes of the Contention (and 2 Henry VI.)."[293]

The comparison seems even more apt when the proximity of Faversham to Ashford is considered. Jack Cade, who in Holinshed is described as being Irish, is described in the play as "John Cade of Ashford" (Henry VI, 2, 3:1.356) Marlowe was from Canterbury, also in Kent, a little more than twelve miles from either Ashford or Faversham.

Rosalind Barber, in her 2019 contribution to Notes and Queries noticed something else about the Jack Cade scene unique to Ashford, in particular Dick the Butcher's description of Jack's origins:

> DICK [Aside] Ay, by my faith, the field is honorable,
>   and there was he born, under a hedge; for his father
>   had never a house but the Cage.
> H VI 2, 4.2.39–52

> "The word 'cage' is glossed by Shakespeare's modern editors as 'a pen, lock-up, small prison compound'. But in all the versions of the play published up to and including 1623, the word is capitalized. . . . which raises the possibility that a specific place was being referenced. If it was, that place would be in Ashford."[294]

The Cage, in fact, was "a small cell (8 ft long, 4 ft wide, and 6 ft high) underneath Ashford's market hall where local troublemakers, such as drunks, would be locked up overnight ."[295]

The Jack Cade scenes are the same scenes that Craig and Kinney, after much careful stylometric sifting, were ultimately prepared to concede "fit Marlowe's patterns quite closely."[296] Barber's conclusion was that such specific knowledge re-enforced the stylometrics favoring Marlowe's authorship of Henry VI Part 2. Similarly, it also lends credence to Marlowe's authorship of Arden of Faversham as being parallel to that part of his world that found its way into another of his plays as yet another form of signature.

Kinney, on the other hand, did his best to find Shakespeare's presence in what he is convinced is a collaboration. Breaking the Arden text into four uneven blocks of "contiguous scenes", the first being scenes i through iii with 7,892 words, the second being scenes iv through vii with 1,965 words, the third being scenes viii and ix with 2,598 words and the fourth made up of the final scenes, x to xvi with 7396 words. The division of these scenes was guided by a Marker Word "training" test which indicated which individual scenes appeared more "Shakespearean". Thus, he was able to group those scenes that he pre-judged to be the very thing he was looking for, in particular the scenes in the second group which he judged to be "all in the Shakespearean part of the graph." Not only is this the smallest group, the group that clearly is well below any amount considered a minimum for accurate testing, it is also, by definition, the group that is most likely to result in a false positive. It would have been better to have combined groups 2 and 3 for a total of 4,563 words, still short of the recommended 5,000, but not by so very much as the two groups individually. But, if he did that, then he would have no hope of finding what he wanted to find.

Kinney tested all four scene groups for both Marker Words (lexical) and Principal Components (function) against larger groups of similar types of words drawn from the individual canons of Christopher Marlowe and Thomas Kyd, having previously eliminated Peele, Greene, Lyly, Lodge, Nashe, Wilson and Munday in his "training" tests. Sure enough, he discovered that "Arden of Faversham is a collaboration; Shakespeare was one of the authors; and his part is concentrated in the middle of the play".[297] Which is to say that the smallest segment, number two, with 1965 words, appeared to be the most similar to Shakespeare.

Two pages earlier, he concluded that "Marlowe does not appear to be the, or a, collaborator in the play" despite the fact that in the very same paragraph he admits that his own tests clearly show that "two clusters of known Shakespeare and Marlowe segments overlap a great deal."[298] These are segments one and three, totaling 10,490 words. The second section, the one he pre-judged to be the most Shakespearean, "falls in a shared territory, and is about equally close Shakespeare as to Marlowe." Meanwhile, The fourth section, which is composed of 7,396 words and had previously landed "in the non-Shakespeare group" of plays by all the combined, previously eliminated playwrights as well as Marlowe and Kyd in the Marker Word "training test", now appears to have shifted its position to entirely within the Shakespeare side of the Function Word chart. How this movement was accomplished cannot be traced, however, because no actual figures are given, just dots of grey or black representing clusters of words in a pair of "word clouds" inside a square chart. It should also be noted that there is no explanation as to why the Function Word test is considered more conclusive than the Marker Word test or whether or not the results would change if the order of testing was changed.

Altogether, the Marlowe share of the various tests in the order given shows him potentially responsible for a combined total of 12,455 words in the first three segments, over 60% of the play, but Kinney views all of that as belonging entirely to Shakespeare because his word "cloud" supposedly overlaps parts of Marlowe's. Even more mysteriously, Kinney does not credit the final, newly shifted group four to Shakespeare. He confirms this when he concludes that Shakespeare's part "is concentrated in the middle of the play." Again, actual figures, never mind the specific words themselves, are not provided. Which means that none of this can be independently verified.

More recently, Jack Elliot and Brett Greatley-Hirsch tackled Arden with a series of tests, including Delta, Zeta and something they called "random forest"[299], which employs algorithmic "decision trees" to "predict" word preferences of various authors. They used a selection of "well-attributed, sole-authored plays, 1580 - 1594" to distill the marker words suitable for testing and, after eliminating all the other usual suspects, they turned their attention to Marlowe and Shakespeare. The Marlowe plays included Tamburlaine 1 and 2, Jew of Malta, Edward II and The Massacre at Paris, the Shakespeare plays included The Comedy of Errors, The Taming of the Shrew, Richard III and The Two Gentlemen of Verona.

It should immediately be obvious that the issue of the effect of genre in the selection of word preference is unavoidable, in particular since the play being studied has nothing to do with battles, armies or governments. The tests, therefore, should attempt to control for this, but instead the authors, by virtue of what they explain is the 8% to 20% error rate of the decision tree algorithm, appear to "hold out" Edward II altogether. Given that Arden quotes Edward II extensively (see note 45), this seems a rather unfortunate error. Edward II does manage to make an appearance, however, in the middle of the results for George Peele and, not surprisingly, it thoroughly overlaps the word cloud for Arden.

Regardless, the authors find that Shakespeare, based on the word preferences associated with the four plays credited to him, is the most likely author of Arden of Faversham. Unfortunately, the underlying data is not provided for this result, just a series of charts showing word clouds on either side of a diagonal separating the tested author from Arden or not, depending on the overlap of one cloud into another. While it is difficult from the generalized display to deduce alternative explanations, it does appear that Marlowe, even in the absence of Edward II's contributions, runs a very close second with his word cloud appearing to crowd the diagonal at least as much as Shakespeare's. Which is to say that, word forests and algorithmic decision trees notwithstanding, Elliott and Greatley-Hirsch raise a lot more questions than they answer.

By way of comparison, Mendenhall printed not only the results of his tests, but the actual numbers of syllables counted with citations for the texts that provided them. Mendenhall's observation that the chief merit of his statistical method was that "the conclusions reached through its use would be independent of personal bias"[300] seems particularly relevant. It is notable that researchers such as Eder have more recently observed that "contrary to common sense, randomly excerpted 'bags of words' turned out to be much more effective than the classical solution, i.e. using original sequences of words ('passages') of desired size."[301] Which is to say that rather than test selected sections, tests should ignore placement and usage altogether, as Mendenhall recommended long ago.

Given the sample sizes used in the Arden of Faversham tests, not to mention the other possible issues with stylometric studies in general, it is probably too much to expect that the authorship attribution issue could be settled purely with data driven tests. What the tests can prove is that certain things cannot be proved. Rather than try to prove what something is, at least prove what it is not. Shakespeare, for instance, cannot be proved to be the author of Tamburlaine or Dido. No stylometric test can account for the fact that there is no evidence that Shakespeare was writing plays in 1587. Marlowe, on the other hand, cannot be proved not to have metamorphosed into the writer known today as Shakespeare. In fact, the stylometric tests all suggest that this is quite possible and, more importantly, that this is possible for no one else. The continuum exists only between Marlowe and the author known today as Shakespeare.

It is also important that stylometric tests should be consistent with known facts. Tests that run contrary to known, citeable facts must therefore be suspect. The list of citable facts supporting an attribution of <u>Arden of Faversham</u> to Christopher Marlowe includes: 1. his personal knowledge of the incident and its location, 2. the temporal and contextual links between Jack Cade of Henry VI Part 2 and Black Will and Shakebag, 3. the multiple parallel quotes appearing in his attributed, contemporaneous work, 4. the multiple quotes appearing in subsequent work attributed to his "editor" ie: Shakespeare, and 5. the characteristic and entirely unique use of his translations of Ovid's <u>Amores</u> to dramatic effect as opposed to mere ornamentation. Soon after this, Marlowe began work on <u>Hero and Leander,</u> the Ovidian themed poem which strings together so many critical events in his life and further ties him to <u>Arden of Faversham.</u>

Contrary to John Bakeless's assertion that the style and theme of <u>Arden of Faversham</u> "are entirely different from his", <u>Arden</u> is very much in the "style and theme" of Marlowe, with its mixture of comic and tragic elements, its subtle and piercing exploration of the various murderer's inner motivations and its poetic range. It is a novel work of enduring theatricality written in a period when Marlowe was constantly exploring and mapping new dramatic territory. As E. H. C. Oliphant declared:

> "If, then, the style of Marlowe is to be found in <u>Arden</u>, it is to be regarded as the work of Marlowe, unless good reason can be shown to the contrary. It is, in fact, more Marlovian than <u>Edward II,</u> which is sufficiently unlike

earlier plays by the same writer to make one feel sure that Marlowe's authorship would not have been unanimously conceded had his name not been put to it. If his part-authorship of Arden be granted, one sees Marlowe from a new angle; and, if he be regarded as in any way responsible for the creation of those two amusing ruffians, Black Will and Shakebag, a new conception of his versatility will have to be entertained."[302]

The fundamental flaw with current stylometric studies regarding Marlowe is not merely confirmational bias, but also sample size and genre. The collection of plays that are accepted as Marlowe's is a deliberately limited sample which excludes other plays that, if included, would tend to change the nature of the results and the signature revealed. None of the tests published to date include Edward III, Arden of Faversham, or Timon in the Marlowe sample, even though, as shown above, empirical evidence both textual and contextual, as well as substantial scholarly judgement inclines toward all three and would increase the number of words and word combinations under consideration by at least half. These tests do not even consider adding to the textual record those parts of the three plays of Henry VI that they confirm and which are now accepted are by Marlowe. All of which, or rather, the absence of which, cannot help but tend to skew the result of any stylometric test that focuses on marker words, function words, N-grams or even word forests now and forever.

Other than the brute force of computer aided counting, nothing about stylometrics is new, particularly not their susceptibility to bias, either in interpretation of results or in the design of tests. When Craig and Kinney admit that "occasionally the methods get things wrong, or at least fail to give an unambiguously right answer,"[303] they are tipping their hand. Mendenhall is significant because he anticipated this and despite the laboriousness of his counting method, his results are free of bias. There is no "right" result, merely a result.

Moreover, Mendenhall comes the closest to working with a "bag of words". If modern stylometrics proves anything, it proves the efficacy and reliability of his methods.

The fact that modern computerized tests do not and, in fact, are not designed to control for the potential that they are comparing not two separate authors, but a single author with himself is never considered. A test that does not control for this possibility cannot therefore be considered an accurate test.

When Craig and Kinney, on the basis of no external evidence at all, but merely on the notion that Shakespeare and Marlowe resembled each other on the page, declare that "we can now lay claim with some certainty that the two playwrights did know each other and worked together - at least on Henry VI - and that the Marlovian echoes that critics have perceived in the early Shakespeare are probably due to Marlowe's strong poetic voice,"[304] a skeptical observer might just have to wonder whether or not they are being entirely serious. In fact, unlike Greene's reports of Marlowe dining with Alleyn, or the Old Bailey's report of Marlowe being caught with Watson in a fatal brawl or Kyd's confession that they "shared a room", no one saw Marlowe together with Shakspere, or reported or commented upon any other sighting, real or imagined, or refuted or denied any anecdotal account of them in the same room, building or stage anywhere anytime ever.

If he collaborated on any of the three parts of Henry VI, neither Greene nor Chettle made any mention of it. So far as the literary record is concerned, Shakespeare is invisible until his sudden appearance in June 1593 with Venus and Adonis, a poem owing its source, concept and multiple lines to the yet unpublished Hero and Leander of Christopher Marlowe.

While the formal and somewhat grudging acknowledgement of Marlowe's responsibility for most, if not all of Parts II and III of Henry VI is fairly recent, the belief that Shakespeare was frequently a collaborative writer is not. No sooner did critics begin questioning the likelihood of his authorship than his defenders began to discover collaborators for many of the plays. The list has grown over the years to include Thomas Kyd (Edward III, also attributed to Marlowe), Thomas Nashe (Henry VI), George Peele (Titus Andronicus), Ben Jonson (Sejanus), George Wilkins (Pericles), John Fletcher (Two Noble Kinsmen, Henry VIII, and Cardenio, which is lost), and Thomas Middleton (Macbeth, Measure for Measure, All's Well that Ends Well, and Timon of Athens).

The New Oxford Authorship Companion ratifies all of this and adds several anonymous contributors as well. Modern scholarship, augmented by computerized models and word counting, pairing, prefixing, suffixing and coining data banks, is now able to find Shakespearian collaborators almost everywhere. As the technology continues to progress, it almost begins to seem as if Shakespeare did not write without collaborators.

And yet, of all the allied pens upon which Shakspere would have to have relied, the one that has had the least mention over the years is Marlowe. Now that Marlowe is getting attention, this seems to have shifted, but only insofar as it can be said that Shakespeare surpassed his mentor. Shakspere and Marlowe, it seems, had a close working relationship, one that went unmentioned by anyone else on the scene. Gabriel Harvey never noticed it, neither did Nashe, nor Greene, not even Chettle. All of them were frequently in print complaining about anyone who crossed them, including Marlowe, but none of them ever wrote about Shakspere. Not even Kyd, when he was on the rack giving up names to save his skin and admitting to sharing a workspace with Marlowe, mentioned Shakspere being anywhere in the vicinity. This can only be because Shakspere just wasn't there.

Chapter Eleven

Theatrical Agents

All the hurly burly over the several centuries spent trying to wedge the Man-Who-Wasn't-There into the midst of the Groats-Worth quarrel has largely obscured the most important fact about it: Greene's "upstart crow" warning appears to have had the desired effect. In the middle of 1592, Marlowe broke with Alleyn and started a new company with the backing of Lady Pembroke and the assistance of Richard Burbage.

The reasons for this move were personal, professional and political, the same forces that drove his career from the start. The first two involved his relationships with two people, Ned Alleyn and Tom Watson, the third overlapped the other two and included his political mentors, Francis Walsingham and Lord Burghley. Although his theatrical career got its biggest push from his teaming with Ned Alleyn, Marlowe had to know early on that it was a partnership that could not last.

As every theatrical producer knows, casting is everything. But, working with Ned Alleyn was no simple matter. For one thing, his ego did not allow for sharing the stage or the applause even with the most formidable author of the age. Regardless, or perhaps because of that, audiences loved him and packed his theaters from the moment he first thundered out Tamberlaine's boast: "Is it not passing brave to be a King, and ride in triumph through Persepolis?" But, Alleyn wasn't content merely to be the voice for bold speeches, he wanted to own them and, if he couldn't write them himself, he wanted to own the writers too.

No one knows for certain how Christopher Marlowe met Ned Alleyn, but Robert Greene has his own version of meeting the great scene stealer and while it puts Alleyn in the worst possible light, attributing all the vanity and cunning typically alleged against members of the theatrical breed by their ubiquitous critics, Alleyn emerges as a self-aware dramatic entrepreneur with an eye toward maximizing his assets and enlisting assistance with his deficits where and when he needed it to advance himself. In short, He knew he could thunder out Hercules well enough, he just needed good writers who could put bold words in his mouth. He offered to pay Greene for the privilege and he would certainly have done nothing less for Marlowe.

What would have caused Marlowe to suddenly write Tamburlaine? Still feeling the recent loss of Phillip Sidney and not altogether pleased with his apprentice work for the Queen's Men he devised a play well out of the mainstream that featured a role that no one in the Queen's Men could play. When Alleyn says he played Hercules and that he thundered the part on tour, it's not unreasonable to suppose that Marlowe would have seen him do it. Greene tells us that Alleyn hired him to write plays for him. Did Greene tell Marlowe about this? Did Alleyn ask Greene who else he knew that he could also hire? Somehow, Marlowe and Alleyn teamed up and Tamburlaine was the result. The idea that Alleyn commissioned a play from Marlowe that would show off his talents and that Marlowe wrote Tamburlaine specifically for Alleyn is less far-fetched than that Marlowe just appeared in London with a play in hand that so suited Alleyn that they were both catapulted to fame. The idea dovetails quite nicely with Greene's summation of his own experience of Alleyn before his London fame. Alleyn had an eye out for playwrights with the intent of hiring them for his own purposes. He knew from the beginning that it would be valuable to him to have signature properties and he was aggressively on the look-out for playwrights who could provide him with what he wanted. His partnership with Marlowe was built into his way of working.

If Alleyn did make such a proposal, Marlowe did not immediately take him up on it; both Tamburlaines and Faust were sold directly to Henslowe and the Admiral's Men, a fact that would become something of a problem for Alleyn soon after he'd made himself a superstar in both roles. For most of 1587 to 1589, however, Marlowe and Alleyn were teamed together in a revolutionary run in English theatre, exciting audiences and often alarming authorities. An oft quoted letter from Philip Gawdy dated November 16, 1587 reporting on the Act V, scene 5 shooting of the Governor of Babylon in II Tamburlaine described just how raucous all this could be:

> "My L Admirall, his men and players having a devyse in ther playe to tye one of their fellowes to a poste and so to shoote him to deathe, ... missed the fellow he aymed at, and killed a chyld, and a woman great with chyld forthwith, and hurt another man very sore".[305]

Live ammunition on stage? Not a problem in an era without fire marshals.

At the same time that he and Alleyn were all but setting fire to the London stage, Marlowe appears to have continued working behind the scenes in the employ of the Walsingham network, keeping a close eye on possible agitators opposed to Elizabeth. Chief among these were Stuart loyalists who, when they were not advancing the cause of Mary Stuart, Queen of Scots, had hopes for the advancement of Arbella Stuart, Mary's niece. As noted in Chapter One, Arbella was a ward of her grandmother, Bess Hardwick, and had been kept in "protective isolation" at Hardwick Hall in Derbyshire since her mother's death in 1582. That the "Morley" mentioned in Lady Hardwick's September 21, 1592 dispatch to Lord Burghley, could have been Marlowe is a possibility that was first raised in a 1937 letter to the Times Literary Supplement by E. St John Brooks. More recently, John Baker asserted that, in the absence of any other known and unoccupied "Morley" holding an MA, Marlowe was most likely Arbella's tutor.[306] Others, including Rosalind Barber, who observed that "writers were frequently employed in this capacity and Marlowe's experience as an 'intelligencer' would make him well suited to such a sensitive position,"[307] and Peter Farey, who looked at all those coming down to Derbyshire for the preceding twenty years and found "only one person fitted the bill – Christopher Marlowe"[308], have concluded the same. As tutor to the teenage Arbella, Marlowe would have cut quite the dashing figure. A leading playwright and poet, tutor to the Queen's niece, and inside intelligencer, Marlowe's career was moving him swiftly upward in all the circles that counted in Elizabethan England.

Personal fame can cause unanticipated difficulties, however, and Marlowe had his share, many of which appear to have come out of his association with Ned Alleyn. On September 18, 1589, Christopher Marlowe got tangled up in a dispute with William Bradley in Hogg Lane, not far from his good friend Thomas Watson's lodgings in Norton Folgate. Bradley owed £14 to Ned Alleyn's innkeeper brother, John who had threatened suit through his attorney, Hugh Swift, Thomas Watson's brother-in-law. In response, Bradley had his friend George Orrell threaten Swift, which caused the attorney to seek an injunction from the Queen's Bench against Bradley and Orrell. In the upshot, Bradley, who had been stalking Watson, confronted Marlowe sometime between two and three in the afternoon when he appeared outside Watson's door. Words were exchanged prompting Bradley to draw on the playwright who defended himself as best he could until Watson finally arrived and Bradley turned on him. "Arte thowe nowe come, then I will have a boute with the"[309] Bradley said and, as Marlowe stepped aside, went at Watson with sword and dagger, driving him "to the edge of the ditch at the north end of Hogg Lane"[310] where the desperate Watson got the better of him with a final, fatal thrust.

Knowing better than to run, they both awaited the constable who then took them to Newgate Gaol and the following day the county coroner held an inquest with a jury of twelve and found in favor of their plea of self-defense. Marlowe was released on bail, but Watson had to remain in Newgate until they both received their official pardons on December 3. This was the incident with which Greene in <u>Francescos Fortunes</u> mocked Alleyn for claiming that had he been on the scene he would have defended Marlowe just as Cicero defended Archais. If anything, had Alleyn been on the scene it would have been him facing Bradley's sword, not Marlowe. And it would have been Alleyn, saved by Watson's frantic stab, who would have been fortunate to be pleading self-defense before the coroner after spending a night in gaol.

While Greene was highly skeptical of Alleyn, he did not report that Marlowe had any response. It was out of this same incident and subsequent fortnight in gaol that Richard Baines later claimed Marlowe boasted to him of learning how to counterfeit coins from a man named "poole a prisoner in newgate who hath greate Skill in mixture of metals."[311] It is notable that Baines has Marlowe boasting foolishly while Greene, who certainly knew him better, describes Marlowe, with better cause to speak against Alleyn, keeping his thoughts to himself, which would be expected of the man trusted to tutor Arbella Stuart.

While traditional biographers persist in citing the Hogg Lane incident as indicative of Marlowe's supposedly contentious nature, even though he was clearly an innocent victim of an unprovoked attack, rare mention is made of John Alleyn's role in this or of his aptitude for finding his path to the center of any conflict. Not only was he the proximate cause of the Hogg lane affray, he also can be found embroiled in a subsequent dispute with the Burbages over the Theatre's finances. On November 16, 1590, John Alleyn took sides in a quarrel at the Theatre between the Burbages and Mistress Brayne, widow of Burbage's "problematic partner in the building and operation of the Theatre."[312] About 8 days later, Alleyn "and his fellowes" had their own argument with Burbage for "some of the Dyvydent money betwene him & them growing also by the vse of the said Theater."[313] Burbage refused and Alleyn threatened to take him to court, which he eventually did in 1592, adding in testimony that Burbage, "in a Rage" swore that he would use them the same as he used widow Brayne. It was this and disputes like it that resulted in the eventual separation between the Alleyn's and the Burbages in late 1592.

Caught between these quarrelsome producer/managers, Marlowe meanwhile, for all his supposedly disreputable associations, continued to pump out plays profitable to all while trying to find more stable ground for his work. His best friend during this time, the man who fought and killed William Bradley in his defense, was Tom Watson who remains one of the most enigmatic of the Elizabethan poet-intelligencers. Horatio to Marlowe's Hamlet, he was eight years his senior, a student of Roman law, well-traveled throughout Europe, fluent in Latin, Italian and French, had been a "friend and poetic ally"[314] of Philip Sidney and was also close friends with Thomas Walsingham. Watson could lay claim to having introduced the art of sonnet writing to England with Hekatompathia or Passionate Centurie of Love (1584), a series of one hundred eighteen line poems dedicated to Edward de Vere, the Earl of Oxford. When Thomas' "uncle" Sir Francis died in April, 1590, Watson wrote and published Melibœus, an elegy in both Latin and English which included lines evoking his days with Thomas in Paris as a couriers for Sir Francis. Posthumously praised by Francis Meres as among the playwrights "best for tragedy"[315] with Marlowe, Peele and Shakespeare, Watson also lived the intelligencer's double reality and his presence in Marlowe's life underscores Marlowe's own uncertain position in the aftermath of Philip Sidney's death. A dashing, worldly poet and adventurer, Tom Watson appears to have filled some of the void left by Marlowe's boyhood hero.

Watson was also something of a con-artist in the mold of Robert Greene, if not nearly so debauched in his reputation. His affiliation with the lawyer Hugh Swift included marriage to his sister Anne, both of whom were siblings of Thomas Swift, one of William Cornwallis' retainers, who attempted to win the affections of their master's daughter with Watson's assistance. Watson may have owed his position to Sir Francis Walsingham who has been supposed to have placed him with Cornwallis "so that he could be Walsingham's ears during the official inquiries into the recusancy of the father, Sir Thomas Cornwallis of

Brome in Suffolk, who was under surveillance from 1587."[316] According to Cornwallis, who took Swift before the Star Chamber and Lord Burghley, Swift's interest in his daughter got turned into a scam which included an attempt to blackmail Cornwallis with what Cornwallis declared was a forged marriage contract. Albert Chatterley, Watson's modern translator and biographer, reports the rather incredible upshot of the affair:

> "Although according to records Watson died in the September of 1592 before Cornwallis could involve him, the burial may be a fiction since it happened at exactly the right time for him to escape serious trouble and since Anne's younger brother Hugh, the attorney who drew up the contract used for the blackmail, and whose burial is recorded in the same church register a couple of weeks later, seems to have reappeared in London after a few years."[317]

Support for Chatterley's suspicions regarding Hugh Swift is advanced by Mark Eccles who reports that "Mr. Hotson has found him acting as an attorney in Queen's Bench in 1595."[318] Chatterley may have been wide of the mark when it came to Watson, but Swift it seems provides another source of inspiration for Marlowe's own disappearance the following May. At the very least, Marlowe cannot be said to have invented the idea of a staged death.

Although widely published and admired for his poetry, nothing of Watson's theatrical enterprise survives, at least not with his name on it. Watson, it seems, was more often than not a plot maker rather than author of dialogue. In his complaint to Burghley, Cornwallis asserted that "devising 'twenty fictions and knaveryes in a play' was his 'daily practyse and his living'",[319] which speaks more directly to inventing action than dialogue or verse.

As a collaborator, Watson would have been well matched to Marlowe, not only in temperament and education, but also in how they viewed the theatre and those who lived in it, Ned Alleyn in particular. Just as Greene and Nashe highlighted Alleyn's excesses, so Watson joined with Marlowe to take advantage of them. Together, they both used Alleyn's talent and had fun with it, sometimes at Alleyn's expense. This probably started with Arden of Faversham, Marlowe's first venture in a contemporary setting.

Recently, Gary Taylor and Rory Loughnane have credited Watson with co-authorship of Arden of Faversham. According to Dalya Albrege in The Guardian:

> "Among other biographical evidence, Taylor draws parallels between Arden and Watson's defence of Marlowe when he was attacked [by William Bradley] in the street in 1589: 'The husband who would be famously murdered is defended by a friend in an earlier attack. That incident in the play is not in the historical sources. It's totally made up by the playwright. The friend is also totally made up.'
>
> "Taylor has compared Arden with Watson's surviving literary prose and poetry, using databases of playwrights working between 1585 and 1595. The study revealed that 'some features of Arden are shared with no one but Watson.'"[320]

As noted in Chapter Ten, Taylor and Loughnane, as well as many others, go well out of their way in their attempt to establish through fundamentally flawed stylometrics that The-Man-Who-Wasn't-There was co-author of Arden. There is, of course, absolutely no trace of an iota of any factual, historical or verifiable connection whatsoever in any record or rumor of a record between Shakespeare and Watson. While they would be loathe to admit it, Taylor and Loughnane's findings much more strongly support the likelihood that Marlowe and Watson, who were practically blood brothers, worked together on Arden. Indeed, it is very difficult to imagine how Watson could have worked on any play set in Marlowe's own neighborhood without involving him. Moreover, on the basis of strikingly similar evidence, Arden was probably not the only play Marlowe and Watson produced in tandem.

The same type of friend and defender as Franklin is of Arden is found in Romeo and Juliet's Mercutio, whose defense of Romeo more directly compares to the Bradley incident than Franklin's defense of Arden and is also an invention, not found in any written source for either play.

There is good reason to date Romeo and Juliet as early as 1591 when both Marlowe and Watson would have been free to collaborate on plays. The Nurse's line: "'tis since the earthquake now eleven years" (I.3.24) and its repetition: "And since that time it is eleven years" (I.3.35) suggests one of two quakes, either in 1580 or 1584, with the earlier one much more notable in London, magnitude 5.7 to 5.8[321] in nearby Dover versus a similarly sized 1584 quake in Agile, Switzerland. The Dover quake was widely reported, and even memorialized by Gabriel Harvey in his "earthquake letter" to Edmund Spencer, both familiar with Marlowe from his days at Cambridge. The Agile earthquake was not similarly noted by anyone in England at the time. Dover, of course, is barely twenty miles south east of Marlowe's Canterbury home, which as noted above, was ten miles south east from Faversham. Traditional scholars lean heavily on the Agile quake because it allows them to insert Shakespeare after 1593, but the plain evidence favors Dover by four years and five hundred fifty miles.

Watson's familiarity with Italy is not merely documented fact, it is fundamental to his identity as a leading poet. While Geoffrey Bullough believes that the play's "main and perhaps sole source was Arthur Brooke's long poem The Tragicall Historye of Romeus and Juliet"[322] (1562), which was itself based on a novella version of Luigi da Porto's Istoria novellamente ritrovata di due Nobili Amanti (1530), Watson could be reliably counted upon to know not only da Porto's original, but the town and people of Verona itself. How else to explain the topical, political and civic details found by Richard Paul Roe in both the text and in Verona which were not included in any published source? For instance, Roe discovered the native sycamore grove as described in Q1, I: 1.116-121.[323]

Traditional critics assert that the playwright included sycamores "by analogy with a tree he knew in England whose leaves looked similar,"[324] which is a variation on the assertion that "he invented a peculiar Italy of his own, with colorful nonsense about what was there"[325] but this explanation does not account for the co-incidence of invention with fact. Watson, on the other hand, spent "a lustrum and a half"[326] traveling throughout France and Italy and "probably carried out his study of the Roman law in Italy, where the foremost schools in his time were in Padua and Bologna."[327] Padua, not twenty miles from Verona and:

> "backed by the wealth of Venice, now ranked first among European universities. More foreigners came to it than any of its rivals, not only because of the eminence of its professors, but also because it was the university town of Venice, the irresistible magnet that drew all travelers."[328]

One or two data points could be chalked up to co-incidence, but the author of <u>Romeo and Juliet</u> knew more about the town than sycamores. According to Roe, he knew all about Freetown and its location, i.e.: Villafranca de Verona,[329] the Castle of Prince Escalus ten miles outside Verona,[330] the "common judgement place" of Free Town, the site for Prince Escalus' mediation of the dispute between the Montagues and the Capulets. Roe noted that "No other teller of this story had called it old or mentioned anything about public judgements."[331]

Roe further noted that medieval rules of equal treatment are not accorded to the Montagues. This accurate depiction of local legal standards, and the unfair application of them, meant to him that "the playwright knew the truth of Veronese traditions" and he suspected that the author had been "in Verona, himself."[332] Watson, no mere tourist, could be counted upon to have studied not only the terrain, but the laws and customs of the country surrounding Padua.

Finally, Roe discovered the location of St. Peter's Church, mentioned in Q1, III.5 but unknown for centuries, directly on the path between Juliet's house and the monastic cell of her confessor:

> "Both in the sixteenth century, and in the days of the story of Romeo and Juliet, the diocesan records reveal that this was, indeed, a parish church. Founded in 955, in the thirteenth century it came under Franciscan jurisdiction and remained so for the next six hundred years."[333]

Apart from Roe's discoveries, there is also the presence of the two twelve line sonnets included in the Prologue and in Act I, Scene 5 of the First Quarto (a third, the prologue to Act II, was added later in the Folio version). Just as Marlowe signaled his interest in the sonnet form in Arden of Faversham with his quotes from Ovid's Amores, so he and Watson, who was already famous for his sonnets, continued this exploration begun in the contemporaneous tragedy. This is part of the continuity from Sidney to Marlowe with Watson adding his influence as Sidney's successor in Marlowe's imagination.

This partnership appears to have continued in some form to develop with Two Gentlemen of Verona, fraternal twin of Romeo and Juliet. Many scholars, such as Bullough, cite Boccacio's "tale of Tito and Gissipo (Decameron X.8)"[334] as one of several sources for the play. Watson, who wrote sonnet LXXI of his Hekatompathia on the theme "that Love not only worketh alteration in the minds of men, but also in the very Gods themselves"[335] in direct reference to Boccacio's tale, could well have provided not only that, but many of the other sources for the play in their originals, in particular Nicolas Collin's 1578 French translation of the widely accepted "primary source for the story of Julia"[336], Jorge de Montemayor's Diana Enamroada (1559), which would have short cut the need to scout out "a manuscript of Bartholowmew Yonge's English version"[337], not published until 1598, seven years after Two Gentlemen's composition but nevertheless advanced as an entirely plausible alternative by stalwarts of the orthodoxy academy.

Again, Roe provides a detailed outline of the contributions Watson would have been able to provide for Two Gentlemen of Verona:

1. Knowledge of the location of Milan's previously suspect harbor and of the canal route from Verona to Milan, which today is unused and is covered by miles of landfill.[338]

2. The actual location and importance of St. Gregory's Well, mentioned significantly as a meeting place in IV. 2, which most critics have been satisfied to assume could have been visible on a contemporary map available in London, but was in fact, a burial ground for plague victims. "The playwright chose the most ominous of all places in Milan for Proteus to frighten Thurio into going home to Verona."[339]

3. The period correct route described in V. 2 from Milan to Mantua.[340]

4. The fact that the V. 1 encounter with the Outlaws takes place in a "wilderness" between Milan and Verona, not a forest as academic editors often assume.[341]

5. Knowledge that the "forest" specifically referred to by Elgamour in V. 1 is nine miles from the gates of Milan.[342]

Scholars generally agree that Two Gentlemen and Romeo and Juliet were written at roughly the same time, although they tend to debate which came first as if creation must be sequential. What is more likely is that the plays were written almost simultaneously, the one being the mirror of the other and so being conceived as a pair. This would have been Watson's chief contribution, taking a plot idea and flipping it inside out to produce a reverse image, one play tragic, the other comedic, proving that comedy is simply tragedy played double-time. Marlowe, with his undeniable facility for character and phrasing, would provide the dialogue as if from a fountain.

The technique was so successful that repetition was inevitable. The result was The Taming of A Shrew and A Midsummer Night's Dream, which bear surprising similarities with different effects, in particular with how they target Ned Alleyn. One of the most singular things about A Shrew is that there is no direct source material for the Ferando (aka Petruccio in The Shrew) / Kate story. In absence of this, most commentators explain that it "is by its very nature of immemorial antiquity, and is found, in different forms, in the literature of all countries"[343] of which "this is a variant of the Shrew theme common in fabliaux from classical times."[344] They then proceed to list a number of similar tales without making any further attempt to positively attribute to any of them the identity of an actual source. What is uniformly overlooked is that the basis for this part of the play was not a previous play or poem, but was Alleyn himself. Both plays feature a central mating ritual with a lead figure lampooning the great Roscius. In A Shrew it is Ferando and in Midsummer it is Bottom. Where Ferando ridiculously misquotes Tamburlaine and Faustus[345], Bottom proposes to play all the parts in the rustics' play within the play, both in obvious mockery of Alleyn. It is almost as if Alleyn, too vivid perhaps to play the teenage Romeo and disappointed with having to play Mercutio (as Burbage is said to have done in the revision), demanded better parts that would not die in act three and would also make better use of his bold acting style with the result that Watson and Marlowe decided to skewer him twice with his own vanity.

Despite all the evidence of Marlowe's hand in all the borrowings from his other plays, traditional critics have always been very reluctant, even unwilling to credit Marlowe with A Shrew. Alexander Dyce asserted that the play is too effective a comedy to have been written by Marlowe "to whom, we have good reason to believe, Nature had denied even a moderate talent for the humorous."[346] Albert Tolman argued that it "was the work of a single author, and that this author was an admirer and imitator of Marlowe rather than that poet himself."[347] F. S. Boas opined that:

> "the more narrowly the borrowings are scrutinized in relation to their source, the less credit do they throw upon the conveyor. In some cases they convict him of curious ignorance of mythological lore, and in others they are grotesquely inappropriate to their new context."[348]

Which is exactly the point if Ferando is intended to appear absurd. Critics who reject a mere sense of humor for a man who was quoted by his worst enemy as saying "all they who love not Tobacco and Boies [are] fooles" are saying more about their own lack of wit than Marlowe's supposedly narrow range.

The similarities between A Shrew and Midsummer do not end with Alleyn's comeuppance. Both plays also feature two pairs of subsidiary lovers who encounter difficulties in their seductions that Alleyn's characters easily overcome in their own romances with bluster and nonsense. Also, both plays are built around plays within plays, Shrew being framed by the Christopher Sly device and Midsummer employing Peter Quince to stage manage a lampoon of Romeo. Finally, both plays are set in Athens which, in the case of Midsummer, Roe asserts was the "Italian Athens" of Sabionetta, "la piccola Atena", near Manutua.

Built by Vespasino Gonzaga (d. 1591), it was conceived as model city following the style of the ancients, including a small theater designed by Vincenzo Scamozzi, and was used as a center for the celebration of the arts.[349] The Ponta della Vittoria, the town's main gate, also known as "il Quercia dei Duca" or "the Duke's Oak", opens onto an oak forest which Roe identified as the site of the rustics' play rehearsal in I. 2.[350]

Finally, Roe pinpointed the "Temple" mentioned in IV. 1. as "la chiesa dell' Incororrnata,"[351] a small, chapel adjacent to Vespanio Gonzaga's octagonal mausoleum. Founded in the late 16th century, Sabionetta, was capital of its small state, both strategically located and a noted musical center, which would have had an unavoidable attraction for Watson, well known for his interest in madrigals and Italian music. Among the composers with whom Watson became familiar, Luca Marenzio, one of the most renowned composers of madrigals, took part in the wedding festivities for Vincenzo Gonzaga and Margherita Farnese in 1581 and spent five years in the family's service.[352] There is no record of Watson actually meeting Marenzio, nor of them visiting Sabionetta together, but in 1590, at about the same time that he would have been collaborating with Marlowe on, among other plays, <u>Midsummer Night's Dream</u>, and with "la piccola Atena" fresh in his mind, Watson published <u>Italian Madrigals Englished</u>, a collection of 28 madrigals featuring lyrics by Watson, 23 of which were composed by Marenzio. This is the type of inter-textual, autobiographic detail that is woven throughout the Marlowe / Watson collaboration.

Other internal jokes mirror external realities. The Christopher Sly reference to Marlowe in <u>Shrew</u>'s framing play is too broad to miss and the use of Thomas Kyd's most successful device, the play within a play that served to distinguish <u>The Spanish Tragedy</u>, suggests that he may either have joined in the fun as well or even have been a lesser target in it. Then there is the combination of Puck and Oberon, suggestive of the Marlowe / Watson team, with its manipulation of Alleyn's Bottom, not to mention Lysander, Demetrius, Hermia and Helena, in the same manner that Watson manipulated Lord Cornwallis' daughter with that supposedly forged marriage contract with Watson's friend, Hugh Swift. This self-referential doubling and repetition suited Marlowe, who not only delighted in quoting from his own work, but persistently returned to prior work, rewriting and recasting it anew even after he left London.

Watson was nine years Alleyn's senior and doubtless viewed him with diffidence, perhaps not as disdainfully as Greene, but no less cynical for all that. For his part, Alleyn must have enjoyed, at least in part, being the butt of Watson's multilayered jokes when it suited him, as it must have when he overplayed Bottom's death scene to great guffaws and subsequent applause. He would not have failed to notice, however, Watson's ability to steer Marlowe's talent and, if Greene's report is to be trusted, he eventually tried to play that role as well.

If Watson made Alleyn bearable for Marlowe, eventually Alleyn tried to push Watson aside. But where Greene was jealous and given to empty threats, Watson was worldly and unintimidated. All of this would come to a head in the Spring of 1592 when Marlowe had his famously mis-comprehended fight with Alleyn, the upstart crow and Shake-scene, and went forward with his plan to establish an independent company with the patronage of his deceased mentor's sister, Mary Sidney, then better known as Lady Pembroke. As always, politics played a significant role in any new venture, particularly in the theatre, and Marlowe would first have to convince the hardheaded Burghley that it would serve his interests to allow his talented intelligencer to skewer Ned Alleyn once more, with gusto.

Chapter Twelve

Enchanted Summer

While the team of Marlowe and Watson steadily produced play after play for the Admiral's Men, Ned Alleyn, perhaps resentful of their importance to the troupe, decided to cut a side deal with Fernando Stanley who was moving forward with both his court career and his family's theatrical company, Lord Strange's Men. Previously noted for the talents of its tumblers, the company had dropped out of view in the mid 1580s only to return to London in 1589 with a new company, composed of former members of Leicester's Men who began making a name for themselves by satirizing the supporters of the Martin Malprelate pamphlets, the notorious and illegally printed attacks by anonymous Puritans on the English church. If these performances were intended to draw favor from the authorities, they fell far short, instead drawing criticism from the Privy Council for depicting matters "vnfytt and vnreuerent to be handled in playes, bothe for divinitie and state..."[353] It was for this, and their defiance of an order on November 5 from the Lord Mayor of London to suspend performances by playing that same afternoon at Cross Keys, that they spent the night in jail, after which the company appears to have quietly left the scene.

Subsequently, the company reorganized and, taking some time to reconsider their repertory, returned to London so successfully that they were able to play court performances at Richmond on December 27, 1590 and at Greenwich on February 16, 1591. It was at this point that the company formed some kind of an alliance with Ned Alleyn who recruited several members of the Admiral's Men to join him in performing at court with Strange's Men. Notably hedging his bet, Alleyn continued to wear the Lord Admiral's livery even while starring in The Jew of Malta, a play he personally owned, for Strange.

The Admiral's Men did not appear at court that year, instead going on tour without Alleyn and for the next two years Lord Strange's Men took pride of place at Henslowe's Rose. Both Tamburlaines and Faust were owned by the Admiral's & Henslowe, however, leaving Alleyn without two of his most famous roles.

Alleyn's dual allegiance has been the source of much comment and confusion, but he may have simply been hedging his bet on the newer company as he was soon to marry Joan Woodward, Henslowe's step-daughter, and in time become more of a promoter than strutting actor. For the time being, however, he was enjoying his notoriety and command of all the best roles written for two companies. His collaboration with Strange's company also enabled him to take better advantage of Thomas Kyd, who "entered Strange's service in 1587-88"[354] and whose Spanish Tragedy competed heads up with Marlowe's Tamburlaine as Alleyn's most successful vehicles to date. In addition to Kyd's Jeronimo, Alleyn was making do with Marlowe's Edward III and the various roles provided by his partnership with Tom Watson.

Kyd, who testified in a June, 1593 letter to Lord Puckering to "wrytinge in one chamber towe yeares since"[355] with Marlowe, also claimed to have first met him "upon his bearing name to serve my Lo[rdship]". Although Kyd does not specify the identity of this Lord, it is understood to be Strange as he asserts that the Lord knew him only "in writing for his plaiers, for never cold my L.[ord] endure his name, or sight . . ." This observation is frequently added to the pile of supposed evidence against Marlowe's character, but Lord Strange may have had other reasons for not wanting to get too close to Marlowe, reasons which were more political than theatrical and would have escaped the less worldly Kyd.

In May, 1591, Lord Burghley, who had assumed control of the intelligence network after Walsingham's death, intercepted a letter from the Jesuit priest Robert Persons to Lord Strange.

Singled out by Burghley in his <u>Execution of Justice</u> (1583) as one who "who yet hideth himself in corners to continue his Trayterous practise,"[356] Persons was considered "one of [Queen] Elizabeth's deadliest foes",[357] and was actively working with other English Catholic exiles to usurp the throne and, as part of their conspiracy, possibly murder the Queen. According to Thomas Phelippes, Burghley's master cryptographer and code breaker, Persons was involved in a conspiracy whose design "was that the Queen should be killed, Sir William Stanley enter the realm with a number of men, and joining some competitor make head against all the rest, till more force and further directions came from the Pope."[358] The "'competitor' (that is, partner) was to be his cousin, Lord Strange."[359] Not all of this was even this clear when Marlowe applied sometime in mid 1591 for a position with Lord Strange's Men, but it would have been an unnecessary waste of an opportunity for Burghley not to have made use of Marlowe's talent for intelligence in the household of a suspected traitor and Marlowe, who had already served a similar purpose "tutoring" Arbella Stuart, would be in no position to refuse the assignment which, in any event, served his theatrical purpose equally well. Once again, he would find himself mirroring Watson who continued to keep an eye on Lord Cornwallis for the same purpose. If Strange thought he was being watched by Marlowe, it would certainly explain why, as Kyd claimed, he could not stand the sight of him or "endure his name."

In late December of 1591 or early January of 1592, in the middle of the holiday season and the rise of Strange's Men with Alleyn, even as he was being celebrated as the company's latest literary acquisition, Marlowe was apparently given a new intelligence assignment and travelled to the Dutch town of Flushing. Taking lodgings with Richard Baines, who by then had a decade long career as an intelligencer for Walsingham, Marlowe seems to have been on a mission for Lord Burghley to uncover a counterfeiting ring allied to Lord William Stanley, "a by-word for treachery, a bogey man"[360] who had returned the town of Deventer back to the Spanish after the battle at Zutphen where Phillip Sidney had been killed. Stanley had then switched sides to the Spanish and had ever since been the leader of a "rag-bag of English, Irish, Italians, Burgundians and Walloons" loyal to Spain and Catholicism. Reports had Stanley employing Edward Bushell, a servant of his cousin, Lord Strange, who had stolen £1,800 worth of gold plate from Winchester Cathedral which was then melted and coined for use in a variety of potentially treasonous schemes. "Burghley had an inkling that conspiracy was afoot"[361] and dispatched Marlowe and Baines to investigate.

Perhaps to establish a cover for his mission, Marlowe apparently arranged for the publication of his translation of Certaine of Ovid's Elegies, a work that would have been banned by the English censor but which was printed in Middleburgh, Holland.[362] There is some dispute about the date of this work: "there are two undated surreptitious printings"[363] of it before 1599 when it was entered in the Stationer's Register as a book "jointly condemned".[364] Percy Simpson made the case that it was printed in 1590, but in 1590 Marlowe was in London writing Arden of Faversham, inclusive of the twin quotes from Elegy # 13. The only time Marlowe is known to have been in the vicinity of Middleburgh was in late December 1591 at the start of his assignment for Lord Burghley. It makes sense then that he took the time to seek a printshop near Flushing for his new work, unpublishable in London, as cover for his other project.

Almost inevitably Flushing must have had unpleasant associations for Marlowe. Philip Sidney had been Governor there shortly before he was killed and had looked to Leicester for support with his undermanned and ill-equipped garrison. The thought of pursuing Stanley, the turncoat who profited at Sidney's expense, would have been fraught with uncertainty and Marlowe could not have looked at the business without misgivings. He wasn't any kind of soldier, his encounter with Bradley proved that well enough. What would he do if the mission got hot and how was he supposed to infiltrate a band of roughnecks in a foreign land? It was one thing to have a book of erotic poems published, quite another to pose as an apostate and not risk his neck in the process.

The plan that developed included the assistance of a third party, Gifford Gilbert, a goldsmith who was encouraged to try his hand at counterfeiting in a scheme that could get Marlowe "a step closer to the Stanley conspirators at Brussels and Nijmegen."[365] Unfortunately, the plot blew up as soon as the first forged coin, minted in pewter, was put it into circulation and promptly discovered. Marlowe, Baines and Gilbert were arrested, taken before Governor Robert Sidney, Philip's younger brother, and interrogated. In a letter to Burghley, the Governor reported that:

> "the men being examined apart never denied anything, only protesting that it was done to see the goldsmith's cunning. And indeed they do one accuse another to have been the inducers of him, and to have intended to practise it hereafter, and have as it were justified him unto me."[366]

Governor Sidney also reported that Marlowe claimed to be "well known both to the Earl of Northumberland and my Lord Strange," a remark that suggests that he, Sidney, may not have been that familiar with Marlowe despite his earlier links with his older brother. What makes this more odd is that within three months Marlowe would begin promoting a new theatre company with his sister, Mary Sidney, Lady Pembroke. Perhaps Robert simply wanted to keep his distance because Baines and Marlowe were angrily accusing each other "of intent to go to the enemy, or to Rome. . ." Lacking further insight or direction, Sidney packed them off to Burghley.

It seems reasonable to ask at this point to ask whether or not any of this was at all palatable for Christopher Marlowe. Various biographers have tried to present this episode as yet another example of Marlowe's unsavory character. As if counterfeiting came so naturally to him and making mischief was his chief occupation. What goes unobserved is the fact that Marlowe's involvement in Baines' counterfeiting escapade was of a piece with his service with the conspirator Lord Stanley's "contender", Lord Strange. The fact that the person accusing Marlowe of an interest in counterfeiting is Baines also goes unremarked, as if Baines could be trusted on any account. All of these calumnies against Marlowe find sympathetic ears in the persons of traditional scholars who inevitably are more interested in shoe horning The-Man-Who-Wasn't-There into the picture. What goes unrecognized by these scholars is that the Lord High Treasurer put his agent, Christopher Marlowe, in position to investigate the two people, Lord Stanley and Robert Persons, who he considered to be the greatest threats against his Queen since the Babington Plot which led to the exposure and ultimate downfall of Mary Stuart, Queen of Scots.

Unfortunately for Marlowe, he also had the task of keeping a close eye on Richard Baines, who had confessed to Catholic sympathies even while in Walsingham's service ten years before.[367] Apparently, Baines did not take well to being minded by the younger, more intelligent and far accomplished poet. When the counterfeiting was discovered (and who can believe that Marlowe would have been the one to propose attempting to circulate it?), Baines immediately accused Marlowe of treachery.

Although he must have been well known to Lord Burghley both through Walsingham and the Privy Council and may well have had direct contact with him when writing the Southampton Sonnets, this is Marlowe's first recorded interview with the Queen's Lord High Treasurer and Secretary of State. Traditional scholars have never known quite what to make of this interview and have even been puzzled by the fact that, rather than penalize Marlowe, Burghley set him free. This is easily understood, however, if Marlowe was working for Burghley all along. Burghley would want to know why the mission went awry, but he would not be more harsh with an agent who he already had placed in the Strange company for the purpose of gathering intelligence.

The Stanley business in Flushing would have been Burghley's chief interest, but Marlowe probably could not add much on that score since his counterfeiting gambit had been so quickly exposed. Regardless, this would have been an opportune moment for Marlowe to advance a different proposition, one more suited to his long term interests. He would not be the first clandestine operative to want out of the service. He would also know that the price of his freedom would have to be more than he could provide as a mere intelligencer.

Whether or not Marlowe had worked all of this through in his mind before he came face to face with Burghley that day in March, 1592, the fact is that within four months' time he was leading a brand new theatrical company under the patronage of Lord and Lady Pembroke, formerly Mary Sidney, the sister of the man who had inspired his personal motto. The question of how this transformation came about can be best answered by thinking as he would think at that moment when he spoke to Burghley and what he might have to offer as a substitute for bumbling forgeries and counterfeits in Flushing.

Marlowe had surely seen enough of plots and intrigues in the underground to know that he preferred to write them for the stage rather than play them with his own life in the balance. While he could return to Strange's Men, he probably would not be very useful as an informant once Fernando Stanley had been alerted to him. Better for him to advance the Tudor cause by way of literature and theatre, staging plays that communicated the crown's preferred self-portrait and supported its legitimacy. Moreover, he had just the vehicle in a new play, Henry VI.

Not yet produced, he could assure Burghley that the company expected it would be at least as successful as The Jew of Malta which had been in performance at court when Marlowe left for Flushing. In fact, Henslowe had recently completed an expansion of the Rose, his "playe howsse"[368] from 1,600 to 2,500 seats[369] at a cost of £105 and Lord

Strange's Men, then in residence, was preparing to become the unchallenged leader of the London stage. Henry VI was to be Ned Alleyn's next triumph and the big draw at the renovated Rose. If Lord Burghley wanted to counter Strange, he needed to worry less about tulips in Flushing and more about the Rose in London.

Marlowe could propose an alternative. He could shift his playwrighting from Strange to a new company sponsored by Lord and Lady Pembroke. As Philip Sidney's sister, Mary had already begun to move herself forward as a patron of poets and as a poet in her own right.

Thus, rather than promoting Strange's company, he could challenge it with a new one more closely allied with the crown. He already had in mind two sequels for Henry VI and he could also propose organizing it with Burbage, who had been fighting with Alleyn and Henslowe. Although the old Burbage was cranky, the son, Richard, was a good actor and more dependable. More importantly, Burbage had been renovating his theater as well. On February 25 1591/92, while Marlowe was still in Flushing, Bryan Ellem was deposed in the Brayne v. Burbage case (stemming from the fracas in November, 1590) and testified that "the said defend^{t}es or one of them haue bestowed in further buildings and Reparacions of the Theater there {and other houses in hollywell aforesaid} [struck out] wtin the vi or vii weeks passed/to the value of xxx or xl^{li} as this depo^t dothe estymate the same."[370] Although this was not as much as the £105 that Henslowe spent on the Curtain, it was not inconsiderable and, as Manley and MacLean have since noted: "It would have been a logical response for Burbage to renovate the Theatre for Pembroke's Men, a company formed around some key members of Strange's Men, like Richard Burbage, and perhaps around some key plays . . . as well."[371]

If Marlowe did propose this, Burghley would likely have been skeptical, disinclined to change tactics and concerned that any sudden departure by Marlowe from Strange would draw too much attention. Marlowe could counter by suggesting that he invent a reason for leaving, such as an argument with Ned

Alleyn who could be depended upon to behave atrociously, especially if he had another hit onstage to feed his ego. That would provide a cover story and he could move on without raising suspicion in an already distrustful Strange.

Burghley would have listened to this carefully; the support of the Pembrokes would be crucial as a counterweight to Strange with both the Admiral's and the Queen's men already suffering in comparison. If Marlowe had read Burghley's Execution of Justice, a blunt argument against various forms of political unrest which, in fact, made specific mention of Robert Persons, one of the people linked to Lord Stanley, then he could emphasize that his plays would support Burghley's argument against treason. He had already written Edward III in this vein. Burghley had written of "lawes of Parliament made in King Edward's time"[372] as authority for justice against contemporary traitors "maintayning and adhearing to the capitall enemy of Her Maiestie and her Crowne"; Marlowe could carry the same message of legal authority onstage for the public to hear and see. If Marlowe could pull it off, he would want Burghley to see to it that court performances would be available.

Whether or not a deal was struck with Burghley, Marlowe returned to Lord Strange's Men and immediately staged Henry VI to instant and overwhelming success. Henslowe made his first note of a performance of Henry VI (*"Harey vj"*) on March 3, 1592 at the Rose Theater in Southwark. He referred to the play as "ne", which typically meant "new, and recorded that it raked in £3.16s.8d, a "remarkable sum"[373]. Altogether it had fifteen performances in the three and a half months before the theaters were again closed due to plague on June 23, 1592.

Thomas Nashe reported a scene from the play in 1592:

> "How would it have joyed brave Talbot (the terror of the French) to think that after he had lien two hundred years in his tomb, he should triumph again on the stage, and have his bones new embalmed with the tears of ten thousand spectators at least (at several times), who, in

the tragedian that represents his person, imagine they behold him fresh bleeding."[374]

This stretch, between March and June of 1592, would have been the opportune time for Marlowe to begin work on the second and third parts of the Henriad. It would have been in that period when the incidents detailed in Greene's Groats-Worth took place. That would have been a perfect moment to have a blistering argument with Ned Alleyn, stuffed with the success of Barabbas the Jew, Talbot the savior and Jeronimo the avenger, over whether or not he could bombast out a blank verse of his choosing in defiance of his playwright. With thousands in daily attendance and the streets packed with roused groundlings, housewives and tradesmen celebrating the adventures of Kings and misers, it would have been the very stage for what apparently got Marlowe hauled before the Middlesex Justice of the Peace on May 9, 1592.

Marlowe may not even have been the chief culprit; it was Greene who made a stink in print, after all. But Marlowe had to post a bond of £20 against his appearance the following October's session "and in the meantime . . . keep the peace toward all subjects . . . and especially toward Allen Nichols, Constable of Holywell Street . . . and Nicholas Helliot, subconstable of the same."[375] £20 would be no small sum even for the most successful playwright in London.

No mention is made in the Middlesex bond of the cause of the complaint, if there was any, against Marlowe. In the absence of further detail, nothing more than general rowdiness can be assumed. This has not, however, stopped any number of biographers from claiming that he "threatened the Constable of Holywell Street,"[376] who "knew him as a street fighter and violent man"[377] and that "they may have rejoiced to be rid of him without more trouble."[378] As if what might easily be, based on the lack of any more serious complaint, comparable to nothing greater than a traffic ticket is an indicator of anything deeply personal. Regardless, it would not stretch anyone's credulity for Marlowe to quit his rehearsals and leave town in compliance with the court order, promising not to return until the Fall.

What better time for him to visit Wilton House, home of Lady Pembroke where her brother Philip had written most of Arcadia, Astrophel and Stella and The Defense of Poesy? All of which influenced his own work so deeply. Mary was by then not only a leading patron of poets but a poet in her own right having completed a translation of Robert Garnier's Tragedy of Antonie and was working on her own, revised, edition of Sidney's Arcadia. Although Thomas Nashe had published an unauthorized version in 1590, she was preparing to publish her version and had registered it with the Stationers on May 3, 1592. Marlowe, a close student of the original manuscript, could certainly help with revisions if she asked him. At the same time, he could show her the plays he had written for her theatre and, with so many actors unemployed, have a few out for a staged reading or two; precisely the sort of thing professionals do for their patrons when embarking on a new enterprise.

Mary's son, William Herbert, third Earl of Pembroke, had turned twelve on April 8 and, with the plague keeping the theaters closed in London, would have had the opportunity to witness and engage in rehearsals with the new company that was to bear his name. Included in the company repertory would have been The First Part of the Contention Between the Famous Houses of York and Lancaster (Henry VI Part 2) (1600), The True Tragedy of Richard the Duke of York (Henry VI Part 3) (1595), The Taming of a Shrew (1594), Titus Andronicus (1594), Edward II (1594) and possibly A Midsummer Night's Dream (1600). There would have been other boys there, company members, to play the young women's roles and William would not have been denied the opportunity to join in the fun with parts like Helena, Hermia, Puck, Katherine and even Edward's Queen Isabella available to him. Burbage, who had apprenticed as a player of female roles, would have made an able tutor for the Earl's effervescent son. William's main tutors Samuel Daniel and Hugh Sanford were hovering about as well as were John Florio and Gabriel Harvey, hoping for patronage. Tom Watson would have been in and out consulting with Marlowe on various plot lines and the recently elevated Thomas Walsingham whose sister had once been married to Philip would have been welcome.

Out of this summer of poetic immersion three commemorative sonnets, numbers 18, 19 and 20 in the published sequence, appear to have been composed in young William's honor, either on the occasion of his name day or shortly after when Marlowe assembled the company and began preparations for the fall when it was hoped that the theaters would be allowed to reopen:

18

"Shall I compare thee to a summer's day?
Thou art more lovely and more temperate.
Rough winds do shake the darling buds of May,
And Summer's lease hath all too short a date."

19

"Devouring Time, blunt thou the lion's paws,
And make the earth devour her own sweet brood,
Pluck the keen teeth from the fierce tiger's jaws,
And burn the long lived phoenix in her blood;
Make glad and sorry seasons as thou fleet'st,
And do what'er thou wilt, swift-footed Time,
To the wide world and all her fading sweets.
But I forbid thee one most heinous crime:
O, carve not with thy hours my sweet love's brow,
Nor draw no lines there with thine antique pen;
Him in thy course untainted do allow
For beauty's pattern to succeeding men."

While sonnets 18 and 19 are almost delicate, comparing the young lord to "a summer's day" and forbidding "Devouring

Time" from carving William's brow with "thine antique pen", sonnet 20 is absurdly ribald, mixing sexes as easily as boys played women:

> "A woman's face with nature's own hand painted
> Hast thou, the master-mistress of my passion;
> A woman's gentle heart, but not acquainted
> With shifting change as is false women's fashion;
> An eye more bright than theirs, less false in rolling,
> Gilding the object whereupon it gazeth;
> A man in hue, all hues in his controlling,
> Which steals men's eyes and women's souls amazeth.
> And for a woman wert thou first created,
> Till nature as she wrought thee fell a-doting,
> And by addition me of thee defeated
> By adding one thing to my purpose nothing."

It is not difficult to imagine William wearing woman's weeds and having played a young lover in Shrew or Midsummer being saluted by the summer's gathering of players and poets, dancers and jugglers, musicians and romantics, all celebrating a rare season of hope and adventure. The idea of honoring young William with his three sonnets read aloud to the assembly would seem inevitable, especially with the punchline being:

> "But since she pricked thee out for women's pleasure,
> Mine be thy love and thy love's use their treasure."

There was undoubtedly a heady atmosphere at Wilton in the Summer of 1592. In fact, if the sonnets are any guide, it appears that Marlowe fell in love there and then and he expressed it in the four sonnets immediately following the three sonnets honoring William Herbert, starting with 21:

> "So is it not with me as with that Muse,
> Stirred by a painted beauty to his verse,

> Who heaven itself for ornament doth use
> And every fair with his fair doth rehearse,
> Making a couplement of proud compare
> With sun and moon, with earth and sea's rich gems,
> With April's first-born flowers, and all things rare,
> That heaven's air in this huge rondure hems.
> O! let me, true in love, but truly write,
> And then believe me, my love is as fair
> As any mother's child, though not so bright
> As those gold candles fixed in heaven's air:
> > Let them say more that like of hearsay well;
> > I will not praise that purpose not to sell."

Many scholars, including John Kerrigan of the Penguin edition of the Sonnets and Katherine Duncan-Jones in the Arden version, have noted the strong affinity between sonnet 21 and 130, both of which reject "the conceit of poets who habitually make extravagant comparisons with stars, jewels and flowers, in favor of truthful (and private?) cogency."[379] Sonnet 130, of course, is practically the signature sonnet in the "Dark Lady" series. The mistaken focus made by some scholars on the woman's dark "eyes", as if this is an identifying feature, has led many down blind paths of misidentification. In fact, Marlowe's "raven black" eyes in sonnet 130 are, as Kerrigan noted, "shadows"[380] of Watson's "sparkling eyes" in sonnet VII of his Hekatompathia.

The notion that 21 and 130 are related has been one of the reasons many scholars to assume that the sonnets are therefore out of order, jumbled up in some way in order to disguise their true meaning. This is not necessarily true. Sonnets 21 and 130 are related because they appear to be addressed either to the same person or to two different people for the same reason with Watson being used as a foil for both sonnets. The fact that they separated in the printed text by one hundred ten other sonnets does not automatically mean that they were printed out of order. Instead, it may mean that there is a cause and effect relationship and that the author, Marlowe, chose to revisit the theme in order to take advantage of the prismatic perspective created by the passage of time. Regardless, even scholars who can't identify either the writer or the person addressed appreciate the connection which generated not only these, but many more sonnets in the complete collection.

As to the beloved's identity, it seems fairly clear that it is not a man because neither the Dark Lady nor Tom Watson's subject are men. Which means that neither William Herbert nor Henry Wriosley are Marlowe's beloved. Nor are Tom Watson or Thomas Walsingham or any other "fair youth" that has been proposed over the years. She should be young, however, if the question in sonnet 22 is to be trusted: "How can I then be elder than thou art?" 22: 9. This line eliminates Lady Pembroke. Marlowe, who was just 28 at the time, must have been addressing someone well his junior to describe himself in such terms.

In that summer of rehearsals and performances, poetry and romance, Marlowe was so very much in love that he feared, like an actor's nightmare, he had forgot how to speak:

> "As an unperfect actor on the stage,
> Who with his fear is put besides his part,
> Or some fierce thing replete with too much rage,
> Whose strength's abundance weakens his own heart;
> So I, for fear of trust, forget to say
> The perfect ceremony of love's rite,
> And in my own love's strength seem to decay,
> O'ercharged with burden of mine own love's might.
> O, then let my books be then the eloquence
> And dumb presagers of my speaking breast,
> Who plead for love and seek recompense
> More than that tongue that more hath more expressed.
>   O, learn to read what silent love hath writ;
>   To hear with eyes belongs to love's fine wit.
>
>   Sonnet 23

To have been the first to receive what may have been Marlowe's first confession of earnest love must have been as amazing to his beloved as it has been for so many who have wondered at it ever after. It is not difficult to imagine them being posted to one of the many trees at Wilton, just as Orlando attached his poems to Rosalind in <u>As You Like It</u> not much later.

Finally, to round out the sequence and place it firmly at Wilton, Marlowe links it directly to Sidney's <u>Astrophel and Stella</u> sonnets, composed in an earlier summer under the same canopy:

> "Mine eye hath played the painter and hath stelled,
> Thy beauty's form in table of my heart;
> My body is the frame wherein 'tis held,
> And perspective that is best painter's art."

>> 24: 1 - 4

Some editors wrongly amend the printed text to read "steeled", which not only mars the rhyme but also jars with "painter's art" which uses brush and paint not engraver's ink. Later sonnets speak of a portrait, perhaps a miniature, in particular sonnet 47: "With my love's picture then my eye doth feast, / And to the painted banquet bids my heart" which might have been a gift given at Wilton to Marlowe by his beloved.

The sonnet carries the attention to eyes further:

> "Now see what good turns eyes for eyes have done:
> Mine eyes have drawn thy shape, and thine for me
> Are windows to my breast, where-through the sun
> Delights to peep, to gaze therein on thee;"

>> 24: 9 - 12

This recalls Sidney's sonnet 42:

> O eyes, whose humble looks most glorious prove
> Only loved tyrants, just in cruelty,
> Do not, O do not from poor me remove;
> Keep still my zenith, ever shine on me.

>> 42: 5 - 8

Sidney's sonnet, the source for Marlowe's Motto would be later recalled in sonnet 73 and in Pericles.

By linking these sonnets to Sidney, Marlowe was expressing his deepest feelings. This was no ordinary infatuation, this was a love that, as even the most uncertain scholars have noted, carried throughout the remainder of the sonnets. The identity of this person may not yet be known, but it is certain that she was one of the most important people in his life.

Chapter Thirteen

Strange Brew

Once Pembroke's Men had been set up, Marlowe took the opportunity to circle back to Canterbury, with time to visit Thomas Walsingham's Scadbury estate where he was to spend enough of the following year to be sought there by the Privy Council's warrant in mid-spring of 1593, and to pay a call at Kirtling Hall, home of Lord North, once a personal friend of Philip Sidney's uncle, Robert Dudley, Earl of Leicester. While it is not certain that Marlowe visited Kirtling Hall, what is certain is that he read George North's unpublished manuscript, A Brief Discourse of Rebellion and Rebels, because it provided the only known source for the grass eating scene in the Jack Cade portion of The First Part of the Contention Between the Famous Houses of York and Lancaster.

In North, the poetic lament of Glendower when he is reduced "To feed on moss, for famine great / on mire and filthy mud"[381] immediately precedes the Jack Cade episode which begins on the same page. In The Contention, Scene 22, after he enters, "Jack Cade lies down, picking of hearbs and eating them" and when he is discovered and challenged by Eyden he retorts:

> "Brave thee and beard thee too, by the best bloud of the realme, look on me well, I have eate no meat this fiue daies, yet and I do not leaue thee and thy fiue men as dead as a door nail, I pray God I may neuer eat grasse no more."[382]

As Dennis McCarthy and June Schlueter explain:

> "All other accounts of Cade's death record simply that Iden killed Cade in a fight in the garden. No other text

even suggests that Cade was hungry, let alone emaciated and famished nearly to death and forced to eat grass."[383]

The North manuscript is described in the first chapter of Rebellion & Rebels (2017) as having been completed in 1576 by George North who signed, dedicated and presented it to Roger, 2nd Lord North, "while living in the nobleman's Cambridgeshire manor, Kirtling Hall."[384] It goes further to say that "it generated no known copies or contemporaneous allusions to it."

The manuscript was discovered by the authors in the 1927 Myers & Co. Illustrated Catalogue of Fine and Rare Books. A year after finding this notice, they were able to track it down as a 1933 acquisition of the British Library. So far as the authors could discover, the manuscript remained in private hands until being acquired by the Library.

Household accounts "indicate that both George North and Thomas were living at Kirtling Hall when George presented his manuscript to Roger."[385] Thomas, Lord North's brother, is separately famous as the English translator of Plutarch's Lives which was printed by Thomas Vautrollier in 1579.

One of the most interesting things about the North manuscript is that its influence on Marlowe does not end with the grass eating scene in The Contention. In fact, as McCarthy and Schleuter show, it touches many more plays, including Henry VI, Part 2, Henry VI, Part 3, Richard III, King Lear and Coriolanus. As the titles suggest, however, these are versions of earlier plays that were completed after the incident at Deptford. This would mean that Marlowe, who cannot have taken the sole manuscript with him was so affected by it that he worked from memory when referencing it. The manuscript itself serves as a veritable bridge between the two periods of his playwrighting career, before and after Deptford.

McCarthy and Schleuter offer no explanation for how the North manuscript might have made its way to the attention of Marlowe. One path might have been through the agency of

Gabriel Harvey who, in addition to being an influential university lecturer on rhetoric at Cambridge where he met Marlowe as a student, was also a mentor, roommate and possibly "bedfellow"[386] of Edmund Spenser and influenced his Faerie Queene (1590), which became one of the most significant poems in the English language. Spenser's poem had been in circulation well before its publication and Harvey added a commendatory poem to the first edition. It is not clear how Marlowe came across the manuscript, perhaps by way of Harvey, perhaps by way of Raleigh, who also added a poem to the first edition, but the playwright made the most of it, quoting from it in 1587 in The Second Part of Tamburlaine:

> "Whose tender blossoms tremble every one
> At every breath that thorough heaven is blown."
>
> IV, iii, 123-124
>
> "Whose tender locks do tremble every one
> At every little breath, that under heaven is blowne."
>
> Faerie Queene

In addition to the work of Spenser, Harvey also had a copy of George North's Description of Swedland, Gottland and Finland (1561) in his personal library. This book, which is now in the Folger Shakespeare Library, is annotated by Harvey and includes the following character assessment of its author:

> "a fine courtier, & brave soldier. A great man with the King of France, the King of Spain, the Emperor, and the Pope, who made him the general of his wars."[387]

So, perhaps it was Harvey who introduced Marlowe to the manuscript.

Or, perhaps it was Roger, 2nd Lord North who, hearing of the activity at Wilton House and always fond of the theatre, paid a call and after a rehearsal of The First Part of The Contention and enjoying Richard Burbage's portrayal of Jack Cade as a send up of Alleyn's Tamburlaine, suggested that Marlowe might want to stop by Kirtling Hall in Kent and review his cousin's manuscript. Roger was undoubtedly on familiar terms with Marlowe because, as McCarthy and Schlueter point out:

> "Alice Arden, the *femme fatale* of [Arden of Faversham] was the step-daughter of Edward, 1st Lord North and half-sister of Roger, 2nd Lord North. She lived for a while at Kirtling Hall, which is where she met her lover, Mosbie, a household servant of the Norths who conspired with her to murder her husband. We also know that Roger, 2nd Lord North, the powerful owner of Kirtling Hall, was a patron of the theatre and that in the 1570s and 1580s his manor was at times a venue for acting troupes, including Leicester's Men and the Queen's Men."[388]

Roger Lord North was a natural adversary to Lord Strange. He was present at the secret marriage of the Earl of Leicester to Lettice Knollys, Essex's mother and mother to Penelope Rich, Sidney's Stella. If Lord North was aware of Burghley's suspicions toward Lord Strange and his likely support of Lord Stanley's catholic plotting, he would have been at least cautiously skeptical as well. The manuscript of Rebellion and Rebels reads very much like Burghley's own Execution of Justice and by providing it to Marlowe, North would have been signaling his sympathy with the Protestant enterprise.

Indeed, it is hard to imagine that Lord North was not the most likely means for the North manuscript to find its way to Marlowe given that he would necessarily have to have been familiar with the playwright of a popular play about events in his own family that, if it hadn't been performed in his own house, would certainly have been brought to his attention wherever it was played. Jack Cade was another of Kent's more notorious characters and if Lord North did not put his cousin's manuscript in the playwright's hands for the express purpose of setting straight the record of Cade's treason, he never objected to its use as inspiration as "it generated no known copies or contemporaneous allusions to it."

Which gives two entirely separate viable paths. It should be worth taking a moment to consider how well all of this links up and re-enforces itself. How even something like the Discourse, unknown for four hundred fifty years, can suddenly be discovered and fit directly into the pattern, supporting what is already known about Marlowe, his interconnected life, how it was reflected in his work and artistic process, enhancing its meaning, instead of contradicting it.

To properly attribute passages from the plays with North's manuscript, McCarthy and Schlueter explain that they used WCopyfind plagiarism software, distributed by Lou Bloomfield of the University of Virginia, and the EEBO, Phase II database (containing 60,000 fully searchable early modern English texts) in the book's comparative research. This allowed them to map word usage to determine influence and frequency and "eliminate the possibility of happenstance by distinguishing the commonplace from the unique." They emphasized that this technique is particularly applicable where "the question of attribution does not apply."[389] Their conclusion was that unlike most other sources for the plays which typically are limited in influence to a single script:

> "a few special works have had a more sizable impact, affecting multiple plays both substantively and verbally. George North's A Brief Discourse of Rebellion and Rebels may now be placed into this more rarefied group of source texts."[390] p. 27

By continuing to employ A Discourse, Marlowe was declaring his allegiance to Burghley's original assignment to monitor and oppose Lord Strange who was still in action after Marlowe's departure from Deptford.

During this same period, Marlowe found the time to stop off in Canterbury. He might have been visiting family and may have been in the market for new clothes in anticipation of the Fall debut of his new company. While there, he got into a tangle with the tailor, William Corkine. It was an odd dustup and something of a domestic affair with both parties bringing assault charges against each other. Marlowe's father posted the bond for his son and Corkine's son later set Marlowe's Passionate Shepherd to music in his Second Booke of Ayers (1612).

This incident, which was quietly settled out of court, has frequently been cited as yet another demonstration of Marlowe's propensity for making "a physical attack"[391] while "accumulating a substantial criminal record."[392] This record included being attacked in the street by a thug, William Bradley, with a grudge against someone else, being accused by the liar Richard Baines, and arguing with a pair of overly earnest constables who may well have served as the models for Dogberry and Elbow. Meanwhile, Corkine senior went on to appear in court a total of fifteen times in the space of eight years. "He had one indictment for assault, was the Plaintiff in nine cases, the Defendant in five."[393] Corkine, as Cynthia Morgan observed, "was not shy when it came to using the court system" and "many other men in Canterbury had difficulty with this tailor."[394]

While the Corkine suit was a minor distraction, Marlowe received more unfortunate news when he returned to London, the worst of which was that Thomas Watson was reported dead. This, and the string of increasingly malign events leading up to the incident at Deptford, have been detailed in Chapter Three, Four and Five. It remains here merely to note that, despite the loss of one of his dearest friends, Pembroke's Men enjoyed such remarkable success that they almost immediately made an appearance at court for two days-worth of performances on December 26, 1592 and January 5, 1593. Lord Strange's Men played for three days, December 27, 31 and January 1. This sequence, while it would not allow a consecutive performance of the three Henry VI plays starting with Strange's Henry VI (unless two plays were played on the 5th), it would have enabled direct comparison between the two versions, with Alleyn in one and Burbage in the other two, which may have been the point.

Scholars have been debating the sequence of composition of the three parts of Henry VI for decades, with one camp asserting that because Henslowe tended to identify sequels, but not first parts, Part I "could not be a Part Two or Part Three but could easily be a Part One."[395] The opposite point of view, first expressed by E.K. Chambers and amplified by many others, including R. B. McKerrow is that the success of The Contention and The True Tragedy produced a demand for a prequel, the reasoning being in part that "if 2 Henry VI was originally written to continue the first part, it seems utterly incomprehensible that it should contain no allusion to the prowess of Talbot."[396] This assertion, of course, ignores the fact that "the first part of Pembroke's serial play advertised itself as a competitor with the Henry VI play".[397]

The reason nobody in what is known today as Henry VI Parts 2 & 3 refers to Talbot is because Ned Alleyn played Talbot and when Marlowe went to Lady Pembroke with Parts 2 & 3, Part 2 being the one Alleyn tried to co-opt, Marlowe didn't want to promote Alleyn's play, Part I. This was the play that Henslowe referred to as Harry 6th. This was also the play that Nashe wrote about so glowingly. It was so successful, Marlowe started the two plays, originally intended to compete directly with Harry 6th and which were combined with it in the First Folio as sequels. Marlowe's intended triumph would be to have these two independent Henry VI plays performed before the court making no reference to Henslowe's Harry. The highlight would certainly have been the Jack Cade sequence, performed by Richard Burbage as a parody of Alleyn.

From the perspective of most scholars, Marlowe appears to have been rattling around, writing plays, getting into trouble and going nowhere fast. From another perspective, however, he appears to have been learning a craft and forming a plan which he began to execute with Pembroke's Men. He had the patron he preferred in Lady Pembroke and an actor he trusted in Richard Burbage. He had the broad outline of a series of plays that the crown would support whole heartedly and he had the connections to make the most of his talent and stay out of the kind of trouble that the Alleyns seemed to attract.

There is no reason to suppose that Marlowe had no consideration or concept of a career path for himself even before he officially entered the professional theater. By joining up with the Queen's Men he showed that he had purpose and the intelligence to take advantage of his personal connections to the people who organized the company. When he made the jump to the London theater, it would have been foolish for him to have done so without seeking the approval of those who had secured his first placement, and who continued to show an interest in his chosen career so long as he remained available for the task of intelligencer. For this reason, Thomas Walsingham, still working for his "uncle" Francis, and Tom Watson, a fellow poet, Thomas' close friend and also a sometime agent, became steady company. Marlowe's success with Tamburlaine probably surprised them, as it surprised everyone. Regardless of whether or not they recognized the revolutionary nature of the piece, no one could have anticipated that the previously little known Edward Alleyn would suddenly explode into prominence in the role.

Despite the initial success, tension and uncertainty would remain while Marlowe worked to prove that he was no flash in the pan. As a sequel, Part II of Tamburlaine satisfied the appetite, but it was challenged by the similar success of The Spanish Tragedy, also in Alleyn's hands and it wasn't until several plays later, following Faust, Edward III, and Arden of Faversham, that with The Jew of Malta the duo of Marlowe and Alleyn ignited the stage to the same degree.

The fracas with Watson and William Bradley and Marlowe's subsequent imprisonment, not to mention the Alleyn's public feud with the Burbages, had to have colored his relations with Ned Alleyn. Greene could not have been the only one who found him overbearing and Marlowe, after four or five years of working closely with him, may well have felt that he needed to prove to himself that he could succeed without him.

While his assignment in Flushing may have seemed an inconvenience at the time, one he could hardly avoid when called to duty by Lord Burghley to investigate the possibility of sedition in the low countries, his encounter with Sir Robert Sidney, brother to Philip, could not help but remind him of a connection he had left unattended for too long. The fact that Pembroke's Men kick started barely six months after Marlowe's return to London could not have been an accident. Sponsored in honor of William Herbert, son of Lady Pembroke and Philip's sister, Mary, it featured Marlowe as its chief playwright and leader from the start.

It is interesting to note that while commentators like Kuriyama, Nicholl and Riggs magnify Baines' self-serving allegations, the set to with the constables and the suit over the suit, all in an effort to show how disreputable Marlowe had become, as if his success had gone to his head, they simultaneously ignore the fact that Marlowe was swimming in deep water on assignment. He was working for the crown to uncover plots against the life of the monarch. This is not work he was trained to do, he had to learn it on the fly. No one could teach him, because no one had done it that way before. In this, he was no loose cannon, he was part of a front line protecting a vision of a Protestant England that was constantly under threat. The poems and plays he was writing were entirely consistent with the politics of his government and he supported it in word and deed.

In order to free himself to pursue these goals he struck a fairly one sided deal with Ned Alleyn who bought both <u>The Jew of Malta</u> and <u>The Massacre at Paris</u> from him. Marlowe may not have been happy about the resulting productions of either. Both plays exhibit the strong possibility of rewriting and editing that do not appear to have been by Marlowe. The struggle over ownership, prefigured in Greene's <u>Orlando</u>, may have been an issue that added further friction to the already strained relationship. Alleyn, who never veered from his commercial interests, did not fit a plan which emphasized political advocacy. Marlowe may have let Massacre go in order to get away from Alleyn, or it may have been just another straw. It does not really seem like the kind of play that would appeal to Alleyn and although it opened to packed houses, it was not often revived while The Jew, with its broad leading character and carnival of excesses, made Alleyn more popular than ever.

There was clearly some argument over which company had the rights to the Henriad. This is reflected in the very titles of the Pembroke's Men's versions, ie: The True Tragedy and The First Part of the Contention. This dispute appears to have carried over to Titus Andronicus which was played by all three companies, Strange, Pembroke and the Admiral's Men in the winter of 1592/93.

It was clearly at this point that Marlowe began to put in place the fullness of his plan for a cycle of English History plays that would culminate in the confirmation of Elizabeth's reign. This project would suit the purposes of the regime quite well and Pembroke's Men were the ideal company to promote it. The concept was so good, that even after his disappearance, the crown made certain to continue it to fruition. Three of the plays in the Henry cycle and Richard III were onstage and four or five others were in some form of draft by the time Marlowe spent the afternoon at Ms. Bull's house on Deptford strand. In addition, Romeo and Juliet, The Taming of A Shrew, and A Midsummer Night's Dream speak to the range and ambition that he alone could bring to the new enterprise.

By the end of 1592, despite all the difficulties and the loss of close friends and mentors, Marlowe was riding a wave of success and the future could not have looked more promising. Unfortunately, despite all his training and theatrical skill as a playwright and stage magician, to say nothing of his familiarity with the shifts of the political winds and the hidden motives of his adversaries, he could not possibly have foreseen the way that the following year would turn all of his accomplishments inside out. But, as Chapters Four and Five have explained, that is exactly what happened.

Just as suddenly as it burst into the lead of the London stage in late 1592, by mid 1593 Pembroke's Men had disbanded. The obvious reason for this collapse was the sudden, inexplicable disappearance of Christopher Marlowe. The circumstances of this were so unusual and so upsetting that no one even wanted to discuss it openly. If anyone had asked Thomas Kyd what he knew about it, his answer, recounting his torture at the hands of the Star Chamber's inquisitors, would have yielded little more than further unease. Actors play heroes, playwrights write about them, producers profit from them; very few of those people actually live lives exposed to mortal danger or high risk in the trenches of government. Not surprisingly, there is little from that period that remarks on the fate of one of the most ambitious theatrical projects of the era.

What survives is one notable sentence in a letter dated September 28, 1593, from Phillip Henslowe to his son-in-law Edward Alleyn then on tour with Lord Strange's Men. Delivering primarily household news, discussing incidental business matters and reporting on the status of the ongoing but slackening plague, Henslowe finally responds to a question that Alleyn appears to have asked in a previous letter, no longer extant:

> "& as for my lorde a penbrokes wch you desier to knowe wheare they be they ar all at home and hauffe ben t{his} v or sixe weakes for they cane not saue ther carges w{th} trauell as I heare & weare fayne to pane the{r} parell . . ."398

It is tempting to try to imagine what the rumor mill in the tight theatrical community must have been like in the summer of 1593. The expectation even after the theaters had been closed by the plague in January must have been that Pembroke's would reassemble at Wilton House in the early Summer and rehearse a batch of new plays delivered by the endlessly prolific pen of Christopher Marlowe. But, by mid-September there was no word of any new production and the once commanding company was silent. For Ned Alleyn to be in the dark about all this, for him to write to his father-in-law about it, confessing ignorance of the whereabouts of his chief competition and that all the actors around him and those they met on tour must also have heard nothing must have been more than a little unusual. They were in the business of gathering and spreading the news and for there to be none at all even now seems odd.

But this is one letter and the standard history of the incident in Deptford suggests that it might already have been old news for some in September, as unlikely as that seems today. What is certain is that the theaters remained closed by plague until the Spring of 1594 when two new companies were organized and the London theater world showed signs of reviving. But, not before the mysterious death of Lord Strange, Fernando Stanley, the man Marlowe had been assigned to attend and whose Catholic and possibly treasonous relations he was investigating in Flushing in early 1592.

By the end of 1593, Fernando Stanley had come under increased suspicion. On September 27, about the same time that Henslowe was composing his reply to his son-in-law Alleyn, Stanley, who had become the new Earl of Derby upon his father's death two days before, received a letter personally delivered by Richard Hesketh who "had been sent as an emissary from Catholics abroad to sound out Stanley on his willingness to take up the claim to the English throne that descended to him from his mother"399 Margaret Stanley, Countess of Derby, whose maternal grandmother was Mary Tudor, the third daughter of Henry VII. The former Lord Strange then accompanied Hesketh to London where they conferred with the Countess who had been under house arrest since 1579 when she was accused of using sorcery, attempting by means of a horoscope drawn up by her physician (who was later hanged) to predict the date of Queen Elizabeth's death. In the end, Stanley turned Hesketh over to the authorities and Hesketh was interrogated and hanged.

It speaks to the tenor of the times that the new Earl's delay in turning over Hesketh was viewed with at least as much suspicion as if he too had been casting horoscopes. With the plague continuing to limit movement through 1593, there seemed to be little he could do to restore his reputation. Then, in mid-April, after a public quarrel with Essex over his protection of a former Stanley retainer who Fernando felt was threatening him, the Earl of Derby fell suddenly ill. William Camden, who was encouraged to write a history of Elizabeth's reign by Lord Burghley's son, Robert Cecil, describes what happened next in a passage that was not published until 1630, when all the participants, including Camden himself, were safely dead:

> Ferdinand Stanley Earle of Darby . . . expired in the flowre of his youth, not without suspition of poyson, being tormented with cruell paynes by frequent vomitings of a darke colour like rusty yron. There was found in his chamber an Image of waxe, the belly pierced thorow with haires of the same colour that his were, put there, (as the wiser sort have judged, to remove the suspition of poyson). The matter vomited up stayned the silver Basons in such sort, that by no art they could possibly be brought againe to their former brightnesse... No small suspicion lighted upon the Gentleman of his horse, who; as soone as the Earle tooke his bed, tooke his best horse, and fled".[400]

There were accusations on both sides, that the Catholics poisoned him for refusing the crown and exposing the plot and that the crown poisoned him for dabbling with Catholics. There were even allegations of witchcraft and to this day the mystery is unsettled. It is speculated, however, that tainted mushrooms were involved.

In a world in which everything was political, when marriages, churches, playhouses and patronage confirmed or undermined alliances, when newly minted Earls could be poisoned in their palace beds and the culprits remain forever unknown, when death most of all was subject to partisan exploitation, is it at all unlikely that the fate of Christopher Marlowe could be any less strange?

Chapter Fourteen

Enter Shaxpere[401]

Imprinted by Richard Field, and are to be sold at
the signe of the white Greyhound in
St. Paul's Church-yard.
1593.

At some point between May 31st and Tuesday, June 12th when the first copy is known to have been sold to Richard Stonley (a Burghley employee and one of the four Tellers of the Exchequer of Receipt, whose usual taste, as recorded in his diary, was for sermons and histories), William Shaxpere (aka Shakspere[402] aka Shaxspere[403]) agreed to have his name, somewhat buffed up, attached to a page dedicating Venus and Adonis to the Earl of Southampton. The reasons why he did this are still not entirely clear. Some will forever maintain that he did this because he wrote it, but then they should also explain how a man who never went to any school high or low that kept any records of anyone ever going to that school ever managed to learn enough about Ovid to decide to write a poem about a pair of minor characters that occupied 200 lines in one chapter of an Ovidian poem that included 250 characters in 15 chapters and almost 12,000 lines in Latin. This man would necessarily be unknown to any other poet of the period who attended either of the two universities or any other school of learning high or low that kept records of any kind because, despite the fact that every other poet worth his salt who typically or occasionally or almost never made a habit of commenting about his contemporaries or rivals or even passing strangers, in particular poets like Robert Greene, Thomas Nashe, Gabriel Harvey, Thomas Watson and Thomas Kyd and all their friends, never had anything to say about him when he was alive. This man would also have to be familiar enough with the seventeen unpublished Southampton Sonnets and Marlowe's unpublished Hero and Leander in order to have freely, almost purposefully, borrowed from them for Venus and Adonis. And he would have to have some notion that dedicating such a poem, which was admired as much for its ribald sexuality as for its poetic ingenuity, to the Earl of Southampton, who never admitted to knowing him before or after, would not get him into trouble especially if, instead of presenting it to him privately, he dared to publish it for public sale.

The publisher, Richard Field, was also from Stratford and may have been familiar with Willim[404] who was five years his junior. Field was also familiar with Lord Burghley because he had been apprentice to and had married the widow of Thomas Vautrollier, a Huguenot printer frequently employed by Burghley. Shakspere may not have known anything about how much time and effort Burghley had already put into encouraging a marriage between his grand-daughter and the Earl, but Field would know enough not to print anything that might displease Burghley. Despite being one of the most thoroughly researched humans in the last 400 years, there is no mention of William, Willim or Will in any correspondence in any connection with or in any vicinity of any of these people and no way to know whether or not he had any idea that Lord Burghley might or might not approve of his intrusion into his private plans for Southampton's future.

Much has been made of the supposed relationship between Shaxspere and Field. Catherine Duncan-Jones confidently asserts, on the basis of absolutely no evidence whatsoever, that Willim "regularly used Field's printing house in Blackfriars, near Ludgate, as a working library, and even did his writing there."[405] Had he done anything of the kind in 1593, he would have found stacks of text books on French, Italian and Spanish, a dozen or more titles arguing against the Pope and Catholicism in general, various speeches and sermons and a translation of Orlando Furioso. He would not have found anything written by Ovid. He might have found a copy of Thomas North's translation of Plutarch, but only if Field, who did not reprint Vautrollier's 1579 version until 1595, allowed him to rummage through his old stock. According to his innumerable hagiographers, Shakspere got his formidable education by means of Field's library, although why Field would entertain the idea of having his country "cousin" thumbing through stock he hoped to sell is a question left unanswered. Had he applied himself more assiduously than his history to that point would suggest, Shaxspere could have come away from Field's shop with a good grasp of continental languages and anti-Catholic propaganda, but very little in the way of the classics or English history.

Clearly, Burghley had good reasons for wanting to put Venus and Adonis into print and have it dedicated to Southampton. What is not clear is why the poem was put up for sale to the public making it available for Richard Stonley to purchase. Most poems dedicated to worthy persons and potential patrons did not end up being printed for sale. They were presented as gifts. This was true of Edmund Spenser's Fairie Queene, which was published and presented to Queen Elizabeth at the poet's expense. This was true of The Countess of Pembroke's Arcadia, dedicated to her brother, Philip Sidney, which was originally published privately at the Countess' expense and distributed among friends. This was also true of Tom Watson's Hekatompathia, which was dedicated to the Earl of Oxford at the expense of "Watson's Friends". John Clapham's Narcissus, the first poem dedicated to Southampton, was printed by Thomas Scarlett and was not put up for sale. George Chapman's The Shadow of the Night (1594) which was to later figure so prominently in the "rival poet" sonnets, was dedicated to Mathew Roydon, published by William Ponsonby and printed by none other than Richard Field very soon after Venus and Adonis, but was not marked for sale. Compared to these texts, Venus and Adonis appears to be most unusual for seeking patronage even while marketing itself to the general public. It almost makes Southampton appear ungenerous. Which may have been the point.

If anything, it's a little embarrassing to have someone publicly panhandling a peer for his patronage. That is not how these things are done. When this is added to Burghley's displeasure over Southampton's continued refusal to marry his grand-daughter it begins to appear deliberate. Burghley was a seasoned pamphleteer in his own right, long since having faced down the Catholic agitators in England and overseas with his Execution of Justice and he "saw propagandist advantage in a controlled output of French news at a time when English troops were supporting the Huguenot cause." He "encouraged" Vautrollier to produce books in French and about French affairs and "Field inherited this role enthusiastically."[406] If Burghley wanted to avoid associating Venus and Adonis with an anti-Catholic propagandist publisher, he easily could have done so. Instead, it was published with a dedication to a known Catholic sympathizer and put on sale to the public by a publisher known to have connections with Burghley himself.

When its first printing promptly sold out, he could have suppressed it. Instead, he encouraged his followers to purchase it and allowed Field to print as many subsequent copies as he could sell.

This begs the question of whether or not the poem had ever been intended for sale in the first place. Neither of Burghley's earlier commissions had been made public, so why was this commission different? The answer may have much to do with the circumstances of its author's sudden departure from London.

The sole surviving copy of the first printing of Venus and Adonis is in the British Museum's Bodelian collection. It has been rebound and thus is not in original condition. The page count of the original printing is uncertain, however the body of the poem itself is intact and each page is numbered, 3 through 52, 48 pages in all, with four neat stanzas on each page except for the first, page 3, which has three. The pages of this text include printer's marks B through G, making six leaves printed in quarto with eight pages per leaf, four to a face for a total again of 48. Printed this way, with six leaves folded twice, once horizontally and once vertically, and stacked one on top of the other to be bound together along the left edge, the body of poem makes a simple insert for a separately printed cover which could fold around and wrap the poem in a single leaf like a slipcase. This cover could also be quarto and could include the title page, a blank reverse, the dedication page, a blank reverse and four blank pages after the body of the poem. The rebound original does not, however, include any blank pages at the end of the book. Finally, the surviving first four pages are not numbered and do not include any printers mark, such as "A", to indicate its placement in the final assembly. This alone suggests that the Title page was printed after the body because it would not then be possible to confuse or mingle it with the previously assembled poem.

It is also possible that a separate title page, complete with the seven other pages completing the folded leaf and bearing a printer's mark "A" was discarded and replaced. This would only be necessary, of course, if Marlowe's name had been originally featured on the title page or in its dedication, if indeed there was one.

Printed and bound alone, the poem could have been presented as a gift outright but it's obvious similarities to other work of Marlowe's, in particular to the sonnets already in Southampton's possession, would have made that impossible. It was also impossible to let such a thing go to waste; Burghley still wanted to get Southampton to marry his niece. With Marlowe suddenly in exile as the result of Essex's meddling, a new name would be needed and quickly.

The fact that no one knew Willim Shaxpere in May, 1593 was actually very useful if the purpose was to use his name to paper over the disappearance of the actual author of <u>Venus and Adonis</u> who had been forced to skip town at that very moment. No one who was familiar to any of the other poets jostling for patronage in that plague infested period could be used for that purpose, as much as they might want to be, because all of their friends and readers would know immediately whether or not they were capable of such a poem.

The name could belong to anyone as long as it was otherwise unknown and its owner could be trusted. For that, Richard Field would have to vouch and must have. This was therefore done on the spur of the moment; there wasn't time to audition anyone for the role and broadcasting the need in that way would have been dangerous for all involved. The plan would be that the name would be used once and never called upon again. The idea that this might become repeated, or worse, permanent would not have occurred to anyone; it would have seemed improbable and unnecessary. Most of all, Shaxpere, who was quickly learning to be a businessman, would want to be assured that the use of his name in this fashion would not spoil future opportunities, whatever they might be.

Printing the poem for the public and putting it up for sale would be another innovation. Where the Sonnets had been private, Burghley, in the aftermath of the debacle at Deptford, must have felt that it was time to use the public to add to the pressure on Southampton because, for one thing, time was running out. Southampton would be twenty-one in little more than a year and beyond Burghley's authority. Perhaps he thought that celebrating him in public with a brilliant poem dedicated to his "metamorphosis" would serve better as both flattery and a warning that private appeals had not.

Finally, including Marlowe's translation of an excerpt from Ovid's 15th Amore on the title page would add to the intrigue by signaling the absent author, quoting an antique exiled poet to draw attention to a modern match in the making, increasing interest and comment while further leveraging the reluctant suitor, Southampton.

There would be the inevitable rumors. Essex could be counted upon for that. Others would dissect the poem and wonder at its skill from such an unknown, but with Marlowe's other work still unpublished, there would be less with which to compare it. And, if Marlowe's disappearance added something to the mystery, that would not be an entirely bad thing. Southampton would pay attention. That the poetry rises above all of that guaranteed that much more notoriety.

This is all speculation, of course, but informed speculation given that Shakspere appears to literally have come from nowhere.

Even as copies of Venus and Adonis were flying off of John Harrison's bookstall, a separate sequence of poems was taking shape. By the time Richard Stonley bought his copy, Christopher Marlowe had been on the Continent for more than a week, stuck in Flushing or someplace like it, awaiting further instructions. During this time he maintained a correspondence with his patron, Thomas Walsingham, that had begun before his departure from Deptford and was to last for at least seventeen years. The initial stage of the journey was described in a sequence of twelve sonnets, starting with the 25th and ending with the 36th, which depicted his growing awareness of the seriousness of his exiled state and tentative acceptance after overcoming a profound shock. It is at this point that Christopher Marlowe takes over from all of his biographers; there is no other source.

Sonnet 25 is the first in the entire collection to suggest that his prospects are threatened:

> "Let those who are in favor with their stars
> Of public honor and proud titles boast,
> Whilst I, whom fortune of such triumph bars,
> Unlooked for joy in that I honour most."

Sonnet 25, 1-4

The poem sets the tone for most of what follows, braving adversity by asserting love for the one person who knows his true value. Sonnet 26 furthers the tale by making it clear that he is separated from his patron by fate and his willingness to endure it:

> "To thee I send this written ambassage,
> To witness duty, not to show my wit -"

> "Till whatsoever star that guides my moving
> Points on me graciously with fair aspect,
> And puts apparel on my tattered loving
> To show me worthy of thy sweet respect."

    Sonnet 26, 3-4, 9-12

The journey, however, is difficult and his isolation takes an increasing toll, with his solitary solace thoughts of his ever more distant love:

> "Weary with toil, I haste me to my bed,
> The dear repose for limbs with travel tired;
> But then begins a journey in my head
> To work my mind when body's work's expired;
> For then my thoughts, from where I abide,
> Intend a zealous pilgramage to thee,"

    Sonnet 27, 1 - 6

Even as he expresses confidence in his protector, the more doubt grows that he can soon return to the life and favor he once knew:

> "How can I then return in happy plight
> That am debarred the benefit of rest,
> When day's oppression is not eased by night,
> But day by nigh and night by day oppressed,
> And each, though enemies to either's reign,
> Do in consent shake hands to torture me,
> The one by toil, the other to complain
> How far I toil, still farther off from thee?"

    Sonnet 28, 1 - 8

Then, with Sonnet 29, he comes face to face with despair, his only support being his faith in Walsingham:

"When in disgrace with Fortune and men's eyes,
I all alone beweep my outcast state,
And trouble deaf heaven with my bootless cries,
And look upon myself and curse my fate,
Wishing me like to one more rich in hope,
Featured like him, like him with friends possessed,
Desiring this man's art, and that man's scope,
With what I most enjoy contented least;
Yet, in these thoughts myself almost despising,
Haply I think on thee, and then my state,
Like to the lark at break of day arising
From sullen earth, sings hymns at heaven's gate;
    For thy sweet loved remembered such wealth brings
    That then I scorn to change my state with kings."

Sonnet 29, 1 - 14

The phrase "sullen earth" recalls line five of Franklin's sixteen line sonnet in Arden of Faversham: "Then fix his sad eyes on the sullen earth", a line that would be soon be repeated as "Why are thine eyes fixed to the sullen earth?" in Henry VI, Part II, the as yet unfinished re-write of The First Part of the Contention Betwixt the Two Famous Houses of York and Lancaster, linking all three as part of a continuing meditation on the crude source of jealousy. In Arden, Franklin reflects on Arden's distrust of his wife, not realizing that Arden has good reasons for it. Reusing that phrase immediately recalls the premise that jealousy is more often without substance and recasts its ironic twist in the new poem, suggesting the underlying uncertainty that suffuses the entire sequence. In the rewritten Contention the line would be expressed by Dame Eleanor, wife to Glouscester, the leading plotter against Henry VI, echoing again the dishonor inherent in jealous thoughts.

    Sonnet 30 carries forward the assertion of solace in faithful friendship, but it seems uncertain and almost forced:

> "When to the sessions of sweet silent thought
> I summon up remembrance of things past,
> I sigh the lack of many a thing I sought,
> And with old woes new wail my dear time's waste;
>
> > "But if the while I think on thee, dear friend,
> > All losses are restored and sorrows end."
>
> Sonnet 30, 1 - 4, 13 - 14

It comes as no surprise to find doubt and even morbid notions crowding into the text:

> "Thy bosom is endearèd with all hearts
> Which I by lacking have supposèd dead;
> And there reigns love and all love's loving parts,
> And those friends which I thought burièd.
>
> > "Their images I loved I view in thee,
> > And thou, all they, hast all the all of me."
>
> Sonnet 31, 1 - 4, 13 - 14

High on that shared list of deceased friends would be Tom Watson. Sir Francis would be in his mind as well and most of all, perhaps, would be Philip Sidney who was a friend and inspiration to all of them. Marlowe would not be wrong in thinking that but for their demise his fate would have been very different. By recalling them in this way, he would have to hope that Thomas Walsingham would feel an equal need to preserve what remained.

Thoughts of other deaths inevitably conjured the possibility of his own which he had so narrowly escaped:

> "If thou survive my well-contented day,
> When that churl Death my bones with dust shall cover,
> And shalt by fortune once more resurvey

> These poor rude lines of thy deceasèd lover,"
>
> "O, then vouchsafe me but this loving thought:
> 'Had my friend's Muse grown with his growing age,
> A dearer birth than this his love had brought
> To march in ranks of better equipage;
> > But since he died, and poets better prove,
> > Theirs for their style I'll read, his for his love.'"
>
> Sonnet 32, 1 - 4, 9 - 14

When he wrote this, Marlowe does not seem to have known that another name had already been attached to one of his poems and if Walsingham knew, he hadn't told him. The irony of this, and of what was to come amid his repeated assertions that his poetry would be his legacy, would not become apparent for months, if not years. Instead, Marlowe focused on how quickly fortunes could change and how he feared that might affect his guardian's commitment:

> "Even so my sun one early morn did shine
> With all triumphant splendor on my brow;
> But out, alack, he was but one hour mine,
> The region cloud hath masked him from me now."
>
> Sonnet 33, 8 - 12

With Sonnet 34 Marlowe begins to question whether or not he has been deceived in his trust. It is as if he has discovered that what he believed would be a brief interruption was being reconsidered, that he would not be returning any time soon and he thus wants assurance that he will not be abandoned:

> "Why didst thou promise such a beauteous day
> And make me travel forth without my cloak,
> To let base clouds o'ertake me in my way,
> Hiding thy brav'ry in their rotten smoke?"

> "Nor can thy shame give physic to my grief;
> Though thou repent, yet still I have the loss.
> Th'offender's sorrow lends but weak relief
> To him that bears the strong offence's cross."

    Sonnet 34, 1 - 4, 8 - 12

There seems to have been some communication following this sonnet, some assurance which calmed Marlowe's emotions. Knowing better than to remain at odds with the one friend he has left, he promptly forgives Walsingham in Sonnet 35:

> "No more be grieved at that which thou hast done:
> Roses have thorns, and silver fountains mud,
>
> "Thy adverse party is thy advocate -
> And 'gainst myself a lawful plea commence.
>
>> "That I an accessory needs must be
>> To that sweet thief which sourly robs from me."

    Sonnet 35, 1 - 2, 10 - 11, 13 - 14

Finally, after shock, anger, denial, and accusation comes acceptance:

> "Let me confess that we two must be twain,
> Although our undivided loves are one.
> So shall those blots that do with me remain
> Without thy help by me be borne alone.
>
> "I may not evermore acknowledge thee,
> Lest my bewailèd guilt should do thee shame;
> Nor thou with public kindness honor me,
> Unless thou take that honor from my name.
>   But do so; I love thee in such sort

As, thou being mine, mine is thy good report."

Sonnet 36, 1 -4, 9 - 14

The terms of the bargain are very hard. Marlowe has no assurance that he can return any time soon, if at all. By that time the Queen's coroner had declared him officially dead, a body had been displayed and buried and Shakespeare's name had been substituted for his on a poem that had London buzzing. Sonnet 36 makes it clear that Marlowe understood there was real danger in continuing to agitate for restoration. His escape from Deptford was a respite, not redemption. All this and more he would have to accept and, realizing this, he promised to make his peace with it.

At this point it seems fair to step back and observe something important about the first 36 sonnets: they are in a sequence that corresponds with the events of Marlowe's life. These are not the only sonnets he wrote during this period; there are others he wrote for <u>Arden of Faversham</u> and <u>Romeo and Juliet</u>, but these are the first 36 included in the published collection and they are not individual musings or poetic experiments, they tell a story. The first seventeen relate directly to his involvement in Burghley's attempt to arrange the marriage of the young Earl of Southampton to his granddaughter. The eighteenth, nineteenth and twentieth were gifts to the young William Herbert, scion of Pembroke and nephew of Marlowe's hero, Philip Sidney. These three poems followed the first seventeen in sequence as sonnets 25 to 36 followed them.

Not yet included in this accounting are sonnets 21 to 24, all four of which are addressed to a person with whom the author was deeply in love. The difficulty with these poems is that it is not entirely clear to whom they are written. In the context of a life or in the context of a specific period in that life poems that lack sufficient specificity remain puzzling. Various individuals have been proposed, including William Herbert, who was twelve at the time and was already addressed in sonnets 18, 19 and 20, but to whom the following four would seem to be far too passionate and too intimate to be acceptable for all that in sonnet 22 the author claims to be "elder than thou". Southampton has been suggested, but in the absence of any real relationship between Marlowe and the young Earl this seems very unlikely. Although he was five years older than Marlowe, Thomas Walsingham must be included; Marlowe spent a lot of time at Scadbury in late 1592 and early 1593 and Thomas is definitely the person being addressed in sonnets 25 to 36, 72 and 73 and 78 through 96. A case could also be made for Tom Watson because Marlowe worked so closely with him on so many plays in that short period. There is also the equally likely possibility that they were written to someone else altogether, someone not yet suspected. For now, however, this is one part of the story remains uncertain because it was so private. It is enough to say that these four sonnets fall neatly into the space between Marlowe's greatest success and his sudden disgrace, which is often the case with love stories.

By the time he finished Sonnet 36, Marlowe appears to have taken stock of his position. If the opening lines of Sonnet 50 are any guide:

> "How heavy do I journey on the way,
> When what I seek, my weary travel's end,
> Doth teach that ease and that repose to say
> 'Thus far the miles are measured from thy friend.'"

then he was far from his intended destination. While he naturally hoped for an end to his exile and a return to London, he understood that no one, certainly not Walsingham, could tell him when that time might arrive. The sonnet continues, describing in literal terms his miserable journey:

> "The beast that bears me, tired with my woe,
> Plods dully on, to bear that weight in me,
> As if by some instinct the wretch did know
> His rider loved not speed being made from thee.

The bloody spur cannot provoke him on
That sometimes anger thrusts into his hide,
Which heavily he answers with a groan
More sharp to me than spurring to his side;
    For that same groan doth put this in my mind:
    My grief lies onward and my joy behind."

Sonnet 50 1 - 14.

Chapter Fifteen

The Unfortunate Traveler

"Right Honorable,

"I know not how I shall offend in dedicating my unpolished lines to your Lordship, nor how the world will censure me for choosing so strong a prop to support so weak a burden; only if your Honor seem but pleased, I account myself highly praised and vow to take advantage of all idle hours till I have honored you with some graver labor. But if the first heir of my invention prove deformed, I shall be sorry it had so noble a godfather and never after ear so barren a land, for fear it yield me still so bad a harvest. I leave it to your honorable survey, and your Honor to your heart's content, which I wish may always answer your own wish and the world's hopeful expectation.

    "Your Honor's in all duty,
    "William Shakespeare"

Anyone even vaguely aware of Marlowe's difficulties in the Spring of 1593, as the search for the author of the Dutch Church Libel and the subsequent arrest of Thomas Kyd all but assured that anyone owning a pen would have been, would have been equally suspicious of this "dedication". Putting aside the teasing reference to "graver matters", a rival poet could not help but observe that the "first heir" of the author's invention could not be the poem itself, being itself that very invention, nor the person to whom it was dedicated, Southampton, who was supposedly its "noble godfather," but indeed was the possibly "deformed" person represented by the name affixed to it. Meaning that someone other than that person was responsible for the thing bequeathed.

This, coupled with the Ovidian extract on the title page, almost begged the question of its authenticity. The extract, from <u>Amores</u> Book I Epistle XV reads:

> *"Vilia miretur vulgus: mihi flavus Apollo*
> *Pocula Castalia plena ministret aqua"*

which Marlowe had previously translated as:

> Let base-conceited wits admire vild things;
> Fair Phœbus lead me to the Muses' springs.[407]

The extract continues in Marlowe's translation:

> About my head be quivering myrtle wound,
> And in sad lovers' heads let me be found.
> The living, not the dead, can envy bite,
> For after death all men receive their right.

There is plenty in this for those interested in Marlowe's work to be suspicious of the sudden appearance, under what can only be called Marlowe's stamp, of another, previously unknown writer claiming to be the author of a poem immediately recognizable as something precious few poets other than Marlowe could have written. Southampton may or may not have been a literary critic, but he had many friends who were and if he showed any of them his collection of sonnets and compared them with his new gift the similarities between them would have been all too obvious.

Two people who took particular notice were the young and fiery Thomas Nashe, a "university wit" and aggressive satirist, and the plodding Gabriel Harvey, a Cambridge pedant and self-appointed literary critic, a pair well known to Marlowe from his Corpus Christi days. Already engaged in a pamphlet war over the Marprelate controversy, their published squabbles had become increasingly vitriolic after the recent death in September, 1592, of Nashe's mentor, Robert Greene.

The highly publicized and notorious fracas known today as the Martin Marprelate controversy, which eventually became the backdrop for Marlowe's predicament, started up in 1588 when a small band of Puritan protesters, led by John Penry who owned the original printing press, published a pamphlet titled An Epistle which in witty and irreverent fashion accused the Anglican clergy of corruption. The Church responded with An Admonition to the People of England by Thomas Cooper, Bishop of Winchester, which "was too long and too dull to appeal to the same class of readers as the Marprelate pamphlet"[408]. The Martinist response, Hay Any Worke For The Cooper, was such a popular hit that Dr. Richard Bancroft convinced Archbishop Whitgift to allow him to enlist professional writers to respond in more abusive kind. This group included John Lyly, Robert Greene and Thomas Nashe who attacked Martin Marprelate with "an armory of quips and quiddities, but with a fatal tendency to flavour their literary raillery with ribald allusions and positive grossness."[409]

Somehow dragged or perhaps leaping into this affray, "astrologer, theologian and controversialist"[410] Richard Harvey, younger brother of Gabriel, wrote or co-wrote or was believed to have contributed to Plaine Percivall the Peace-Maker of England (1590) which took aim at both sides urging them to "shake hands and be friendes" while casting broad aspersions in both directions. The back and forth continued and not long after Robert Greene published A Quip to an Upstart Courtier (1592) in which he heaped derision on Gabriel Harvey's peculiar advocacy of English hexameter verse and lambasted the Harveys one by one before concluding that while Harvey's rope-maker father was decent enough, "honest parents may have bad children". Sales of this pamphlet were among Greene's best, which made things that much worse for Gabriel Harvey. Soon after, Greene died, possibly of the plague, and in memoriam Chettle published the previously dissected Groats-Worth.

Ever thin skinned and holding firmly to a grudge, Harvey promptly trampled all over Greene's grave with <u>Foure letters, and certaine sonnets especially touching Robert Greene, and other parties, by him abused</u> (1592). Puritanically moralistic, Harvey attributed Greene's death to dissipation and drink. Sonnet 18 gives a short sample of the general tone:

> SONNET XVIII.
> Iohn Harueys Welcome to Robert Greene.
> Come fellow Greene, come to thy gaping graue:
> Bidd Vanity, and Foolery farewell:
> Thou ouer-long hast plaid the madbrain'd knaue:
> And ouer-lowd hast rung the bawdy bell.
> Vermine to Vermine must repair at last:
> No fitter house for busy folke to dwell:
> Thy Conny-catching Pageants are past:
> Some other must those arrant Stories tell.
> These hungry wormes thinke long for their repast:
> Come on: I pardon thy offence to me:
> It was thy liuing: be not so aghast:
> A Foole, and Phisition may agree.
> And for my Brothers, neuer vex thy selfe:
> They are not to disease a buried Elfe.

In furious defense of Greene, Nashe then published <u>The Apology of Pierce Penilesse, or Strange News of the intercepting certain letters and a convoy of verses as they were going to victual the Low Counties</u> (1593) in which he blasted Harvey, dissecting his earlier pamphlets and roundly abusing his character.

All of this personal and ultimately insignificant behavior was being played out as a somewhat entertaining sideshow to the real and very intense manhunt for the anonymous authors of the Marprelate pamphlets. Archbishop Whitgift in particular had become incensed at the repeated attacks on his clergy and general authority and had long since turned for satisfaction from pamphlets to police. By early 1593, Penry, John

Greenwood, Henry Barrow and dozens of other suspects had been rounded up and were being interrogated at Fleet. Greenwood and Barrow were convicted and hung in March while Penry was kept waiting until May 30, 1593 for his fatal appointment, all of which preceded and somehow dovetailed with Marlowe's own disappearance from Deptford the following night.

As a participant, however remote, and follower in and of these events, Gabriel Harvey was openly suspicious of Marlowe's disappearance. Evidence for this is provided by the publication of his <u>A Nevv Letter of Notable Contents With a Straunge Sonet, Intituled Gorgon, or The Wonderfull Yeare</u>. The letter, twenty-six pages dated September 16, 1593, and addressed to the printer, John Wolfe, expresses Harvey's pride in the English language and praises his two friends and poetic heroes, Philip Sidney and Edmund Spenser, thereby polishing his own bona fides while continuing in separate censorious smears his public feud with Thomas Nashe. The letter is followed by a poem that scholars of Elizabethan literature have found notoriously obscure:

>   Gorgon, *or the wonderfull yea*re
> St Fame *dispos'd to cunnycatch the world,*
> *Uproar'd a wonderment of* Eighty Eight:
> *The* Earth *addreading to be overwhurld,*
> *What now availes, quoth She, my ballance*
>   *weight?*
> *The Circle smyl'd to see the* Center *feare :*
> *The wonder was, no wonder fell that yeare.*
> *Wonders enhaunse their powre in numbers odd:*

The fatall yeare of yeares is Ninety Three :
Parma *hath kis*t; De-Maine *entreates the rod*d:
Warre wondreth, Peace and Spaine in Fraunce to see.
Brave Eckenberg, *the dowty* Bassa *shames*:
The Christian Neptune, *Turkish* Vulcane *tames*.

> Navarre *wooes* Roome: Charlmaine *gives* Guise *the*
> Phy:
> *Weepe Powles, thy* Tamburlaine *voutsafes to dye.*

> L'enuoy.
> *The hugest miracle remaines behinde,*
> The second Shakerley Rash-Swash to binde.[411]

[all italics are original to Harvey]

While most scholars can agree on the people involved, in particular Marlowe aka "Tamburlaine" and Thomas Nashe, who is taken to be the "second Shakerley", there is little unanimity with regard to Harvey's intent behind the poem. As Thomas Nashe's Biographer, R. B. McKerrow admits, "it was doubtless intended to have some meaning, but ... I have in vain attempted to discover what this may be."[412] Those who have ventured an interpretation have generally read the poem as a warning to Nashe, although a warning of what is considered indecipherable.

Peter Shakerley, the man being held up as an example of ridicule, was "one of those self-publicising Elizabethan oddballs who found their way into the public's imagination."[413] More importantly, Shakerley died in September, 1593, and was buried in St. Gregory's-by-St.-Paul's Churchyard on September 18th, not far from where the printers kept their shops. Charles Nicholl is of the view that "it was Shakerley's death, not Marlowe's, which occasioned the poem."[414] This idea, however, would not explain the "Gorgon" title, or the reference to "the wonderment of eighty-eight" or the statement that "Tamburlaine vouchsafes to die".

As A. D. Wraight has pointed out, however, Harvey's title recalls a defiant line from Marlowe's Tamburlaine Part I (IV.i.18) where Zenocrate's father insists that he will not retreat "were that Tamburlaine as monstrous as Gorgon, prince of Hell".[415] Harvey, therefore, can be understood to be asserting that he will not retreat from the subject of his verse. This makes two references to Marlowe, one at the beginning and one at the end of the sonnet.

In Shakespeare Authorship Doubt in 1593, Rosalind Barber provides an interpretation for some of the poem's other references from the perspective of a Gabriel Harvey suspicious of their attribution with interesting results: First, that "Fame and deceit are the opening notes: the world is easily conned where fame is concerned."[416] Second that "'A wonderment of Eighty Eight' has also been suggested as Marlowe, whose 'atheist Tamburlan' was first mentioned this year by Robert Greene."[417] Third that "Harvey then moves on to the present tense and the present year [1593] and lists a series of 'amazing events[418] (for the most part welcome rather than dire ones)'[419] from the current year." And Fourth that if the reference to 'Tamberlaine' indicates Marlowe (as it has been taken, for example, in the Dutch Church libel), the word 'vouchsafe' seems to suggest an "element of collusion, on Marlowe's part, in his own death."[420]

Then comes the tag, titled "L'envoy" which Barber translates:

> "the sentence structure does not allow Nashe to be both 'the second Shakerley' and 'the 'hugest miracle' that remains behind 'to binde' Nashe, or for Nashe to bind. Interestingly, the overlooked verb 'bind' supports the argument that the 'miracle' to which Harvey is referring is a recently published pamphlet. . . . For Harvey to believe that Venus and Adonis is a work of Marlowe's that Nashe has brought to press is not unreasonable."[421]

What makes this belief even more reasonable is the fact that Harvey, having come to London to sort out the affairs of his brother, John, stayed "apparently at the house of John Wolfe in St. Paul's Churchyard."[422] Wolfe was then a leading member of the Stationers' Company and had recently been appointed Printer to the City of London, having spent the early part of his career in running battles with the authorities due to his "penchant for piracy".[423] More importantly for the story of these events, Wolfe somehow obtained the publishing rights to Marlowe's Hero and Leander which he entered in the Stationer's Register on the 28th of September, 1593, not two weeks after Harvey published his letter addressed to his host and excoriating Thomas Nashe. Gabriel Harvey, very familiar with Christopher Marlowe and his work, could easily have been among the very first to make the connection between Venus and Adonis and Hero and Leander being in a time and place where both the published and manuscript texts were readily available to him, practically spread out on John Wolfe's kitchen table for better comparison of the two side by side. The two poems, so similar that the published work has long been accepted by generations of critics as the sibling of the other, then unpublished work, with this "heir" attributed to a complete unknown, improbably named Shakespeare, must have seemed to Harvey an absolute "miracle" indeed.

And since no one willingly "vouchsafes to die", Harvey was off to the races, as much as accusing Nashe in print of having a hand in Marlowe's disappearance. This would be tantamount to getting crosswise with the Privy Council if it was a faked murder because Marlowe, after all, was still under house arrest when he disappeared. Harvey would see Nashe's participation, possibly including writing the suspect dedication with its clever language about "graver matters", as being worthy of exposure. Harvey, obviously thinking he had Nashe by the short hairs, gleefully tried to tie him up with Marlowe. While his rant may seem obscure today, to Nashe it would have been a very real threat.

What isn't clear in any of this is why Harvey thought Nashe was involved at all in Marlowe's disappearance. That Marlowe and Nashe were friends is not the issue. For all his vehemence, Harvey failed to provide even the most obscure evidence for his allegation that Nashe was the one "to bind" Venus and Adonis. Apparently, all he had were his suspicions and a belief that Nash knew more than he was telling.

Nor is it clear what John Wolfe thought of all this. He wasn't just a member of the Stationers' Company, he was its Beadle, the enforcer of its rules against publishing pirated manuscripts, the very thing for which he'd been notorious early in his career. He was the Printer for the City of London. Richard Field, who printed Venus and Adonis, was a junior member of the same guild. It was Wolfe's job to know what the publishers were printing and why. Wolfe had in his possession the manuscript for Marlowe's Hero and Leander; he entered it in the Stationers' Register and he printed Harvey's allegations that Nashe was the man "to bind" Venus and Adonis. If Wolfe thought Harvey was off his nut, not only did he not have to print his screed, he could have had it censored outright. If he knew, and who else would know, that Thomas Nashe had nothing to do with publishing a poem that strongly resembled a poem written by Christopher Marlowe but was credited to a complete unknown, why did he let Gabriel Harvey address his public letter containing that accusation to him and then publish it himself?

There has never been an explanation of how Wolfe got his hands on Hero and Leander. David Riggs has suggested that the poem was inspired by Lady Pembroke who, in the words of Abraham Faunce in his Third part of the Countesse of Pembrokes Yuychurch, Entituled, Amintas Dale (1592):

> . . . wills euery man to remember
> Some one God transformd, or that transformed an other:
> And enioynes each nymph to recount some tale of a Goddesse
> That was changd herself, or wrought some change in an other:[424]

Marlowe had earlier written his prefatory letter to Watson's posthumous Aminta Gaudia dedicating the book of poems to his theatrical patron, Lady Pembroke, boldly stating that she was "infusing the spirit of an exalted frenzy, whereby my poor self seems capable of exceeding what my own ripe talent is accustomed to bring forth." Riggs sees this conveying Marlowe's "response to Lady Pembroke's call for Ovidian poetry."[425] The result was Hero and Leander. It is not certain that she ever saw the poem in manuscript, but who better to hand it off to Wolfe?

Especially if she is the other person mentioned in mysterious terms in Harvey's address, one who must also have had a strong reaction to the publication of Venus and Adonis. Harvey calls her "a Gentlewoman rare, with Phenix quill in diamant hand of Art" who muzzled "the redoubtable Bullbare," and played "the galliard Championesses part." Although A. D. Wraight asserts that "Harvey's 'Gentlewoman rare' has never been identified,"[426] it seems pretty clear that this is a reference to Lady Pembroke, Mary Sidney, whose version of her deceased brother's Arcadia was also published in 1593, qualifying her not only with a phoenix quill, but also as the muzzler of Nashe who wrote the preface for an unauthorized and quickly withdrawn version of Philip Sidney's Astrophil and Stella in 1590. That Harvey further credits her in the same stanza with "The mightiest miracle of Ninety Three", an apparent reference to that Arcadia, pretty much resolves the issue.

Lady Pembroke's connection to Christopher Marlowe is well established at this point, so Harvey can be understood as comparing Venus and Adonis and its miracle of impersonation with Lady Pembroke's Arcadia and its miracle of resuscitation to Marlowe's detriment although both are acknowledged "miracles". What the Countess may have thought of being hauled into Harvey's contretemps with Nashe is probably not favorable to either, but she would have to have understood the implications regarding her protegee Marlowe's disappearance. Which means that the circle of people suspicious of Venus and Adonis and its attribution is much wider than typically assumed.

All of this interpretation of a supposedly obscure poem may be pure conjecture, but scholars who insist that Harvey was actually celebrating the miracle of Shakespeare's first publication should explain why it is that Harvey never mentions his name in the poem or in his larger letter to Wolfe, not once, but spends all of his time writing about Sidney, Spencer and Marlowe. It is the curious review that fills pages focused on someone other than the author of the work being reviewed, an author whose name is conspicuously displayed in a peculiar dedication to a very prominent Earl. Those who insist that he is warning Nashe that he too could end up in "the pitt" need to do a better job of explaining why he thought Marlowe's death in 1593 and the possibility of Nashe's similar demise was so miraculous.

Given the uproar over the Groatsworth that preceded all this, it is not surprising that Nashe stayed clear of further engagement with the volatile Harvey. Instead, he surfaced in early 1594 with the first printing of Dido, Queen of Carthage, including himself as a smaller typeface co-author below Marlowe's more prominent name above. Significantly, Nashe appears to have chosen this occasion to include "an elegy on Marlowe, affixed to the 1594 quarto of Dido."[427] This elegy has not survived. Edmund Malone tracked down Thomas Warton, the author of an early mention of it, and included his recollection in a note affixed to the Bodelian copy of the play:

> "He informed me by letter that a copy of this play was in Osborne's catalogue in the year 1754; that he saw it in his shop (together with several of Mr. Oldys's books that Osborne had purchased), & that the elegy in question "on Marlowe's untimely death" was inserted immediately after the title-page; that it mentioned a play of Marlowe's titled The Duke of Guise and four others; but whether particularly by name, he could not recollect. Unluckily, he did not purchase the rare piece, & it is now God knows where."[428]

It is puzzling that an elegy would not have been included in the original printed text, but was instead inserted. This may have been Nashe's way of responding to Harvey without acknowledging his allegation that he was somehow involved in publishing Venus and Adonis, but the parallel that the elegy makes by way of its insertion with the insertion of the dedication in Venus and Adonis is striking. If Nashe did "bind" Venus and Adonis as Harvey seemed to believe, then he might well have taken the opportunity to refute the charge by making a last minute edit of Dido and unintentionally repeated himself by way of an elegy with its echo of an earlier dedication.

Nashe was not done with his parallels, echoes and remarkable literary co-incidences. The same year that he published Dido and composed his elegy to Marlowe, he published The Unfortunate Traveller (1594). The number of parallels in this book with Marlowe's life up to that point are rather astonishing.

Nashe's protagonist, Jack Wilton, begins his tale at an English military encampment in Flanders, where he meets "an vgly mechanical Captaine" and convinces him to spy on the enemy camp. The Captain is immediately captured and accuses Jack of suborning him, not unlike Richard Baines who accused Marlowe of treasonous counterfeiting during their assignment in Flushing. Wilton then digresses, describing the sweating sickness that caused him to "runne out of England" like the plague then running amok in London.

After the war was "blowen ouer, and the seueral bands dissolued," Jack travels to Munster, Germany, and witnesses the massacre of John Leyden's Anabaptist faction by the Emperor and the Duke of Saxony, a historical event which prefigured the St. Bartholomew's Day Massacre and, in the context of the novel, echoes Marlowe's Massacre at Paris. Jack reflects on religious conflicts and then resolves to return to England, but before he can arrive he encounters Henry Howard, Earl of Surrey, his "late master" and one of the originators, with Sir Thomas Wyatt, of the English sonnet, who has pledged to defend the honor of his beloved Geraldine in an Italian tournament. Nashe uses this part of his tale to satirize the conventions of chivalry. Critic Katherine Duncan-Jones has noted "that it is above all these conventions as illustrated in [Philip] Sidney's Arcadia that Nashe takes as his material."[429] These connections with tournaments and poetry and Sidney's fame in both, particularly in the development of the English sonnet, all pair the novel's Earl of Surrey with Sidney, another echo of a major presence in Marlowe's life. Indeed, if Nashe's reference to "late master" is taken literally, it would seem to confirm the possibility that Marlowe had been a page for Philip Sidney.

On their way to Italy, Surrey and Wilton travel together to Wittenberg, home of the fictional Dr. Faustus, and meet his stand-in, "the greatest coniurer in Christendome," Corneilus Agrippa, who shows them a magic mirror with an image of Surrey's beloved "weeping on her bedde." Seeing this, Surrey renews his journey to Venice, but not before exchanging identities with Wilton to enable him to "to take more liberty of behaviour." In Venice, they fall in with a prostitute who gives Jack "a great deale of counterfeit gold" which they try to pass to a "gracelesse fornicatresse" only to be arrested and put in jail, just as Marlowe had similarly been apprehended with Richard Baines in their counterfeiting scheme. There Jack meets Diamante, "a pretie round faced wench . . . with blacke cie browes, a high forehead, a litle mouth, and a sharpe nose" who has been falsely accused of adultery and cast out by her husband, are soon freed by their inquisitor, Pietro Aretino, who is included not for his connections to Marlowe but because Nashe judges him "one of the wittiest knaves that ever God made".

Surrey, Jack, and his new love, Diamante, finally arrive in Florence, where Surrey finds Geraldine and then competes in the tournament for her honor. As Duncan-Jones points out, the conception of this contest "is close to that of Philantus' tournament in Book I of the New Arcadia." It also bears close comparison with the parade of emblems and the subsequent joust in Pericles. Nashe, like Sidney, makes it clear that although Surrey defends Geraldine's honor just as Philantrus defends Artesia's, "the whole affair is an empty show, and proves nothing either about the lady's beauty or her champion's nobility."[430]

Jack and Diamante then leave Surrey and Gerldine behind and travel to Rome where Esdras of Granado and his lackey Bartol the Italian break into the house where Jack and Diamante are lodging. Esdras rapes the virtuous matron of the house, Heraclide, who commits suicide after an eloquent oration, not only mirroring the action of Lucrece in Book II of Ovid's Fasti but anticipating the same set of events portrayed in The Rape of Lucrece. Heraclide's husband accuses Jack of the rape, but another English character known as the "banished English Earl" comes "to heare his confession, and see if hee knew him" after which he "desired the execution might be staid." This character bears a striking resemblance to William Allen, a Cardinal of the Roman Catholic Church who was significant in Marlowe's history as one of the major actors with the Earl of Stanley in the English Catholic insurgency that Marlowe had been deployed to investigate.

The final episode of The Unfortunate Traveller reveals the fate of Esdras, murdered by Cutwolf, brother of Esdras's lackey Bartol. At Bologna, Jack and Diamante attend Cutwolf's public execution. Standing before the crowd, Cutwolf describes how he revenged his brother, tracking down Esdras, forcing him to blaspheme God and then firing a pistol into his mouth, thereby damning his soul eternally in death. "This is the fault that hath called me hither" he claims, "No true Italian but will honour me for it." Regardless, he is brutally executed and Jack and his newly-wed Diamante leave "the Sodom of Italy", heading back toward the English encampment in France where the story began.

Throughout The Unfortunate Traveller, Nashe appears to be improvising a tale based on Marlowe's life as a forecast of his friend's future in exile which, as the final episode, echoing Ovid's tale of Lucrece, suggests that he can only return when some form of justice has been realized for his sacrifice. Considering how much The Unfortunate Traveller appears to reveal about Nashe's insight into Marlowe's personal history, it is surprising that more has not been made of the story and its appearance less than a year after Marlowe's disappearance. More often than not, Nashe's work is reported by scholars to be "a storehouse of oddity and fantastic wit."[431] Others dismiss it as a travelogue of stereotypes: "The French, Italians, and Dutch, Anabaptists, Saracens and Jews, among many other groups such as women and Catholics, appear as exaggerated types who pose many dangers to the unwary Englishman."[432] This superficial treatment is utterly oblivious to the relationship between the novel's specific characters and their parallels to real people and situations in the life of Christopher Marlowe.

Although it closes with a signature date of June 27, 1593, exactly four weeks after Marlowe's disappearance, suggesting that Nashe completed the first draft in that time, The Unfortunate Traveller was not published until 1594. Preceding it, Nashe published Christ's Tears Over Jerusalem (1593) in which he proclaimed his desire "to be at peace with all men" and made a special apology to "Master Doctor Harvey," his first address to him after the accusations in Gorgon, "whose fame and reputation (though through some precedent injurious provocations, and fervent incitements of youngheads) I rashly assailed, yet now better advised, and of his perfections more confirmedly persuaded, unfeignedly I entreat of the whole world, from my pen his worths may receive no impeachment." In fact, the entire purpose of Christ's Tears seems defensive. While it laments the deaths, presumably from plague, of "rich merchants, poor artificers, ploughmen, gentlemen, high men, low men, wearish men, gross men and the fairest complexioned men", it also attacks "blasphemies and scripture-scorning ironies," as if in response to Harvey's attacks, Nashe was attempting to protect himself "from that taint of atheism and sedition which surround[ed] Marlowe"[433] in the summer of 1593.

Notably, Nashe dedicated The Unfortunate Traveller to Southampton, addressing him as "a dere lover and cherisher you are, as well of the lovers of Poets, as of Poets themselves." Thus, a book based not too loosely on Marlowe's life and bearing a date within a month of Marlowe's disappearance and the publication of Venus and Adonis with its famed dedication to Southampton, was the only work Nashe himself dedicated to Southampton. It was not put up for sale until its second printing, also in 1594 "newly corrected and augmented," and neither was acknowledged by the Earl. In fact, although he has been constantly reported by his biographers to have aided various poets far and wide, "if he did, all record of these benefactions has been lost."[434]

The novel's success, evidenced by being revised and reprinted in its first year, was probably due less to its wandering narrative or Nashe's effervescent style than to the fact that, as J. J. Jusserand obliquely put it, "readers were on the look-out for allusions; they took his historical heroes for living people but thinly disguised, and lined Nash's story with another of their own invention."[435] Which is another way of saying that at least some of them saw the Marlovian references and suspected that Nashe knew more than he was telling. It was a controversy he seems to have anticipated as he promptly replied in A Comparative Admonition to London "annexed" to his revised Christ's Tear's (1594): "I am informed there be certain busy wits abroad that seek in my Jack Wilton to anagrammatize the name of Wittenberg to one of the universities of England, that scorn to be counted honest plain-meaning men like their neighbours, for not so much as out of mutton and pottage but they will construe a meaning of kings and princes." Insisting that he meant no aspersion to anyone except for the Harveys, "who, if they should once grow into the least liking of me, I would sinfully loathe myself while I lived," his response was, in effect, a non-denial denial:

> "Grave learned courteous gentlemen, in a word I will end with you; I had no allusion in sentence, word or syllable unto any of you when I writ the entertainment at Wittenberg, and let so much suffice to your contentment."

In short, unless their name was Harvey, there was no reason why anyone attending Cambridge or Oxford at that time should think that Nashe was writing about them. On the other hand, if they thought he was writing about Marlowe, as Harvey evidently did, Nashe had nothing more to say. If Nashe was doing this unwittingly, then somebody other than Gabriel Harvey needed to explain to him what it looked like he was doing so he could stop. On the other hand, if he was trying to divert the suspicion Harvey had heaped on him while putting a finish to the danger of further speculation, then he appears to have staged a clever dodge which, with a nod and a wink, he had Harvey's cake and ate it in front of him.

Chapter Sixteen

Marlowe and Rape

If Marlowe had any impatience with his continuing exile, he only needed to consider the political situation in London to recognize the need for restraint. Not only had the newly minted Earl of Derby's difficulties over the Hesketh affair which, regardless of whether or not it ultimately resulted in his death by way of poisoned mushrooms, had entirely undermined his place at court and all but shut down his theatre company, but Essex had discovered letters addressed to the Queen's Royal Physician, Roderigo Lopez, that had the entire court alarmed at accusations of yet another assassination plot. This while plague continued to keep London on edge and the public under a blanket of uncertainty.

Elizabeth's court had always been fueled by tales of conspiracy and threats, real and imagined, against her crown and her life. Burghley and Walsingham had put down several of these in succession, most spectacularly the Babington Plot which had led to Mary Queen of Scot's execution. But there never seemed to be an end to the plots with Catholics in England and on the Continent continuing to agitate and recruit and scheme against the Protestant Queen. With Walsingham's death, Burghley and his son, Robert Cecil, had maintained their vigilance and, with the help of agents like Robert Poley, Thomas Phelepes, Richard Baines and, prior to his Deptford escape, Christopher Marlowe, kept a firm hand on a variety of threats, actual and potential as the Earl of Derby could attest. At the same time, however, internal challenges arose and Essex's personal feud with Robert Cecil had become the most serious. Marlowe's exile, the direct result of this rivalry was not even its most serious consequence in 1593; that distinction has to be awarded to the Lopez affair which, like Marlowe's, had the common root of Essex's personal enmity.

Rodrigo Lopez enjoyed a high degree of success and honor when he made the fatal mistake of revealing in a letter to Antonio Perez, Secretary to King Philip of Spain, that he had on more than one occasion treated Essex for syphilis.[436] Essex set Phelippes on Lopez's trail and shortly uncovered secret correspondence between him and a pretender to the Portuguese throne, Dom Antonio, Prior of Crato. Lopez had once been engaged by Francis Walsingham to contact members of the Spanish court, but after Walsingham's death, Lopez had no official permission to correspond with either court. This lapse of protocol gave the inflamed Essex sufficient excuse to have Lopez arrested and tortured in early January, 1594. Subsequent revelations of additional correspondence, including information on the English court passed on to the Spanish, sealed his fate. Lopez, who had been a useful informant for Burghley regarding the Spanish court, was quickly tried on February 28, 1594 and sentenced to death.

The entire scandal, exposing a plot that allegedly threatened the life of the Queen with poison from her own physician, even though Lopez protested his innocence throughout, was a tremendous coup for Essex and momentarily restored momentum to his contest with Robert Cecil after the unsatisfying fracas at Deptford.

In the middle of all this intrigue and blight, holiday celebrations at court were somewhat diminished. Both Derby's and Pembroke's companies were unwelcome, so entertainment was provided by the Queen's Men, Walsingham's old company, making a return on January 6, 1594, for the sole court performance that year and the last for the old favorite. For those seeking something more up to date, a revived Sussex's Men and the new Earl, Robert Radcliff, whose father had died in early December, leaving him his estate, the Earldom and an acting company "which had many ex-Strange's and ex-Pembroke's players in its ranks"[437] and had taken residence in the reopened Rose on December 26, 1593. Sussex's repertory, however, did not include a single play by Christopher Marlowe, the author who had dominated both companies and the court festival not one year before. For that, Sussex's Men had to reach beyond their own ranks. Titus Andronicus, salvaged from Pembroke's Men which had liberated it from Strange's, was the run's big hit, playing three performances in two weeks, January 24, 29 and February 6. Sandwiched between was Ned Alleyn, returning to the Rose in The Jew of Malta on the 4th. Receipts for that week were the strongest the run, but fears of resurgent plague closed the theaters immediately after.

While the reason for closing the Rose seems clear, what led to it is less often explored. The Sussex repertory during their January run consisted chiefly of provincial plays which were never published and have not survived. The titles included God Speed the Plough, Huon of Bordeaux, Abram and Lot, The Fair Maid of Italy and King Lud. It is only Titus and Jew which survive from this run and both of those appear right at the end, in the final two weeks. It is not unreasonable to conclude that the provincial plays of Sussex were not quite the draw that the gore filled Titus and The Jew, with its own share of horrible deaths, were. Audiences apparently crowded into the Rose for both with the further draw being the addition of Ned Alleyn in the return of his most popular role. Contagion spreads in crowds, so the success of the season was also the cause of its abbreviation.

There is another reason to consider, however, and that is the fact that both of these two more popular plays can be tied to Marlowe. Titus Andronicus was published in 1594 without attribution and while the first scene of the play is usually credited to George Peele, the remainder of the play has typically been attributed to The-Man-Who-Wasn't-There largely on the basis of being included in the Folio and more recently by fundamentally flawed stylometric tests that have been built on comparisons with texts such as Romeo and Juliet and The Taming of a Shrew which Chapter Eleven has shown were actually collaborations between Marlowe and Tom Watson.

Titus has the distinction of being recorded in Henslowe's diary as "ne", generally interpreted as meaning "new", even though by the time Henslowe noted it, it had been in performance for at least a year and possibly for as long as five. If Ben Jonson is to be trusted, it might have been older than that, as he famously observed in the preface to Bartholomew Fair, published in 1614, that: "He that will swear, Jeronimo, or Andronicus are the best plays, yet shall pass unexcepted at here, as a man whose judgement shows it is constant, and hath stood still these five and twenty, or thirty years."

Traditional scholars like Jonathan Bate, editor for the Arden Titus Andronicus, cannot bear to read Jonson's statement plainly as it would mean that Titus must be dated circa 1590 at the latest, which would then mean that despite all efforts to backdate the presence of The-Man-Who-Wasn't-There, the play could not possibly be originally his. Instead, Bate asserts that Jonson was indulging in "exaggeration" and tries to prove this by claiming that the same prologue "inflates the length of performance" and that it "inflates ticket prices."[438] In fact, however, Jonson says the play, Bartholomew Fair, would last two and a half hours, which is by no means an exaggeration, and lists five ticket prices available to the buyer ranging from six pence to half a crown, each equal "to the value of his place, provided always his place is not above his wit," an admonition Bate would do well to observe.

Undaunted by facts, Bate goes further to claim that "the image of Lavinia's husband's dead body being used as a pillow while she is raped exactly replicates a detail in Nashe's 1593 Unfortunate Traveller"[439] and therefore must have been written after it. For some reason not explained, it does not occur to Bate that Nashe could be the one making the replication and that Esdra's rape of Heraclide, the most dramatic scene in the novel as with "her husbands dead bodie he made a pillow to his abhomination," all witnessed by Jack Wilton "through a crannie of my vpper chamber vnseeled," is based on the most shocking scene in the hugely popular play. Nor does Bate make the obvious connection, one made spectacularly by Nashe himself, that Marlowe, impersonated by the unseen Jack, is the author of the play which inspired the scene in Nashe's novel based on incidents in Marlowe's life.

What then were the additions to the script which caused Henslowe to mark it as "ne"? Very likely sequences such as this from Act 4, scene 3:

> Enter the Clown with a basket and two pigeons in it.
>
> Titus: News, news from Heaven! Marcus, the post is come.
> Sirrah, what tidings? Have you any letters?
> Shall I have justice? What says Jupiter?"
> Clown: Ho, the gibbet-maker? He says that he hath taken them down again, for the man must not be hanged till the next week.

This has been recognized as a reference[440] to the fact that on March 31, 1593, two Puritans, John Greenwood and Henry Barrow, both known to Marlowe from his Cambridge days, Greenwood being a former student for whom Marlowe had made buttery allowance,[441] had their executions in relation to their Marprelate pamphlet activities delayed for a second time in barely a week. They were first taken out of prison for execution on March 24th, the day after their sentencing, but were respited for a week during which, apparently, "Lord Treasurer Burghley endeavoured to save their lives."[442] One week later, the pair were then taken to "the gallows, and after the ropes had been placed about their necks were again respited."[443] Finally, they were executed on April 6th, after all appeals had failed.

The twice delayed executions were notorious because their victims were widely read and hotly debated for several years, even managing to be published while jailed. Elizabethan audiences would have been well aware of a reference to their deaths slipped into an already popular play. This grotesque sequence was echoed more personally for Marlowe with John Penry, another Marprelate participant, who was convicted on May 23rd, 1593, but not hanged until the 29th at the "unusual hour of 4 p.m."[444]. "A man of Marlowe's own age and status," Penry "was suddenly and secretly executed only four miles away from Deptford, where Kit's own life is alleged to have ended on the following day." As David More and others have noted, if a substitute body was needed to help in Marlowe's escape, "Penry's corpse would still have served well for Marlowe's."[445] Would the audience suspect that the line "the man must not be hanged till the next week" might better fit the lone Penry than the duo of Barrow and Greenwood? All of them were cut from similar cloth, but the switch from a plural "he hath taken *them* down" to the single "*man*" that must not be hanged suggests that Marlowe was thinking of Penry as the last of the three.

Titus Andronicus appeared "just a few months before"[446] The Rape of Lucrece with which it shares Marlowe's continuing fascination with Ovid. In fact, one reason for dating the play before 1593 is that Nashe echoes the rape of Lavinia with the rape of Heraclide in The Unfortunate Traveller which is in turn echoed by Lucrece, all three of which are traceable to Ovid's tale of Philomel in Book Six of the Metamorphoses, cited in Titus by Marcus when he recognizes that Lavinia has been injured more severely than the classic heroine:

> Fair Philomena, why she but lost her tongue,
> And in a tedious sampler sewed her mind;
> But, lovely niece, that mean is cut from thee.
> A craftier Tereus, cousin, hast thou met,
> And he has cut those pretty fingers off,
> That could have better sewed than Philomel.

Titus Andronicus II:3: 38 - 44

Lavinia then employs another Ovidian strategy from Book One, mimicking Io who, transformed by Jupiter into a heifer to conceal his rape, revealed his crime by writing in the dust with her hoof. Similarly hobbled, Lavinia manipulates a stick with her mouth to draw her rapist's name in the sand.

It is scenes like that which caused John M. Robertson to assert that "by common consent Titus is the most horrible play in the whole Elizabethan drama."[447] Robertson was alluding to the play's outright quantity of gore, but the judgement has been held against its artistic quality as well. T. S. Elliot called it "one of the stupidest and most uninspired plays ever written."[448] Harold Bloom summed up this strain of modern critical opinion thus:

> "Something about Titus Andronicus is archaic, in an unpleasant way. Everyone onstage is very remote from us, the rigid Titus most of all, except for the engaging Aaron the Moor, who is an improvement upon Richard III in the possible contest to surpass Barabas, Jew of Malta, who is the most self-aware and self-amused of villains."[449]

On one level, Titus, like Taming of a Shrew, is a satire, in this case not of an actor like Ned Alleyn but of Thomas Kyd's Spanish Tragedy, the revenge plot of which Robertson observed: "In truth, Titus is exactly the type of that of the Tragedy, only heightened to the point of horror-a chain of revenges in which the central personage partly feigns madness."[450] Jonathan Bate outlines the similarities between the two plays:

> "Each action begins at the end of a war, with a parade of prisoners, prominent among whom is the enemy monarch's son. . . . The life of the chief prisoner is spared, leading to amorous intrigue and eventual dire consequences. Public disputation occurs over a point of honor; love is a means of vengance . . . . A *locus amorenus* (bower, forest glade) is established, then darkened and violated. A dramatically crucial and highly

> emotional *anagnorisis* takes place in the form of a linguistically charged soliloquy: Hieronimo's gradual recognition of his murdered son, Marcus' recognition of his raped an mutilated niece. . . . Assumed madness and theatre are the revenger's two means of speaking and acting in public."[451]

And where The Spanish Tragedy ends spectacularly with Hieronimo's staging his son's murderer's murders by casting them in a play within the play, Titus goes further still and stages a banquet featuring the baked corpses of his daughter Lavinia's rapists which he feeds to their mother, Tamora.

Like A Midsummer Night's Dream, another play from the same period shown to be the work of Marlowe and Watson and a thematic mirror of Shrew, Titus is "brimming with references to the Metamorphoses"[452] and the links to Ovid, which permeate Marlowe's work.

Audiences in 1594 would have had no more difficulty recognizing Marlowe's spirit in Titus as revived by the lead actors in his company, Pembroke's Men, than they would have in finding him restored in the person of The Jew of Malta as portrayed by the irrepressible Ned Alleyn. No less conspicuous would be the heightened meaning of the play's prologue spoken by the character Machevill:

> "Albeit the world think Machevill is dead,
> Yet was his soul but flown beyond the Alps;
> And, now the Guise is dead, is come from France,
> To view this land, and frolic with his friends."

Robert Greene had accused Marlowe of studying "Machiavellian policy" in his Groatsworth and Machevill had been named in the Dutch Church Libel, the broadside credited to Marlowe that started his problems with the Privy Council. The Guise, meanwhile, was the lead villain in Marlowe's Massacre at Paris. Machevill even provides a link with Titus, proclaiming in the same prologue that: "I count religion but a childish toy, And hold there is no sin but ignorance" which directly echoes Aaron's response to the accusation "Thou believest no god" with "What if I do not? - as indeed I do not." V.1. 71 - 3.

There were plenty of people in the theatre and elsewhere capable of making these connections and, in an age when suspicions of conspiracy could be deadly for all concerned, anything pertaining to the mysteriously vanished poet would be unwelcome, especially onstage. When Titus alluded to the deaths of Greenwood, Barrow and Penry and then was immediately followed by The Jew bombastically flaunting "the Guise's" flight to Switzerland, the presence of plague at the Rose becomes an almost convenient pretext for shutting down what was suddenly a too overtly charged series of politically awkward performances.

Did discomfort with these messages add to the reasons to have the Rose closed? Plague or no plague, it was certainly a political time.

If Marlowe knew anything about any of this, he never mentions it in his correspondence with Walsingham which in 1593 and 1594 was primarily concerned with coming to terms with the reality of his exile and keeping his lifeline intact. Compartmentalization was a discipline that was essential to his intelligence service and it was what enabled him to carry on a literary career while simultaneously serving the crown. Exile did not change the need for the discipline; if anything it intensified it. Any work that he did from that time on would naturally be kept separate from his correspondence which, being limited to the Sonnets, was itself in a form of code.

The work that primarily occupied Marlowe in his first year of exile was The Rape of Lucrece (1594). Although the dedication says nothing about the genesis of the poem, its subject clearly indicates what was on Marlowe's mind while he composed it. A poem that highlights a signal moment in the history of Rome, depicting an act that precipitated the disgrace of Rome's last king and the creation of the Republic, it also includes clear references to two of the men who had played significant roles in Marlowe's life, Ovid and the Earl of Essex.

Ovid had been a significant inspiration for Marlowe well before his rushed departure from Deptford. He had twice included translations of the "Dawn Song", Elegy 13 in <u>Arden of Faversham</u>. He had taken inspiration for the falsely attributed <u>Venus and Adonis</u> and the unpublished <u>Hero and Leander</u> from Ovid's <u>Metamorphoses</u> and the most recent time he had been across the Channel he had published <u>Certaine of Ovids Elegies,</u> ten translations of selections from Ovid's <u>Amores</u>. Apart from his influential poetry, Ovid was perhaps most famous for having been banished into exile to the town of Tomis on the coast of the Black Sea in AD 8 by Augustus Caesar. That parallel would not have escaped Marlowe in 1593.

Which is why it makes perfect sense that he would find inspiration in Ovid's unfinished <u>Fasti</u>, also known as "The Book of Days", a six book dramatic poem structured as a series of eye-witness reports and interviews by the poet with Roman deities who explain the origins of Roman holidays and customs. Starting with the first of January, the poem ends at the midpoint of a year with the 30th of June. In a separate work, <u>Tristi</u>, Ovid explains that he worked on both while he was in exile, including an additional six books of <u>Fasti</u> that would complete the full year, but those have since been lost or were never completed. One of the longest passages in the six surviving poetic books, lines 685 to 855 of Book II (The Regifugium, February 24), details the fall of the Roman King Tarquin as the result of his son's rape of Lucrece, wife of the patriarch of Collatium. This passage is considered by scholars to be the chief classical source for the <u>Lucrece</u> that was registered with the Stationer's on May 9, 1594 and, like <u>Venus and Adonis,</u> was dedicated to the Earl of Southampton.

Scholars are very fond of asserting that <u>Lucrece</u> addresses the promise made in the dedication for <u>Venus and Adonis</u> that:

> "only if your Honor seem but pleased, I account myself highly praised and vow to take advantage of all idle hours till I have honored you with some graver labor."

It is hard to imagine a more glaring example of the *post hoc ergo propter hoc* line of false reasoning that dominates Shakespearean scholarship. As if Lucrece is at once more serious, ie: "graver", than Venus and Adonis and was even then contemplated by its actual author.

What supposedly would have been published instead if Venus and Adonis had not "but pleased"? Something less "grave", perhaps? Some more pleasing poem now forever lost? And, for that matter, how does anyone purport to know what Southampton thought of Venus and Adonis since he never acknowledged it in any way, shape or form?

It would be one thing for Shakspere to publish the erotic fairy tale of Venus and Adonis (where did he get the money?)[453] in all innocence, but the overtly political Lucrece? If he was actually involved, he could not by then be unaware of the danger of intruding upon the dispute between Burghley and his ward. The plague was rampant and, just like Marlowe, people could disappear no matter how well connected. Consider Kyd, who was raked and tortured and forced to accuse Marlowe of atheism and who wrote letters to another Privy Counsellor, Lord Puckering, trying to exculpate himself and who finally died in August, 1594, in disgrace. And to once again put a poem dedicated to Southampton out for sale? Without Burghley's express permission? These were dangerous times.

The point to the "graver labor" reference is not that it is a reference to a "graver", more serious poem that had not been written or even imagined at that time. It is instead an ironic hint that the genesis of the person supposedly dedicating Venus and Adonis to Southampton, or rather that the reason why Marlowe's name does not appear, would be revealed to Southampton if Southampton pleased to take the poem's suggestion and get married. The "graver labor" is the story of

245

Marlowe's faked death, not a promise of a more substantial sequel.

By the end of 1593 it had to be obvious to everyone involved that the Earl of Southampton was never going to marry Lord Burghley's grand daughter, Elizabeth DeVere. The effort to persuade him had begun quietly, proceeding from family urging to poetic suggestion in private to lyric encouragement and public pressure, none of which achieved the hoped for result. Burghley did not become Lord Treasurer by lacking determination, however, and if nothing else would work then he seemed perfectly willing to employ public shaming as a last resort. To achieve this, he had a very capable aide in Christopher Marlowe who never would have thought to do anything like that on his own, especially not with his own life in peril thanks to Essex, Southampton's confidant and political tutor, but with Burghley's sanction Marlowe threw his full energy into the task and infused the poem with enough of his own grievance to give it added weight. The result was a work that blended all of his dismay and anger at his personal injury, the larger issues of England's political destiny, and the very deliberate intrusion of Essex into the private affairs of the younger Southampton within a publication that could serve, as Barbara Parker observed, "a warning to an impressionable youth, and future statesman, of the perils of following such a master."[454]

Lucrece is a mediation on power and monarchy. It is also highly allegorical and as such is purposefully open to multiple interpretations which can simultaneously reflect and enhance each other. In one reading, Lucrece is Elizabeth herself threatened by Essex in the guise of Tarquin. In another, Lucrece is Marlowe unfairly maligned by Essex and his followers after Marlowe's patrons and supporters boasted of his honesty.

Many critics, unable or unwilling to investigate the author's personal intentions, have taken a fairly political view of the poem, locating an implied criticism of Elizabeth in favor of the establishment of republican values which were historically the result of Lucrece's violation. Andrew Hadfield, for instance, "takes the poem's dedication to Southampton, a member of the Essex circle, as a sign of its anti-absolutist spirit."[455] Similarly, Annabel Patterson argues for the republicanism of the poem[456] and Michael Platt describes the poem as "republican in sentiment and focus."[457]

Feisal Mohamed, on the other hand, asserts that "The Rape of Lucrece does not embody a republican spirit so much as it reflects late Elizabethan skepticism on sacred kingship and fears of self-seeking factions awaiting to seize power after the death of the heirless queen."[458] In his view, "the point on good monarchical government receives strong emphasis in the poem."[459] Lucrece sits at the center of this government's authority because, as a chaste wife, Lucrece is "the character against whom political legitimacy is measured." This perspective echoes that of Robert Miola, who observes:

> "Lucrece resides in the middle of the Aristotelian and Ciceronian series of concentric circles that expand outward to include the family, household, city, nation, and world. . . . Tarquin's rape of Lucrece violates all the circles of social order that surround her."[460]

Penny Garnsworthy appears to agree that the issue is one of character, observing that Lucrece:

> "seems to argue that any political system can only be as good, just, and effective as its component individuals. Rather than demonstrating a system in which the character of individuals flows from their political organisation, [it] demonstrates a society whose system takes on the character of its individuals."[461]

Thus, the question of monarchy versus republicanism is beside the point; it is the people and not the system which makes justice possible. From this perspective, Essex would be intolerable whether he were monarch or magistrate.

The allegorical nature of the poem even allows Christy Desmot to declare that <u>Lucrece</u> includes "opportunities for cross-gendered identification that aligns them with both victim and perpetrator in the rape".[462]

Barbara Parker asserts that <u>Lucrece</u> "contains three levels of allegory" which she identifies as those that "replicate transpiring political events in Rome," those that mirror "the events culminating in the ruin of Troy", Troy being "equated with England as well as with Rome, both 'second' Troys," and finally, "the correspondence between the poem's milieu and England's."[463] Within this this matrix of relationships, she further clarifies that "at the time <u>Lucrece</u> was written, England's political milieu notably resembled the poem's. . . the Court was dominated by faction - by the Essex-Cecil rivalry for control not simply of policy but of the Queen herself."[464] And yet, even though she correctly observes that "the dedication to Wriothesly actually serves as a warning against aligning himself with anti-Elizabeth forces,"[465] Parker confesses that, from her perspective, "why Shakespeare dedicated <u>Lucrece</u> to Southampton we can only guess."[466] Parker has properly evaluated the essence of the poem's political importance, but when it comes to reasons for Shakespeare's dedication she falls short primarily because she understands precisely how improper it would be to deliberately link one's patron to an enemy of the crown. On the other hand, if the author had permission, or if he had been instructed to make that connection then the guesswork ends.

Shakspere's motives regarding <u>Lucrece</u> are unclear simply because, beyond lending a glossy version of his name to the dedication, he had nothing to do with it. Marlowe's motives, however, could not be more self-evident and a fourth level of allegory appears that would help resolve Parker's issue. If cross-gendered identification is within the reach of an author whose every female character was originally played by teenage boys, then it would not seem to be out of character for Marlowe to see himself as Lucrece at the hands of Essex's Tarquin.

The dedication to Lucrece did not have to be the rush job that the dedication for Venus and Adonis must have been, so it is disappointing that it has none of the latter's inventiveness. It is instead a dry, brief and formulaic note that could have been written by anyone. It was certainly not written by Marlowe:

> To the Right Honourable Henry Wriothesly, Earl of Southampton, and Baron of Tichfield.
>
> THE love I dedicate to your lordship is without end; whereof this pamphlet, without beginning, is but a superfluous moiety. The warrant I have of your honourable disposition, not the worth of my untutored lines, makes it assured of acceptance. What I have done is yours; what I have to do is yours; being part in all I have, devoted yours. Were my worth greater, my duty would show greater; meantime, as it is, it is bound to your lordship, to whom I wish long life, still lengthened with all happiness.
>
> Your lordship's in all duty,

This is an altogether different dedication from the one that graced Venus and Adonis. It is plainer, less playful and less witty, more direct, specific and rather formal. Supposedly, it was written by a poet who had a personal relationship with Southampton, but there is nothing in it to indicate that this is the author of the most successful poetic debut of the decade, one that had gone through two printings in the previous year,[467] that was commented upon and imitated repeatedly and had been dedicated to the same person being addressed anew. Nowhere is there any reference to previous accomplishment or success which even modesty would permit in recognition of generous patronage. Worse, it not only fails to account for the license taken in putting the previous poem up for sale, it makes no mention of repeating the act in the context of a much less flattering subject, one that directly linked Southampton to the person believed by many to be threatening the queen. As if a short grouping of platitudes could override the seriousness of the allegory. Barbara Parker is quite right to wonder that anyone would dedicate The Rape of Lucrece to Southampton.

The key to understanding this dedication is in the word "warrant" which makes the poem "assured of acceptance." "Warrant" is a legal term which, as a noun, the Cambridge Dictionary defines as meaning: "a legal document that gives someone, for example, the police, the authority to do something" and in the verb usage means: "to make a particular activity necessary, . . . to say that it is certain that something will happen."[468] In May, 1594, the only person in all of London who held a "warrant" over the Earl of Southampton was his legal Guardian, Lord Burghley. Southampton would reach his majority when he turned 21 on October 6th, 1594; until then he could not refuse to accept from his guardian a warning against consorting with Essex, even if it was written up as a poem and put up for sale to the public.

As Southampton's guardian, Burghley "was entitled to take all the ward's land under his control and . . . was supposed to account to the heir when he came of age (hand over the profits made from the land during the wardship) and was similarly liable for waste."[469] Therefore, when the dedication says: "What I have done is yours; what I have to do is yours; being part in all I have, devoted yours," it is referencing Burghley's supervision of Southampton's estates under his guardianship, not some coy reference to poems and plays written and unwritten. Similarly, "Moiety" in the context of the contract implied by "warrant" is understood to mean a share or half of one of two parts of property ownership,[470] and "superfluous" is an adjective meaning more than is sufficient or required; excessive.[471] A "superfluous moiety" would be a part of that property or partnership which exceeds what is sufficient. Southampton's estate was essentially owned by Burghley during the period of his supervision. The advice included in the poem was superfluous to that ownership. Finally, the closing line: "Were my worth greater, my duty would show greater;

meantime, as it is, it is bound to your lordship," refers directly to Burghley's obligation to make an accounting to his ward, Southampton, for his stewardship of his estates which he pre-emptively asserts would be greater if he himself had more riches. This is all couched in the kind of legal formality with which Burghley is expert, all of which goes to show Burghley's hand. Southampton would immediately recognize this. It was the type of letter he had received from his guardian many times.

As usual, Burghley was prescribing strong medicine but, by the same token, he remained hopeful that Southampton would take it. As implied by the legal term "moiety" and in his closing statement, Burghley makes it clear that he views his ward as a partner, and while he is senior he does not presume to be greater. The poem itself, while unsparing in its treatment of Essex, is not aimed at Southampton but only at the company he chooses to keep.

It would be preposterous for any supposedly hopeful protégé to write anything so salutary and then put it up for sale to the public. To attach such a pointed critique of Essex to Southampton's name could not be perceived as complimentary by anyone, especially not by anyone determined to follow Essex. Which is what Southampton did, very much to his detriment. The one person who held a "warrant" which assured "acceptance" of the public and unwelcome warning against that course was Lord Burghley who commissioned Marlowe for the purpose. What Marlowe wanted was an opportunity to prove his continuing loyalty and usefulness and he got that with The Rape of Lucrece.

Southampton would inevitably know that the poem was written by Marlowe. He would have heard the rumors; Essex would have seen to that. And the continuity from Venus and Adonis through Titus Andronicus and finally Lucrece would be self-evident, the most striking thing being the scenes with Lavinia and Lucrece, both horribly raped and referencing the brutally silenced Philomel. It all spoke to a continuity in that period pointing to Essex as the perpetrator.

Nor was Southampton the only one who understood this. Thomas Nashe added his own perspective with <u>The Unfortunate Traveller</u> in which Jack Wilton witnesses Heraclide's rape at the hands of Esdras, mirroring both Lavinia and Lucrece with the added implication that Jack can only return to England when some form of justice has been realized for her sacrifice. It matters little whether or not Nashe was anticipating <u>Lucrece</u> or imitating it as they both draw on <u>Titus</u> and all of them make the case against Essex by allegorical means.

Almost thirty years later, Ben Jonson would revisit the business of poetic dedications and offer his own advice on how to interpret the dedications to <u>Venus and Adonis</u> and <u>The Rape of Lucrece</u> in his epigram on the cover of the Folio:

> To the Reader:
>
> The Figure that thou here seest put,
>   It was for gentle Shakespeare cut;
> Wherein the Graver had a strife
>   With Nature to outdo the Life.
> O, could he but have drawn his Wit
>   As well in Brass, as he has hit
> His Face, the Print would then surpass
>   All that was ever writ in Brass.
> But since he cannot, Reader, look
>   Not on his Picture, but his Book.

There is the obvious point that Jonson makes a specific difference between the Figure and his Wit, that they are different things and that his Wit is the better of the two. The Graver, however, could not draw Wit. Jonson could have said "Engraver" but he did not. Instead, he linked the <u>Folio</u> to Shakespeare's first appearance in print, his first impersonation of a poet by borrowing the word "graver" from the dedication to <u>Venus and Adonis</u> which has so often been taken to anticipate <u>The Rape of Lucrece</u>. Jonson is well aware of both dedications and he does not agree that the "graver" in the dedication for Venus and Adonis was a reference to any sequel. He says the Face has been drawn, that this is Nature, but that the Life, the Wit is not visible. Shakespeare, being that Face for the invisible Wit which can only be Marlowe, he recommends that the Reader look not on his/Shakespeare's picture, but on his/Marlowe's book. For Jonson, the "graver" is the hand substituting an image for the real thing. Jonson doesn't go so far as to say so directly, but that hand can only belong to Lord Burghley.

All that would come later, however. The Rape of Lucrece was entered in the Stationer's Register on May 9, 1594 and published shortly after. At that point, Shakspere's embellished name had been use twice, once to cover Marlowe's escape from Deptford and once as an alias for Lord Burghley. It would not have been necessary for anyone to imagine that it would ever be used again. In fact, once Southampton reached his maturity, there would be no likely occasion for it. In June of 1594 it is quite possible that the name Shakespeare might never have been printed again and it would have remained attached to two poems of inexplicable origin and remarkable promise unfulfilled. Events and politics, however, would soon require otherwise and the name would resurface in the most improbable way. The plague was on the wane and the theaters were about to reopen.

Chapter Seventeen

The Night of Errors

If the testimony of the Gesta Grayorum (1688) can be taken literally, then it seems perfectly reasonable to observe that the first performance of The Comedy of Errors was the most significant first performance of any play in Elizabethan history, including the first performance of Tamburlaine. Not only did it mark the coming out of a new theatrical company, The Lord Chamberlain's Men, it featured the onstage debut of the very person that all of literary London had been anxious to meet for over a year: William Shakespeare himself, who before that moment had been little more than a name on a pair of dedications for two best-selling poems.

As is typical of all things Elizabethan, there is some dispute about the date of this performance. The Gray's Inn production was on Holy Innocents' Day, December 28th, but the Master of Revels' account, dated March 15, 1595, shows a payment to Richard Burbage, Will Kempe and "Shakespeare", for a Court performance on the same day.[472] This is the first record of Shakspere's connection to the Lord Chamberlain's Men which had been revived the previous June with Burbage, Kempe and other players from Pembroke's Men. E. K. Chambers asserted in The Elizabethan Stage (1923) that the date for the Court performance must have been the 27th and that the Master of Revels was mistaken about the 28th because he thought it was unlikely that the company could have played both venues on the same day. On the other hand, that is exactly what the Lord Admiral's Men did on the 28th, playing Faustus at the Rose and at Court on the 28th.

The notion that Holy Innocents' Day could have accommodated the two London companies traveling back and forth across town to entertain both the Court and the public has no less validity than the notion that Shakespeare was actually present at Gray's Inn on the Night of Errors, as he most certainly was, but not in the way that popular history usually reports it. Both ideas add to the sense of heightened excitement that the evening is reported to have generated. Not only would Faust be followed by the newly minted Lord Chamberlain's Men at Court, but the whole conception of resuming the battle of the playing companies, suspended in 1593, would be highly anticipated. On top of which, if Shakespeare really was in attendance at the Court or Gray's Inn performance of Errors, it would inevitably have been looked upon by many as an opportunity to make sense out of the ruckus kicked up by Gabriel Harvey's Gorgon, which appeared to assert that the author of Venus and Adonis was not the person named on the title page. That controversy had not abated in the least with the appearance of Nashe's Unfortunate Traveller and the publication of The Rape of Lucrece, all of which had been dedicated to Southampton who was naturally expected to be in attendance. Shakespeare, meanwhile, was for most people only a name. Whatever might be claimed today, contemporaneous readers and audiences would not be of a single mind on the issue of whether or not Shakespeare was who he was purported to be just as Harvey and Nashe were themselves on opposite sides from the start.

The reappearance of two major playing companies at Newington Butts the previous June was itself a cause for excitement after almost two years of plague driven scarcity. Andrew Gurr has speculated in the absence of any documentation that "the Lord Chamberlain's Men and the Lord Admiral's Men were created by their patrons as a duopoly to replace the monopoly of the former Queen's Men."[473] This ignores the fact that a duopoly already preceded it in Strange's and Pembroke's Men and that both of them relied heavily on the plays of Christopher Marlowe as the basis of their repertory. The Admiral's Men was, in fact, a continuation of the same company that had featured Ned Alleyn who briefly joined Strange's but quickly found his way back to his father-in-law's company when Strange fell into disrepute. The Lord

Chamberlain's Men, meanwhile, was patched together by Burbage and Kemp out of the remnants of Strange's and Pembroke's companies with the patronage of Henry Carey, by then the Lord Chamberlain, in charge of court entertainments. James Burbage, who had a connection to Leicester's Men dating back to the 1570s when the Theater opened under his management, had been affiliated with Henry Carey, Lord Hunsdon, since the break-up of Leicester's Men. Leicester's contributed players to The Queen's Men who later lost players to both Lord Strange's and Pembroke's Men. Richard Burbage, James' son, worked with Pembroke and Marlowe and had played the leads in most of Marlowe's Pembroke plays before Marlowe disappeared.

Gurr argues that the two companies were "given similarly strong repertories of plays, Shakespeare to the one, and Marlowe to the other."[474] It was not actually necessary, however, to give anything to anybody; the Admiral's Men already owned Tamburlaine Parts I and II, and Faust, while Ned Alleyn, their star player owned The Jew of Malta and The Masacre at Paris outright. The Lord Chamberlain's Men, meanwhile, possessed by way of Pembroke's The True Tragedy of Richard, Duke of York, The Contention, Edward II, and The Taming of a Shrew. Both companies could lay claim to Titus Andronicus, Henry VI, Romeo and Juliet and Midsummer Night's Dream, but as Pembroke's claim was more recent, these too went with the Chamberlain's Men. Thus, the division was not according to authorship, but strictly on the basis of ownership. The restoration of the Pembroke repertory would therefore be cause for much excitement in itself as it included, as shown in Chapter Twelve, most of Marlowe's most recent work.

Just as there are no records of the Privy Council's activities from the months between August 27, 1593 and October 1st, 1595, so there are no records for Lord Chamberlain's performances at all except for those made by the intrepid Henslowe at Newington Butts with the Admiral's Men shortly after their formation in June, 1594, their regular court appearances and the occasional mention in contemporaneous correspondence. While they attempted to buy the Blackfriars for indoor winter performances in late 1594, they were not able to complete that plan until 1608. For all practical purposes, therefore, they were direct competitors with Henslowe's company in 1594, much as Marlowe must have originally envisioned Pembroke's would be with Strange's in the Spring of 1592. Most scholars assert that the Lord Chamberlain's company was doing similar business as the Lord Admiral's so well documented by Henslowe, but since Burbage's records, if there ever were any, do not survive, there is no certainty of this. Most likely, they were playing Marlowe's <u>Henry VI</u> plays, <u>Romeo and Juliet</u>, <u>Shrew</u> and others, but even this is not certain. Meanwhile, the continued absence of Marlowe from the stage and the speculative potential for his return in light of the publication of <u>The Rape of Lucrece</u> following <u>Venus and Adonis</u> and the unending pamphlet war between Nashe and Harvey, would have been an added source of anticipation when the students of Gray's Inn sent out December 13th "invitations for a blowout season of plays and entertainments to rival anything ever seen or staged before in England."[475]

As with the actual date of the performance, the question of whether or not <u>The Comedy of Errors</u> debuted then or had been in performance before has been disputed. The Grayorum, however, refers to it in such a way, "like to Plautus his Menechmus", as if it had previously been unfamiliar. The idea that the play could have been composed specifically for this occasion, as events themselves suggest, has been debated primarily because traditional scholars have found it inconvenient to imagine that the play could have any purpose other than mere entertainment, particularly if that purpose runs contrary to traditional theories of authorship. Although Taylor and Loughnane date it from 1594, they are unwilling to allow more than that "the play's Plautine plot seems particularly suitable for the learned audience at Gray's Inn."[476] Strong arguments have been made, however, in favor of a commissioned play. Specifically, the limited setting (it is one of only two Shakespeare plays to observe the Classical Unities of Time, Place and Action, its brevity (shortest in the Folio at 1777 lines), along with the wealth of legal terminology, has led both Sidney Thomas[477] and Charles Wentworth[478] to argue that the play was indeed written specifically for the Gray's Inn performance.

If the play was already in the Lord Chamberlain's repertory, then Shaxpere's presence at the Gray's in performance is part of a continuum of the revived company. If not, then the play signifies something deeper is afoot and Shakspere's role in it is significantly altered from that of a first time author to a player in a larger production. On the evidence, the latter possibility appears almost certain.

In 1594, Lord Burghley had been a member of Gray's Inn for almost forty years and his family and the Walsingham's had dominated it throughout. Gray's Inn was the house where Burghley took his law degree. Admitted in 1541 and elected an Ancient 1547, Burghley continued his affiliation with Gray's Inn all through his life, sending his son Robert Cecil there to study law as well. The invitation to the Inner Temple, which included Essex and Southampton among its most influential members, could not have been made without Burghley's personal approval. The entire purpose of the event, which was staged with the mock seriousness and elaborate display of the court rituals it satirically embraced, was to make peace between the two legal clubs and, chiefly, its most important members whose disputes, chief of which was Southampton's rejection of Elizabeth deVere, Lord Burghley's grand-daughter, had become the subject of "evil Reports that some Enviers of our Happiness had sown abroad." The event was supposed to make peace between them, but many anticipated further trouble.

Southampton turned 21 on October 6th, but not before Burghley as his guardian had taken his £5,000 bounty. The newly independent Earl was undoubtedly still smarting from the expense, a condition which Essex surely expected to turn to his further advantage. Other men might have resolved to move on from such an affair and its foreseeable result and perhaps

Southampton, left alone, would have been of that mind, but Essex was not such a man. Instead, he had to be considered a continuing threat to the survival of Christopher Marlowe, a man who had played an intimate part in Burghley's effort to force Southampton's hand and who had so far escaped Essex's reach.

Traditional scholars make little mention of these circumstances, as if those in attendance that evening had no agenda other than holiday celebrations and Shaxpere's presence amid them was hardly notable for all that he supposedly acted in the company. In fact, however, Marlowe's disappearance had been the subject of rumors and printed speculation for more than a year and many of those attending Gray's Inn that evening would have this question and its possible relationship to Southampton and his marriage negotiations very much in mind. While the objective of the invitation was not solely to settle this issue, its resolution was nevertheless central to its success. As for the play which was to be featured, no author was credited, not even in the Grayorum published ninety-four years after the event, a fact that would only have heightened the suspense over its outcome.

Essex, meanwhile, was in a somewhat awkward position due to the publication of A Conference About the Next Succession of the English Crown (1594). Printed in Antwerp but then circulating in London with a dedication to Essex, the book argued that he and Burghley were effectively on opposite sides of the question with Essex supporting James IV of Scotland and Burghley favoring Arbella Stuart, a subject Elizabeth naturally found distasteful and others found seditious. Essex had worked too hard to advance himself in the Queen's regard to have an anonymous pamphlet upset his position. The possibility of a staged reconciliation between his alma mater and Burghley's would both lower the temperature and serve his interests. The only question was what he could get for it in return.

The festivities stretched over two weeks, starting on the 20th of December, St. Thomas's Eve, concluding on January 3,

1595, and began with a gathering of several dozen hosts and an equal number of guests in the Great Hall. After a carefully staged round of introductions, salutes and a reading of the titles and tributes of the Prince or Purpoole, a Norfolk gentleman, Mr. Henry Helmes, "one accomplished with all good parts, a very proper man of personage, and very active in dancing and reveling,"[479] specially elected to preside over the event, made several declarations including a general pardon, in the excruciatingly elaborate language that characterized the event, for:

> "All and every publick Person and Persons, whether they be Strangers or Naturals, within Our Dominions be by virtue hereof excused, suspended and discharged from all, and all manner of Treasons, Contempts, Offences, Trespasses, Forcible Entries, Intrusions, Disseisins, Torts, Wrongs, Injuries, Over-throws, Over-thwartings, Cross-bitings, Coney-catchings, Frauds, Conclusions, Fictions, Fractions, Fashions, Fancies, or Ostentations: Also all, and all manner of Errors, Misprisions, Mistakings, Overtakings, Double-dealings, Combinations, Confederacies, Conjunctions, Oppositions, Interpositions, Suppositions and Suppositaries: Also all, and all manner of Intermedlance, or Medlance, Privy-searches, Routs and Riots, Incumberances, Pluralities, Formalities, Deformalities, Disturbances, Duplicities, Jeofails in Insufficiencies or Defects: Also all, and all manner of Sorceries, Inchantments, Conjurations, Spells, or Charms: All Destructions, Obstructions and Constructions: All Evasions, Invasions, Charges, Surcharges, Discharges, Commands, Countermands, Checks, Counter-checks and Counter-buffs: Also all, and all manner of Inhibitions, Prohibitions, Insurrections, Corrections, Conspiracies, Concavities, Coinings, Superfluities, Washings, Clippings and Shavings: All, and all manner of Multiplications,

Inanities, Installations, Destillations, Constillations, Necromancies and Incantations: All, and all manner of Mis-feasance, Non-feasance, or too much Feasance: All Attempts or Adventures, Skirmages, Assaults, Grapplings, Closings, or Encounters: All Mis-prisonments, or Restraints of Body or Member: And all, and all manner of Pains and Penalties, Personal or Pecuniary whatsoever, committed, made, or done against Our Crown and Dignity, Peace, Prerogatives, Laws and Customs, which shall not herein hereafter be in some sort expressed, mentioned, intended, or excepted."

The twenty exceptions to the pardon included:

"All such Persons as have, or shall have any Charge, Occasion, Chance, Opportunity, or possible Means to entertain, serve, recreate, delight, or discourse with any vertuous or honourable Lady or Gentlewoman, Matron or Maid, publickly, privately, or familiarly, and shall faint, fail, or be deemed to faint or fail in Courage, or Countenance, Semblance, Gesture, Voice, Speech, or Attempt, or in Act or Adventure, or in any other Matter, Thing, Manner, Mystery, or Accomplishment, due, decent, or appertinent to her or their Honour, Dignity, Desert, Expectation, Desire, Affection, Inclination, Allowance, or Acceptance; to be daunted, dismayed, or to stand mute, idle, frivolous, or defective, or otherwise dull, contrary, sullen, male-content, melancholy, or different from the Profession, Practice and Perfection of a compleat and consummate Gentleman or Courtier."

"All such Persons as shall maliciously and willingly burn or cut, or cause to be burned or cut, any Conduit, or Trough, Pipe, or any other Instrument used as means

> of Conveyance of any Liquor, Water, or other kind of Moisture."

and notably,

> "All Fugitives, Failers and Flinchers, that with Shame and Discredit are fled and vanished out of the Prince's Dominions of Purpoole, and especially from his Court at Graya, this time of Christmas, to withdraw themselves from His Honour's Service and Attendance, contrary to their Duty and Allegiance, and to their perpetual Ignominy, and incurable Loss of Credit and good Opinion, which belongeth to ingenious and well-minded Gentlemen."

Which is to say that, if anyone was still paying attention after all of this extravagant legalistic buffoonery, the fugitive, Christopher Marlowe, was not among the pardoned but was instead, specifically excluded.

With the welcomes, presentations and pardons exhausted, the first evening came to an end.

One week later on Innocents-Day Grays' Inn resumed its festivities with an unanticipated crowd. According to the <u>Grayorum,</u> "the common Report amongst all Strangers was so great, and the Expectation of our Proceedings so extraordinary, that it urged us to take upon us a greater State than was at the first intended." Apparently news had got out that something was up at Gray's Inn and a substantial audience had unexpectedly mobbed the Great Hall. A stage for the mock dignitaries, including the Prince of Purpool and the Lord Ambassador from the Inner Temple and their followers, had been set up at one end where they would be featured above the banquet and could view the planned entertainment, but "too many of those in attendance that night felt that their status warranted them a place on the stage, with the Prince"[480] and in the resulting tummult:

> "The Lord Ambassador and his train thought that they were not so kindly entertained as was before expected, and thereupon would not stay any longer at that time, but, in a sort, discontented and displeased. After their departure the throngs and tumults did somewhat cease, although so much of them continued, as was able to disorder and confound any good inventions whatsoever."

Despite this embarrassment, the evening continued more or less as planned, concluding with the debut of The Comedy of Errors which, "like to Plautus his Menechmus," presented two pairs of characters being confused for each other, much as the mock dignitaries who "in the fantasy of Purpool"[481] were purposely mistaken for the real Lords who remained behind to supervise the event which then came to be known as The Night of Errors.

As reported in the Gesta Grayorum, the "confusion" was the work of "a Sorcerer or Conjurer" and created such an outrage that he was brought back the following night to face a mock trial with charges including:

> "How he had caused the Stage to be built, and Scaffolds to be reared to the top of the House, to increase Expectation. Also how he had caused divers Ladies and Gentlewomen, and others of good Condition, to be invited to our Sports; also our dearest Friend, the State of Templaria, to be disgraced, and disappointed of their kind Entertainment, deserved and intended. Also that he caused Throngs and Tumults, Crowds and Outrages, to disturb our whole Proceedings. And Lastly, that he had foisted a Company of base and common Fellows, to make up our Disorders with a Play of Errors and Confusions; and that that Night had gained to us Discredit, and it self a Nickname of Errors. All which were against the Crown

and Dignity of our Sovereign Lord, the Prince of Purpoole."

For those in the remaining audience believing at that moment that this new play might indeed have been written by Christopher Marlowe, they would only have to recall that Robert Greene had referred to Marlowe as "bred of Merlin's race",[482] that he was often compared with his creation, the magician, Faustus, and that in The Unfortunate Traveller Nashe had included Cornelius Agrippa, "notorious in the sixteenth century as a magician . . . and it is in that role that he provides Marlowe with a prototype for the character of Doctor Faustus."[483]

Just as The Unfortunate Traveller featured an extended section in which Jack Wilton, under the influence of Agrippa, exchanges identities with Philip Sidney's stand-in, the Earl of Surrey, in order to allow them to travel undiscovered in Italy, so The Comedy of Errors underscored the significance of the event while allowing its authors to exchange covert allusions in plain sight. For all the ornamental triviality of the festival, the play was at the center of the event; it gave its name to it and it was included as a charge against the "Sorcerer".

Unmentioned in the charges, but included in the extant script of The Comedy of Errors, are direct responses to the ongoing war of words between Nashe and Harvey which itself was emblematic of the unresolved feud between Burghley and Essex. Specifically, in Act IV, Scene 4, when Dromio of Ephesus is introduced to Antipholus of Ephesus' wife Adriana, he remarks: "Mistress, *respice finem*, "respect your end" or rather, to prophesy, like the parrot, "beware the rope's end." In addition to outlining the line's sexual innuendo, The Arden Shakespeare further unpacks this line to explain that it "may also be alluding to Nashe's Strange News which satirizes the academic Gabriel Harvey being 'bidde, *Respice finem*, 'looke back to his father's house.' Harvey's father was a rope-maker, thus, says Nashe, 'thou dost liue by the gallows.'"[484]

Putting the ongoing conflict between Nashe and Harvey smack in the middle of The Comedy of Errors would not have gone unnoticed by the attendees at the Gray's Inn performance on Innocent's Day's night. Harvey would not have been irrational to view Dromio's "beware the rope's end" remark as a response to the closing lines of his Gorgon which appear to include a warning to Nashe (the Bull-beggar) by comparison with both the destruction of St. Paul's steeple by lightning in 1561 and "a hugyer thing" ie: Marlowe's own fall:

> Powles steeple, and a hugyer thing is downe:
> Beware the next Bull-beggar of the towne.

Earlier in the play, Dromio of Syracuse calls forth an image of Nashe's mockery of Harvey's parentage by echoing Robert Greene's description of "a bibulous, greedy and pitiless sergeant who arrests debtors"[485] in his Quip to an Upstart Courtier and it's allusion to a "rope-maker" whose eldest son fits Harvey's description. This sequence of pop culture references might seem obscure today, but would not have been to the "great Presence of Lords, Ladies, and worshipful Personages" in attendance on the Night of Errors, who knew of Quip as a best seller of six separate printings.

In this way a dispute that had begun as a principled, pseudonymous attack on ecclesiastical excess devolved into a personal argument over literary style which quickly descended via Greene and Nashe to ad hominem with a sudden, inconvenient detour into conspiracy theory by way of Harvey with Marlowe somehow stuck in the middle of Harvey's fevered allegations against Nashe. The question for Lord Burghley, the host of the Gray's Inn festivities, was apparently what to do about a squabble that had grown so public that it threatened to haphazardly expose all manner of carefully contrived deceptions. Having The Comedy of Errors featured as the main entertainment reveals that Marlowe had his own ideas about how best to handle his literary rivals. What no one quite foresaw was how this comedy might be received by others also implicated in the Nashe/Harvey discharge.

Together, the rope-maker wisecracks from the twin Dromios could easily be understood to be Marlowe's response to Harvey's allegations against Nashe in Gorgon with a warning no less salient, to wit: "Lay off or suffer the consequences." Of all the speeches that might have resonated most with the remaining members of the Inner Temple, this none too camouflaged warning would have been just the thing. This group, sponsors of the departed "Ambassador's Train" included the Earls of Shrewsbury, Cumberland, and Northumberland, the Earl of Southampton and the Earl of Essex, the author of Marlowe's exile. And yet, rather than follow their make-believe peers out the door, they remained, presumably because they agreed with the sentiment.

So, what was Shakspere's role in all of this? He is known as one of the three payees for the same day's court performance with Burbage and Will Kempe, but that doesn't necessarily mean that he also appeared at Gray's Inn. If he did appear at Gray's Inn with the cast of The Comedy of Errors, what did he actually do? Gabriel Harvey, who could lay claim to tutoring Edmund Spenser and was an authority on all things poetic, had never heard of him and was saying so in print, accusing Nashe of concocting a ruse to cover someone else's tracks, "binding" Venus with somebody named Shakespeare. Then, suddenly this man was onstage in front of an audience "so exceeding great, that thereby there was no convenient room for those that were actors."

Most scholars assume that Kempe, as the company's leading clown, played Dromio of Syracuse and Burbage Antipholus of Syracuse, these being the larger roles for of each pair twins, but Shakspere, for all the unbridled speculation given to his activities, has never been accused of playing major roles onstage. Why, then, would he be one of the three men paid for the performance? Up to that moment, Shakspere had been the invisible man; despite his modern reputation, at that time and place there was no record of him being involved with any of these people, Greene's "shake-scene" reference to Ned Alleyn notwithstanding.

It seems unlikely that he would have been considered the "Sorcerer or Conjurer that was supposed to be the Cause of that confused Inconvenience." That was a title that belonged more appropriately to the author, Marlowe, who was presumably out of town. He may, on the other hand, have "caused the Stage to be built, and Scaffolds to be reared to the top of the House, to increase Expectation." This would be very much in keeping with the role of a theatrical promoter, which many scholars accept as one of Shakespeare's occupations.

At the same time, Doctor Pinch, a character who appears only in Act IV, Scene 4, the scene with all of the Nashe/Harvey references, is repeatedly called a "conjurer" and attempts to exorcise a demon "housed within this man", Antipholus of Epheseus. Kent Cartwright in Appendix 3 of The Arden Shakespeare: The Comedy of Errors suggests that Shakespeare "as false conjuror has metatheatrical appeal."[486] This would be triply applicable if Shakspere, playing a role identified with Harvey due to his "saffron face"[487] is also understood to be standing in for Marlowe, aka "Merlin", as he works a spell on one of two theatrical twins.

The Harvey/Pinch identification is furthered by the published script which describes Pinch as a "schoolmaster", a title not included in the dialogue. Harvey, of course, was one of Marlowe's instructors at Cambridge, noted for his advocacy of hexameter verse and his close relationship with another student poet, Edmund Spencer. What could be more metatheatrical than having Shakspere play Pinch, a role identified with Harvey, the man who, in reference to the publication of Venus and Adonis the previous year, asserted that Nashe, "*dispos'd to cunnycatch the world*", knew that "*The hugest miracle remaines behinde*" after "*Tamburlaine voutsafes to dye*," especially if that "miracle" was understood to be Shakespeare, the man credited with writing that same poem, dedicated to the Earl of Southampton who was then watching that very performance? Sitting next to Southampton would be the Earl of Essex, the man that the similarly dedicated Rape of Lucrece had warned against. Shakspere, making what may have been his first public appearance, impersonating not only Harvey but also the man believed by some to be the true author of both poems, not to mention impersonating Shakespeare as well, the fictional person created by the poems, being warned onstage by a mis-identified servant twin to "beware the rope".

Shakspere in the role of Pinch could then be considered the "Conjurer that was supposed to be the Cause of that confused Inconvenience" because his very presence was not only the center of confusion but the very subject of the ongoing controversy between Burghley's Gray's Inn and the Essex's Inner Temple. As a result, the "conjurer" was detained, rechristened "The Prisoner" and, in keeping with the Night of Errors, was brought forth by the members of Gray's Inn before their guests of the Inner Temple the following evening, "arraigned at the Bar", and then allowed to plead his own case. He was certainly glib enough, claiming that:

> "all the Knavery and Juggling of the Attorney and Sollicitor, which had brought all this Law-stuff on purpose to blind the Eyes of his Excellency, and all the honourable Court there, going about to make them think, that those things which they all saw and preceived sensibly to be in very deed done, and actually performed, were nothing else but vain Illusions, Fancies, Dreams and Enchantments, and to be wrought and compassed by the Means of a poor harmless Wretch, that never had heard of such great Matters in all his Life."

These words have the ring of authenticity amid all the over written phrasing in the larger Grayorum. This being a law court, the Defendant could have had help preparing his testimony, but it is almost as if it is Shakspere himself who steps forward, full of brass, repeating ideas found in the play and improvising a perfect imitation of his betters to the crowd's surprise and delight. It is a performance consistent with his later reputation of having "a natural wit, without any art at all," a verdict reported as current among the locals by the Reverend John Ward, appointed vicar of Stratford upon Avon in 1662.[488] Consistent with the play's theme of mistaken identity and misapprehended messages, he argued that he was more confused than anyone, had never heard of or understood anything about any disputes between Nashe and Harvey, Prelates and Marprelates or Burghley and Essex (ie: "such great Matters") and could not thus be responsible for the audience's furious disarray.

Rather than accuse an absent magician, he put the blame on "the Negligence of the Prince's Council, Lords and Officers of his State, that had the Rule of the Roast, and by whose Advice the Commonwealth was so soundly mis-governed." Which is to say, he blamed Burghley. Amazingly, the Prince of Purpoole, perhaps speaking for Burghley, agreed and "thereupon the Prisoner was freed and pardoned" while "the Attorney, Sollicitor, Master of the Requests, and those that were acquainted with the Draught of the Petition, were all of them commanded to the Tower" ending the case.

Of course, no one actually went to the Tower as this was yet another fictive element in a fictitious parade of imitation jurists in an imaginary court for an audience of ersatz nobles. The one reality in all of this was that Shakspere, the counterfeit poet, had been publicly substituted for the real one and could thereafter carry on as if he was the true original. This wasn't an accident, this had been the entire purpose of the revels, the performance which had been interrupted by the previous Night of Errors but which, with a little improvisation, had been finally accomplished. It had all been for show; Burghley and Essex had obviously agreed on the design in advance and both recognized that the substitution had to be done publicly in order to put an end to the rumors being amplified by people like Gabriel Harvey. The success of the venture was assured by its very public presentation, leaving no doubt who endorsed it.

With the matter thus settled, the festivities were able to resume according to plan and the Inner Temple invitees were brought back on January 3rd for the grand conclusion, the third revel, a celebration of amity between Grays' Inn and the Inner Temple. With both inns gathered, a "Device" was presented which included a parade of classical friends, including Theseus and Perithous, then Achilles and Patroclus, then Pilades and Orestes; then Scipio and Lelius; each pair coming arm in arm, offering Incense upon the Altar to the Goddess of Amity, "which shined and burned very clear, without Blemish; which being done, they departed." The final pair, Graius and Templarius also offered incense but, burning dark and smoking, it was not accepted until the "Arch-Flamen" added some mystical chants and got the flame burning "more clear than at any time before" which finally satisfied the Goddess. The Arch-Flamen then pronounced the two Inns "True and Perfect Friends" "And Lastly, denounced an heavy Curse on them that shall any way go about to break or weaken the same; and an Happiness to them that study and labour to eternize it for ever."

The ceremonies closed as they had opened, with the Prince of Purpool making a proclamation, this time outlining "strict Rules of Arms, and Civil Government, religiously to be observed," including among a variety of absurdities, such as "No Knight of this Order shall have any more than one Mistress, for whose sake he shall be allowed to wear three Colours: But if he will have two Mistresses, then must he wear six Colours; and so forward, after the rate of three Colours to a Mistress." A string of similar rules followed, concluding with a declaration that "Every Knight of this Order shall endeavour to add Conference and Experience by Reading; and . . . also frequent the Theatre, and such like places of Experience."

Obviously, there was a lot of silliness mixed with a serious purpose. As the author of the Grayorum attested, the invitation and festivities represented a deliberate and successful effort to make peace between the two Inns of Court; it:

"was devised to that End, that those that were present might understand, that the Unkindness which was growing betwixt the Templarians and us, by reason of the former Night of Errors, and the uncivil Behaviour wherewith they were entertained as before I have partly touched, was now clean rooted out and forgotten."

The presentation of The Comedy of Errors by the Lord Chamberlain's Men, a play celebrating mistaken identities and doubles performed by the company patronized by Essex's uncle Henry Carey, Lord Hunsdon, swapping out Marlowe the Sorcerer for Shakspere the Wretch, resolved the issue of Marlowe's safety. While some innocent feathers got ruffled, in the end Shakspere was formally installed as Marlowe's double for all to see. No less significantly, Essex would have control through his uncle of the leading theatrical troupe at court and Marlowe would continue to write for it under an assumed name.

The irony is that the scholars who have been so busy speculating about Shakspere's activities have never stopped to consider that the Night of Errors could actually be the first documented appearance of their favorite, recorded in his own words, using his wits to charm an audience of skeptics. It is the very kind of performance that suits his character in contemporaneous accounts.

Consider the preparation needed to pull this off. Marlowe writes the bitter Lucrece in advance of Southampton's 21st birthday and afterward concocts the conciliatory Comedy of Errors. While there are no accounts confirming this, in fact all Privy Council records from this period are missing,[489] there are some separate reports that suggest how it might have been accomplished. Specifically, Robert Poley, the senior intelligencer present at the incident in Deptford, is known to have made three trips to the Continent between May, 1593, and December, 1594. On July 14th, 1593, he was "paid for couriering letters to and from France," in September he was "arrested in the Netherlands and examined by the States

General" after which he was released, and on August 19th, 1594, he was "paid for couriering letters to and from Brussels."[490] There is no record of the contents of Poley's courier's pouch, but his travels encompass the territory a recently exiled fellow English intelligencer familiar with the region could be expected to inhabit.

It is also worth noting that William Warner, the successful attorney of the common pleas and author of Albion's England, the same man who published the first notice of Marlowe as a playwright with his mention of Timon in his preface to Syrinx or A Sevenfold History (1584), is the same man whose translation of Menachmi (1595) is considered by many scholars to have been a possible source for Errors although, as Geoffrey Bullough admits, the author "doubtless knew enough Latin to read him in the original."[491] Warner's translation was registered with the Stationer on June 10th, 1594 but was not published until well after the Gray's Inn festivities, so Marlowe would have to have seen it in manuscript, if at all. More importantly for Marlowe, however, is the fact that Warner enjoyed the patronage of Henry Carey, Lord Hundston, the Lord Chamberlain, sponsor of the newly christened Lord Chamberlain's Men and uncle to Robert Deveraux, the Earl of Essex. A member of neither Gray's Inn nor the Inner Temple, he may have been capable of acting as a disinterested party, an honest broker between rival houses, helping to negotiate a much needed peace with Marlowe as the ultimate offering, guaranteeing his own safety by agreeing to work exclusively for Essex's uncle with The Comedy of Errors the first fruit of the bargain.

The Dr. Pinch scene, which derives from no prior source, was aimed at Harvey and probably was not intended to give other offense; that was instead accomplished by the over-crowded stage which caused the Inner Temple's Ambassador to depart "in a sort, discontented and displeased." Whether the subsequent trial of the Gray's Inn "Wretch" for this "mischanceful Accident" was improvised or pre-planned, the play also enlarged upon another scene not original to Plautus, the final reconciliation between Egon, the father of both Antipholi, and Emilia, his wife who survived the shipwreck that separated them with one of their sons and had since become an Abbess at Ephesus. This scene was the real point of the play and Marlowe clearly intended its message of reunion and restoration after untimely separation to carry the day. Bullough attributes this scene to John Gower's <u>Confessio Amatis</u>, but more personally and more significantly for Marlowe it echoes Philip Sidney's <u>Arcadia</u>, book 3 chapter 23, where Pyrocles is reunited with Philoclea, his wife separated from him and thought dead after a shipwreck. That this same excerpt inspired the denouement of <u>Pericles</u> fifteen years later is one more irony in the continuum of Marlowe's exile which not only did not end but was only beginning after The Night of Errors.

The <u>Gesta Grayorum</u> concludes with a report on the following month of activities, which included a mock embassy to Russia, a flotilla of fifteen barges on the Thames, a horseback procession "through Tower-street, Fen-church-street, Grace-church-street, Corn-hill, Cheap-side, and so through St. Paul's Church-yard; where, at St Paul's School, His Highness was entertained with an Oration," and finally, on to the court itself where:

> "there was fighting at Barriers; the Earl of Essex and others Challengers, and the Earl of Cumberland and his Company Defendants: Into which number, our Prince was taken, and behaved himself so valiantly and skilfully therein, that he had the Prize adjudged due unto him, which it pleased Her Majesty to deliver him with her own Hands; telling him, that it was not her Gift; for if it had, it should have been better; but she gave it him, as that Prize which was due to his Desert, and good Behaviour in those Exercises; and that hereafter he should be remembred with a better Reward from her self. The Prize was, a Jewel, set with

>seventeen Diamonds, and four Rubies; in value, accounted worth an hundred Marks."

This was how the agreement that Andrew Gurr imagines had been made between the Chamberlain's and Admiral's Men was actually formalized. It was part of a larger treaty between Essex and Burghley which, in fact, could not have been concluded until Essex managed to have his way with Southampton, keeping him out of Burghley's orbit. Burghley meanwhile got to take his pound, or £5,000, of equity from his former ward who was by then free to marry Essex's sister, which he finally did in 1598.

All of this was conducted in plain sight, celebrated in fact. The Queen was well aware of the entire festival and applauded its success. When the ceremony veered off course and the Templar's amateur ambassador was squeezed off the stage, Essex and Burghley improvised and turned an embarrassment into a showcase. In the process they had found an unlikely prodigy. Thrust into the spotlight, Shakspere performed better than they had any right to expect. He survived his baptism of fire and fully earned his place as a sharer in the Lord Chamberlain's company. He was, so to speak, a made-man. Not really an actor, certainly not a writer, he was, if the charges made by the Attorney and Sollicitor of Gray's Inn properly described him, a stage manager and promoter who "caused the Stage to be built, and Scaffolds to be reared to the top of the House, to increase Expectation" and "caused divers Ladies and Gentlewomen, and others of good Condition, to be invited to our Sports." In this role he fit perfectly into the Lord Chamberlain's company which lacked exactly that, someone to keep the playhouse in order. He was, in short, a business man presented with a golden opportunity and, if he kept his nose clean and didn't ask too many questions, he could count on the support of some of the most powerful people in England. It says quite a lot about him that he was able to pull it off. No one really knows what brought him to London in the first place, or when he first arrived, but he made the most of his opportunities with the same skills that he could have learned trading grain in Stratford.

Whatever else he may have been, however, he was not a writer. The student prosecutor of the Night of Errors did not charge him with writing anything pleasing or unpleasing. They all knew the difference between a poet and a promoter and they knew enough about the methods of writers to discern the source of the entertainment, which was "like to Plautus his Menechmus". The man who was to become in time the person known today as "William Shakespeare" was not then fully formed with an identity that had become a brand name capable of itself being purloined for other's use. He had just then stepped out on stage with contours that were even then being formulated. He had talent and he had energy. He had charm. He would do well. All of that was in the future. For the moment, he fit the bill and that would be enough for many years. He literally stepped into Marlowe's shoes when he took over the producer's chair for Pembroke's Men, a company formed by Marlowe, producing plays written specially for them by Marlowe, and then renamed with their new patron, the Lord Chamberlain under Essex's control.

The biggest loser in all of this was, of course, Christopher Marlowe. True, his safety had been secured, for the time being, but his hoped for return and restoration was even less likely than before. Where once there had been a vacuum he could hope to fill, suddenly there was someone in his way occupying that very space. What was left to him was poetry and playwrighting which he would shortly prove he could do better than anyone else, even if he had to do it in exile.

Chapter Eighteen

Publish or Perish

People who doubt that any group of conspirators high or low could have kept secret the identity of the author of the plays attributed to Shakespeare would do well to consider the contemporaneous example of the author of the Martin Marprelate pamphlets, a controversy which involved many of the same individuals and yet, despite the murderous and unending hostility of Archbishop Whitgift and his use of the full powers of the Privy Council, the Star Chamber and the minions of Anglican enforcement and notwithstanding the fact that the Archbishop was eventually able to destroy all the Marprelate printing presses and imprison and ultimately hang all of the suspects in the perpetration of the pseudonymous author's attacks on a corrupt clergy, to this very day that same antagonist has never had his identity discovered. None of the conspirators ever spoke his name even when racked, whipped, starved and interrogated for hours at a time by teams of hardened prelates who would not have been found wanting for employment in the Spanish Inquisition. Not all the scholars in the following four hundred years have been able to uncover the evidence that would tie the surreptitiously penned pamphlets to a specific hand. They know who printed them, who carried the type in what form and face from whence in Belgium and when, who owned and worked and hid the presses and who supplied them with paper and ink, who moved them and from what place to what place and when. They know who tended the printed pages, who folded them and stitched them together, who distributed the finished pamphlets, how many and to whom, how they were sold and how quickly, and for how much at what profit or loss. They know who searched for them and where, who tipped off the searchers and who kept silent, and how by the unlucky accident of an upended cart spilling its oddly shaped leaden contents in a village lane, they were ultimately discovered, and where and when. To the minute. But, they don't know who wrote the pamphlets; they don't know his name.

Martin Marprelate was important because he demonstrated the true power of the printing press to spark protest and undermine authority. His operation was necessarily small and his tenure brief, cut short by the extreme exercise of ecclesiastical excess he dared to expose and his destruction was intended to serve as an example to any others who might similarly aspire. But he shook the foundation of the English Church and made a madman out of Whitgift who ever after was on the watch for any future expression of discontent. Some people believe the real Martin was John Greenwood, hung in March of 1593 and alluded to in Titus Andronicus and As You Like It. Still others think he may have been Henry Barrow, who dared to visit Greenwood in jail and, having walked through the gate of his own accord, was himself never allowed to leave. Others believe Martin may have been John Penry, who died the night before Marlowe disappeared and may have had his body substituted before the Queen's Coroner to conceal Marlowe's escape. Still others think Martin may have been Marlowe. All of them went to Cambridge and were divinity scholars at about the same time. Marlowe once "yielded his place"492 in commons for Greenwood at Cambridge.

Gabriel Harvey was at Cambridge too. In his mind, the printing of Venus and Adonis became a mirror image of Martin Marprelate; although printed by Field, its issue was hurried and its author a pseudonym. When he accused Nashe of binding it, he added another layer of skuduggery. When Harvey wrote about the "*wonderment of* Eighty Eight" in Gorgon, *or the wonderfull yeare*, he was not referring just to the Armada, but also to the publication of the first Marprelate pamphlet, The Epistle, which was secretly published and distributed in that same year of 1588. When Harvey wrote: "*The fatall yeare of yeares is* Nintey Three" when "*thy* Tamburlaine *voutsafes to die*" he was comparing Martin Marprelate's Epistle with

"Shakespeare's" Venus and Adonis and drawing the conclusion that both were published under pseudonyms. And though the targets of the two pamphlets were very different, the first being Whitgift and the latter being Essex, both were members of the Privy Council and both wanted leverage over the crown which explained why criticism of them must be made from behind a mask. The Dutch Church Libel was of a piece in this. The proof is that the authorities reacted in a very similar fashion, rounding up Kyd, stretching him on the rack and searching his lodging for secret papers. Kyd, like Harvey, pointed to Marlowe who, whatever else may be said about him, left behind a mystery as enduring as the fate of Martin Marprelate.

Initially, the mystery was merely a name, made up more or less out of a simpler original, that floated like a "miracle" over St. Paul's churchyard. Later, that name was attached to a "wretch" who stood trial at Gray's Inn and, after arguing his own case before a heckling assembly of scholars, apprentices and hangers-on, was made a partner of the Lord Chamberlain's Men despite having no known talent or background in law, theatre or public address. The question remained however, as 1594 gave way to 1595, what this newly minted man of the theatre would do with this unexpected opportunity.

Between the date of his marriage license on November 27, 1582, when his name was spelled Shaxpere, the bond for the same on November 28, 1582, when his name was spelled Shakspeare, and the death of his unfortunate son, Hamnet, whose last name was spelled Shakspere, on August 11, 1596, nothing is known of the activities of Willim Shakspere except that he was paid under the name of William Shakespeare on March 15, 1595 with William Kempe and Richard Burbage by Sir Thomas Heneage "for twoe seuerall Comedies or Enterludes shewed by them before her maiestie in Christmas tyme laste paste viz vpon St Stephens daye & Innocents daye,"[493] December 27, 1594, which preceded the same evening's Night of Errors entertainment at Gray's Inn. At that point, two new biographies emerged out of the one fantasized biography of Shakespeare. The one is for Shakspere the businessman and the other is for Marlowe the poet and former intelligencer, both of whom followed very different paths from the one painted by modern scholarship and hagiography.

Shakspere, of course, was a very different person from the one depicted in legend. For one thing, he may not have been altogether literate. Certainly not in the sense of having mastery of the classics of antiquity, Ovid, Plutarch or Musaeus.

Inevitably, traditional scholars must confront the indisputable fact that there is no record of Shakspere ever attending any school anywhere ever. "Why should there be?"[494] some respond, exasperated with the very question, the answer to which is that by comparison the education of every other writer of any note in this period can be easily traced because, no matter what modern gatekeepers say, the acquisition of classical literary competency was unusual in the 16th century and the government, for reasons practical, religious and political, kept good records of who those highly literate people were, where they were and how they got there.

Standardized printing by means of moveable type was itself a recent innovation and the business of publishing for the general public was in its infancy and tightly controlled, the Stationers' Company having been chartered only in 1557. Books were not so plentifully cheap that they were featured on remainder shelves, there were no public libraries, no newspapers, and even by the end of the century, literacy was atypical:

> "Those who could read still came from the aristocracy and middle class; it depended on the occupation of the family whether a child would have the opportunity for a complete education. Only by the end of the seventeenth century, well after Shakespeare's death, was there a real interest in education for the poor with the development of 'charity schools.'"[495]

Traditionalists argue that John Shakspere, Willim's father, was "middle class", despite the fact that in 1576, when Willim would have been about twelve:

> "John decided to, or was made to, withdraw from public life in Stratford. He had been excused levies that he was supposed to pay by supportive townsmen and business associates and they kept his name on the rolls for a decade, perhaps hoping that in that time he would be able to return to public life and recover his financial situation, but he never did so."[496]

Both John and his wife, Mary, were illiterate as were both of Willim's daughters.

In the total absence of any record of any formal education or connection with anyone who may have tutored him with sufficient care to have ever made the slightest mention of taking the time or making the effort, traditional scholars frequently point to Richard Field as the most likely source for Willim's education and familiarity with the classics. As a native of Stratford and subsequent owner of a successful London print-shop, Richard Field seems like an ideal candidate for this task. Only two and a half years Shakspere's senior, contemporary records show that he apprenticed for six years under Thomas Vautrollier who published the 1587 edition of Holinshed's Chronicles, had the rights to Timothy Bright's Treatise of Melancholy, Ovid's Metamorphoses and Fasti in Latin, Thomas North's English translation of Plutarch's Lives and dozens of grammar books for Latin, French, Spanish and Italian.

When Vautrollier died in 1587, Field became partners with his widow, Jaqueline Vautrollier, a printer in her own right. In 1589 he married Jaqueline and succeeded to his master's business, becoming in time a leading member of the Stationer's Company. He did not, however, have and never had any of the larger collection of texts identified as source material for the plays and poems attributed to Shakespeare, including the

Geneva Bible, the Bishop's Bible, and The Book of Common Prayer, The Decameron, Arthur Brooke's, The Tragical History of Romeus and Juliet, Holinshed's Chronicles of England, Scotland, and Ireland, Samuel Daniel's The Civil Wars between the Two Houses of Lancaster and York, the plays of Plautus and Terence, or the Gesta Danorum (Deeds of the Danes) by Saxo Grammaticus.[497] On top of which, Field essentially severed his relationship with Shakespeare the "poet" in mid 1594 when he sold the rights to Venus and Adonis to publisher and bookseller John Harrison the Elder who also published Lucrece. Field continued to print for Harrison, including several additional issues of Venus and Adonis, but did not print Lucrece and did not print any of the plays. While traditional scholars consistently assert that a close friendship existed between poet and printer, the actual record reveals no sign of that and no reason why Field would want to allow anyone to nose around in the back of his shop reading manuscripts he was bound to protect or thumbing copies of books he hoped to sell.

In 1594 and 1595 very little is known of Shakspere's activities. Apart from the court performances, there are no records for any other performances by the Lord Chamberlain's Men and no records for Shakspere the man in these years. He may have been friends with the Burbages and other members of the company, including possibly John Hemmings who shows up as payee with George Bryan for the 1595 court performances and, along with Richard Condell and Burbage, made it into Shakspere's will.

The Lord Chamberlain's Men did not keep the close records that Henslowe famously did for the Lord Admiral's Men. Whether or not Burbage, Hemmings or Shakspere wrote down much of anything, none of it has survived. What little is known of their activities is that on February 6, 1596, John Burbage bought property in Blackfriars, site of a former monastery, apparently with a plan to convert the rooms into England's first purpose-built indoor theater. The plan was blocked by a petition in the neighborhood, which included signatory Richard

Field acting nothing like a man who wanted Shakspere and his chums hanging about. Instead, the space was rented to The Children of the Chapel, a boys company under the management of Nathaniel Giles who had taken to impressing children against their parent's will. Challenged over the legality over this exercise of his warrant in 1600[498], he nevertheless continued to stage entertainments with boys for the crown until the fashion waned in 1608 without further interference from the neighborhood.

The Lord Chamberlain's Men are known to have played from June 3rd to the 13th 1594 with the Lord Admiral's Men at Newington Butts. They are also credited with performances on December 26th and 27th, 1594 at Court and Grey's Inn on the 27th, and on January 3rd, 1595 at Court. The following year they played at court on December 26th, 27th and 28th and on January 6th, and February 22nd, 1596. Presumably, they continued to play at The Theatre throughout, but there are no records for any of it. Most of their activities in 1594 and 1595 can only be traced in the sale of scripts. In fact, they appear to have been very much in the business of making a market in play scripts, a practice which got its real start with John Lyly in 1584 but, with Lyly, fell out of fashion until it got a significant boost from Robert Greene and Christopher Marlowe.

When he died in 1592, Greene unquestionably owned the title of "the most successful English print author."[499] With 31 titles then in print, including nine that had been reprinted by then and one, <u>A Quip For An Upstart Courtier</u>, the volume that figured so prominently in the Harvey/Nashe squabble and which was referenced in <u>The Comedy of Errors</u>, reprinted six times in 1592 alone, Greene almost singlehandedly created the idea of the professional writer. Of all of this activity, however, none of his many plays had made it into print by 1594. The distinction of making playwrighting in print a profitable sideline seems to have been an innovation of the Lord Chamberlain's Men with an unintended boost from

Christopher Marlowe who left them in possession of a collection of very valuable, decidedly marketable plays.

While Lyly's plays had been reprinted multiple times in 1584, in particular Campaspe and Sappho and Phao, and three others, Endimion, Galathea, and Midas had seen print in 1591/2, Lyly's plays were primarily played by boys companies for court audiences. It was not until the publication of Marlowe's Tamburlaine the Great in 1590 that the market potential for plays performed for the general public was established. Originally printed as a single edition combining both parts one and two, it was reprinted in single parts in 1590 and again as a combined edition and separate individual parts in 1593500. Tamburlaine was so successful as a two part volume that the 1591 first edition of The Troublesome Raigne of King John apparently tried to mimic the format and was titled The First and Second Part even though it was merely one play.

Subsequent publications between 1591 and 1594 include Marlowe's Arden of Faversham, Lyly's trio, Kyd's Spanish Tragedy and Soliman and Perseda, "essentially an elaboration of the play-within-a-play in the last act of The Spanish Tragedy"501 and Marlowe's Edward II. While none of these matched the runaway success of Tamburlaine, it was clear by 1594 that a larger market was ready to be tapped if saleable scripts could be found. As it happened, when the Lord Chamberlain's Men pulled itself together in early 1594, it found itself in possession of a trove of plays written by Christopher Marlowe, the most popular playwright on stage and soon to be in print. This included scripts for Arden of Faversham, Edward II, Edward III, The Contention, The True Tragedy, Henry VI, Midsummer Night's Dream, Richard III, Romeo and Juliet, The Taming of A Shrew, Titus Andronicus and Two Gentlemen of Verona.

Again, without any record of performances it is difficult to assess the financial state of the company, but for whatever reason it soon decided to test the potential of its stock in the new territory of publishing. Selling rights to publish did not necessarily mean that any right to perform had to be surrendered, so the only question was whether or not a publisher would take the risk of advancing capital on an unknown commodity. The best way to overcome that hurdle was to offer recognizable product from a proven hand.

An ordinary person who comes to London with no particular skill but with an eye for opportunity and an interest in business, falling in with a group of actors whose main asset during an extended period when the play house is closed is a collection of plays by a well-known, popular and notorious playwright and who notices perhaps that another play written for a competing company, <u>Dr. Faustus</u> perhaps, has recently been published and, like <u>Venus and Adonis,</u> is selling out at St. Paul's, might suggest that selling some of this same author's plays would be a way to sustain the company in the short run, especially if, despite selling the them to a publisher outright, the company could retain the right to continue to perform them.

It wouldn't take a genius to observe that in mid 1594, the moment at which Shakspere had his notoriety publicly confirmed and his presence accepted by the social and political elite, that the publishing world had simultaneously been deprived of several of its most profitable authors, Greene, Harvey, Kyd and Marlowe. Into this gap stepped Shakspere with a trove of riches that seemed to be his alone to plunder. That all of these plays once belonged to Pembroke's Men and now were the property of the Lord Chamberlain's was simply opportune. That they had been written by Marlowe was especially beneficial because of their innate quality and sudden notoriety.

It has frequently been observed that Pembroke's Men sold off their plays almost as quickly as they sold off their costumes. Still, somebody had to step forward to negotiate such sales of texts, to find publishers willing to take the risk and to split the proceeds appropriately. Once Shakspere stepped forward, with his knowledge of trading in grain and land, he would have seemed as logical a choice as he was for the role of theatrical manager, doing a job that no one else wanted to do and providing for his company by doing it. Presumably, as one of the Company's three senior shareholders, none of the scripts could be sold without his approval.

The first to be published, of course, was <u>Titus Andronicus</u> most likely because its disputed ownership meant that whoever sold it first would reap the greatest benefit. This was quickly followed by the registration of <u>Edward II</u> and <u>The Massacre at Paris</u>, both of which also had equally uncertain provenance. This is characteristic of a man of business thinking carefully about his prospects for success. The investment cost him nothing and he could keep a separate share for himself as the agent funneling texts to the publishers.

This was a man who had not been involved in any of the politics that had so consumed London and its theaters for the previous decade. None of that seemed to bother him very much. Shakespere was just such a man.

Even when he was dragged into the middle of it on the Night of Errors, he appears to have shrugged it off as if either he didn't understand it or didn't care to concern himself with it. It must have seemed all rather remarkable to him, a bit like walking into the middle of war zone during a brief cease fire. And strangely, it seemed as though he had been drafted by both of the chief generals which meant that everyone involved had to be nice to him whether they wanted to or not. The first publisher he engaged, Thomas Millington, had registered <u>The Jew of Malta</u> and was soon to handle most of Marlowe's original Pembroke Plays.

From 1584, when the first Elizabethan era play was printed to 1589, only four plays were registered:

> April 6, 1584, Thomas Cadman: <u>Sappio</u> by Lyllye: "if he get ye comedy lawfully allowed to him."

> November 12, 1584, Thomas Hackett: <u>Fedele et Fortuna</u>. The deceits in love discoursed in a Commedia of il Italian gent, and translated into English.

April 1, 1585, Gabriel Cawood: <u>Tityrus and Galaten</u>. A Comedy.

Oct. 28, 1588, Richard Jones: Pageant before Martin Calthrop, L. Mayor, 29th Oct. 1588, by G. Peele. "Upon condition that it may be licensed."

None of these were by Marlowe. From June, 1590, through February, 1593, twelve plays were registered[502], four of them by Marlowe, including <u>Tamburlaine Parts 1 & 2</u>, <u>Arden of Faversham</u>, and <u>Edward II</u>. <u>Tamburlaine Parts One and Two</u> were printed together in one volume in 1590 and promptly sold out. Separate copies of each play were also printed and also sold out. Second editions of both the combined and individual plays were printed in 1592. As no other plays were reprinted in this period, Marlowe could be counted as having eight of sixteen total plays then in circulation. And then there is <u>The Massacre At Paris</u>, registered by Nicholas Ling and Thomas Millington on May 17, 1594, published in an undated octavo, but performed as <u>The Tragedy of the Guise</u> by Lord Strange's Men on January 26, 1593. Suspicion that the octavo was a pirated reconstruction[503] makes it possible to slip it in under the wire, to give Marlowe a hypothetical nine of the total seventeen plays printed or registered in the thirty three months between June of 1590 and February of 1593. Anyone who can credibly claim to be responsible for more than half of an entire genre has to be considered a market maker.

It is well worth taking a moment to examine more closely the sequence of Marlowe's early plays as they were published:

1. <u>Tamburlaine Parts I and II</u>, The two comical discourses of "Tomberlein the Cithian shepparde.", August 14, 1590. Richard Jones, publisher/printer was an innovative and "discerning publisher"[504]. During his long career, beginning around 1564 and probably ending with his last entry in the Stationers' Register in 1602, Jones worked

as bookseller, publisher, and printer. He is now of interest to cultural bibliographers because of the way he articulated his role as a publisher and discriminating reader through the "virtually unrivalled amount of prefatory material" he wrote for the books he published.[505] Jones specialised in publishing and printing broadside ballads and small to median-sized books of vernacular poetry, including verse anthologies like A Handefull of Pleasant Delites, A Gorgious Gallery of Gallant Inventions and Brittons Bowre of Delights. Poetry books were attractive to publishers because they sold reasonably well, with "a sufficient – if not great – number of customers", and there was always a "steady supply of new material"[506].

2. Doctor Faustus, entered in Stationers' Register on December 18, 1592, though the records are confused and appear to indicate a conflict over the rights to the play.[507]

Although the first performance references are to the Lord Admiral's Men's repertoire at the Rose in 1594 - with Edward Alleyn in the lead, there are indications that the play had been performed at least two years earlier. According to Simon Trussler, "the Admiral's are conjectured to have purchased the prompt-book from the company of Pembroke's Men which may have performed the play at court during the Christmas celebrations of 1592, and possibly at the Theatre in Shoreditch during a brief abatement of the plague in 1593."[508]

As for the dating of the play's composition, according to the Warwick Centre for the Study of the Renaissance, the jury is still out:

"if some scholars argue that The Tragical History of Doctor Faustus has been composed around 1592 - at the peak of Marlowe's dramatic career, others believe it followed shortly after the composition of his Tamburlaine, thus dating back to 1588/90."[509]

3. Massacre at Paris, June 19, 1593(?). Lord Strange's Men acted a play titled The Tragedy of the Guise, thought to be Marlowe's play, on January 26, 1593. The only surviving text is an undated octavo edition, that at 1,250 or so lines seems too short to represent the complete original play. Printed by A. E. for Edward White.

4. Edward II, 1594, by Christopher Marlowe, "As it was sundrie times publicly acted in the honorable citie of London by the Lord Pembroke's Men." Entered in the Stationers' Register on July 6, 1593, five weeks after Marlowe's death. The earliest extant edition was published in octavo in 1594, printed by Robert Robinson for William Jones.

5. Dido, Queen of Carthage, 1594. by Christopher Marlowe and Tos. Nashe. Printed by the Widdowe Orwin for Thomas Woodcocke.

6. The Jew of Malta, entered in the Stationers' Register in 1594 by Thomas Millington and Nicholas Ling,

The question arises as to how the scripts found their way to their publishers. Greene's comment that he sold the rights to Orlando Furioso to both Ned Alleyn and The Queen's Men suggests that authors were well aware of the marketability for their scripts. Marlowe was not a dope. Seeing the profits turned by Tamburlaine would inevitably cause him to want to take part more directly in the sale of his scripts. If Greene acted as his own agent, Marlowe could too, so he could as easily have been the conduit for publication as anyone and like Greene with Orlando he appears to have sold directly to Alleyn with The Jew of Malta. His movement between companies during this period, culminating with the formation of his own company, Pembroke's Men, increases the likelihood that he chose when and to whom his scripts would be sold and under what license.

When Marlowe disappeared, there was a sudden gap in that connection between the scripts and their publishers. Meanwhile, there were half a dozen scripts extant that were unpublished. Most of these scripts were in the hands of the remnants of Pembroke's Men. Who then stepped up to move them into print? The new face on the scene was Shakspere.

By virtue of having his embellished name attached to Venus and Adonis, and his relationship, whatever it may have been, with Field, it is reasonable to say that Shakspere was familiar with some of the leading printers of the day. From June, 1593, he could easily have been the main conduit for moving Marlowe's plays into the print. Knowing Field, but not being a writer, it would have been in his interest to find out as much as he could about the guild that controlled the trade. He could do that by peddling scripts to the highest bidder, making a market in texts that had a proven audience both at the playhouse and in the bookstalls: Marlowe. Alleyn wasn't about to sell Jew and Tamburlaine was already gone; that left the bulk of Marlowe's product under Shakspere's effective control. Publishing a play did not mean giving up performance rights and selling them one by one to various dealers meant that the name would stay in the public mind while the theaters were closed while providing the company the income to keep itself afloat. And there was the added benefit of the missing person controversy, kept afloat by Harvey and Nashe, to boost sales.

In 1594, the following plays that can be attributed to Marlowe appeared in print: Titus Andronicus, The First Part of the Contention Between the Two Famous Houses of York and Lancaster, The Taming of A Shrew, The most famous Chronicle History of Leire King of England and his three daughters, The tragedy of Richard III. Also appearing that same year was another play with a very unusual connection to Marlowe, Locrine. The continuity in these sales argues that they were part of an evolving market strategy that a man of business with a talent for trading in goods would have been better capable of implementing than a landlord or actor, as the Burbage's were. Each of these is worth reviewing more closely.

1. Titus Andronicus, 1594, "As it was plaide by the Right Honorable the Earle of Darbie [nee Lord Strange], Earle of Pembroke and Earle of Sussex their Seruants". Printed by Jon Danter to be sold by Edward White & Thomas Millington. No author credit; entered into Stationer's Liber B on February 6, 1594.

   Titus was still a popular play, but its ownership appears to have been in some dispute with both the Admiral's Men, by way of Strange, and the Lord Chamberlain's Men, by way of Pembroke, able to lay claim to it. This could be the primary reason why it got published when it did. In order to prevent the Admiral's Men from trying to cash in on a play they no longer controlled but still possessed, the Lord Chamberlain's Men decided to publish it first, precluding the possibility that the Admiral's Men could do the same. Millington is particularly important here because his presence establishes a link with Pembroke's archive that continued through The Contention and The True Tragedy.

2. The First Part of the Contention Between the Two Famous Houses of York and Lancaster, 1594, produced by Lord Pembroke's Men, printed by John Creed for Thomas Millington, no author credit; entered to the Stationer's Register, Liber B on March 12, 1594 as "the firste parte of the Contention of the two famous houses of York and Lancaster with the deathe of the good Duke Humfrey and the banishement and Deathe of the Duke of Suffolk and the tragicall ende of the prowd Cardinall of Winchester / with the notable rebellion of Jack Cade and the Duke of Yorkes ffirste clayme vnto the Crowne."

   The early printing of the Henry VI duo and Shrew suggest that these were the first to be replaced with new versions. If so, 1594 is very early for this. Also,

Shakspere has not yet been introduced via Errors, so the question is whether or not he played a role in these sales.

3. The Taming of A Shrew, entered in the Stationers' Register May 2, 1594, performed "sundrie times" by Pembroke's Men; no author credit. Printed by Peter Short for Cuthbert Burbie. Burbie published The Unfortunate Traveller.

4. The most famous Chronicle History of Leire King of England and his three daughters. Entered in the Stationers' Register May 12, 1594 for Thomas Creede. Marlowe's contribution to this play is discussed in Chapter Eight.

5. The tragedy of Richard III., wherein is shown the death of Edward IV., with the smothering of the two princes in the Tower, with a lamentable end of Shores' wife and the conjunction of the two houses of Lancaster and York. An enterlude. Entered in the Stationers' Register June 19, 1594, for Thomas Creede. This was part IV of the Henry VI plays, not the Queen's Men version.

6. Finally, there was Locrine which was not written by Marlowe but appears to have come to the Lord Chamberlain's Men by way of Marlowe's association with Sir Francis Walsingham. It also stands as an early attempt, not just by Shakspere but by anyone, to pursue a branding strategy between two venues, publishing and the theater, not as a playwright but as an editor.

   On July 20, 1594, The Lamentable Tragedy of Locrine, the Eldest Son of King Brutus was entered into Stationers' Liber B by Thomas Creede. Printed sometime between November 1595 and March 1596, the title page bears the line "Newly set foorth, ouerseene and corrected, By W.S." and thirteen quarto copies exist for the 1595 publication

Registered only four months after The Contention, the W.S. attribution suggests that Shakspere may well have been working closely with the Lord Chamberlain's Men even before they played with the Admiral's Men at Newington Butts. According to Michael Delahoyde, "Locrine seems to have belonged to the Queen's Men despite the absence of any record of performance."[510] Various scholars, from Baldwin Maxwell[511] to R. B. McKerrow[512], have assumed that the W.S. must refer to another writer with those initials such as Wentworth Smith for whom no other works survive. His career, however, as recorded by the intrepid Henslowe lasted barely two years, starting in April, 1601 and lasting into March, 1603.[513] There is also the case of William Smith; sometimes mistaken for Wentworth Smith, he was a poet and friend of Edmund Spenser and was active between 1591 and 1596.[514] Other scholars, including Katherine Duncan Jones[515] and Lucas Erne[516], focusing on the nuances of what may be implied by "Newly set foorth, overseene and corrected," suggest that these initials may well refer to the first appearance of Shakespeare's initials in print as a reviser or editor of the play, which is generally believed to date from some years earlier.

Supporting this analysis is the fact that the first attribution of the play was to Charles Tilney, one of the Queen's personal bodyguards[517] before he was executed in 1586 for being part of the Babington Plot. Master of Revels Edmund Tilney's twenty-five year old cousin, Charles was credited with the authorship of Locrine in a handwritten note attached to an autographed copy of the 1595 quarto by Sir George Buck, Edmund Tilney's "relation by marriage"[518] and successor as Master of Revels[519]. Walsingham could then have handed it off as a curiosity for evaluation to Marlowe or Watson, which would account for the fact that, as Benjamin Griffin summarized it, "investigations of the revision-process have suggested that the Marlovian rant and crude gigantism of Locrine belong to the revisions."[520] Whether the actual reviser was Marlowe, Watson or Peele under the influence of Marlowe, it would have been Marlowe who kept the manuscript with him during the creation of Pembroke's Men so that when that company dissolved it, along with so many other scripts actually written by Marlowe, fell into the lap of the Lord Chamberlain's Men.

Members of Pembroke's Men who knew Marlowe, in particular Richard Burbage, would have been able to tell Shaxper that Locrine was not Marlowe's play and W. S., who had already had a version of his name tacked onto Venus and Adonis and Lucrece, both of which had been approved by Burghley, apparently could not resist the opportunity of adding his initials to an otherwise unattributed play. He might have asked Burghley about it, if he could get word to him, but Burghley might not have cared even if he knew that Tilney was the source or he might have been amused at the idea. At any rate, W.S. took advantage and got his name in print as a man of the theatre for the first time. As Katherine Duncan-Jones asserted, "such a link would be a good selling point for what is, in truth, a fairly undistinguished 'medley' play."[521] No one would think Shakspere had actually written it because it was too old for that. But, he could have "corrected" it and then added his initials as an experiment which, apparently, did not go well because he would not try it again until nearly five years later in 1598.

What Edmund Tilney thought of all this is another matter. He was still Master of Revels in 1595 and it was his unfortunate, some would say traitorous, nephew's manuscript that was being appropriated after all. If he wanted all memory of that incident to remain buried, then having the play suddenly resurface cannot have been a welcome sight. It's hard to think of any good reason that he might have had to want to see it published, but published it was.

Katherine Duncan-Jones, who devoutly believes that Shakspere wrote all the poems and plays credited him via his nom-de-plume, nevertheless pictures his activities in this period as less than literary:

> "he perhaps fulfilled the offices of book-keeper and stage keeper. His book-keeping job was to prepare the master copy of each play performed, and also to pen the 'parts', with cues, to be conned by individual actors. His stage-keeping job was to direct performances to ensure that performers were ready on cue, that all physical action, including dumb shows, was correctly performed, and perhaps to act as prompter."[522]

This seems like a fair description of the roles that an uneducated country boy could have handled. With the theaters closed, he may also have acted as literary agent to the publishers, a role he could have been expected to understand. In this way, he would be providing support for the entire company while netting a percentage for himself. It would be much less of a stretch to add to these duties the odd sale of an old, neglected script as opposed to the wholesale creation of a completely new one.

Two other plays of Marlowe's were published shortly after the initial burst in 1594. This essentially cleaned out the Pembroke closet as new plays and revisions began to appear, including The Comedy of Errors and Love's Labour's Lost.

7. The True Tragedy of Richard Duke of York (later Henry VI, Part 3), 1595, produced by Lord Pembroke's Men, printed by P. S. [Peter Short] for Thomas Millington who, with Nicholas Ling, entered The Massacre at Paris in the Stationers' Register in 1594, no author credit;

8. Edward III, 1596, printed by Cuthbert Burby, no author credit; entered in Liber C of the Stationers' Company on December 1, 1595 as "The Raigne of King Edward the Third as it has been played sundrie times about the citie of London." Attribution of this play to Marlowe is supported by A. D. Wraight[523], Robert A. J. Matthews[524], Thomas V. N. Merriam[525], and most recently, but qualified as "purely speculative", by Richard Proudfoot and Nicola Bennett[526], editors of Edward III for the Arden Shakespeare. More importantly, Robert Greene, Marlowe's contemporary, attributed it to him in 1590 in Francesco's Fortunes.

Except for Locrine, which Marlowe may have touched up, all the plays sold by the Lord Chamberlain's Men in this period were by Marlowe. When Shakspere put his initials on Locrine he was not claiming to be an author, he was claiming to be an editor with the clear intent of linking himself to the other plays then being put on the market. As the only person identified in the process other than the publishers and printers, he must inevitably be considered the one most likely to have acted on behalf of his company partners as an agent for the sales. Diana Price argues against the possibility that any of this was done surreptitiously:

> "Any financial interest in play scripts that Shakspere retained as a theatre shareholder, or retained as the owner, was subverted by the theft of Shakespeare plays. Shakspere therefore stood to lose hard cash from any unauthorized sale of the Shakespeare plays - *unless Shakspere himself stood to gain by that sale.*"[527]

The fact that so many plays were sold so quickly argues that they were sold by agreement among the company sharers, not by unauthorized parties. Shakspere was evidently the middleman in the exchange and when it was possible for him to add his name to an otherwise unattributable script, he did so.

Apparently, the fact that Locrine was tied to a man accused of being a notorious traitor was not sufficient to discourage him from taking advantage of the opportunity to add his name to its publication. It wasn't the first time he'd done something like that. In a business where John Wolfe, the enforcer of the Stationer's company had started in the business as a pirate of manuscripts, and in an era when one of the most popular authors wrote under the pseudonym of Marprelate and who remained obscure despite all efforts to uncover him, Shakspere found he could fit right in.

Chapter Nineteen

Love on the Run

While Shakspere was out making a market in Marlowe's old scripts and otherwise cleaning up backstage, Marlowe was stuck in Flushing or someplace like it brooding about how he'd been sacrificed to Essex's ambition and trying to write his way back into London's good graces. By then he'd unloaded his anger by attacking Essex via Lucrece and had played along with Burghley's hostage swap by way of the Night of Errors. When neither gambit resulted in the restoration he'd hoped for, he seems to have thought that perhaps by reminding the court of the good old days and his connection with Philip Sidney he could win them over at last and gain a measure of forgiveness, perhaps even redemption. The result was a play presented in the 1594/5 holiday season, Love's Labour's Lost.

Something like a sequel to the Night of Errors and the Gray's Inn Revels, Love's Labour's Lost satirized and celebrated the brief peace that had been made between the Essex and Burleigh factions while weaving it together with themes and characters inspired by Sidney's own court entertainments, notably The Lady of May, which "was written specifically for her [the Queen's] entertainment during a visit to Leicester's house at Wanstead, in Essex, in May, 1578."[528] A brief one act, The Lady of May centers around the romantic competition between two shepherds and their four supporters for the hand of the title character. The play climaxes with the Queen choosing between the suitors, but not before a pedantic pedagogue named Rhombus pontificates in theatrical pig Latin on the nature of the contest and its rivals, a device that is echoed in Love's Labor's Lost with the competition between Don Armado and Costard over Jacquinetta as overseen by Holofernes. Love's Labor's Lost expands on the original, giving the four additional shepherd/suitors their own romantic

297

interests, specifically the King of Navarre and three courtiers who swear to live and study three years at court keeping apart from all distractions including the fairer sex. This vow of celibacy is promptly challenged by the arrival of the Princess of France and three of her most attractive chamber maids who have come to Navarre seeking repayment of a debt due to the King of France. Apart from the intrigue and playful wit that ensues, what makes this source material most interesting for scholars is the fact that The Lady of May was not in fact published until 1598, making it very difficult for them to understand how it could have been the basis for a play performed in December, 1595.

The extraordinary hesitancy of Stratfordian scholars with regard to drawing conclusions from the facts is the natural consequence of their understandable fear of venturing too far out on the narrow and unstable scaffolding supporting their precarious point of view. One clear example of this timidity is their general inability to confirm that George Chapman is indeed the "rival poet" of sonnets 74 to 86 because doing so repudiates the notion that Shakspere had any hand in writing those sonnets. A very similar demonstration of this behavior is the connection between the personality of Holoferenes and Rhombus which was first noticed by Samuel Johnson who wrote that he "considered the character of Holofernes as borrowed from the Rhombus of Philip Sidney who, in a kind of pastoral entertainment exhibited to Queen Elizabeth[529], has introduced a schoolmaster so called, speaking 'a leash of languages at once' and puzzling himself and his auditors with a jargon like that of Holofernes."[530] Despite this clear insight, modern editors such as H. R. Woudhuysen have difficulty accepting Sidney's The Lady of May as a source for Love's Labour's Lost, asserting that "unless he had access to a manuscript version, how could Shakespeare have seen it?"[531] The answer, of course, is that Shakspere didn't, Marlowe did. With his personal motto attesting in 1585 to his familiarity with Sidney's then unpublished Astrophel and Stella, Marlowe demonstrably had ample access to Sidney's poetry well before he spent the summer of 1592 under Lady Pembroke's wing creating a theatre company in honor of her son and her deceased brother Philip Sidney's nephew.

The origin of Holofernes has also been traced to Sidney's Defense of Poetry. Richard Proudfoot cited its criticism of "a self-wise-seeming schoolmaster" as a source for the character in Essays and Studies[532] and H. H. Furness noted in the New Variorum Shakespeare that the connection has been made as early as 1863.[533] The Defense of Poetry was not published until 1595 and, like The Lady of May, was available only in manuscript before publication. In fact, Love's Labor's Lost, which was not published until 1598, is so indebted to Sidney that Samuel Coleridge observed as early as 1836 that its "mere style of narration . . . seems imitated with its defects and beauties from Sir Philip Sidney".[534]

Unable to explain how Shakespeare could possibly have such intimate knowledge of Sidney's personal life and poetry, Modern scholars perpetually attempt to discover alternate avenues by which he could have gained substitute inspiration that "just may as well have come out of common Renaissance literary culture."[535] This claim, that the author could "reverse engineer" familiarity with Sidney's world view falls flat because, very simply, it would require a working knowledge of that world view in order to replicate it. It is again, the same type of *post hoc ergo propter hoc* reasoning that assumes Shakespeare had an education because he is credited with plays and poetry that would require an education to create.

Sidney's resonance in Love's Labour's Lost goes well beyond the setting or the connection to Holofernes. Specifically, Glynne Wickham has pointed out that when Katherine, one of the Princess' ladies in waiting, remarks that she had seen Dumaine "at the Duke of Alanson's once", I.1.61, it is not only the first of three references to this meeting, but it is more significantly a direct allusion to Sidney's famous Four Foster Children of Desire tiltyard entertainment presented before the Queen in May, 1581 upon the visit of her then suitor, the Duc d' Alençon, heir to the French throne. Wickham makes clear that this was not merely a topical refence to a dimly remembered event, but that it signals a deeper presence in the plot by outlining the similarities between the play and the Four Foster Children:

> "the four noble knight-jousters are transformed into the King of Navarre and his three courtier-companions: Berowne, Dumaine and Longaville. The emblematic cipher of Perfect Beauty (alias the Virgin Queen Elizabeth and her virginal attendants) is similarly metamorphosed into the Princess of France and her ladies-in-waiting: Rosaline, Maria and Katherine. The two day assault in the tiltyard on this 'Castle' is likewise maintained in the double encounter between the men and the women in the play - first through the Masque of Muscovites, and then through the Pageant of the Nine Worthies."[536]

The importance of this pageant has been discussed earlier in Chapter Seven, "Philip Sidney's Device". A. C. Hamilton described it as "devised for a highly politicized occasion, it is a unique cultural text, the only one written by a major Elizabethan poet who knew the Court and the life of a courtier at first hand."[537] Elizabeth and her 1595 court would have recognized the similarity between the play and the pageant immediately. The pageant was originally performed in 1581, about the time of Sidney's composition of Astrophil and Stella which notably produced the source for Marlowe's motto. That Marlowe would build a play based on this original is entirely fitting if what he hoped to do was link himself in the mind of the court with its sainted poet and his mentor.

Not surprisingly, Glynne also finds parallels among the specific characters, notably Berowne, the lead character who "is as convincing a portrait as may be imagined of the romantic Renaissance ideal of young manhood that Sidney himself sought to present to the world."[538] Berowne, who soon falls in love with Rosaline, starts the play quibbling about the specifics of his three year commitment to isolated scholarship:

> "O, these are barren tasks, too hard to keep:
> Not to see ladies, study, fast, not sleep."

Act I.1.47-8

Although he complains about being forbidden the company of women, he simultaneously asserts that he is impervious to love:

> "I, that have been love's whip,
> A very beadle to a humorous sigh,
> A critic, nay a night-watch constable,
> A domineering pedant o'er the boy,
> Than whom no mortal so magnificent!"

Act III.1.169-73

Then, admitting that he has fallen in love, describes his nemesis:

> "A whitely wanton with a velvet brow,
> With two pitch-balls stuck in her face for eyes;"

Act III.1.191-2

All of this is consistent with Sidney's unfortunate failure to complete his father's agreement with Lord Burghley to marry his daughter and Sidney's later failure to marry Penelope Deveraux who was "golden-haired with dark eyes"[539] and later was known to be the inspiration for Sidney's <u>Astrophel and Stella</u>. This, coupled with all of the other influence of Sidney visible in the play make Berwone a clear echo of Sidney in Marlowe's conception.

Similarly, Boyet, the courtier most despised by Berowne, is modeled after the Earl of Oxford who was Sidney's particular antagonist. Sidney famously and embarrassingly had had a confrontation with Oxford in front of the Duke of Anjou in 1579 at a tennis court when Oxford, "born great, greater by alliance, and superlative in the Prince's favor"[540] demanded that Sidney cut short his match and give up the court. It was Oxford who married Burghley's daughter, Anne, who had first been pledged to Sidney and then spent years in an unhappy marriage to his arrogant, better heeled rival. Those who now imagine that the Earl was actually the hand behind the work attributed to Shakspere invariably assert that Boyet is Oxford's version of Sidney and that Berwone is his personal stand-in, but this gets the question exactly backward. Berwone asserts that Boyet: "pecks up wit as pigeons pease / And utters it again when God doth please."[541] Whatever else could be said of Philip Sidney, no one could claim that he lacked wit. Oxford, on the other hand, despite the extravagant claims made by later devotees, was never in Sidney's poetic league. Regardless, by the time Love's Labour's Lost was performed, "the violent Earl of Oxford"[542] had long since fallen from grace while Sidney's legend continued to grow. Which is to say that in a play effectively dedicated to Sidney, jokes at Oxford's expense would have offended no one.

Nor should it be forgotten that Oxford's wife, Anne, was the mother of Elizabeth, the grand-daughter of Lord Burghley who he so avidly sought to marry to the Earl of Southampton, the pursuit of which set off the chain of events that resulted in Marlowe's disgrace. It makes perfect sense, therefore, that Marlowe would employ Sidney's stand-in, Berwone, to attack Oxford's surrogate, Boyet. Southampton and Essex, to say nothing of Penelope herself, could certainly be counted upon to make the connection.

Chief among the other major influences active in Love's Labour's Lost expressing Marlowe's perspective is the Gesta Grayorum, which appears both in the masque of worthies sequence in Act V involving the four pairs of lovers in Muscovite disguise and in the character of King Ferdinand. As Sophie Chiari observed, the King "is more of a Prince of fools unable to bring his shows to an end, and as such, quite comparable to the incompetent 'Prince of Purpool' who presided over the Christmas festivities of Gray's Inn"[543] and added that "the very phrasing of Ferdinand's edict (1.1.137-46) . . . echoes the wording of the Inns' mocking regulations."[544] At one point in the masque Rosaline describes Ferdinand as "Seasick, I think, coming from Muscovy" (5.2.393), a remark that has been likened by John Nichols as echoing Purpoole's staged return from the "Russia" described in the Revels, which was shorthand in fact for a night of carousing the town after which, apologizing from exhaustion "and presumably his drunkenness", he declined to pay a pre-planned visit to the Queen.[545] Most scholars have acknowledged the link, but H. R. Woudhuysen disputes this, asserting that "there are few if any verbal links between the two and the elements they share are generic rather than specific: courts, real and imaginary, enjoyed entertaining ambassadors, and witty debate played a part in the entertainments."[546] Regardless, it is a fact that Lord Burghley was simultaneously a regent of Gray's Inn and a major shareholder in the Muscovy Company which had a royal monopoly on Russian shipping. That the entire mock Russian embassy in the Grayorum was a satire of Burghley seems too obvious to contest, especially since Burghley would have to have approved it in advance. More significantly from Marlowe's point of view, the Muscovy Company's main office and port was in Deptford, not far from Mistress Bull's establishment, where Marlowe met with Poley, Frizer and Skeres before he made his escape from London in May, 1593. No one other than he would make such a connection between that, the Night of Errors and Love's Labour's Lost.

The connection to the Gesta Grayorum, which recall was not published until 1688, is further confirmed by Act III, Scene 1's wrangle over "l'envoy" between Holofernes, Moth, Armado and Costard. A direct reference to Gabriel Harvey's "l'envoy" which sums up his Gorgon, or a Wonderful Yeare where he claimed that Thomas Nashe had a hand in publishing Venus and Adonis after Marlowe escaped London. When Moth asks Armado: "Is not l'envoy a *salve*?", meaning "salvo" or opening, with a pun on "balm", Armado replies: "No, page, it is an epilogue or discourse to make plain / Some obscure precedence that hath tofore been sain." He follows this by way of example by challenging Moth to solve the famous riddle:

> "The fox, the ape and the humble-bee
> Were still at odds, being but three."

Moth solves the riddle with:

> "Until the goose comes out the door,
> And stayed the odds by adding four."

While there are many ways of interpreting this riddle, and scholars have puzzled over it endlessly, the key must be found within the confines of the dispute outlined in "l'envoy" and the individuals described in Gorgon, its source. This includes Gabriel Harvey as its author, Thomas Nashe as its target, Christopher Marlowe as referenced by the "Tamburlaine" allusion in Gorgon and a fourth person who Harvey threatened to expose. The solution to the riddle lies in matching the animals depicted in it, a clever fox, a dull witted ape, an annoying bee, and finally a goose that is tricked, with the people indicated in "l'envoy". Since Costard concludes that "a fat l'envoy - ay, that's a fat goose", it would then seem that Harvey, author of "l'envoy" is the goose and the other three are Marlowe, the clever fox who escaped pursuit, the dull witted, imitative Shakspere who Harvey threatened to expose, and the annoying Nashe, who had been called a "bug" by Harvey in a previous pamphlet, Pierce's Supererogation[547]. With the riddle, Marlowe is saying that he, Nashe and Shakspere tricked Harvey. This is the argument that threatened to explode until the Night of Errors and The Comedy of Errors, with its admonition to "'beware the rope's end'" (IV.4.44), advised Harvey to keep his suspicions to himself.

The play goes further to identify Holofernes with Harvey when he enters in Act V's Parade of Worthies portraying a character named "Judas". Holofernes claims he portrays Judas Maccabeaus, but the young Lords will have none of it, asserting that he is indeed Iscariot, the betrayer. There is no textual or narrative reason for the Lords to insist on this label; any other joke would suffice to ridicule Holofernes. It is the author himself who views Holoferenes as a Judas and in Marlowe's eyes, although he had been betrayed by others, Gabriel Harvey was among the worst.

As if these connections weren't enough, the King in Love's Labour's Lost agrees in the final scene to delay further courtship of the French Princess for "twelvemonth and a day", V.1.865, out of respect for the death of her father. In fact, the Lord Chamberlain's Men performed at court on December 28, 1595[548], exactly one year and one day after the Night of Errors, December 27, 1594 at Gray's Inn. Thus, if the events of The Gesta Grayorum are partial inspiration for Love's Labour's Lost, then the play's dance of Muskovites and debate over l'envoy represent the events of the prior year which its subsequent performance commemorates in a self-referential, meta-theatrically temporal loop on the agreed upon day, one year and a day later, which simultaneously makes it clear that the performance was indeed at court on December 28, 1595.

Love's Labour's Lost is esoteric only in that it defies orthodox interpretation. Respectable scholars who nevertheless insist that Shakspere wrote it and three dozen other plays, not to mention more than a hundred fifty sonnets and poems, all without ever having a trace of an education, inevitably fall back on statements like: "it is easier to put forward theories about what is really going on in the play than to disprove them."[549] As if to say that the very plethora of theories proves that they must all be false or incomplete, without ever acknowledging that their own traditional theory is very much included in that summation. Meanwhile, context is everything. Love's Labour's Lost is, by its own admission, a sequel to The Comedy of Errors and a continuation of the argument that the first play initiated which, in short, was: what is to be done with Marlowe?

It is here that the play's invocation of isolation and scholarship makes the most sense. Traditional scholars refuse to see this because it doesn't fit the paradigm they have been trained to accept. To them, the play is "an enigma, a riddle only those in the know could solve: and those inevitably turned out to be the factions at court and London's literary elite."[550] For people who knew or who suspected that Marlowe was in exile, none of this is enigmatic. With this play, Marlowe was communicating that, like Berwone, he would accept a period of isolation if it led to a better future. The irony is that by incorporating a historical reference into the play, Marlowe created a temporal loop; by stating that the play was itself a representation of what occurred one year and a day before, he left its resolution stuck in its own repetition. If the princes and princesses are to meet again in a year and a day from the time of the play only to repeat the play then the period of separation will never end. The implication is that an outside force will have to break the spell.

The character of Marcade could represent that force, but his message that the King of France is dead, restarts the separation. The oddly named character has a very brief moment onstage, but suddenly ends the party and brings about a complete change in tone. The significance of his message coupled with the his unlikely name has puzzled scholars. A. C. Wood thought the source of the character's name might derive from The Cobler's Prophecy (1594) a play by Robert Wilson with a character who is inspired by the god Mercury, who he calls "Markedy"[551] and Woudhuysen compares him to the character of Mercury in Marston's The Malcontent (1603) "where he makes a late arrival in the play as the presenter of a masque of the dead."[552] That said, the name "Marcade" is more easily assembled by taking one syllable each from Marlowe and Jack Cade, the most popular character in The First Part of the Contention Between the Two Famous Houses of York and Lancaster, the first part of the Henry VI duet written by Marlowe for

Pembroke's Men. It is certainly significant for Marlowe to present a character one year and a day after the Night of Errors and his latest prior appearance, that reminds his audience of his presence at the moment when the bargain of one year and a day is struck between Ferdinand and the new Queen of France and their retinues. Throughout the play, Marlowe continues to insert important reminders of his presence, even at the very end.

The final song has resisted interpretation, but scholars have noted its connection to Nashe's Summer's Last Will (c. 1592) and the more obvious fact that it contrasts Spring with Winter and appears to prefer Winter because "spring is full of fear, winter of merriness."[553] Overlooked in this is the fact that Marlowe's exile began in the Spring of 1593 and both Comedy of Errors and Love's Labour's Lost, not to mention the Gray's Inn Night of Errors, all were performed at Christmas. By looking ahead to a reunion one year and a day hence, the play is clearly nodding to a resolution in some future Winter.

Shakspere, meanwhile, appears to be represented by the character of Costard, a country bumpkin with Stratfordian roots originally played by Will Kempe, one of the Lord Chamberlain's company's stars. The character's name means "apple" and Stratford is in the southwestern part of Warwickshire, "noted for orchards and market gardening."[554] Like Antipholus of Ephesus, one of the twins in Comedy of Errors purged by Dr. Pinch, the character played by Shakspere during the Night of Errors, Costard is first put in jail by Armado for the crime of pursuing Jacquinetta, a maid who the braggart Armado also desires. Later freed by Armado, Costard immediately confuses two letters he is given to deliver, creating an instant comparison with Marlowe who gave more trustworthy service as a courier for the crown. Later, he participates in the "l'envoy" sequence and solves the riddle by revealing that the "goose" is "a fat l'envoy" meaning that the joke is on Gabriel Harvey, author of "l'envoy". Finally, when recruited into service as part of the presentation of nine worthies, Costard admits he does not know anything about the man he is supposed to impersonate: "For my part, I know not the degree of the Worthy, but I am to stand for him." He is the only one of the players who portrays a worthy unknown to him, much as Shakspere does for Marlowe, a man he supposedly had not met.

It is also very interesting that when Armado promises to remunerate Costard for delivering his letter, Costard remarks:

> "'Remuneration'! O, that's the Latin word for three farthings. Three farthings - remuneration. 'What's the price of this inkle?' 'One penny.' 'No, I'll give you a remuneration.' Why, it carries it! 'Remuneration'! Why it is a fairer name than French crown."

III.1.134-38.

As "French crown" was commonly known as slang for "a bald head caused by syphilis, the 'French disease'"[555], Costard is likening Armado's remuneration to venereal disease and thereby links Armado to Dr. Lopez whose unfortunate fate was brought on by his inopportune correspondence informing a confederate Spaniard of the Earl of Essex's similar malady. Essex found out and accused Lopez, the Queen's physician, of conspiring to poison her with the result that Lopez was arrested, tried and hung in mid 1594. Armado is the only Spanish character in all of the plays and it would seem unlikely that the reference would escape the court audience.

If the link by way of Syphilis to Dr. Lopez and Essex seems perhaps too scandalous for light entertainment to bear, consider that a second link to another contemporary Spaniard with echoes of Marlowe's exile is also recognizable, specifically, Antonio Pérez, the former secretary of King Philip of Spain who had recently fled the country after escaping jail and charges of attempting to murder Juan de Escobedo, secretary of Don Juan of Austria, King Philip's half-brother. Pérez had come to England in 1593 as was a guest of Sir Frances Bacon at the Night of Errors[556] and became a political agent in the service of the Earl of Essex. He was the target of several assassination attempts, one which included plotters implicated in the Lopez affair. His parallels with Marlowe even go so far was having his Pecados de Historia o Relaciones published by Richard Field. Gustav Ungerer, in A Spaniard in Elizabethan England, argued that there were many similarities between Pérez and the character Don Armado, including their prose style and love life.[557] An exiled courtier and intelligencer standing in for Marlowe arguing with Shakspere's substitute Costard over a serving wench? What could be more innocently amusing?

Shakspere never knew Philip Sidney, he never read Sidney's Arcadia; he could care less about Philip Sidney and if he had read Love's Labour's Lost and someone explained to him that Holofernes was funny because he was like a character out of The Lady of May he would not have had the faintest idea what they were talking about. He certainly would have heard about the notorious Dr. Lopez, he may have met Antonio Pérez before performing for him; regardless, the story of Essex's malady was broadly rumored. He doubtless knew what "French Crowns" were.

Marlowe was undoubtedly aware of Shakspere. The mention of the "ape" in "l'envoy" and all the jokes at Costard's expense make this abundantly clear. What must Shakspere have thought being the butt of these jokes? Did he console himself that he was in charge, a free man having the benefit of Marlowe's labor? Did he resent him?

Consider that Love's Labour's Lost was performed at court for an audience that probably included not just Southampton, Essex and Penelope Rich, but all of their most important friends and enemies. Oxford had been banished, so jokes at his expense would not have been unappreciated. Sidney was a national hero and the court audience would happily approve a play calling upon his poetry even then in print. In no way would these people confuse Shakspere with the author of Love's Labour's Lost even though the play was the first one published under his name when it finally appeared on the bookstalls in 1598, the same year as Hero and Leander. As for who among them might have been considered a friend to Shakspere, of all people that would most likely have been someone like Essex who benefited from his presence as much as anyone; Essex who had run Marlowe out of London, who continued to stand between him and any hope of return and who got the benefit of his family's patronage of the Lord Chamberlain's Men.

The one thing that is probably most true about the mythology encrusted over Shakspere is that he generally kept his opinions to himself. According to A. L. Rowse, "He was evidently a quiet, tactful, prudent man, not one for getting into trouble, intent on his own affairs"[558] while Stephen Greenblatt laments that "if anything, Shakespeare often seems a drabber, duller person, and the inward springs of his art seem more obscure than ever."[559] In the context of a man hired to act as a shield for another, however, this behavior does not appear so incongruous.

Marlowe had his own opinions and, apart from making jokes at Shakspere's expense, he could also reflect on his situation with a fair amount of irony. From time to time that method could be found in the plays, in particular in Love's Labour's Lost, but the arena he chose most often for this was the sonnets.

Correspondences between Love's Labour's Lost and the Sonnets have often been noted. C. F. McClumpha went so far as to observe that "the great similarity between certain sonnets and the play almost forces one to think of an equally close relationship as regards time of composition."[560] The first lines of the play, "Let fame, that all hunt after in their lives, / Live registered on our brazen tombs, / And then grace us in the disgrace of death" have frequently been compared with the similar sentiments of sonnets 55, 60 and 63:

> "Not marble nor the gilded monuments
> Of princes shall outlive this powerful rhyme,
> But you shall shine more bright in these contents

Than unswept stone, besmeared with sluttish time."

   55: 1 -4

"And yet to times in hope my verse shall stand,
Praising thy worth, despite his cruel hand."

   60: 13-14

"For such a time do I now fortify
Against confounding Age's cruel knife,
That he shall never cut from memory
My sweet love's beauty, though my lover's life.
   His beauty shall in these black lines be seen,
   And they shall live, and he in them still green."

   63: 9 - 14

Other scholars have shown the many affinities of theme and imagery of the three internal sonnets with the larger collection. As Sidney Lee put it, "in phraseology the sonnets often closely resemble such early dramatic efforts as Love's Labour's Lost and Romeo and Juliet."[561] And yet, despite all of this detailed investigation, scholars and critics alike are typically reduced to compiling mere lists of similar lines and phrases without correlated significance. No interpretation is possible because no life attaches to the word strings. They seem to dangle in mid-air like fuzz connected only to each other but not to any real time, place or person. It is a strange form of criticism that provides so much detail devoid of actual sense.

   It should not go unnoticed, for instance, that the King's opening speech in Love's Labour's Lost is made as a declaration of the self-imposed exile he has chosen for himself and his retinue. While Geoffrey Bullough asserts that "no precise literary source has been found for the story of the courtier's oath . . ."[562], the King's decision reflects Marlowe's similar condition of exile and clearly signifies its temporal and personal immediacy.

Whatever else he hoped to accomplish with Love's Labor's Lost, Marlowe was not able to use it as a springboard for redemption and restoration. Reminders of Sidney and happier times, unravelling of the complicated threads of so many intertwined lives and mockery of his misfortune, none of that resulted in any end to his disgrace. Instead, he remained in exile, trapped into what appears to have been a rather one-sided bargain. Although he would continue to make similar appeals throughout his life and many of the plays reflect his state of mind, they do not reveal the true nature of this bargain. It involved much more than a staged death and hasty exit in order to secure protection from Essex. In time, even Essex would fall away and still the exile continued.

At this point Marlowe was almost thirty-one years old and stuck in Flushing. Sidney had been 31 when he died not far from Flushing after being stationed there a year. Like Sidney, he had taken inspiration from Ovid and found himself more exiled than Sidney could ever have imagined.

As Love's Labor's Lost suggests, however, exile was not Marlowe's sole concern. He had modeled himself after Sidney, but where Sidney had declared his love more or less openly in Astrophel and Stella, if Marlowe had a similar love he had so far concealed it from the public. In his private correspondence, however, he was more direct. Who might this person be and why did Marlowe choose to compare himself to Sidney at this moment? The answer to these questions can only be found in the autobiography known today as The Sonnets.

Chapter Twenty

Love's Wound

For all the detailed inventories of rare words, parallel phrases and thematic echoes, one connection that is rarely, if ever, made between Love's Labor's Lost and the Sonnets is with Costard's "French Crown" quip and sonnet 37's admission that the author has been "made lame by Fortune's dearest spite." Both indicate contemporaneous effects of venereal disease. Both statements are echoed in sonnet 89's promise: "Speak of my lameness, and I straight will halt." Together, these declarations and others such as Sonnet 35's "loathsome canker lives in sweetest bud;" 35: 4, have convinced many scholars that the author may have been "part of a love triangle in which all three parties contracted venereal disease."[563]

Syphilis was indeed common enough in England at that time. It is no stretch to infer that in addition to suffering from his separation from Walsingham, Marlowe also believed he had "an unwanted legacy of infection"[564]. Based on the sequence of the sonnets, it does not appear that he thought he had this infection until after he left London. Indeed, as John J. Ross attests:

> "I can find only 6 lines referring to venereal infection in the 7 plays of Christopher Marlowe. However, 55 lines in Measure for Measure, 61 lines in Troilus and Cressida, and 67 lines in Timon of Athens allude to venereal disease."

The sonnets, meanwhile, make consistent reference to venereal infection, but only after sonnet 35 which also marks the conclusion of the escape from London.

Marlowe does not appear to blame himself for the disease, nor for giving it to anyone. At first, he describes it as something of an accident typical to the situation and mingles it with forgiveness for staging the escape from Deptford:

> "No more be grieved at that which thou hast done:
> Roses have thorns, and silver fountains mud,
> Clouds and eclipses stain both moon and sun,
> And loathsome canker lives in sweetest bud;"
>
> 35: 1 - 4

Then it becomes a theme, an image and a metaphor to which he returns again and again, sometimes delivered directly and sometimes mingled with other layers of meaning, often in the context of love and its complications:

> "And gilded honour shamefully misplaced,
> And maiden virtue rudely strumpeted,
> And right perfection wrongfully disgraced,
> And strength by limping sway disablèd.
>
> 66: 5 - 8

> "Ah, wherefore with infection should he live
> And with his presence grace impiety,
> That sin by him advantage should achieve
> And lace itself with his society?"
>
> 67: 1 - 4

> "Say that thou didst forsake me for some fault,
> And I will comment upon that offence.
> Speak of my lameness, and I straight will halt,
> Against thy reasons making no defence."
>
> 89: 1 - 4

> "How sweet and lovely dost thou make the shame
> Which, like a canker in the fragrant rose,

Doth spot the beauty of thy budding name!"

    95: 1 - 3

"But for his theft, in pride of all his growth
A vengeful canker eat him up to death."

    99: 11 - 12

"Pity me then, and wish I were renewed,
Whilst, like a willing patient, I will drink
Potions of eisel 'gainst my strong infection;"

    111: 8 - 10

"But since I learn, and find the lesson true,
Drugs poison him that so fell sick of you."

    118: 13 - 14

The penultimate sequence known as the "Dark Lady" sonnets, numbers 127 to 152, are no less rife with references and allusions to what could be considered venereal disease:

"Th' expense of spirit in a waste of shame
Is lust in action;"

    129: 1 -2

"Beshrew that heart that makes my heart to groan
For that deep wound it gives my friend and me;"

    133: 1 - 2

"In things right true my heart and eyes have erred,
And to this false plague are they now transferred."

    137: 13 - 14

> "Only my plague thus far I count my gain,
> That she that makes me sin, awards me pain."
>
> 141: 13 - 14
>
> "My love is as a fever, longing still
> For that which longer nurseth the disease,"
>
> 147: 1 - 2

The affinity between sonnets 21, written at Wilton House, and sonnet 130, the signature sonnet in the "Dark Lady" sequence and the earlier sonnets of Tom Watson has been noted in Chapter Twelve but bears closer inspection here. It was Tom Watson, not Spencer, who became the first English poet to make a reputation as a sonneteer.[565] He published his <u>Hekatompathia or Passionate Century of Love</u>, one hundred sonnets dedicated to the Earl of Oxford, in 1582. Watson was Marlowe's partner in playwrighting and a respected poet, but his verse appears stilted today, featuring what Sidney Lee complained were "conventional appeals to his wayward mistress, and . . . expressions of amorous emotions [where] there is no pretence of a revelation of personal experience."[566] Sonnet VII from his collection is a particularly notable example:

> "Hark you that list to hear what saint I serve:
> Her yellow locks exceed the beaten gold;
> Her sparkling eyes in heav'n a place deserve;
> Her forehead high and fair of comely mold;
> > Her words are music all of silver sound;
> > Her wit so sharp as like can scarce be found;"

As Dr. Daniel Cook observed, the author of sonnet 130 "clearly read these poems as a young man. Years later, in his own sonnet sequence, we find a devastating reworking of Watson's bleary blazon:"[567]

> "My mistress' eyes are nothing like the sun;
> Coral is far more red than her lips' red;
> If snow be white, why then her breasts are dun;
> If hairs be wires, black wires grow on her head.
> I have seen roses damasked, red and white,
> But no such roses see I in her cheeks,
> And in some perfumes is there more delight
> Than in the breath that from my mistress reeks."

If Watson's sonnet V asked:

> "If't be not love I feel, what is it then?
> If love it be, what kind of thing is love?
> If good, how chance he hurts so many men?
> If bad, how haps that none his hurts disprove?
>   If willingly I burn, how chance I wail?
>   If gainst my will, what sorrow will avail?"

Sonnet 135 took Watson's innocent "will" and retorted with one more overtly sexual:

> "Whoever hast her wish, thou hast thy Will,
> And Will to boot, and Will in overplus;
> More than enough am I to vex thee still,
> To thy sweet will making additions thus."

The comparison is not one to one, but it is surely deliberate. It would be impossible for Walsingham, intimately familiar with Watson, not to recognize the echo. There are more sonnets from Marlowe than there are of Watson, they are less repetitive than the <u>Passionate Centurie</u> and have a broader canvas, but the connection is there. For Thomas Walsingham, there probably never was a "Dark Lady", there was only Marlowe mocking Watson.

    Although Kerrigan asserts that "Sonnet 21 has the same role in the first group of sonnets (1 - 126) as 130 in the second (127

- 152)"[568], it never seems to occur to him that they could both be addressed to the same person because he makes the mistake of assuming that the first 126 sonnets are all written to someone other than the "Dark Lady", the so called "fair youth". This, despite the fact that a woman is identified almost immediately after the subject of sonnet 35's canker is introduced:

> "Gentle thou art, and therefore to be won;
> Beauteous thou art, therefore to be assailed;
> And when a woman woos, what woman's son
> Will sourly leave her till she have prevailed?"
>
> 41: 5 - 8
>
> "That thou hast her, it is not all my grief,
> And yet it may be said I loved her dearly;"
>
> 42: 1 - 2

To whom are sonnets 41 and 42 referring? The evidence would include someone with a relationship with Thomas Walsingham who might have been of an age to have had a fling with Marlowe sometime before 1593, perhaps in 1592 when sonnets 21 to 24 were written, but not much earlier. There is one woman already identified within the sonnets who fits this description. She is only woman other than the Queen who can be positively identified in the sonnets. This is the woman for whom Hero and Leander was completed by the "Rival Poet", George Chapman, who dedicated it to her and who, according to a scurrilous legend of the time, memorialized in an anonymous poem, "O Ladies, ladies howle & cry", had syphilis:[569] Audrey Walsingham, nee Shelton.

Alastair Bellany and Andrew McRae[570] provide context for the poem which accused Lady Audrey and the Countess of Suffolk, Catherine Howard, of having affairs with Robert Cecil and causing his death in 1612 by "infection":

"A Song"[571]

O Ladies, ladies howle & cry,
For you have lost your Salisbury.
He that of late was your protection,
He is now dead by your infection.[1]
Come with your teares bedew his lockes,
Death kild him not; it was the pockes.[2]

Lett Suffolke now, & Walsingham.[3]
Leave their adulterous lives for shame:
Or else their Ladiships must know,
There is noe helpe in Doctor Poe.[4]
For though the man be very cunning,
He canne not stay the poxe[5] from running.

And now these lecherous wretches all,
Which plotted worthy Essex fall,[6]
May see by this foule loathsome end,
How foulie then they did offend.
And as they all deserv'd this curse,
Oh lett them all die soe, & worse.

And lett all, that abuse the King,
Themselves to greatnes soe to bring,

---

[1] infection: Syphilis

[2] pockes: Syphilis

[3] Suffolke...Walsingham: Cecil's two alleged lovers, Audrey, Lady Walsingham, wife of Sir Thomas Walsingham and Mistress of the Robes to Queen Anne (Croft, "Reputation" 58), and Catherine Howard, Countess of Suffolk, wife of Thomas Howard, Earl of Suffolk.

[4] Doctor Poe: Leonard Poe, one of Cecil's physicians.

[5] poxe: syphilis.

[6] Cecil was frequently accused, both at the time and in the libellous epitaphs, of engineering the fall and 1601 execution of Robert Devereux, 2nd Earl of Essex

> Be forc'd to travell to the bath,7
> To purge themselves of filthie froath:
> And when they back againe returne,
> Then lett the pockes their bowells burne.
>
> Soe shall the King, & state be blest,
> And subjects all shall live in rest,
> All which long time have been abused
> By tricks, which divellish whores have used.
> But now the cheife is gone before,
> I hope to see the end of more.

Some might say that a romantic triangle marred by venereal disease explains most of the mystery about the sonnets and that if Southampton is the patron being addressed that Shakspere is then the author. But that explanation would not resolve the meaning of sonnets 73 and 74 and their reference to Marlowe's Motto or "Death's second self", the "coward's knife" or the "fell arrest" that carried their author away. It would not explain why there is no mention of Southampton having venereal disease when others, such as Essex, Lady Audrey and Robert Cecil were all reported with it. Nor would it explain all the other relationships or the context of that period which have nothing to do with Shakspere and everything to do with Marlowe. It certainly does not explain why Shakspere would care one whit about discovering that George Chapman had completed <u>Hero and Leander</u> or why he would be upset with and complain to Southampton about it.

When could Marlowe, a mere poet and sometime intelligencer, make the acquaintance of Audrey Shelton, grand-niece to Anne Boleyn? If the time line of the <u>Sonnets</u> is any guide, then that period when Marlowe was rehearsing his new company of players, Lord Pembroke's Men, during the summer of 1592 at Wilton House, the Pembroke escape from plague afflicted London, under the eye of Mary Sidney even then

---

7 the bath: Cecil died on his return journey from taking the waters at Bath.

editing her version of Philip's Arcadia, would have been most propitious and welcoming. This would have been the same summer when Marlowe composed sonnets 18, 19 and 20 to Mary's son William and then wrote sonnets 21 to 24. This would have been the ideal moment for Audrey to pay a call, attend a rehearsal and make her presence felt.

In mid-summer 1592 Audrey, then 24, would have found Wilton House bustling with activity, rehearsals, recitals and romance. Both Marlowe and the dashing Watson, alive with creative energy, attractive and amusing, could be certain to turn almost any young woman's head. This means that Watson was on hand for sonnet 21's mockery of his own Hekatompathia, putting Audrey in the middle of a competitive collaboration with Marlowe. Afterward, when Watson died and Marlowe retreated to Scadbury under Walsingham's protection, she apparently transferred her affection to the Lord of the Manor and her future husband.

When sonnet 40 declares:

"Take all my loves, my love, yea take them all;
What hast thou then more than thou hadst before?
No love, my love, that thou mayst true love call;
All mine was thine, before thou hadst this more.

Sonnet 40: 1 -4

Marlowe is asserting that he fell in love with her before she married Walsingham. Written after his sonnets of exile, he is also implying that the Walsingham relationship happened after he'd been forced to leave. All of this fits with the sequence of the lives being portrayed, Watson's, Walsingham's, Audrey Shelton's and Marlowe's. If this is the same woman as the one possibly mentioned in sonnet 21, could she then be connected to the woman in sonnet 130?

Audrey, of course, was not of dark appearance. If anything, she was very fair, sharing red hair with her elder "cousin",

Queen Elizabeth. There is one small portrait by Issac Oliver of a lady of the Queen's court that has been identified by A. D. Wraight as possibly being of Audrey[572] and while her eyes appear dark, the portrait is small enough that it is difficult to make much of it. Certainly, Audrey has never been reported to have had uniquely dark eyes. How, then could she be considered the model for the "Dark Lady"?

As discussed in Chapter One, an interval of several years came between the Rival Poet sonnets of 78 to 92 and the reconciliation of 116 to 121, perhaps as much as seven years, during which the Queen died in 1603 (sonnet 107) and Marlowe wrote over a dozen plays. Meanwhile, in London, Lady Audrey Walsingham was making a name for herself as Mistress of the Wardrobe to Queen Anne and for her participation in court masques and other entertainments. On the evening of Sunday, 8 January 1604, Audrey appeared in The Vision of the Twelve Goddesses, Queen Anne's first public masque, written by Samuel Daniel, designed by Inigo Jones and performed in the Great Hall of Hampton Court Palace. In one of the earliest of the Stuart Court masques, staged when the new dynasty had been in power less than a year, Audrey played the role of Astrea, one of the twelve goddesses.

In 1605 Lady Audrey appeared as "Periphere" in the Masque of Blackness by Ben Jonson. Considered risqué because of "the predominant role of female actresses playing what were considered traditionally male roles"[573], it created additional controversy by featuring Queen Anne and the ladies of her bedchamber wearing blackface makeup as part of their costume. One observer, Sir Dudley Carleton, at the time an MP for St. Mawes, expressed his displeasure with the play as such:

> "Instead of Vizzards, their Faces and Arms up to the Elbows, were painted black, which was a Disguise sufficient, for they were hard to be known... and you cannot imagine a more ugly sight than a Troop of lean cheek'd Moors."[574]

The Masque opened with a song:

> Sound, sound aloud
>   The welcome of the orient flood,
>   Into the west ;
> Fair Niger, son to great Oceanus,
>   Now honor'd, thus,
>   With all his beauteous race :
>   Who, though but black in face,
>   Yet are they bright,
>   And full of life and light.
>   To prove that beauty best,
> Which, not the color, but the feature
>   Assures unto the creature.

It was news of this masque which appears to have prompted sonnet 127 and what followed:

> "In the old age black was not counted fair,
> Or if it were, it bore not beauty's name;
> But now is black beauty's successive heir,
> And beauty slander'd with a bastard shame:
> For since each hand hath put on nature's power,
> Fairing the foul with art's false borrow'd face,
> Sweet beauty hath no name, no holy bower,
> But is profan'd, if not lives in disgrace.
> Therefore my mistress' eyes are raven black,
> Her eyes so suited, and they mourners seem
> At such who, not born fair, no beauty lack,
> Slandering creation with a false esteem:
>   Yet so they mourn, becoming of their woe,
>   That every tongue says beauty should look so."

Sonnet 127

Some scholars such as John Hamill[575] speculate that because Rosaline in <u>Love's Labour's Lost</u> is described as the "dark eyed lady" she could be the Dark Lady of sonnets 127 to 154. Rosaline has been identified in Chapter Nineteen as Penelope Rich nee Deveraux who has also been identified as Philip Sidney's "Stella", but she is not the Dark Lady of the sonnets. Marlowe did not have a relationship with Penelope Rich for all that he was aware of her. Nor did Penelope have a relationship with Southampton, who in the mind of traditional scholars would have to be the third part of the romantic trio described by the sonnets. Penelope did have a scandalous affair, with Charles Blount, Baron Mountjoy, who she eventually married in secret after Lord Rich divorced her. As torrid and unfortunate as all that was, it was not the subject of the sonnets.

The "Dark Lady" is the same Lady who has also been accused of having venereal disease. She is the lady about whom sonnet 141 declares:

> "Only my plague thus far I count my gain,
> That she that makes me sin, awards me pain."

141: 13 - 14

In 1608, Lady Audrey appeared in the last of the three masques in which she is known to have performed, the Masque of Beauty, also by Ben Jonson. A sequel to the Masque of Blackness, she portrayed one of twelve "cupids" which included the Queen and other prominent members of her court. The masque presented the former "daughters of Niger" cleansed of the black pigment they had worn on the prior occasion. As if on cue, the final two sonnets address the fate of Cupid:

> "Cupid laid by his brand and fell asleep:
> A maid of Dian's this advantage found,
> And his love-kindling fire did quickly steep
> In a cold valley-fountain of that ground;
> Which borrowed from this holy fire of Love,
> A dateless lively heat, still to endure,

> And grew a seething bath, which yet men prove
> Against strange maladies a sovereign cure."

Sonnet 153: 1 - 8

The cupid sonnets have been taken to mean that their author sought the same hot bath cure that other sufferers from syphilis had endured with occasional success. While this may or may not be literally true, the reference is plain and the irony of them being the last in the collection, connected both to Audrey's career as a masquer and to the rumor of her own malady is more telling. It was shortly after these two sonnets that the collection was assembled and published.

One other connection between Love's Labour's Lost and the Sonnets must be mentioned. Three of the sonnets from the play and two separate sonnets were printed with fifteen other poems credited to W. Shakespeare in William Jaggard's 1599 compilation The Passionate Pilgrim. The separate sonnets reappear in 1609 as sonnets 138 and 144, bracketing the first part of the "Dark Lady" sonnets. Written at least six years before, these two sonnets are clearly not part of the continuity with the other Masque of Blackness sonnets, so the question is, why are they placed out of sequence? They appear to be the only two out of sequence in the entire collection, and the reason may be that they provide a link to the period when Chapman's version of Hero and Leander was published and the dispute between Marlowe and Audrey first began. Coming at the end, the two sonnets signify a reconsideration of the entire event and its aftermath.

If 138 and 144 are out of sequence, it makes sense to restore that sequence which, interestingly, appears to follow sonnet 37, the second time that venereal disease is mentioned: "So I, made lame by Fortune's dearest spite", which follows on sonnet 35's "And loathsome canker lives in sweetest bud." This would be followed by 138, which begins: "When my love swears that she is made of truth / I do believe her, though I know she lies." Read this way, they imply both that Marlowe loved Audrey and that he believed she was somehow responsible for making him "lame".

Sonnet 144 would then follow sonnet 42, which would be counted 43 if 138 is restored as 38 and counted as well. Read this way, "That thou hast her, it is not all my grief, / And yet it may be said I loved her dearly;" is followed by:

> "Two loves I have, of comfort and despair,
> Which like two spirits do suggest me still;
> The better angel is a man right fair,
> The worse spirit is a woman colored ill."
>
> Sonnet 144: 1 -4

In this context, Audrey's ill color is not that of blackness, as is so often assumed, but rather her brazen red hair which was so strong that at her christening she was also called Ethelred. (It is also possible that the "ill color" refers to local skin discoloration brought on by venereal disease.) Both sonnets 138 and 144 were printed as part of the Dark Lady sequence, but the person to whom they were addressed would not have considered them solely part of that series. While some might assert that rearranging the sonnets to create juxtapositions is highly speculative and nothing new, it is singular how these two sonnets, 137 and 144, can work simultaneously in their dual positions and expose new features of them and the sonnets affected by them and their positioning. These two sonnets don't have to be inserted after sonnets 37 and 42, but they were generated at about the same time because they ended up being published with the other sonnets of similar generation from Love's Labour's Lost and they resonate with 37 and 42 in a remarkable way, so linking them appears reasonable. Thus, an ill-colored woman can mean both dark and red (or even diseased) individually or both in either or both positions while making it more clear that it is the already identified Audrey all the while.

It might even be possible to say that at this point, starting at sonnet 37, the sonnets are first thought of by their author as a composite whole. Not to say that they were conceived of as a finished product, but that they formed a sequence, starting perhaps with #18 telling a story that started in the Summer of 1592 at Wilton House and that by 1595 had become a story about Marlowe, Walsingham and Audrey. It was, in short, a story in the making and where it would end only time would tell.

Many of these sonnets were addressed to Audrey even though Thomas doubtless read them as well. They included various attacks on Audrey, mockery, allegations and even the deepest feelings of betrayal mixed with a continuing hope for restored love. At some point, a reconciliation with her became inevitable. How or when this was accomplished is not altogether clear, but it is telling that in its published form, 144's venom is followed by a sonnet which describes Marlowe's recognition of Audrey's better self:

> "Those lips that Love's own hand did make,
> Breathed forth the sound that said 'I hate',
> To me that languished for her sake:
> But when she saw my woeful state,
> Straight in her heart did mercy come,
> Chiding that tongue that ever sweet
> Was used in giving gentle doom;
> And taught it thus anew to greet;
> 'I hate' she altered with an end,
> That followed it as gentle day,
> Doth follow night, who like a fiend
> From heaven to hell is flown away.
>   'I hate', from hate away she threw,
>   And saved my life, saying 'not you'.

145: 1 - 14

While this and the sonnets that follow are typically grouped with the "Dark Lady" sonnets, in fact that group really includes only 127-136 and 138-143 all of which lampoon variously <u>The Masque of Blackness</u> and Tom Watson's <u>Passionate Century</u>. Sonnet 144 starts a new sequence as Marlowe wrestles anew with his mixed feelings for Audrey who has continued her court career apparently against his wish.

No sooner has he considered reconciliation than Marlowe turns critic and in sonnet 146 appears to take Audrey to task for participating the court masques:

> "Poor soul, the center of my sinful earth
> [ ] these rebel powers that thee array,
> Why dost thou pine wihin and suffer dearth,
> Painting thy outward walls so costly gay?"

146: 1 - 4

For centuries various scholars have been doing their best to fill in the two mysteriously absent syllables in line 2 of this sonnet, suggesting, among many other unlikely emendations, "Foiled by", "Soiled by", "Spoiled by", "Swayed by", "Starved by", "Thrall to", "Yoked to", "Prey to", "Fooled by", "Bound by", Grieved by", "Galled by", "Vexed by", "Pressed with", "Served by", "Ruled by", "Feeling", "Hemmed with", and "Leagued with"[576], none of which explains why the blank is left unfinished. The Arden version boldly inserts "Feeding" "on the advice of Helen Vender"[577] and attempts to explain the omission as the result of "either eye-slip or careless dictation," which nevertheless does not explain why this choice is better than any other. With this in mind, it may be worth pointing out that "Audrey" not only fits the meter, but also explains why it obviously could not be printed even though it would be well understood by the recipient of the original.

Perhaps he has heard the rumors about Audrey and Robert Cecil. Knowing that she is infected and what that infection can lead to, he warns her very directly:

> "Why so large a cost, having so short a lease,

> Dost thou on thy fading mansion spend?
> Shall worms, inheretors of this excess,
> Eat up thy charge? Is this thy body's end?"

146: 5 - 8

Marlowe vents angrily in the six ensuing sonnets, veering between spiteful predictions and pitiful excuses, as if he is driven mad by the uncertainty of his future and of the love he feels for Audrey, a love that is compromised by time and doubt and, as always, returns him to the subject of infection and its consequences:

> "Then, gentle cheater, urge not my amiss,
> Lest guilty of my faults thy sweet self prove;
> For, thou betraying me, I do betray
> My nobler part to my gross body's treason;"

151: 3 - 6

The final two cupid sonnets do not so much resolve the issue as bring it to a rest. Audrey did not heed their warning, but instead continued on the path that they contested and, ultimately, was memorialized in scurrilous verse that, in its way, was as vicious as the Dutch Church Libel, smearing the name of a woman connected to the son of the man for whom Marlowe had been smeared twenty years before.

If Marlowe was perpetually vexed by Lady Audrey, her husband Sir Thomas seems to have taken her court adventures very much in stride. Not long after Marlowe escaped London, Thomas ensconced himself at Scadbury in Kent and rarely participated in the life of the court. He "was occasionally employed on ceremonial duties, such as meeting the French Ambassador, Biron, when he arrived at Dover in the autumn of 1601; but most of the references to him until 1603 are still concerned with his regular county duties" with the notable exception of when he "and his wife walked in Elizabeth's funeral procession."[578] Although he and Audrey were appointed joint Keepers of the Queen's Wardrobe, he evidently left the execution of those duties to her and contented himself with service as MP for Rochester until 1626 but "played no prominent part"[579] in either Elizabeth's or James' Parliaments.

The cupid sonnets were the last of Marlowe's dangerous letters, with whatever remained of the politics that had driven him into exile buried with his reputation. Ten years after his outburst to Thomas over the publication of Hero and Leander in 1598, his passion had been spent. Audrey had her own thoughts on the affair which she would soon reveal. But, before that, there is one more aspect of the story that must be explored.

Chapter Twenty One

The Missing Person

Was there ever a "Fair Youth"? Reading the <u>Sonnets</u> in order and marking the clear links between the three lives represented, Marlowe, Audrey and Thomas, reveals one of the most unexpected relationships of all. In retrospect, it seems inevitable.

However they were originally conceived and composed, for whatever disparate purposes and over a period of almost twenty years, the sonnets were finally assembled and published in almost the exact order in which they were written. The sole exceptions being sonnets 138 and 144 which, as Chapter Twenty shows, were deliberately reordered. There were other sonnets not included in the collection, those written specifically for <u>Romeo and Juliet,</u> and <u>Love's Labour's Lost</u> and one for <u>King Lear</u> which did not appear until the <u>Folio,</u> fourteen years later, but the collection gathers up everything else and puts it in an order which literally reads like excerpts from an autobiography.

Much has been made over the centuries of the "sugared sonnets" mentioned by Meres in <u>Palladis Tamia,</u> primarily in an attempt to date the composition of the entire collection circa 1598. This is true for some, but not for all or even most. The first seventeen written to Southampton and the following three which appear to have been written for William Herbert may be all that Meres had in mind when he claimed that they were witnessed "among his private friends, etc." Later sonnets, such as the first sonnets of exile, 25 to 35, or even the "Rival Poet" sonnets could not have been considered "sugared" even though they were composed no later than 1598. Others, such as the reconciliation sonnets of 115 to 125, which may be sweet enough, or the "Dark Lady" series which certainly are not, are all too late for Meres to have referenced. It is interesting, in fact, that Meres includes Marlowe and Chapman in his overview of poets as twin "imitators" of Musaeus' source for Hero and Leander while making no mention of the sonnets directed squarely at Chapman's plagiarism. If anything, Meres confirms Marlowe's fears by matching him with Chapman while, for obvious reasons, the sonnets protesting the appropriation remained private.

There is another reason why those later sonnets would have been kept private: they touch upon the murky details of both the Walsingham marriage and the birth of their son, Thomas Walsingham, Junior. The implications of this are more readily observed when the sonnets are matched with the timeline of the three intertwined lives of Christopher Marlowe, Audrey Shelton and Thomas Walsingham.

Sonnets 1 to 17: As discussed in Chapter Three, these sonnets were written by Marlowe as a complete set commissioned by Lord Burghley in anticipation of the seventeenth birthday of his ward, the young Earl of Southampton, on October 10, 1590. Burghley had the simple motive of hoping to use them to persuade the Earl to marry his grand-daughter, Elizabeth DeVere, and thereby allow Burghley to control Southampton's considerable fortune after he reached the age of majority, twenty-one. While the young Earl was doubtless pleased with the gift, he steadfastly refused to marry Elizabeth. It was this commission and its failure to achieve Burghley's intent that set in motion the conflict resulting in Marlowe's exile at the hands of Robert Deveraux, second Earl of Essex.

Sonnets 18 to 20: These three charming sonnets were written in celebration of William Herbert, third Earl of Pembroke, who turned twelve on April 3rd, 1592. They may have been written on that occasion or shortly after, in the summer, when Marlowe assembled a group of actors and began rehearsing a new collection of plays at Wilton House in preparation for the fall when it was hoped that the theaters would be allowed to reopen. While the company carried

William's banner, it was supported by Lady Pembroke, the deceased Philip Sidney's sister and Marlowe's close friend.

Sonnets 21 to 24: Addressed to Audrey Shelton, these are the first revelation of Marlowe's affair with her in the summer of 1592 (See Chapter Twelve: Enchanted Summer). It should also be noted that these four sonnets put an end to the notion that the first 126 sonnets are uniformly addressed to a single "fair youth" or a young man with whom the author was supposedly in love. In fact, the first 24 sonnets are addressed successively to two young men, separated by age and family, neither of whom was the love interest of the poet, and Audrey who, at 24 years, was considered a great beauty by all later report and most certainly was the recipient of the poet's deepest feeling.

Sonnets 25-36: Sonnets of Exile, written to Thomas Walsingham; Summer, 1593. As discussed in Chapter Fourteen, these sonnets record the moments immediately after the incident at Deptford, when Marlowe is grateful for Walsingham's assistance in his escape, through his growing doubts, regret and dismay at the implications of his declared "death" and finally to his uncertain acceptance of what must be endured, his separation and disgrace, at least in the short term. This was an almost hopeless situation and his sole connection with his former life was by way of couriers like Robert Poley. Judging by his letters, his despair must have been nearly overwhelming.

In Sonnet 35 he first mentions the venereal disease that was to afflict him for the remainder of the entire sonnet sequence: "And loathsome canker lives in sweetest bud;" 35: 3. This also marks a shift from the simpler, romantic messages of the earlier sonnets to a more complex mode where multiple layers of action and relationships are interlocked even as his life contains more complicated patterns. Thus, the temporary resolution of one issue, exile, includes sources of further discontent, his discovery of his sexual ailment.

Sonnets 37 to 42, Fall 1593: To Thomas Walsingham, as discussed in Chapter Twenty, this string also includes sonnet

138 and 144 which appear to have originally appeared in a sequence which would place them at 39 and 44. Once again, this sequence features multiple layers of meaning, including further elaboration on the venereal disease theme, "I, made lame by Fortune's dearest spite," the revelation that Audrey and Walsingham have come together, "That thou hast her, it is not all my grief, / and yet it may be said I loved her dearly;" and a new theme involving Marlowe's dedication of his work to Walsingham. Indeed, Marlowe appears to be accepting a commission from Thomas:

> "If my slight Muse do please these curious days,
> The pain be mine, but thine shall be the praise."

9: 13 - 14

How much time had passed is unclear, but Marlowe's first work in exile would have been <u>Lucrece</u>, a poem warning Southampton against Essex, the man both Marlowe and Walsingham had to despise and who Burghley wanted shamed. Among all the other betrayals implied and stated in that poem, <u>Lucrece</u> would also carry Marlowe's mixed feelings over the loss of Audrey to his patron and protector.

Sonnets 43 to 49: To Audrey, Winter 1593. So many scholars have assumed that these poems were all written to the so-called "fair youth" that it seems outside all possibility that these are all written to a woman. As a group, these sonnets deal with the distance between Marlowe and his beloved who is depicted as the subject of his dreams and the jewel of his heart. As affectionate as he might feel toward Thomas, who saved his life after all, the tone of these poems is much more intimate than anything he has addressed to anyone other than the person portrayed in sonnets 21 to 24, Audrey Shelton. For instance, where he repeatedly refers to Thomas as his love, he describes his feelings for Audrey in terms of his heart, breast, eyes and thoughts, dwelling on her fair beauty and fearing that she is "the prey of every vulgar thief" 48: 8.

Their separation forces them to correspond by way of messengers and he is relieved at their report "Of thy fair health," which, given the context of the previous references to venereal disease, is highly suggestive. Then, in sonnet 49, Marlowe appears to acknowledge a legal barrier to any reunion:

> Against that time when thou shalt strangely pass,
> And scarcely greet me with that sun, thine eye,
> When love, converted from the thing it was,
> Shall reasons find of settled gravity;
> Against that time do I ensconce me here
> Within the knowledge of mine own desert,
> And this my hand against myself uprear
> To guard the lawful reasons on thy part
> > To leave poor me thou hast the strength of laws,
> > Since why to love I can allege no cause.

49: 5 - 14

The lawful reason may be the fact that Marlowe had been declared dead by the Queen's Coroner, a decree that could not be withdrawn. It may also be that by this point, Thomas and Audrey were married.

It is a fact that there is no written record of this marriage even though it is commonly acknowledged in later reports. During this period, from May 1593 to April, 1595, the plague continued to keep London shuttered and the court was largely quiet. A. D. Wraight asserts that "at the time of Marlowe's recorded sojourn at Scadbury in 1593 Thomas was probably still a bachelor, for we hear no mention of a Lady Audrey Walsingham in any official documents of the time, or in reportage of court gossip in which she later figured so prominently."[580] All of this supports the likelihood that the marriage was more or less private and that it took place sometime after Marlowe left London but not later than early 1594 as the sonnet timeline suggests.

Sonnets 50 and 51: To Thomas and Audrey, early 1594. As might be expected, there was a break in the correspondence between the private communication of the marriage and subsequent poems describing the next leg of Marlowe's journey. This pair of poems, the first to Thomas, the second to Audrey, describe a second step in Marlowe's journey away from London. Robert Poley, the intelligencer who acted as a courier for Lord Burghley and who was present at the Deptford incident leading to Marlowe's escape, made a visit to Brussels in August, 1594[581] having been arrested and released in the Netherlands the previous September.[582] This is consistent with Marlowe leaving Flushing and proceeding to Brussels before undertaking horseback travel overland in Europe as described in both sonnets:

> "How heavy do I journey on the way
> When what I seek, my weary travel's end,
> Doth teach that ease and that repose to say
> 'Thus far the miles are measured from my friend.'
> The beast that bears me, tired with my woe,
> Plods dully on, to bear that weight in me,
> As if by instinct the wretch did know
> His rider loved not the speed being made from thee."

> 50: 1 - **8**

> "Thus can my love excuse the slow offence
> Of my dull bearer, when from thee I speed:
> From where thou art why should I haste me thence?
> Till I return, of posting is no need."

> 51: 1 - 4

Earlier in the year, Marlowe completed <u>Lucrece</u> and it had been published that Spring of 1594. In the aftermath, the decision had evidently been made to relocate him further inland, although not so far as to make him unavailable for the odd job like the Night of Errors. As Marlowe saw it, even if he enjoyed the work, he had little choice in the matter:

> "Being your slave, what should I do but tend
> Upon the hours and times of your desire?
> I have no precious time at all to spend,
> Nor services to do, till you require."
>
> 57: 1 - 4

Sonnets 52 and 53: Late Spring, 1594, to Thomas. This pair of sonnets celebrates Thomas as protector and patron even as Marlowe habitually references his separation:

> "Blessed are you whose worthiness gives scope,
> Being had, to triumph, being lacked, to hope."
>
> 52: 13 -14

> "In all external grace you have some part,
> but you like none, none you, for constant heart."
>
> 53: 13 -14

Sonnet 54: Mid-Summer, 1594. Thomas Walsingham II, the "Fair Youth", is christened. To the earlier youths, Southampton, Pembroke and Audrey, can now be added the fourth and most significant in terms of the timeline, the son of Audrey and Thomas Walsingham. It is well worth quoting the sonnet in full:

> "O! how much more doth beauty beauteous seem
> By that sweet ornament which truth doth give.
> The rose looks fair, but fairer we it deem
> For that sweet odour, which doth in it live.
> The canker blooms have full as deep a dye
> As the perfumed tincture of the roses,

> Hang on such thorns, and play as wantonly
> When summer's breath their masked buds discloses:
> But, for their virtue only is their show,
> They live unwoo'd, and unrespected fade;
> Die to themselves. Sweet roses do not so;
> Of their sweet deaths are sweetest odours made:
> > And so of you, beauteous and lovely youth,
> > When that shall vade, my verse distills your truth."

The poem makes use of the canker referenced in sonnet 35, but puts it to new purpose as "summer's breath their masked buds" disclose the "beauteous and lovely youth." The "canker" of course, is venereal disease which did not prevent Audrey from conceiving

Like the marriage of Thomas Senior and Audrey, Thomas Junior's actual birth date is something of an open question. Andrew Thrush, writing for The History of Parliament Online states that in 1602: "his father, offering to compound for his wardship and marriage from the Court of Wards for £50, gave his age as 13."[583] In a note to the same entry, however, Thrush admits that he calculates the younger Thomas' age by virtue of the fact that, while the document offering the compound "is undated", "his fa. who was born in 1561, is said to have been 41."[584] Unfortunately, Thrush does not explain who said Thomas Senior was 41; if it had been mentioned in the document he would presumably have said so, but he did not, leaving the question open. Regardless, Thrush has the date of Thomas Senior's birth wrong; according to The Inquisition Post Mortem on Edmund Walsingham, Thomas was "26 and more" on November 26, 1589 when he inherited his older brother's estate.[585] By this reckoning, therefore, he was born in 1563. Thomas Junior would then be 13 in 1604. This still fits Thrush's timeline, since Thomas served as M.P. for Poole in 1614 when, according to Thrush he would have been 24. Thomas Junior subsequently served as M. P. for Rochester from 1621 to 1640.

This timeline is complicated, however, by the belief, held by A. D. Wraight and others, that Thomas Senior did not marry Audrey Shelton until sometime in 1597-8, following the Queen's visit to Scadbury in October 1597, which according to Thrush would make Thomas Junior illegitimate at birth in ca 1590. Meanwhile, Thrush records that "According to the historians of Chislehurst and his father's inquisition postmortem, Walsingham was born in 1600,"[586] a date that he disputes but which has the advantage of granting legitimacy of birth to the subsequent M.P. but which would make him only 14 when he stood for Poole. A much better answer is provided by the fact that, as Thrush concedes: "The historian of Rochester preferred the date 1594"[587] as Thomas Junior's birth year.

What might help to resolve the question is the fact that the record upon which Thrush bases his timeline, i.e.: Thomas Senior's "offering to compound for his [son's] wardship and marriage from the Court of Wards" was in anticipation of the confirmation of The Great Contract in the first Parliament of King James, legislation which was intended to resolve various taxation issues but which took seven years to negotiate, from 1603 to 1610, and was never completed or enacted. Which is to say that Thomas Senior's undated offer to pay his son's taxes in advance could have been made at any time in that seven-year span. If Thomas Junior needs to be 13 years old sometime between his parents' marriage in or about 1594 and his entry to Parliament in 1614, then it would not be impossible for him to reach that age as late as 1607 and still be eligible to be a youthful M. P. seven years later.

All of this fits very neatly into the timeline laid out by the sonnets affirming again that the poems are sequential and echo events in Marlowe's life, from Burghley's commission of seventeen sonnets for Southampton, to the three written to honor and delight the young Earl of Pembroke and the four celebrating his love affair with Audrey Shelton immediately followed by his hurried exile, his recognition of Audrey's match with his Patron and protector, Thomas Walsingham, his venereal misfortune, the wedding in 1594 and subsequent christening of Thomas Junior, all dovetailing with the times and places of the events being described.

While most of sonnets 1 to 126 are not actually addressed to or on the subject of this fair youth, a good many of them are and it is well worth focusing on those. The first of them is sonnet 54 and the second one is sonnet 55, the first sonnet in the sequence to claim that it will memorialize its recipient "more bright in these contents / than unswept stone, besmeared with sluttish time." Some scholars have likened it to sonnet 19 before it which asserts that "My love in my verse shall live ever young", but the reference there is to enduring love, not to the poem as a monument in itself. The memorial claim may seem odd considering that when 55 was written publication was not contemplated. That said, if the poem is a gift addressed on the boy's behalf to his parents, then it has in effect been published and immortality has been achieved. Note too, the fact that this links it with the first seventeen sonnets as an answer to the advice to "increase, / That thereby beauty's rose might never die".

Sonnet 77: To Thomas Junior, circa 1597/8. The boy would have been about three or four and perhaps is learning to write. A blank book given as a gift to record his thoughts. This becomes subject of a rebuke when Marlowe returns the book to his mother and father. His apology is sonnet 122. Among the multiple ironies is the fact that giving books as gifts becomes the subject of a furious dispute when Thomas Senior gives his wife the "completed" <u>Hero and Leander</u>.

Sonnet 108: to Thomas Junior, circa 1603/4. If, as is often observed, sonnet 107 marks the death of Queen Elizabeth, then sonnet 108 following close after would make Thomas about ten years old and, if the intimacy of the sonnet can be accepted, may well have thought of Marlowe as his uncle:

> "What's in the brain that ink may character
> Which hath not figured to thee my true spirit?
> What's new to speak, what new to register,

That may express my love, or thy dear merit?
Nothing, sweet boy; but yet like prayers divine,
I must each day say o'er the very same,
Counting no thing old; thou mine, I thine,
Even as when first I hallowed thy fair name:
So that eternal love, in love's fresh case,
Weighs not the dust and injury of age,
Nor gives to necessary wrinkles place
But makes antiquity for aye his page,
> Finding the first conceit of love there bred
> Where time and outward form would show it dead."

Sonnet 108

Marlowe "first hallowed" Thomas Junior's name with sonnet 54 and it is interesting to note that this sonnet is that sonnet's numeric double. Marlowe then mirrors the boy with the role of a page, appropriate for his years and perhaps recalling Marlowe's own service with Sidney.

Sonnet 122: To Thomas Junior, 1604. Traditional scholarship, in the absence of context, links this sonnet with sonnet 77 on the basis of a shared object, the book/tablet, and the fact that in its first appearance it is a blank gift while in the second it is filled out. "Some critics believe that this book, filled in and returned to the poet, is the one discussed in 122."[588] Since this observation touched on the sensitive subject of "biographical reference", hundreds of examples are ferreted out to show otherwise. Regardless, if the blank book was a gift to a four year old Thomas Junior circa 1598, then he would have been about ten when Marlowe, having read it, returned it. In general, scholars have been at a loss to explain why the poet would return a gift from his beloved "fair youth", but if the sonnet is actually an apology to the boy for an earlier return of that book not to him but to his parents, then returning the book is less offensive than considerate.

What this also shows is that Marlowe has had actual correspondence with Thomas Junior. The most innocent explanation for his attention could be his interest in his parents, but there is a further intimacy in the patient tone of the poem that suggests almost filial concern.

Significantly, Marlowe excuses his return of the book by citing his prodigious memory which, he claims, "kept it all". Marlowe would have to have had an almost photographic memory to travel so far from home without books while relying on their knowledge and calling them to mind as he continued to write.

Sonnet 123, 1604. As if to answer a quibble to his claim in sonnet 122 that the gift will remain in his memory "Beyond all date, even to eternity - ", he asserts:

"No, Time, thou shalt not boast that I do change."

"This I do vow, and this shall ever be:
I will be true despite thy scythe and thee."

123: 1, 13 - 14

Sonnet 126: For Thomas Junior, 1604-5. Marlowe appears to be offering an adult relative's appreciation and counsel in what would prove to be his final word to Thomas in the sonnet sequence:

"O thou, my lovely boy, who in thy power
Dost hold Time's fickle glass, his sickle hour,
Who hast by waning grown and therein show'st
Thy lovers withering, as thy sweet self grow'st;
If Nature, sovereign mistress over wrack,
As thou goest onwards, still will pluck thee back,
She keeps thee to this purpose, that her skill
May time disgrace, and wretched minutes kill.
Yet fear her, O thou minion of her pleasure;
She may detain, but not still keep her treasure.
Her audit, though delayed, answered must be,
And her quietus is to render thee.

              (   )
              (   )"
         126: 1 - 12

Many critics have noted the fact that there are only twelve lines in this sonnet which is composed entirely of rhymed couplets, the same type of couplet which ends every other sonnet in the sequence. The fact that the printer included two more lines in parentheses is also remarked, and sometimes dropped altogether by some editors. The final couplet followed by the empty, bracketed lines suggest to many scholars "a sense of incompleteness or sudden ending which is re-enforced by the empty parenthesis".[589]

On the other hand, if the poem is taken in context, its message may become more clear. By 1605, Marlowe had been in exile for literally twelve years and in this sonnet he expresses his almost overwhelming obsession with the passage of time. This concern was stated in his first sonnet to Southampton in 1590 repeated in sonnet nineteen written to the twelve year old William Herbert. Meanwhile, Thomas Junior, who may well have been conceived in 1593 immediately before Marlowe's escape from London, is almost the living symbol of Marlowe's exile: each year of his life matches each year of Marlowe's banishment, a fact that Marlowe would know all too well. The twelve lines of the sonnet matches those twelve years and leaves the future uncertain as it was for both of them.

In the sonnets to Thomas Junior, Marlowe expresses fondness and pride, emotions appropriate for a close relative, an uncle or a guardian. To Thomas Senior he usually speaks in terms of friendship, duty, honor and, on those occasions when tensions rose, he wrote in anger or even made threats. It is for Audrey alone that he reserves his passion which he keeps alive throughout the entire sequence, despite the passage of time which he frequently laments. Oftentimes he appears to be writing to Thomas and Audrey together, especially when complaining of his misery and solitude. At other times, it is hard to avoid the idea that Thomas read the same correspondence that was addressed heatedly and directly to his own wife.

At some point the question has to be asked, how could Marlowe expect to continue to write so passionately to Audrey? Why does he feel the freedom to do so even though she is married to his protector? The answer might well be that Thomas was homosexual. Park Honan seems to think so when he asserts that "young Thomas Walsingham and [Tom] Watson melted into each other's ways"[590] as Paris couriers for Francis Walsingham in 1580. When Tom Watson wrote Meliboeus, his elegy to Sir Francis Walsingham, he saved his "fuller picture of escapades in France" with Thomas for his Latin version, prompting Honan to conclude that "Thomas' associates took pains not to embarrass him with revelations."[591] Nevertheless, Watson complained to Walsingham, "How you have changed from those days."[592] Earlier, Watson had offered himself as Ganymede to the Earl of Arundel's Jove in his introductory letter to his translation of Antigone which, even if in jest, suggests his willingness to pursue extra-traditional avenues in seeking patronage.

That said, it is not necessary to conclude that Thomas Walsingham was homosexual to observe that he and his wife lived very separate lives. She loved life at court, he preferred life in the country. Her personal life was public and even scandalous, his was quiet and austere. This pattern started very early and yet they never formally separated as Penelope Deveraux did from Lord Rich. If anything, Marlowe's complaints against Audrey might easily have been Thomas' as well. Except that Thomas does not appear to have contracted venereal disease. When Marlowe writes "Of thy fair health" in sonnet 45, he appears to be addressing Thomas who is neither the fire nor air referred to earlier in the poem. Of all the notables who did contract venereal disease, including Essex and Cecil and many others rumored about at court, Thomas was never among them.

What is now implied by the timeline is that Thomas Junior may actually have been Marlowe's son. This could explain the quiet marriage and the uncertain date of birth for Thomas which would have to have been obscured in order for it not to be discovered. Sir Thomas "became a Kent justice of the peace in 1596" and before that "there are numerous references to Walsingham as an official in Kent."[593] Keeping a wedding or a birth quiet would not have been difficult for him. The christening could have been delayed by several months without significant notice, therefore the birth may have been very near the marriage itself with Audrey just beginning to show.

The notion that Thomas Junior might have been illegitimate finds support, in all places, in Edward Blount's dedication to Hero and Leander in which he expresses the hope that Sir Thomas "would prove more agreeable and thriving to his right children than any other foster countenance whatsoever."[594] Traditionalists would argue that Blount is saying that Sir Thomas will support the new poem as much as he has supported previous poems from Marlowe. That, however, is not what the plain words say. The use of the phrase "foster countenance" is unusual if all that Blount is referring to by "right children" is yet another of Marlowe's poems. The unusual phrasing leaves open the not so very unusual possibility that Blount is referring to an actual child for whom Sir Thomas has provided a "foster countenance." When Blount further says "his right children" he introduces the possibility that Thomas Senior has been a foster parent for Christopher Marlowe's actual child. This unusual interpretation is invited by Blount's phrasing which does not use words like "poem" or "patron".

Puzzling and equivocal statements like those from Blount's dedication make more sense when viewed in a context consistent with the overall narrative of Marlowe's life as recorded in the sonnets. If all of this seems like a stretch, then what do words mean, after all? Why else would Blount refer to Hero and Leander in that particular way? As a foster child, one of many? Don't forget that this would have been the very poem withheld when Marlowe fled London; a poem he may well have been writing for Audrey, as it was when it was completed; a poem that borrowed from the first seventeen sonnets with the subject of "increase" when she was very likely pregnant. If Blount did not suspect any of this when he wrote his unusual dedication, then he somehow managed to stumble into some very personal territory in a highly extraordinary way.

There is one other very significant statement in this regard that Audrey supplied herself which will be fully explained in the next chapter. For now, suffice to say that there was indeed a "fair youth" and he very possibly could have been Thomas Walsingham Junior.

Chapter Two

Mr.W.H.

A Lover's Complaint has very often been given less attention than Shake-speare's Sonnets despite being published in the same volume. As John Kerrigan noted: "Poorly edited because thought peripheral, it has stayed peripheral because poorly edited."[595]

This, despite the fact that the idea of a collection including "a formal connection between sonnet sequence and complaint was thoroughly established"[596] by the time the collection was published. Far from peripheral, A Lover's Complaint is so much a direct response to the Sonnets that there is good reason to doubt that they would have been published without it.

What may be most interesting about A Lover's Complaint is the way that it echoes the narrative of the Sonnets. Viewed from Audrey Walsingham's perspective, the Sonnets relate her love affair with Marlowe from their meeting at Wilton House all the way through the birth of her son, the dispute over the "Rival Poet" sequence, the reconciliation of that dispute and the Masque of Blackness critiques. It was her reaction to the final critiques that apparently prompted her to respond with the Complaint.

At the beginning of the poem, the "fickle maid full pale" is discovered in a vale "tearing of papers, breaking rings a-twain / Storming her world with sorrow's wind and rain." [6 – 7]. She is unflatteringly described as: "The carcass of a beauty spent and done." Then, perhaps to soften that judgement:

> "Time had not scythed all that youth begun,
> Nor youth all quit, but spite of heaven's fell rage Some beauty peeped through lattice of seared age."
> [12 – 14]

Audrey would have been about forty-one in 1609, not so old as to be unattractive but old enough to feel the loss of youth, especially if she had taken sonnets 127 to 152 so much to heart that she might want to tear them apart. Most importantly, the allegations made in those sonnets would be the first connection between them and the <u>Complaint</u> which becomes their direct response as opposed to some arbitrary, unrelated poem.

It soon is revealed that the maid has "a thousand" such "favours", all of which she proceeds to throw into a river. She also has many "folded schedules" which "she perused, sighed, tore and gave the flood;" after which she finds:

> "yet more letters sadly penned in blood,
> With sleided silk feat and affectedly
> Enswathed and sealed to curious secrecy."

[47 - 49]

A better description of privately couriered sonnets, written with passion and careful ambiguity could hardly be imagined. The passage literally begs the question of whether some other volume of sonnets may have been sacrificed in the process of composing the <u>Complaint</u>. Further expressing her anguish, the maid cries: "O false blood, thou register of lies, / What unapproved witness dost thou bear!" which implies the separation between her and the writer of the letters.

An older man, grazing his cattle nearby, is drawn to her side and, asking why she is so upset, is told that she is unhappy in love and that she gave her youthful heart "too early" to "one by nature's outwards so commended / That maiden's eyes stuck all over his face." She then describes person in terms that seem to mirror Marlowe's Cambridge portrait:

> "His browny locks did hang in crookèd curls,
> And every light occasion of the wind
> Upon his lips their silken parcels hurls."

>
> [85 - 87]

and

> "Small show of man was yet upon his chin;
> His phoenix down began but to appear,
> Like unshorn velvet, on that termless skin,
> Whose bare out-bragged the web it seemed to wear;"
>
> [92 - 95]

and

> "His qualities were beauteous as his form,
> For maiden-tongued he was, and thereof free;
> Yet, if men moved him, was he such a storm
> As oft 'twixt May and April is to see,"
>
> [101 - 103]

She also notes his skill as a horseman:

> "Well he could ride, and often men would say
> "That horse his mettle from his rider takes;"
>
> [106 - 7]

which recalls the horse imagery of both Hero and Leander:

> "   a hot proud horse highly disdains
> To have his head controlled,"
>
> [141 - 2]

and Venus and Adonis:

> "Being so enrag'd, desire doth lend her force

Courageously to pluck him from his horse."

[27 - 8]

Physical descriptions aside, the maid portrays this man as fascinating in mind:

> "So on the tip of his subduing tongue
> All kinds of arguments and questions deep,
> All replication prompt and reason strong,
> For his advantage still did wake and sleep.
> To make the weeper laugh, the laugher weep,
> He had that dialect and different skill,
> Catching all passions in his craft of will."

[120 - 126]

All of this and more is consonant with that enchanted summer at Wilton House in 1592 when Audrey first met Marlowe. She even portrays him like a playwright rehearsing his always eager actors:

> "Consents bewitched, ere he desire, have granted,
> And dialogued for him what he would say,
> Asked their own wills, and made their wills obey."

[131 - 133]

She claims have resisted his charms which she thought were false and:

> "Saw how deceits were gilded in his smiling,
> Knew vows were ever brokers to defiliing,
> Thought characters and words merely but art,
> And bastards of his foul adulterate heart."

[172 - 175]

But, once he set siege to her heart, he steadily overcame her resistance, insisting that "For feasts of Love I have been called unto, / Till now did ne'er invite nor never woo" and showing her various "tributes wounded fancies sent me" which, rather than hoard, he offers to her:

> "For you of force must your oblations be,
> Since I, their altar, you enpatron me."
>
> [223 - 224]

The most significant of these is a "device" sent to him by a nun:

> "Which late her noble suit in court did shun,
> Whose rarest havings made the blossoms dote;
> For she was sought by spirits of richest coat,
> But kept cold distance, and thence did remove
> To spend her living in eternal love."
>
> [234 - 238]

This passage reads suspiciously like Audrey accusing Marlowe of boasting about having received a gift from a teenage Arbella Stuart, the potential successor to Elizabeth's throne who was kept in isolation and under house arrest for decades lest various Catholic supporters use her to attempt to displace the Queen. The idea that in her splendid isolation the very beautiful Arbella may have been infatuated with her handsome, charming tutor[597] does not seem at all preposterous when Audrey simultaneously asserts that so many others were as well. In such cases, the truth of the thing is not as consequential as the fact of the accusation.

By 1609, Arbella's circumstances had improved substantially. Following Elizabeth's death and the succession of King James, Arbella came to court and Lady Audrey was there to greet her. In March 1604 the royal family celebrated their Entry to London with a procession, and Arbella followed Anne of Denmark in a carriage with some of the queen's maids of honour. While the subject of marriage had been a major topic of discussion throughout, she was at the time still unmarried. It would be the secret marriage in 1610 to William Seymour, 2nd Duke of Somerset, which would prove her final disaster and result in confinement in the Tower of London until her death in 1615. Audrey, who was even in 1609 rumored to be the mistress of Robert Cecil, could not have foreseen such an end for Arbella, but her rivalry with her was sufficiently personal that she made note of it as a tipping point of the seduction in the Complaint.

In a poem of 329 lines, Audrey has Marlowe taking 49 of them to disavow this "nun" and then end his appeal to her with tears:

> "'O father, what a hell of witchcraft lies
> In the small orb of one particular tear!
> But with the innundation of the eyes
> What rocky heart to water will not wear?"
>
> [288 - 291]

No sooner does she yield, than she accuses him of dishonesty and worse:

> "There my white soul of chastity I daffed,
> Shook off my sober guards and civil fears,
> Appear to him as he to me appears -
> All melting, though our drops this diff'rence bore:
> His poisoned me, and mine did his restore."
>
> [297 - 301]

Just in case the accusation is not altogether clear, she repeats it again and again in the final stanza, expressing her fear that, even knowing what she knows, she might betray herself again:

> "'O, that infected moisture of his eye,
> O, that false fire which in his cheek so glowed,
> O, that forced thunder from his heart did fly,
> O, that sad breath his spongy lungs bestowed,
> O, all that borrowed motion, seeming owed,
> Would yet again betray the fore-betrayed,
> And new pervert a reconcilèd maid."
>
> [323 - 329]

The infection that identified her in the sonnets is the same infection that she claims he gave to her. It is not unusual for accusations to fly in such matters, but Audrey would not have been likely to have been nearly as sexually experienced as Marlowe in 1592. For all the anger Marlowe has hurled at her over the years, the lines that really seem to have stung the worst were the ones that claimed she gave him the pox. From her point of view, that may not only have been untrue, but very unfair. If ever there was a lover's complaint, that is it.

The poem ends there, somewhat unresolved. Will the maid find relief or will she continue to suffer? Will the false lover continue his abuse or will he resolve to do better by her? The poem does not say and perhaps it was not possible to say more at that time. While she professes to accept the past, the fact of the complaint argues against that. On top of which, if Audrey really did have a hand in this, why then was it published?

Although they are her thoughts being expressed, it seems unlikely that Audrey would have composed them on her own. Whether or not they were written independently as a gift or produced on consignment, a woman in her position would have had her pick of poetic assistants, from Samuel Daniel to Ben Jonson and many others among which to choose. In fact, the poet who was very early proposed as the likely author of <u>A</u>

Lover's Complaint may have been a not only convenient but a very apt collaborator.

George Chapman had become the very man that Marlowe feared he would be when he complained about him in Sonnets. Between 1598 and 1608 he wrote ten plays, most of which were performed by The Children of St.Paul's at the Blackfriars, including seven comedies, The Blind Beggar of Alexandria (1598), An Humorous Day's Mirth (1599), both performed by Henslow's company, The Admiral's Men, The Old Joiner of Aldgate, not published but performed by The Children of St.Paul's in February of 1603, All Fools (1605), Monsieur D'Olive (1606), Sir Giles Goosecap (1606) and The Gentleman Usher (1606), three tragedies, Bussy D'Ambois (1607) and The Conspiracy and Tragedy of Charles, Duke of Byron Parts I and II (1608) and one collaboration, Eastward Hoe (1605) with Ben Jonson and John Marston which was also played by The Children of St.Paul's at the Blackfriars and resulted in Chapman's imprisonment.

In fact, both Jonson and Chapman were imprisoned for offending the King with anti-Scottish satire in Eastward Hoe, a situation that was only resolved with their release after months of protracted negotiations which included the Earl of Suffolk, Lord Aubigny (the King's cousin Esmé Stuart), the Earl of Pembroke, the Lord Chamberlain, Robert Cecil (newly created Lord Salisbury), and even King James himself. Eventually, it became necessary to engineer a "large financial payment made by Salisbury to Sir John Murray"[598], a Scottish knight and favorite courtier of the King who had been particularly offended at the play's Scottish satire. Not reported, but always available when the theatre and Cecil were involved, would have been Audrey who would not have been faulted for offering to assist in the release of the man who had dedicated Hero and Leander to her.

Chapman then got into trouble on his own with Charles, Duke of Byron which included a scene in which the French Queen slaps the face of her husband's mistress. The French Ambassador was so upset that the play was suppressed. Later, when the Court left London, the play was performed again by the Boys only to have three of them thrown into prison while Chapman "apparently"[599] avoided a similar fate by leaving town and taking refuge with Ludovick Stuart, Duke of Lennox. James, meanwhile, shut down the theatres only to reopen them after a spell of calm, but not before Chapman wrote to George Buc, Master of Revels, unchivalrously blaming the actors for playing the banned scene.[600]

Throughout this period, Chapman remained close to the Walsinghams and dedicated All Fools to Sir Thomas in a quarto printed in 1605 by George Eld for Thomas Thorpe, the same team that would soon publish the Sonnets. In his dedication, Chapman claimed that though he was "loath to pass your sight / With any such like mark of vanity;" he was only publishing the play "lest by others' stealth it be imprest. / Without my passport patch'd with other's wit,"[601] which is a rather remarkable protest to make in a dedication to the man on whose behalf he had not seven years before patched up Marlowe's Hero and Leander and published under his own name. Apparently, Sir Thomas was not altogether pleased with the dedication because when Chapman subsequently decided to dedicate The Conspiracy and Tragedy of Charles, Duke of Byron to him, he confessed that "hauing heard your approbation of these in their presentment" had "made me hetherto dispence with your right in my other impressions". Nevertheless, and despite that approbation, Chapman wanted to dedicate his most politically inept play to Walsingham's son, Thomas Walsingham, Esquire, "that my affection may extend to your Posteritie":

> "whom I doubt not, that most reuerenc'd Mother of
> Manly Sciences; to whose instruction your vertuous
> care commits him; will so profitably initiate in her
> learned labours, that they will make him florish in his
> riper life, ouer the idle liues of our ignorant
> Gentlemen; and enable him to supply the Honorable
> places, of your name; extending your yeares, and his

right noble Mothers (in the true comforts of his vertues) to the sight of much, and most happy Progenie; which most affectionately wishing; and diuiding these poore dismemberd Poems betwixt you, I desire to liue still in your gracefull loues; and euer,

The most assured at your commandements GEORGE CHAPMAN."

This too was printed and published by the team of Eld and Thorpe not many months before they printed Shake-Speare's Sonnets and A Lover's Complaint. These were the only dedications Chapman made in this period and it is perhaps notable that he was allowed to drift away from the Walsingham orbit soon after. Chapman's decision to dedicate a play about marital infidelity to Thomas Junior, who was by then the same age as the players who had been jailed for performing it, at the very moment that the Complaint was being composed is either a phenomenal blunder or deliberately provocative. The question is who is provoking who. Where does Chapman get the idea that this would be acceptable?

As discussed in Chapter One, George Chapman is the overwhelming contender for the identity of the "Rival Poet" by virtue of the many links between those sonnets and his own work, in particular his additions to Marlowe's Hero and Leander. The sole reason traditional scholars have for not accepting Chapman in this role is that he leads directly to Christopher Marlowe. Despite this, as discussed in Chapter Two, many scholars have also agreed that he is the most likely author of A Lover's Complaint. As early as 1912, J. W. Mackail made the obvious connection that "the poem . . . may be the work of the 'rival poet'"[602] which J. M. Robertson then called "a singularly happy hypothesis."[603]

There would obviously be a remarkable irony in Chapman's collaboration with Lady Audrey in the composition of A Lover's Complaint. It was Chapman's contribution to Hero and Leander which sparked Marlowe's jealousy in the first place. Moreover, the claim that Chapman had "married" his contribution to Marlowe's unfinished original would be matched again by marrying Audrey's complaint to Marlowe's long list of complaints. This makes Chapman's dedication in Hero and Leander all the more telling when it suggests some form of separation between Lady Audrey and Sir Thomas that is addressed by his share in the completed poem:

> "This poor Dedication (in figure of the other unity betwixt Sir Thomas and yourself) hath rejoined you with him, my honoured best friend;"

"Rejoined"? Was the implied separation by virtue of discontent or merely a formal restating of vows or something else altogether? Sonnets 59 to 72 fall within this period and all appear to be written directly to Audrey.

This group of sonnets is less precisely tied to the timeline, although they clearly fall within a period between 1594 and 1598 when Marlowe was apparently still close to home and hoping for a reprieve. This is confirmed by the fact that in June, 1595, Lord Burghley paid £16 to Thomas Drury for courier services in and out of France. This was the same Robert Drury who had been employed by Puckering and Buckhurst in the Baine's business and his accusations against Marlowe in May, 1593 [Chapter Four]. If Burghley's preferred courier, Robert Poley, was being kept closer to home, Drury, who had sought service with Burghley while in prison, appeared to be ready and available and his familiarity with Marlowe's circumstances would have made him useful in the same role.

During this time Marlowe was preoccupied with writing and rewriting a variety of plays which were eventually debuted by the Lord Chamberlain's Men, starting with Comedy of Errors and continuing with Love's Labour's Lost, the rewritten Henry VI Parts 1, 2 and 3 and The Taming of the Shrew. Other new plays included Richard II, The Merchant of

Venice and Henry IV. That these were written in anticipation or as an argument for his restoration is attested to by sonnets 57 and 58, both of which grouse to Thomas about being made a "vassal bound to stay your leisure." While his first two new plays had been aimed at the court and Richard II at Essex in particular, further work was aimed at the general public in support of the Tudor enterprise. As Marlowe saw it, even if he enjoyed the work, he had little choice in the matter:

> "Being your slave, what should I do but tend
> Upon the hours and times of your desire?
> I have no precious time at all to spend,
> Nor services to do, till you require."
>
> 57: 1 - 4

Following these notes, Marlowe appears to turn his attention to Audrey and speaks of their separation in specific terms, either as a body of water:

> "Let this sad interim like the ocean be
> Which parts the shore where two contracted new
> Come daily to the banks, that, when they see
> Return of love, more blest may be the view;
>
> 56: 9 - 12

or as Time:

> "Against my love shall be as I am now,
> With Time's injurious hand crushed and o'erworn;
>
> 63: 1 - 2

and:

> "O, how shall summer's honey breath hold out

> Against the wrackful seige of battering days,
> When rocks impregnible are not so stout,
> Nor gates of steel so strong, but Time betrays?"

    65: 5 - 8

or both:

> "Like as the waves make towards the pebbled shore,
> So do our minutes hasten to their end;
> Each changing place with which goes before,
> In sequent toil all forwards to contend."

    60: 1 - 4

and:

> "When I have seen by Time's hand defaced
> The rich proud cost of outworn buried age;
> When sometime lofty towers I see down-razed
> And brass eternal slave to mortal;
> When I have seen the hungry ocean gain
> Advantage on the kingdom of the shore,
> And the firm soil win of the wat'ry main,
> Increasing store with loss and loss with store;
> When I have seen such interchange of state,
> Or state itself confounded to decay,
> Ruin hath taught me thus to ruminate -
> That Time will come and take my Love away."

    64: 1 - 12

which, in addition to their metaphoric quality, can also be understood to describe an actual separation of a long period by a nautical barrier consistent with Marlowe's exile.

Another repeated motif is that of an image, possibly a miniature portrait, that Marlowe keeps with him and with which he contemplates his beloved. This continues a motif that first appeared in sonnet 24, to Audrey:

> "For through the painter must you see his skill
> To find where your true image pictured lies,
> Which in my own bosom's shop is hanging still,
> That hath his windows glazed with thine eyes."
>
> Sonnet 24: 5 - 8

In sonnet 47, he similarly references a portrait in another poem addressed to Audrey:

> "With my love's picture then my doth feast,
> And to the painted banquet bids my heart."
>
> Sonnet 47: 5 - 6

The most suggestive in this regard may be sonnet 61:

> "Is it thy will thy image should keep open
> My heavy eyelids to the weary night?"
>
> Sonnet 61: 1 - 2

It does not seem likely that Marlowe is referring to a portrait of Thomas Walsingham keeping him awake at night. There is, however, a beautiful miniature of a "Portrait of an Unknown Woman" by Issac Oliver wearing a masque costume which A. D. Wraight speculated may be of Lady Audrey. Now kept in the Victoria and Albert Museum, the portrait would be too late to be like the one that Marlowe describes, but it shows that he may have had something like it to remind him of Lady Audrey. [604] Either Marlowe is writing to Thomas with a passion he has never before expressed or he continues to address his passion to Audrey, despite her marriage and her young son. Or, possibly, he is writing to both, knowing that they will both read the sonnets in turn and letting them sort out which is which. The confusion may be part of his own perspective and daring, part of a personal strategy to continue to argue for his release and return. It hardly seems possible that he would write to Thomas about nocturnal fantasies.

Sonnet 66 sums up the movement of Time amid multiple wrongs and raises the subject of death as a respite from a dishonest world:

> "Tired with all these, from these I would be gone,
> Save that to die, I leave my love alone."
>
> 66: 13 - 14

which is then continued in sonnets 71 and 72:

> "No longer mourn for me when I am dead
> Than you shall hear the surly sullen bell
> Give warning to the world that I am fled
> From this vile world with wilest worms to dwell."
>
> 71: 1 - 4
>
> "O, lest your true love may seem false in this,
> That you for love speak well of me untrue,
> My name be buried where my body is
> And live no more to shame mor me nor you;"
>
> 72: 9 - 12

As a combined series, sonnets 56 to 72 depict the storm of thoughts that preoccupied the interim between the abrupt start of Marlowe's exile up to the point of his break with the Walsinghams over the unexpected publication of Hero and Leander. What they also suggest is that Marlowe had not yet decided to take the Walsingham's marriage seriously, as if he considers it a matter of convenience, a political marriage that cannot be expected to interfere with his love affair with Audrey. He even appears to assume that both Thomas and Audrey are of the same mind with him. This would help explain Chapman's reference to a reunion in his dedication.

The publication of Hero and Leander would then have been Thomas' reply, a statement that the marriage must stand firm. If understood fully by Marlowe, it would be the most painful reason of all for his distress. Whatever the Sonnets had been up to that point, their substance changed radically afterward. Ironically, it is also possible to say that they might not have been published but for the persistence of the Walsingham marriage.

The employment of Thomas Thorpe as publisher for the collection was by no means accidental. Although Sir Sidney Lee claimed that the publication of the Sonnets was unauthorized and characterized Thorpe's presence as the result of "the predatory work of procuring, no matter how, unpublished and neglected 'copy,'"[605] the record of Thorpe's publications argues against Lee's dismissive estimation. Thorpe published four of Ben Jonson's scripts, including Sejanus (1605) and Volpone (1607), three plays of George Chapman, All Fools, The Conspiracy and Tragedy of Charles, Duke of Byron and The Gentleman Usher (1606), as well as one of John Marston's and, his first publication, The First Book of Lucan (1600 posthumous), was a translation from the Latin by Christopher Marlowe. Given this record, Stanley Wells and Gary Taylor concluded that "Thorpe was a reputable publisher, and there is nothing intrinsically irregular about his publication."[606]

What often goes unmentioned in all this is the remarkable fact that in addition to being a part time publisher of poetry and plays, Thorpe was also a sometime intelligencer formerly in the employ of the Essex faction in the 1590s. In fact, Thorpe's activities as a member of Essex's spy network extended at least as far back as 1596 when he traveled to Madrid to follow and later report on a pair of "English fugitives, declared traitors, just as they were urging the

Spanish government to launch a new Armada."[607] This report is included in Thorpe's own testimony before the Court of Exchequer which has been uncovered by Patrick H. Martin and John Finnis and included in an article titled "Thomas Thorpe, 'W.S.' and the Catholic Intelligencers". Detailing Thorpe's career as an intelligencer, Martin and Finnis contend that Thorpe's publishing career was greatly assisted by his Catholic connections through which he obtained the rights to various manuscripts attributed to Catholic sympathizers, including the several plays by Ben Jonson who supposedly converted while awaiting trial at Newgate in 1598. Martin and Finnis do not, however, explain how Thorpe gained possession of the manuscript for Shake-speare's Sonnets and it appears that so far as they are concerned, his Catholic connections had nothing to do with it.

In addition to being a publisher and a spy, Thorpe had another connection to Sir Thomas Walsingham by way of Christopher Marlowe. When Thorpe begin his publishing career with Marlowe's translation of The First Book of Lucan, he obtained the rights to that work by means of his friendship with Edward Blount, who published the first edition of Marlowe's Hero and Leander in 1598 and dedicated it to Sir Thomas. Thorpe, therefore, had a three-part connection to Walsingham, first by being part of a competing spy network, second by virtue of being Blount's friend and third by way of a publishing interest in Christopher Marlowe.

As to who could have put this all together, at the end of the day, the one person who had access to all the elements, the Sonnets and the Complaint, not to mention the history, is Audrey Walsingham. Those sonnets not addressed to her or to Thomas she could have gathered by way of Cecil and Lady Pembroke. Publishing Marlowe's Sonnets with Chapman's Lover's Complaint would at a minimum bookend the version of Hero and Leander which was dedicated to her and included parts also by Marlowe and Chapman. It makes for a very neat package and one that suggests a riposte to the origins of her conflict with Marlowe.

All she would need would be a suitable dedication. In the end, she found one that has baffled scholars ever since:

> TO.THE.ONLIE.BEGETTER.OF.
> THESE.INSUING.SONNETS.
> Mr.W.H. ALL.HAPPINESSE.
> AND.THAT.ETERNITIE.
> PROMISED.
> BY.
> OUR.EVER-LIVING.POET.
> WISHETH.
> THE.WELL-WISHING.
> ADVENTURER.IN.
> SETTING.
> FORTH.
> T.T.

Sidney Lee speculated that the attribution to "Mr.W.H." was in reference to a fellow Stationer, William Hall, who like Thorpe was performing "the irresponsible rôle of procurer of manuscripts". Somewhat later, E. K. Chambers, who thought it more likely that Sir William Herbert, the Earl of Pembroke, was the mysterious Mr. W.H., walked back Lee's notion of the dedicatee being a fellow stationer, saying:

> "there is some unconscious humour in the notion of Thorpe's dedicating the volume to a printer whom he had not employed. To me it seems more difficult, every time I read the dedication, to believe that, even in Thorpe's affected phrasing, the person to whom he wished eternity was any other person than the person to whom the ever-living poet promised eternity."[608]

Donald Foster, chair of Dramatic Literature at Vassar College, recently argued that Thorpe's dedication has simply been misunderstood by modern scholars, that contemporary readers understood that the phrase "onlie.begetter" was a reference not to the person who inspired or procured the Sonnets, but to "the person who wrote the work."[609] He further asserted that the "ever.living.poet" refers to the deity and that "Mr.W.H." is a misprint that most probably should have been spelled "Mr.W.Sh." In this way, he intends to refute all of those who have tried in vain to unravel Thorpe's dedication and identify its dedicatee as someone other than Shakespeare. At the same time, however, Foster admits that the publisher of the second edition of the Sonnets, John Benson, changed the "ever-living" reference to clearly indicate the author of the poems and not a possible deity, thus putting part of Foster's interpretation in doubt.

Perhaps Foster is right and that the entire controversy is merely the result of that old Elizabethan standby for any disputed interpretation, the misprint. Or, perhaps E. K. Chambers has the better notion when he says that he found it difficult not to conclude that "the person to whom [Thomas Thorpe] wished eternity was any other person than the person to whom the ever-living poet promised eternity." After all, Foster's special pleading notwithstanding, it is that rare work of literature that is dedicated to its own author.

While frequently mentioned candidates for the identity of Mr.W.H. include William Herbert and Henry Wriosley, the Earl of Southampton (with his initials reversed), no traditional scholar has ever suggested the name of one particular, special patron of the poetic arts: Thomas Walsingham. His initials, after all, are T. W., which are obviously not a match. But, if the hyphenation of Shake-Speare is at all suggestive, perhaps something similar applies to Walsing-Ham.

Often overlooked is the fact that the words in the dedication are separated either by hyphens or by a period with no empty space, with the sole exception of "ALL.HAPPINESSE." which has an empty space between it and "Mr.W.H." The periods between each word therefore allows the "W.H." to be read either as one or two words simultaneously. In other words, the reader can overlook those periods rather than have to abide by them as they do not necessarily connote separate words or separation of any kind.

Of all the names proposed as "the onlie begetter" of the Sonnets, Thomas Walsingham could well be the most central to the story they tell. The possibility is further supported by the full definition of "begetter": "a male parent; a father or mother; one who begets or one who gives birth to or nurtures and raises a child; a relative who plays the role of guardian."[610] This definition results in a twin set of double entendres within the dedication wherein Sir Thomas is both the guardian/begetter of Thomas Junior, who may actually be Marlowe's illegitimate son, and the guardian/begetter of the sonnets written by Marlowe, not Shakes-speare who meanwhile acts as guardian for Marlowe.

The only difficulty with this is that "Mr.W.H." cannot, in fact, apply to Sir Thomas any more than it can refer to the Earl of Pembroke or the Earl of Southampton as it is inappropriate, especially in a dedication, to refer to a Lord or Knight or an Earl by anything less than his title. "Mr.W.H." is only appropriate if it applies to Thomas Walsingham, Esquire, the son of Sir Thomas. And, of course, the lines wishing "All Happinesse And That Eternitie Promised By Our Ever-Living Poet." apply perfectly to Thomas Esquire who has been wished exactly that in at least half a dozen sonnets printed in the volume.

In 1609, Thomas Junior would have been about 15 years old. By naming Junior as the guardian of the sonnets, Audrey would be declaring that he was old enough to understand the history and that she had explained it all to him, including the details of her illness. Any hesitation in that regard would only breed distrust. The only alternative explanation would be that she simply used her son like a pawn in a showdown with Marlowe, but that also would have alienated Thomas which would run contrary to her apparent purpose. The Sonnets and The Conspiracy and Tragedy of Charles, Duke of Byron are the only works ever dedicated to him, both include the hand of

Chapman and both were intended to promote him in the eyes of the world.

Still, the question has to be, why would Audrey publish what put her own reputation in such a poor light? Sir Thomas would naturally have opposed it, having already expressed his displeasure with having his family name in print. Regardless, the answer may very well be simply to get Marlowe to stop sending his increasingly heated letters. She had had ten years of Marlowe's anger and frustration and probably could not take any more of it.[611] She was isolated from her husband and must have wanted Marlowe to understand that she was tired of having him threaten her with all of this. In fact, he threatened her in the Rival Poet sonnets ten years before. He threatened to "Tell All". More importantly, the threat included Thomas who may well have been his own son.

In the ten years since he had first made his threat, the boy had reached the age when many could consider him a man. In fact, he would be knighted four years later, in 1613 when he was very likely still nineteen. So, ten years after Marlowe had first made his threat, Audrey called his bluff. By 1609, all of the people who could have been threatening to any of them were dead; Essex, Whitgift, the Queen even Burghley and she was Cecil's mistress. She was telling Marlowe the threat is over. If she really had destroyed some of what he had sent, then when she published the rest with her own reply he would know what, if anything, was missing. She might well destroy anything else that he would send her and she could not him help any more than she already had. It had to stop.

And it did. There are no more sonnets. If Marlowe defied her and sent more, she must have destroyed them because no one has ever seen them. It was, in effect, the end of the affair.

Afterwards, everyone went back to their more or less ordinary lives. Sir Thomas Walsingham continued as MP for Rochester until 1614 when he was returned to Parliament as knight of the shire for Kent. He died a wealthy landowner at Scadbury in 1630.

Thomas Walsingham, Esquire, as noted above was knighted at Royston on 26 November 1613[612] when he was approximately nineteen or twenty. In 1614 he was elected Member of Parliament for Poole. He was elected MP for Rochester, the seat his father had held, in 1621 and again in 1628 and held the seat until 1629 and was made vice-admiral of Kent in 1627. He married twice and had three children, naming his Eldest son Thomas. He sold the family estate at Scadbury in 1655 and died at Chiselhurst in 1669.

Lady Audrey spent fifteen more years at court, notoriously keeping company with Robert Cecil who died in 1612, but also was on hand when Anne of Denmark was received at Wells, Somerset on August 20th, 1613 and on December 4th, 1615 when the Venetian ambassador had his final audience with Anne of Denmark at Greenwhich Palace. During this period, the court physician, Theodore de Mayerne is reported to have noted she suffered from serious headaches or migraine.[613] She died in May 1624 and was buried at St Nicholas, Chislehurst, six years before her husband and five years his junior, her health possibly complicated by venereal disease.

George Chapman moved on from the Walsingham family with a promise of stronger patronage by way of Prince Henry VI who had pledged him £300 plus a pension to be remitted upon the completion of this translation of The Illiad. Unfortunately, Henry died in 1612 and his household failed to honor the commitment. Chapman transferred his attention to Lord Somerset and Lady Frances Howard who were soon after mired in scandals of their own and also proved unable to support him. His later years were more obscure, and he supported himself collaborating on a handful of plays and other projects, including a translation of Musaeus' original Hero and Leander (1618), before passing away in 1634.

Christopher Marlowe finally put aside sonnets and other poetic forms but continued writing plays without ever giving up his hopes for redemption and ultimate return to England. Pericles, the play he had begun in honor of Philip Sidney almost 25 years before about the hero's shipwreck odyssey and long delayed reunion of husband, wife and daughter, was a hit in London in 1609 and he completed several more about similarly separated and reunited families, including Cymbelline, A Winter's Tale, and The Tempest.

On June 19th, 1609 none other than Ned Alleyn purchased a copy of the Sonnets, recording his acquisition under "Howshowld stuff": a book Shaksper Sonets, 5d".[614] Sixteen years after he had written to his father-in-law to ask what was going on with Pembroke's Men, what must he have thought and how much did he recognize of the story he found inside that slim volume?

Epilogue

Did Marlowe ever manage to return to London? There are a few hints and one last sonnet that might shed some light on this question. Not included in the 1609 collection and not published until 1623 in the Folio, it is today known as Merlin's Prophecy and is found in Act III, Scene 2 of King Lear:

> "When priests are more in word than matter,
> When brewers mar their malt with water,
> When nobles are their tailors' tutors,
> No heretics burned but wenches' suitors,
> When every case in law is right,
> No squire in debt nor no poor knight,
> When slanders do not live in tongues,
> Nor cutpurses come not to throngs,
> When usurers tell their gold i' th' field,
> And bawds and whores do churches build—
> Then shall the realm of Albion
> Come to great confusion.
>   Then comes the time, who lives to see 't,
>   That going shall be used with feet."

Not included in the 1608 quarto version of the play, the poem is irregular in that its rhyme scheme is aabb ccdd eeff gg, is written in tetrameter rather than pentameter, and its authenticity has long been questioned. According to Richard Knowles, "the Fool's 'Merlin Prophecy,' . . . despite its admirers, has often been thought to be an intrusive irrelevance."[615]

Dennis McCarthy and June Schlueter, however, believe that Merlin's Prophecy has a key connection with George North's manuscript "A Brief Discourse on Rebellion and Rebels" which, as noted in Chapter Twelve, was not published and existed in a single copy kept at Kirtling Hall where it would have been available to Marlowe during his visit to nearby Canterbury in 1592. McClean and Schlueter argue that North's text, which they found to have provided source material for the Jack Cade scenes in The True Contention Betwixt the Famous Houses of York and Lancaster (aka Henry VI Part II), as well as source material for Richard III, Antony and Cleopatra, and Coriolanus, also provides a source for the Prophecy. Consistent with their view that North's text is reflected in many of the plays, they assert that, far from being irrelevant:

> "North's conflating of a prophecy by Merlin with a description of role-reversals in a topsy-turvy world offers a primary example of King Lear's debt to the earlier text. "Discourse" may even have provided the basis for the character of the Fool who quotes Merlin explicitly, emphasizing the sixth century Prophet with whom he has much in common. Or, to be more precise, Lear's Fool resembles the peculiar version of Merlin described in "Discourse".[616]

The poem can be read generally to say that when that which is true is false and that which is false is true, then not only will England "come to confusion", but walking will be done with feet. Howard Dobin seems to have had this reading in mind when he complained that:

> "The Prophecy is sheer nonsense, foretelling things that have always been true or never will be true. The climactic prediction - that people will use feet to walk - is hardly news."[617]

It is also possible, however, to read the sonnet more personally. For instance, the first line, "When priests are more in word than matter" and the tenth, "And bawds and whores do churches build" which bookend the list of true/false statements can be understood as a "shout-outs" to Martin Marprelate's attacks on the clergy. Similarly, line six, "No squire in debt nor no poor knight", recollects Philip Sidney's difficult finances, while line eight, "Nor cutpurses come not to throngs", reminds the theatrical audience of a typical hazard. Closer to home, line seven, "When slanders do not live in tongues" clearly touches Marlowe's disgrace and line four, "No heretics burned but wenches' suitors" sums up the charges against him, being both a heretic and suitor. All of these lines can be understood to create a context which describes significant parts of Christopher Marlowe's life. Which all goes to say that the poem is not so irrelevant as it might seem.

In the tag line for the scene, the Fool states: "This prophecy Merlin shall make, for I live before his time." The fact that, as early as 1588, Robert Greene made a point of comparing Marlowe to "such mad and scoffing poets that have prophetical spirits, as bred of Merlin's race"[618] seems to have gone unnoticed by the majority of commentators on the poem. Regardless, this alone ties it directly to Marlowe and the other, more personal reading of the sonnet flows straight through it.

As for going "with feet"; surely it does not take a Cambridge scholar to observe that "feet" references poetic meter? Could it be possible that Marlowe was making a little joke, saying that his travels have been annotated by his poems? More broadly, could this mean that the poem is saying that when true is false and false is true, then poets like Marlowe will inevitably be banished? If nothing else, that is an interpretation that fits the character and purpose of the Fool.

The timing alone suggests that Merlin's Prophecy was written sometime after the <u>Sonnets</u> and <u>A Lover's Complaint</u> were published. Why would Marlowe add the poem after 1608 and why would it reference North's Rebellion and Rebels? It is only possible to speculate, but Marlowe's affair with Audrey could not be considered ended until 1609 at the earliest because that is when <u>A Lover's Complaint</u> was published. Sometime between that and when the Folio was being edited Marlowe must have taken time to reflect on North manuscript which influenced so many of the plays. Line four of the Prophecy, "No heretics burned but wenches' suitors" closes the first quatrain and recalls events from late 1592 and early 1593, the same period when he met Audrey, fell in love with her and subsequently would have been able to read North's manuscript. One thought leads to another, with the result that the Prophecy is added to King Lear and another trace of Marlowe is added to the timeline.

The final trio of plays on themes of separation and reunion of families, Cymbeline, Winter's Tale and Tempest have been mentioned, but it is worth noting that they were performed, not quite as a series, but in a kind of sequence beginning with Cymbeline in April, 1611, The Winter's Tale in May 1611 and The Tempest on Hallowmas Night, November 1, 1611. What this might mean in terms of Marlowe's hope for a return to London is open to interpretation.

What is more significant in addressing the question of whether or not Marlowe could have returned is the difficulty traditional scholars have in attributing the famous "Fly Scene" in Act III, Scene 2 of Titus Andronicus. The scene, which does not appear in the 1594 quarto or any of its later reprints, is included only in the 1623 Folio version and orthodox scholars generally agree with Gary Taylor and Doug Duhaine that Shakespeare, who died in 1616, "cannot have written the scene."[619] While Taylor and Duhaime employ their usual flawed stylometrics to promote Thomas Middleton as author of the inserted scene, if Marlowe is given proper credit for his own work, then the same stylometric tests confirm him in greater measure.

Flaws in the Taylor/Duhaime model include Literature Online (LION) searches for unique word sequences which match sequences found in Titus 3.2. The idea was to search for strings of two, three and four words which close readers of Chapter Ten, The Stylometric Fallacy, will immediately recognize as violating the first principle of advanced stylometric analysis, avoiding context. In fact, a search for discrete word strings such as "between thy teeth" and "a coal black" (examples given by Taylor and Duhaime) are instantly contrary to the "bag of words" technique that is recommended by Maciej Eder and employed by Dr. Thomas Mendenhall. They go further to ignore the "bag of words" principle and skew their results by filtering "high frequency strings like 'to the' from the output file."[620]

Having performed all of these mathematically unsound gymnastics, Taylor and Duhaime then report that, surprise, the author with the highest number of frequency string matches is none other than Shakespeare with a total of eight, including phrases from Taming of the Shrew, Twelfth Night, King John, Henry IV Part 2, Cymbeline, Henry V and two from Titus Andronicus. The first six of these matches were then tossed overboard because, based on independent scholarly analysis of adjacent scenes and long-standing tradition, they considered it "reasonable to begin with the hypothesis that Shakespeare had died or retired before"[621] Act III Scene 2 was written. As for the two Titus matches, even though they "appear nowhere else in LION's dramatic texts from this period" they were disallowed because, they assert, "Whoever wrote 3.2 must have been familiar with the rest of the play."[622] As a result, Taylor and Duhaime calmly reject the results of their own data search when, in their view, it does not yield the "right" answer.

Proceeding along this predetermined path, they then eliminate half a dozen other authors none of whom manage to string together more than a single match, including Christopher Marlowe who is credited with one. They then carefully consider the two writers they found with two matches, Rowley, Killegrew and Heminge, but put them all aside on the basis that "even two of these extremely rare links are not reliable evidence for the authorship of a passage of this size." Finally, they arrive at Thomas Middleton who they believe "is the likeliest candidate of all" with four of the "rarest parallels".[623]

Note in particular that all of this careful attribution modeling falls on the choice between four versus two data points. It is difficult to imagine a slimmer margin with which to declare authorial certainty. Meanwhile, if Marlowe is given proper credit for his own plays, regardless of Titus, then Taylor and Duhaime's own stylometric tests prove conclusively, with a score of seven to four, that he wrote Scene 3.2. Throw in Titus, with which he was obviously "familiar", and the score jumps to 9 matches, more than double any other candidate. Apparently, the real trouble with stylometics is not that it provides some reasonable results, but that the results do not conform often enough to the predisposition of the analysts and thus must be further manipulated with discarded data and pre-selected input.

There is another, more personally significant, reason for thinking that Marlowe may have written the scene, the death by self-starvation in prison of Lady Arbella Stuart on September 25, 1615. As Taylor and Duhaime hypothesize this event, which has nothing to do with stylometrics, may possibly have been the inspiration for the scene itself:"

> "Like Arbella, the grieving, educated noblewoman Lavinia has lost her husband. Unlike any other passage in Titus Andronicus, the Fly Scene focuses on Lavinia's rejection of food and drink. Arbella stubbornly refused to speak; Lavinia cannot speak. . . . anyone watching or adapting the play after Arbella's imprisonment might have made the connection, and completed the link by adding to Lavinia's tragic, grieving silence a refusal to eat."[624]

Of all the Elizabethan playwrights and their Jacobean comrades, none of them is known to have had more direct relations with Arbella Stuart than Christopher Marlowe who had been her tutor when she was a teenager. To see her imprisonment eventually drive her so "far out of frame"[625] that it ended in suicide must have been deeply upsetting to anyone who knew her in her youth. The Fly Scene, rather than being commissioned to take advantage of a contemporary scandal, is a poet's heartfelt reaction to her bitter martyrdom, with which he could identify perhaps more than any other poet since Ovid himself. If Marlowe did write the "Fly Scene", then he was apparently alive between 1616 and 1623 and well aware of the link between Lavinia's grieving silence and Arbella's sad life. As usual, Marlowe returned to earlier work to comment upon and expand its ironic repetition of themes in his life and the lives of his friends.

Then there is <u>Timon of Athens</u>. Not entered into the Stationer's Register until 1623, it has no record of performance prior to publication and none until 1761. Like <u>Pericles</u>, <u>Timon of Athens</u> has long been assumed to be the work of two writers, in this case Thomas Middleton in the partner's role occupied by George Wilkens for <u>Pericles</u>. Like <u>Pericles</u>, however, <u>Timon of Athens</u> is a rewrite of an earlier play, in this case <u>Timon</u>, which, as discussed in Chapter Eight, may in fact be Marlowe's earliest play of all as it can be dated all the way back to when he entered Cambridge in 1580.

There are very few textual similarities, basically a few lines, between <u>Timon</u> and <u>Timon and Athens</u>. Structurally, however, they are very much the same and follow Lucan's classical dialogue, "Timon the Misanthrope", with the addition of scenes preceding Timon's fall from grace which is where Lucan's version begins. While <u>Timon</u> includes a series of comic scenes parodying Drake's circumnavigation of the globe, <u>Timon of Athens</u> drops them in favor of greater emphasis on Timon's profligacy and the sub-plot involving Alcibiades who eventually revenges both himself and Timon by defeating Athens. Both plays build on Lucan by detailing Timon's life before his humiliation. In both plays a faithful servant repeatedly warns Timon against his extravagance and follows him after his disgrace; in both Timon hosts a mock banquet to abuse his persecutors and both include a scene in which Timon elevates a poor man above his station. In all of this, it must be remembered that Lucan was almost as much a source for Marlowe as Ovid, as his translation of <u>The First Book of Lucan</u> testifies.

The plays differ, of course; <u>Timon</u> is a comedy whereas <u>Timon of Athens</u> is decidedly not. Among their many differences is a brief masque scene in Act I, Scene 2 of <u>Timon of Athens</u> which features Ladies dressed as "Amazons" but which Apemantus, a caustic friend of Timon, curses in terms that seem to echo the attacks found in the "Dark Lady" sonnets, 130 to 154:

> "What a sweep of vanity comes this way.
> They dance? They are madwomen;
> Like madness is the glory of this life,
> As this pomp shows to a little oil and root."
>
> I:2.131 - 135

More importantly, Timon of Athens provides no cheerful reconciliation, but instead marches inevitably toward its bitter conclusion. Timon's last words, after all those who have tormented him have come offering apologies seeking forgiveness for their dishonesty and cowardice, are complete rejection. First, he offers them a tree, which they believe is a good sign, then tells them they had best go hang themselves on it before he cuts it down. Then he exits, saying:

> "Lips, let sour words go by, and language end:
> What is amiss, plague and infection mend;
> Graves be only men's works and death their gain,
> Sun, hide thy beams, Timon hath done his reign."

The final word is his epitaph, read by Alcibiades who has just conquered Athens, his former home:

> "Here lie I, Timon, who alive all living men did hate,
> Pass by and curse thy fill, but pass and stay not here thy gait."

It is almost too much to imagine that this could represent Marlowe's final words on the subject, but the timing of this play's appearance and its link to the original raise that possibility. Where Cymbeline, Winter's Tale and Tempest all preceded Robert Cecil's death in 1612, Timon of Athens followed it. The hopefulness expressed in the earlier plays appears to have been depleted in the aftermath of Cecil's demise. Other than Audrey and Thomas, whose clout in court inevitably diminished with the loss of Cecil, there was no one left who could or would help rehabilitate Marlowe. Indeed, the subsequent political climate, involving the contest for power between Robert Carr, Thomas Howard and their factions, the murder of Thomas Overbury and subsequent trial and pardon of Carr as well as the eventual rise of George Villers, was sufficiently unstable as to make any return highly problematic at least until at least 1619, after Villers had outlasted all challengers for the King's favor. As if to emphasize that uncertainty, it was during that period that Arbella Stuart made the mistake of marrying against the King's wishes and met her sad fate in 1615, locked in the Tower of London, refusing to eat.

The publication history of Timon of Athens also suggests a very late date of composition. Traditional scholars, observing that it "has often been seen as a kind of practice run for Lear, or alternatively as a reprise of that play,"[626] believe that the two were composed in proximity to each other and want to date the former from the latter's earliest recorded performance date, 1606. As outlined in Chapter Eight, however, the links between the two plays include multiple links between them and the original Timon as well as King Lier, both of which were composed much earlier, making the linkage of the two later versions less directly temporal. Which is to say that the fact that King Lear was performed for King James in 1606 does not mean that Timon of Athens was written at the same time.

More significant is the fact that Timon of Athens appears to have been a hasty addition to the Folio. Scholars base this assertion on the fact that the pagination of the Folio shows a gap of eight page numbers between Timon of Athens and the next play in the volume, Julius Caesar. In addition, Troilus and Cressida, which appears to have been originally intended to follow Romeo and Juliet, the play which precedes Timon in the Folio's sequence, is spliced between the Histories and

Tragedies sections even though its pagination begins where Romeo and Juliet leaves off, suggesting that it was the play originally intended for that position but was delayed for some reason and could not be added until the entire volume was almost complete. Finally, many scholars consider Timon "unfinished"[627], hypothesizing that it was written "under conditions of mental and perhaps physical stress, which led to a break-down."[628]

All of that may be true and the play could still be, rather than a draft of King Lear, the final play of Marlowe's career, a statement intended to re-evaluate the entire enterprise from its earliest expression to its ultimate, very bitter completion. The fact that "it is rough and loosely structured, with some segments that are not fully integrated"[629] can simply be the result of late-stage composition, a circumstance that could also account for its relative brevity and awkward location in the final Folio. Taken with the late additions to King Lear and Titus Andronicus, both of them also tied to the very earliest stages of Marlowe's artistic effort, the likelihood that Marlowe, and only Marlowe, was the person making these changes becomes very strong. In combination, these late additions to the canon present a multi-faceted, simultaneously ironic, melancholy and bitterly defiant assessment.

Marlowe never had much luck with editors. The publisher of Tamburlaine noted in his precis that he had cut all the comic scenes from Marlowe's signature epic with the result that generations of scholars have framed the idea that Marlowe never wrote comedies. Faust, The Jew of Malta and The Massacre At Paris all appear to have been published in truncated, abridged or tampered form, so Marlowe would have had good reason not to want to leave the job of editing the Folio to any sundry hands.

All of which goes a long way to suggest that Marlowe had a hand in editing the Folio, right up to the moment when Timon was added in 1623. If so, it would seem unlikely that he could have done it all from outside London. If he did return sometime after 1619 and before 1623, then he would have had the further motive in an opportunity to reunite with Audrey, who died in 1624.

This would mean that Marlowe, in the end, accepted the ruse that had been engineered to protect him because by 1623 nearly everyone involved was past caring. Instead of keeping silent, however, he allowed his work to be published and republished under an assumed name. Of all the things that might be the hardest to believe, that he escaped, that he lived in exile, that he fell in love with Audrey and that they had a son raised by his best friend, the idea that he finally allowed his plays to be published under an assumed name, that he participated in making that happen, that might be the most difficult thing to believe. But that is what happened.

Perhaps it was not such a sacrifice by then. Perhaps he really respected the man who had carried that burden of false identity for so long. Perhaps he did it so as not to disgrace his son. Perhaps he needed the money. Perhaps it was all these things and then some.

Towards a Conclusion

Critics and scholars have written a great deal about the plays and poems attributed to Shakspere in the process of trying to comprehend his supposed genius. Marlowe, the true author of the work, was obviously a genius and much of what the scholars have understood clearly applies to him. But the scholars also tend to see things that aren't there, crediting all kinds of knowledge and context in their search for meaning in what is otherwise not quite as far reaching or esoteric as they imagine. Of course, Marlowe knew the classics as well as any team of academics, but some of the things they suggest by way of interpretation can never have been Marlowe's conscious intent, referencing all sorts of sources, potential influences and so on. It's a lot simpler than that. Just because one or more poet employs similar motifs it does not follow that Marlowe had all or any of it in mind when he wrote this poem or that play.

It is true that many of the scholars who have studied the works have sometimes operated under a lack of adequate information. It was not until 1923 that the Coroner's Report was discovered and Marlowe's portrait with its all-important motto was not unearthed until 1952. But, for the most part, all the evidence has been available since then, with the notable exception of the North manuscript which goes even further to re-enforce the story of Marlowe's journey as told here. Almost all the pieces have been available for at least half a century and yet it is not until now that they have been assembled in quite this way.

In many cases, obvious influences on the work have been overlooked or judged unlikely because, very simply, they necessarily lead away from the preferred conclusion. Philip Sidney's influence is significant in this instance, because no one can properly explain how an uneducated country lad could come to be so familiar with unpublished work by England's leading poet in the 1580s. Marlowe, on the other hand, could be expected to be very familiar with Sidney's work, but admitting this would require further investigation of plays and poems not usually attributed to him, which might force some scholars to wonder whether he actually died at Deptford.

Doubtless, some of the evidence has led to further evidence found in the Sonnets and the timeline, but that is an outgrowth of pursuing a simple line of inquiry that has been obscured by scholars and academics almost universally. So, they cannot be entirely forgiven, especially not the current generation, for having refused to take seriously the evidence of their own eyes.

Inevitably, fixing a historical and fully documented life to the work of a previously hypothetical artist will tend to place limits on what critics and scholars can attribute to that artist's life and work. Marlowe was not the gentle bard, nor was he invisible except to the degree that he has been mischaracterized in order to make room for the idealized figure of "Shakespeare".

In other words, take him all in all, Marlowe was a man who knew a lot, but he did not know everything. The image scholars seem to have of a Shakespeare endowed with super-human insight and talent cannot be sustained once a real person is allowed to step forward. Only a fantasized being could be so all knowing. Which means that accepting Marlowe will inevitably mean accepting someone less than the infinitely superior being Shakespeare has been built up to be in the popular imagination. Marlowe will be restored but the loss will then be felt by generations of Shakespearian idolators who will no longer be allowed to project absurd ideas of spontaneous generation onto a stick figure. It is time to let all the encrusted obfuscation laminated onto the image of an unlettered but savvy rustic fall away and let Marlowe take his rightful place.

What saves all of this from being the sort of inbred conspiracy theory that so many authorship doubters favor is that this is just people doing what people do, complicating each other's lives. It is not a load of acrostic puzzles or symbolistic self-referential circular reasoning in search of some secret message. There is no secret - it is all right there on the page for all to see.

There may never be a way to finally know what happened to Christopher Marlowe, the greatest poet in the English language, the GOAT in every sense good and bad. There may never be enough evidence even with what has yet to be discovered, to know whether or not he ever returned to England and lived to see his work published under an assumed name. But perhaps the scholars of the future, whoever they may be, can seek answers unburdened by the misreading of the past.

Regardless, it is a fact that Marlowe survived the incident at Deptford. It is a fact that he wrote <u>Hero and Leander</u>, <u>Venus and Adonis</u>, <u>The Rape of Lucrece</u>, <u>The Comedy of Errors</u>, <u>Love's Labour's Lost</u>, the <u>Sonnets</u>, <u>Tamburlaine</u>, <u>Arden of Faversham</u>, <u>Lear</u>, <u>Timon of Athens</u>, <u>Edward III</u>, <u>Henry IV</u>, <u>V & VI</u>, <u>Richard III</u>, <u>Romeo and Juliet</u>, <u>The Tempest</u> and so many more, enough to fill a Folio. Enough to fill a thousand theaters and still go unrecognized. Let him be recognized at last.

Acknowledgements

Martin Ouvry for his timely and tremendously helpful editorial encouragement and expertise.

Phil Setren for his steadfast support and enthusiasm.

Elizabeth Bove, Elizabeth Harnet, and Dana Sachs for reading the early drafts and offering good advice.

Chris Morse for some final editorial tips.

Dr. Rosalind Barber for skepticism.

Patti Ann Nordgren for inspiration.

Notes

1 Shake-Speare's Sonnets, London, Thomas Thorpe, (1609), Sonnet 92, line 9.

2 Ibid, sonnet 88, lines 6 & 7.

3 Ibid, sonnet 90, line 1.

4 Francis Meres, Palladis Tamia, Cuthbert Burbie, London, (1598)

5 Acts of the Privy Council, VI, 29 June, 1587.

6 Scott McMillan and Sally-Beth MacLean, The Queen's Men, Cambridge University Press, 1998, p. 27.

7 Rosalind Barber, The Marlowe Papers, St. Martin's Press, New York, 2012, p. 416.

8 Charles Nicholl, The Reckoning, Harcourt, Brace and Company, 1992, p. 295 - 301. Nicholl makes the case that Essex intended target was Sir Walter Raleigh, his rival for the favor of Queen Elizabeth, and that Marlowe was merely a pawn attacked for his connections to Raleigh.

9 Thomas Beard, The Theatre of God's Judgements, S. I &: M. Hand, (1598), p. 92.

10 Ibid, The Reckoning, p. 115.

11 Ibid, Christopher Marlowe, Poet & Spy, p. 131.

12 Riggs, ibid., p. 152.

13 A. D. Wraight & Virginia F. Stern, Christopher Marlowe, A Pictorial Biography, Chichester, Sussex, England, (1965), p. 249.

14 Ibid, Wraight & Stern, Marlowe, p. 250.

15 Edward Blount, [Dedication], Hero and Leander, by Christopher Marlowe, (1598), London, Adam Islip.

16 Henry Petowe, Hero and Leander, London, Thomas Purfoot, (1598).

17 Ibid, Sonnets, Sonnet 78, line 3.

18 Harry R. Hoppe, John Wolfe, University of Florida Press (December 1933), The Library, Series 4 14 (3): 241–287.

19 George Chapman, Hero and Leander, Begun by Christopher Marlowe and Finished by George Chapman, Paul Linley, (1598).

20 John Bakeless, The Tragicall History of Christopher Marlowe, Greenwood Press (1942), Vol 2, p. 114.

21 This type of thinking, of attributing later perspective to a prior circumstance, of assuming that, for instance, a person could know that because his poem was ultimately completed five years later by someone else, he could have foreseen the need to appoint a successor and have time to make that choice, to assume in short post hoc ergo propter hoc, is not just sloppy scholarship, it is fundamentally flawed and illogical. The sad fact is, however, that modern scholarship regarding Elizabethan literature is so permeated with it that examples of it pop up with dismaying regularity. The future, however, cannot affect the past and scholars would do well to keep that in mind.

22 Ibid, Sonnets, Sonnet 80, line 1.

23 Ibid, Sonnet 85, line 7.

24 Ibid, Sonnets, Sonnet 86, lines 5 - 11.

25 Ibid, Sonnet 88, lines 1 - 8.

26 Ibid, Sonnet 90, lines 9-14.

27 William Minto, Characteristics of English Poets from Chaucer to Shirley, Blackwood & Sons, London, (1874), p. 292.

28 John Kerrigan, ed., The Sonnets and A Lover's Complaint, "Commentary", Penguin Books, London, (1986) p. 280.

29 Arthur Acheson, Shakespeare and the Rival Poet, John Lane: The Bodley Head, London And New York (1903).

30 F. J. Furnival, The Leopold Shakspere, The Poet's Works In Chronological Order From The Text Of Professor Delius, With 'the Two Noble Kinsmen' And 'Edward III', And An Intr. By F.j. Furnivall, (1896).

31 "Introduction", Shakespeare's Sonnets, The Arden Edition, Katherine Duncan-Jones ed., Bloomsbury, London (2010), p. 65. Duncan-Jones includes Chapman with John Davies of Hereford, Samuel Daniel and Ben Jonson among the candidates she considers "plausible".

32 Ibid, Acheson, Shakespeare and the Rival Poet, p. 128.

33 MacDonald P. Jackson, "Francis Meres and the Cultural Contexts of Shakespeare's Rival Poet Sonnets", Review of English Studies, n. s. 56, 2005, pp. 224-46.

34 http://www.shakespeares-sonnets.com/sonnet/81

35 John Kerrigan, "Introduction," The Sonnets and A Lover's Complaint, ed., Penguin Classics, 1999, p. 21.

36 Park Honan, Christopher Marlowe, Poet & Spy, Oxford University Press, 2005, p. 328.

37 A. D. Wraight, The Story the Sonnets Tell, Adam Hart, London, 1994, p. 166.

38 John Nichols, The progresses and public processions of Queen Elizabeth : among which are interspersed other solemnities, public expenditures, and remarkable events during the reign of that illustrious princess : collected from original MSS., scarce pamphlets, corporation records, parochial registers, &c., &c. : illustrated with historical notes, Printed by and for John Nichols and Son, (Printers to the Society of Antiquaries), 1823, p. 591.

39 Wraight, ibid., p. 167.

40 Letter of Lady Arabella Stuart to Lord Shrewsbury, dated "Hampton Courte December the 18th," cf. Sara Jayne Steen, The letters of Lady Arbella Stuart (Oxford, 1994), p. 197.

41 A. D. Wraight and Virginia F. Stern, In Search of Christopher Marlowe, Adam Hart, Ltd., Chichester, 1993, p. 263.

42 Edmond Malone, Supplement to the Edition of Shakspeare's Plays Published in 1778 By Samuel Johnson and George Stevens, London: J. Murray, 1780, p 645.

43 Sir Sidney Lee, A Life of William Shakespeare, Smith, Elder & co., London, 1898. p. 204.

44 The New Oxford Shakespeare Authorship Companion, Gary Taylor, Gabriel Eagan, editors, Oxford University Press, (2017), pp. 484 - 592.

45 William Hazlitt, Characters of Shakespear's Plays, LONDON: PRINTED BY C. H. REYNELL, 1817, p. 350.

46 J. W. Mackail, "A Lover's Complaint", Essays and studies by members of the English Association, Oxford, 1912, p. 69.

47 J. M. Robertson, M.P., Shakespeare and Chapman; a Thesis of Chapman's Authorship of 'A Lover's Complaint', T. Fisher Unwin, Ltd., London, 1917, p. 10.

48 Sidney Lee, Dictionary of National Biography, 1885-1900, Volume 56, Smith, Elder & Co. (1900), p. 323

49 Katherine Duncan-Jones, "Was the 1609 Shake-speares Sonnets Really Unauthorized?", Review of English Studies, (1983), n.s. 34, 155.

50 Arthur Marotti, quoted in "Introduction", Critical Essays on Shakespeare's A Lover's Complaint, Shirley Sharon-Zisser, ed., Routledge, May 15, 2017.

51 The direct borrowings from Hero and Leander in Venus and Adonis include:

.	V&A:	Even as the sun with purple-color'd face	1
		Had ta'en his last leave of the weeping morn,	2
		Rose-cheek'd Adonis hied him to the chase	3
	H&L:	(For his sake whom their goddesse held so deare,	I 92
		Rose-cheekt Adonis) kept a solemn feast	93
.	V&A:	Stain to all nymphs, more lovely than a man,	9
	H&L:	Some swore he was a maide in man's attire,	I 83
		For his lookes were all that men desire,	84
.	V&A:	Till his breath breatheth life in her again.	474
	H&L:	He kist her, and breath'd life into her lips,	II 3
.	V&A:	Narcissus so himself forsook,	161
		And died to kiss his shadow in the brook.	162
	H&L:	exceeding his	I 73
		That leapt into the water for a kiss	74
		of his own shadow, and despising many	74
.	V&A:	Love's golden arrow at him should have fled,	947
	H&L:	Thence flew Loves arrow with the golden head,	I 161
.	V&A:	But gold that's put to use more gold begets.	768
	H&L:	Then treasure is abusde,	I 234
		When misers keep it; being put to lone,	235
		In time it will return us two for one	236
.	V&A:	Were beauty under twenty locks kept fast,	575
		Yet love breaks through and picks them all at last.	
	H&L:	The richest corne dies, if it be not reapt,	I 328
		Beautie alone is lost, too warily kept.	329
.	V&A:	O hard-believing love! how strange it seems	985
		Not to believe, and yet too credulous;	986

H&L:	(Love is too full of faith, too credulous,	II
	With follie and false hope deluding us.)	221
		222

52 Ibid, Bakeless, The Tragical History of Christopher Marlowe, p.263.

53 Ibid., p. 293

54 Henry David Gray The Journal of English and Germanic Philology, University of Illionois Press, Vol. 47, No. 4 (Oct., 1948), pp. 365-373

55 Burleigh "died at Cecil House at about seven o'clock on the morning of 4 August, a Friday" 1598. Stephen Alford, Burghley, Yale University Press, 2008, p. 331

56 Ibid., p. 319.

57 Ibid, Sonnet 120, lines 9 - 14.

58 Thomas Thorpe, "Dedication", Lucan's First Book, Translated Line for Line by Chr. Marlowe, Paul Short, London.

59 Patrick H. Martin and John Finnis, "Thomas Thorpe, "W.S.," and the Catholic Intelligencers" in English Literary Renaissance, Blackwell Publishing, vol. 33, issue 1 (2003).

60 G. P. V. Akrigg, Shakespeare and the Earl of Southampton, Hamish Hamilton, London, 1968, p. 5.

61 Ibid., p. 6.

62 Ibid., pp. 33-4.

63 Akrigg, ibid., p. 32

64 Katherine Duncan-Jones, Shakespeare's Poems, The Arden Shakespeare, Bloomsbury, 2007, p. 27.

65 Akrigg, ibid., p. 39.

66 Robert Hutchinson, Elizabeth's Spy Master: Francis Walsingham and the Secret War that Saved England, London: Weidenfeld & Nicolson, 2007, p. 257.

67 Stephen Alford, The Watchers, Bloomsbury Press, 2012, p. 313.

68 Katherine Duncan-Jones, "Introduction", The Arden Shakespeare, Shakespeare's Sonnets, Bloomsbury, 1997, p. 55.

69 Akrigg, ibid., pp. 201 – 207.

70 There are some, such as Hilton Landry in Interpretations of Shakespeare's Sonnets, Berkley, 1963, pp. 129-140, who would argue that the Sonnets addressing Southampton's marriage should include

numbers 18 and 19. These last two, however, do not discuss marriage or progeny.

71 "It was written sometime between 1589 and 1592", https://en.wikipedia.org/wiki/Doctor_Faustus_(play)

72 Bess of Hardwick to Lord Burghley, dated 21 September 1592 (Blanche C. Hardy, Arbella Stuart: A Biography, Dutton, 1913, pp.64–67).
Bess also notes "Morley" had hoped for an annuity of £40 a year (equivalent to £11,100 in 2019) from Arbella based on the fact that he had "been so much damnified [i.e. that much out of pocket] by leaving the University".

73 Stephen Greenblatt, Will in the World, W. H. Norton and Company, New York, 2004, p. 229.

74 Ibid.

75 David Riggs, The World of Christopher Marlowe, John Macrae, Henry Holt & Co., New York, (2004), p. 109.

76 Riggs, ibid., p. 108.

77 Peter Ackroyd, Shakespeare, The Biography, Doubleday, New York, 2005, p. 205.

78 Francis Meres, Palladis Tamia, London, Cuthbert Burbie, 1598.

79 John Bakeless, The Tragical History of Christopher Marlowe, Vol. II, Greenwood Press, Westport, CT, 1942, p. 233.

80 Charles Nicholl, The Lodger, Viking, 2008, p. 177.

81 Maurice Charney, "Marlowe's Hero and Leander Shows Shakespeare, in Venus and Adonis, How to Write in Ovidian Verse Epyllion", in Marlowe's Empery, Sara Munson Deats and Robert A. Logan eds., Newark, University of Delaware Press, 2002, p. 85.

82 Douglas Bush, Mythology and Renaissance Tradition in English Poetry, New York, Norton, 1963, p. 144.

83 Stephen Alford, Burghley, Yale University Press, New Haven, 2008, p. 316.

84 Alford, ibid.

85 Patrick H. Martin and John Finnis, "Thomas Thorpe, 'W.S.,' and the Catholic Intelligencers." English Literary Renaissance, vol. 33, no. 1, 2003, pp. 3–43.

86 The Writings of John Greenwood and Henry Barrow 1591-1593, Routledge, 2004, p.219.

87 Ibid, p. 318.

88 Riggs, Ibid., p. 318.

89 Arthur Freeman, "Marlowe, Kyd and the Dutch Court Libel, English Literary Renaissance, 3 (1973), pp. 44-52.

90 A speech prior to Act I, Scene 1 of the 1633 first edition The Jew of Malta, spoken by a character named Machevill, includes the following:

"Albeit the world think Machevill is dead,
Yet was his soul but flown beyond the Alps;
And, now the Guise is dead, is come from France,
To view this land, and frolic with his friends.
To some perhaps my name is odious;
But such as love me, guard me from their tongues,
And let them know that I am Machevill,
And weigh not men, and therefore not men's words.
Admired I am of those that hate me most.
Though some speak openly against my books,
Yet will they read me, and thereby attain
To Peter's chair; and when they cast me off,
Are poisoned by climbing followers.
I count religion but a childish toy,
And hold there is no sin but ignorance."

There is some question as to whether or not this prologue was written before or after Marlowe's disappearance. The play itself, owned by Edward Alleyn, was not published until well after Alleyn's death in 1626. In his dedication, Thomas Heywood states that "This play, composed by so worthy an author as Christopher Marlowe, and the part of the Jew presented by so unimitable an actor as Mr. Alleyn, being in this later age commended to the stage; as I ushered it unto the Court, and presented it to the Cock-pit, with these Prologues and Epilogues here inserted, so now being newly brought to the press, I was loath it should be published without the ornament of an Epistle." [Italics added]

Robert Green had already referred to Marlowe as Machevill in Greene's Groatsworth and some of his attacks on Marlowe in that essay appear to anticipate much of this speech. Marlowe being equated with Machiavelli was not new, but the suggestion that he had "flown beyond the Alps" would not be contemporary with May 5, 1593.

91 MS BL Harleian 6848, fo. 189.

92 A. D. Wraight, In Search of Christopher Marlowe, Adam Hart, Sussex, 1993, p. 238.

93 Agent's Report on Richard Chomeley, date unknown, probably March 1593, BL Harliean MSS 6848 F. 190, R. and V.

94 Ibid., F. 191.

95 Robert Deveraux, Earl of Essex, letter to Robert Bagot, November 13, 1593, quoted in Nicholl, The Reckoning, Ibid., p. 281.

96 Nicholl, ibid., pp. 282 - 3.

97 Riggs, ibid., p. 321.

98 Riggs, ibid., p. 320.

99 Nicholl, ibid., p. 306.

100 While the dating of the "Libel" is exact, the dating of the "Remembrances" is not. It is noted by Kuriyama as being "possibly March", but this assertion is based on the arrest warrent for Chomeley which is dated March 19, 1593. The warrant, however, was not executed until June 28, leaving Chomeley free to concoct the "Libel" and the "Remembrances" after the registration of Venus and Adonis with the Stationer's company on April 18.

101 Kuriyama, Ibid., p. 122.

102 Kuriyama, Ibid., p. 126.

103 Kuriyama, ibid., p. 218.

104 Privy Council entry, dated May 18, 1593, in In Search of Christopher Marlowe, A. D. Wraight, Adam Hart LTD., Chichester, 1993d, p. 284.

105 Kuriyama, ibid., p. 220.

106 Richard Baines, "A Note Containing the Opinion of One Christopher Marly concerning His Damnable Judgement of Religion", BL Harley MS 6848 ff 185-6.

107 Thomas Drury, Letter to Anthony Bacon, August 1, 1593, LP MS 649, f 246; Bill, p. 29.

108 Charles Nicholl, The Reckoning, Harcourt, Brace & Co., 1992, pp. 290 - 301.

109 Constance Brown Kuriyama, Christopher Marlowe, A Renaissance Life, Ithaca, Cornell University Press, 2010, p. 130.

110 Ibid.

111 Kuriyama, ibid., p. 131.

112 Honan, ibid., p. 338.

113 "The inquest on Marlowe's death was slightly irregular, since the county coroner failed to attend the proceedings at Deptford. However, the authority of William Danby, the Royal Coroner, or Coroner of the Verge, . . . signals that the homicide occurred within twelve miles of the queen."
Park Honan, Christopher Marlowe, Poet and Spy, Oxford, 2005, p.376.

114 William Danby, "Inquisition made in two copies on Detford Strand", June 1, 1593, MS C260/174 no. 127, The National Archives (PRO)

115 Leslie Hotson, The Death of Christopher Marlowe, New York: Haskell House (1925).

116 Park Honan, Christopher Marlowe, Poet & Spy, Oxford University Press (2005), p 325.

117 Leslie Hotson, "Marlowe Among the Churchwardens" in Atlantic Monthly, 138 (July 1926), pp. 37-44.

118 Charles Nicholl, The Reckoning, Harcourt, Brace & Co., 1992, p. 157.

119 Honan, Ibid, p. 344.

120 Thomas Beard, The Theatre of God's Judgements, S. I &: M. Hand, (1598), p. 92.

121 Francis Meres, Palladis Tamia, A Comparative Discourse of our English Poets, Cuthbert Burbie (1598), p. 89.

122 William Vaughan, The Golden Grove, Memorialized in Three Books, Stafford (1600) Book 1, Chapter 3.

123 William Pierce, John Penry, His Life, Times and Writings, Hodder and Stoughton Limited London, (1923), p. 478.

124 Ibid.

125 David More, "Drunken Sailor or Imprisoned Writer?" in Marlowe Lives!, http://www.marlovian.com/essays/penry.html

126 John Waddington, John Penry the Pilgrim Martyr, W. & F.G. Cash, (1854), p. 204.

127 Peter Farey, "HOFFMAN AND THE AUTHORSHIP", 2007
http://www.rey.myzen.co.uk/hoffman.htm

128 Drury, ibid.

129 Thomas Drury, Letter to Robert Cecil, (undated) HMC 4, pp. 366-7.

130 Ibid., pp. 357-8.

131 Nicholl, ibid., p. 319.

132 See note 7 above.

133 Katherine Duncan-Jones, "Introduction", Shakespeare's Sonnets, The Arden Shakespeare, Bloomsbury, 2017, p. 83

134 Bradin Cormack, "Shakespeare Possessed: Legal Affect and the Time of Holding" in Shakespeare and the Law, Paul Raffield and Gary Watt, eds., Bloomsbury Publishing (2008), p. 93.

135 Colin Burrow, "Sonnet 74" in The Oxford Shakespeare: The Complete Sonnets and Poems, Colin Burrow, ed., Oxford (2002).

136 John Kerrigan, op. cit. (1986) p. 268.

137 Thomas Tyler, "Sonnet 74" in Shakespeare Online, Thomas Tyler ed., 20 Aug. 2013. < http://www.shakespeare-online.com/sonnets/74.html >

138 MacD. P. Jackson, "Francis Meres and the Cultural Contexts of Shakespeare's Rival Poet Sonnets", in The Review of English Studies, Vol. 56, Issue 224, 1 April 2005, pp. 224–246

139 MS C260/174, no. 127, National Archives.

140 John Kerrigan, op. cit. (1986) p. 268.

141 Richard Verstagen, CRS 52, p. 174.

142 Nicholl, ibid., p. 391.

143 Akrigg, ibid., pp. 31–2

144 Samuel Schoenbaum, Shakespeare's Lives: New Edition, Oxford: Clarendon Press, (1991), p. 568.

145 A. W. Schlegel, article in Schiller's Horen (1796); repr. in "A Course of Lectures on Dramatic Art and Literature", trans. John Black, London: A. J. W. Morrison (1846), p. 352.

146 John Kerrigan, "Introduction", The Sonnets and A Lover's Complaint, ed. John Kerrigan, Penguin Press (1986), p. 11.

147 G.B. Harrison, "Introduction", The Sonnets and A Lover's Complaint, Penguin Books Limited, (1938), pp. 13-14.

148 John Kerrigan: op. cit., "Commentary", (1986) p. 169.

149 Katherine Duncan-Jones, ed., "Introduction", Shakespeare's Sonnets, The Arden Shakespeare, ed. Katherine Duncan-Jones, Bloomsbury (2010), p. 81.

150 Katherine Duncan-Jones, Ungentle Shakespeare, The Arden Shakespeare (2001), p. 218.

151 Gary Taylor and Rory Loughnane, "The Canon and Chronology" in The New Oxford Shakespeare Authorship Companion, eds. Gary Taylor and Gabriel Eagan, Oxford University Press (2018), p. 574.

152 Richard B. Hovey, "Sonnet 73" in College English, James E. Miller, Jr., ed., National Council of Teachers of English, vol. 23.8 (1962) p. 672-673

153 Barbara Estermann, "Shakespeare's Sonnet 73" in Explicator, Routledge (United States) vol. 38.3 (1980) p. 11-12.

154 John S. Prince, "Shakespeare's Sonnet 73" in Explicator, Routledge (United States) vol. 55.4 (1997), p. 197.

155 Amanda Mabillard, "Sonnet 73" in Shakespeare Online, Amanda Mabillard ed., 8 Dec. 2012. < http://www.shakespeare-online.com/sonnets/73detail.html >

156 Duncan-Jones, Shakespeare's Sonnets, op. cit. (2010) p. 256.

157 To understand this more clearly, consider that the poet says that "In me thou see'st the twilight" he does not say that the twilight is "in us". The poet is identifying himself with twilight and he is also saying that just as it is in him, he is in it. Viewed longitudinally, which is to say, standing on the Earth and looking at the Sun, when the poet is in twilight then anyone standing due North or due South of him, to his left or to his right, is also in twilight. The reader however, cannot be in twilight, the twilight cannot be "in him" because the poet did not include him when he said it was "in me thou see'st".

Further, the reader cannot be to the East of the Poet because then he would be in darkness and not able to see the twilight and/or the Poet. Therefore, the reader must be to the West of the Poet. Physically, twilight has a duration as the Earth rotates in relation to the Sun. It also has a more or less constant reach due to the curvature of the Earth. Each line of longitude is one hour, twilight typically lasts one half an hour. This duration translates into miles on the surface of the globe. For most of Europe, one half hour of sunlight translates to about 600 miles.

600 miles splits the difference between civil twilight, about 400 miles, and nautical twilight, about 800 miles, which are defined as the sun being 6 and 12 degrees below the horizon, or respectively, 1/3 and 2/3 of astronomical twilight which occurs when the sun's center is 18 degrees below the horizon. Sunset actually occurs when the sun's center is 16 minutes below the horizon (since the sun is a disc), a distance of 17.73 degrees. 1 degree of longitude at the equator is 69.5 miles which equals about 1,230 miles total.

So, putting this all together and noting that the Poem opened up with "bare ruin'd choirs" which is either a reference to Canterbury or England, then when the Poet is in twilight he is standing somewhere within 600 miles East of and outside of England with the reader being in England, itself a mere 280 miles across at its widest point.

158 Carl D. Atkins, "Sonnet 74" in Shakespeare's Sonnets: With Three Hundred Years of Commentary. Carl D. Atkins ed., Madison: Fairleigh Dickinson University Press (2007), pg. 198.

159 Duncan-Jones, Shakespeare's Sonnets, op. cit. (2010), p. 256.

160 J. B. Leishman, Themes and Variations in Shakespeare's Sonnets, Hutchinson (1961), pp. 38-9.

161 Philip Edwards, "An Approach to the Problem of Pericles" in Shakespeare Studies, vol. 5 (1952), p 26.

162 Suzanne Gossett, "Introduction" in The Arden Shakespeare: Pericles (2004), p. 49.

163 The New Oxford Shakespeare Authorship Companion, Gary Taylor and Gabriel Eagan, ed., Oxford University Press, (2017), p. 571.

164 Geoffrey Bullock, Narrative and Dramatic Sources of Shakespeare, vol VI, (1966), Routledge and Keegan Paul, Columbia University Press, p. 357.

165 Ibid., p. 358.

166 Henry Green, Shakespeare and the Emblem Writers (1870), Burt Franklin, p. 173.

167 Gabriel Symeoni, quoted and translated in Green, ibid., p. 172.

168 Geffrey Whitney, quoted in Green, ibid., p. 173.

169 MS Corpus Christi, Freeman to Bury, 9 Dec., 1952, in Christopher Marlowe Poet & Spy, Park Honan, Oxford University Press (2005) p. 115

170 Noel Purdon, "Letter of the Corpus Association" in Cambridge Review, vol. 46 (1967), pp. 30-3.

171 Tarnya Cooper, Searching for Shakespeare, Yale University Press (2006), p. 94.

172 Green, ibid., p. 171.

173 Edmund Molyneaux, "Historical Remembrance of the Sidneys, the father and the son", in Raphael Holinshed, The Third Volume of The Chronicles, London, 1587, fols. 1554-5b.

174 Henry Green, Shakespeare and the Emblem Writers, Burt Franklin, (1870)

175 Green, ibid., p. 185.

176 George Whetstone, Sir Phillip Sidney, his honorable life, his valiant death, and true vertues A perfect myrror for the followers both of Mars and Mercury, who (in the right hardie breaking vpon the enemie, by a few of the English, being for the most part gentlemen of honor and name) receiued his deathes wound, nere vnto Sutphen the 22. of September last past, dyed at Aruam the 16. of October following: and with much honor and all possible mone, was solemnely buried in Paules the 16. of February 1586. By G.W. gent. Whereunto is adioyned, one other briefe commemoration of the vniuersall lamentation, the neuer dying praise, and most sollemne funerall of the

sayd right hardie and noble knight. Imprinted at London: [By T. Orwin] for Thomas Cadman, (1587)

177 William Camden, Remaines of a Greater Worke, Concerning Britaine, (1605)

178 https://en.wikipedia.org/wiki/Penelope_Blount,_Countess_of_Devonshire

179 Scott McMillin and Sally-Beth MacLean, The Queen's Men and Their Plays, Cambridge University Press, 1998, p. 127.

180 Ibid., p. 128.

181 Katherine Duncan-Jones, Philip Sidney, Courtier Poet, Yale University Press, New Haven and London, 1991, p. 205.

182 Alan Stewart, Philip Sidney, A Double Life, Thomas Dunne, New York, (2000), p. 238.

183 Duncan-Jones, ibid., p. 247.

184 Stewart, ibid., p. 232.

185 Green, ibid., p. 172.

186 Sidney Blumenthal, The Marlowe-Shakespeare Connection, MacFarland & Co., Inc., 2008, p. 15.

187 Blumenthal, ibid., p. 131.

188 Robert U. Ayres, The Death and Posthumous Life of Christopher Marlowe, 2012, np, p. 69.

189 Ibid., p. 68.

190 Dominicus Baudius to Janus Dousa, 16/26 October 1586, Arnheim. BL Burney MS371, fo. 123.

191 Acts of the Privy Council, 29 June, 1587, PRO London.

192 Ibid.

193 John Dryden, The Poems of John Dryden: Volume One: 1649-1681, ed. Paul Hammond, 1995, repr. Abingdon, Routledge, 2014, p. 339 (l. 16-19).

194 Edmond Malone, "Attempt to Ascertain the Order in Which the Plays Attributed to William Shakespeare Were Written", in William Shakespeare, The Plays of William Shakespeare in Ten Volumes […] To Which Are Added Notes by Samuel Johnson and George Steevens, ed. Edmond Malone, second edition, 10 volumes, London, 1778, 1: 269-346, p. 284.

195 Scott McMillin and Sally-Beth MacLean, The Queen's Men and Their Plays, Cambridge University Press, 1998, p. 125.

196 Ibid., p. 128.
197 **Lucy** Munro, "Young Shakespeare/Late Shakespeare: The Case of Pericles", p. 1, https://doi.org/10.4000/shakespeare.3668
198 Ibid., p. 9.
199 Gary Taylor, Pericles, by William Shakespeare and George Wilkins, A Reconstructed Text, in William Shakespeare: The Complete Works, Oxford, (2005) p. 1059.
200 F. D. Hoeniger, ed., "Introduction", in Pericles, Arden Shakespeare, Van Nostrand Reinhold; 3rd edition (December 31, 1990), p. lxiii.
201 Bullough, ibid., p. 564.
202 Stewart, ibid., p. 2.
203 Thomas Lant, Sequitur celebritas et pompa funebris, 1587.
204 Stewart, ibid., p. 2.
205 Suzanne Gosset, ed., "Introduction", Pericles, The Arden Shakespeare, Bloomsbury, 2004, p. 62.
206 Ibid., p. 115.
207 John Bakeless, The Tragical History of Christopher Marlowe, Greenwood Press, Westport, CT, 1942, p. 89.
208 David Riggs, The World of Christopher Marlowe, Henry Holt & Company, 2004, p. 98.
209 Scott McMillin and Sally-Beth MacLean, The Queen's Men and Their Plays, Cambridge University Press, 1998, p. 27.
210 Ibid., p. 28.
211 Honan, op. cit., p. 65.
212 Ibid.
213 Anthony B. Dawson and Gretchen E. Minton, (ed.s) in "Introduction", The Arden Shakespeare, Timon of Athens, (2008), p. 31.
214 Francis Meres, Palladis Tamia, 1598.
215 William Warner, Pan his syrinx, or pipe compact of seuen reedes, At London, Printed by Thomas Purfoote (1584)
216 Robert Hills Goldsmith, "Did Shakespeare use the old Timon comedy?", in Shakespeare Quarterly, vol. 9.1 (1958), pp. 31-8.
217 Geoffrey Bullough, (ed.), Narrative and Dramatic Sources of Shakespeare, vol. 6 (1966), p. 235.

218 John C. Baker, "Towards a New Date and Suggested Authorship Attribution for the Timon, MS", in <u>Notes and Queries</u>, NS 45 (1998), pp. 300-2.

219 Robertson, ibid., p. 117.

220 John Munro, "Introduction", <u>The Troublesome Reign of King John: Being the Original of Shakespeare's 'Life and Death of King John'</u>, Edited by F. J. Furnivall and John Munro, Chatto and Windus, London, 1913.

221 Munro, ibid.

222 Levin, Carole, "A Good Prince: King John and Early Tudor Propaganda" (1980). Faculty Publications, Department of History. 50.https://digitalcommons.unl.edu/historyfacpub/50

223 Levin, ibid.

224 McMillan and MacLean, ibid., p. 166.

225 SR, quoted in <u>Narrative and Dramatic Sources of Shakespeare, Vol. VII</u>, Geoffrey Bullough, ed., Routledge and Keegan Paul, London, 1973, p. 269.

226 https://eclipse.gsfc.nasa.gov/SEsearch/SEsearchmap.php?Ecl=16051012

227 Geoffrey Bullough, <u>Narrative Sources of Shakespeare, Vol. VI</u>, London: Routledge and Keegan Paul, 1966, p. 234.

228 Ibid., p. 235.

229 Dawson and Minton, Ibid., p. 24.

230 Bullough, Ibid., p. 235.

231 Honan, op. cit., p. 67.

232 Frederick S. Boas, <u>Christopher Marlowe, A Biographical and Critical Study</u>, Clarendon Press, Oxford, 1940, p. 71.

233 McMillan and MacLean, ibid., p. 156.

234 Christopher Marlowe, <u>Tamburlaine, Part I</u>, Prologue, 1-2.

235 McMillan and MacLean, ibid.

236 Ibid., p. 155.

237 Ibid., p. 168.

238 Charles Nicholl, <u>The Reckoning</u>, Harcourt Brace & Company, 1992, p. 5.

239 Lawrence Manley and Sally-Beth MacLean, <u>Lord Strange's Men and Their Plays</u>, Yale University Press, New Haven, 2014, p. 57.

240 Lawrence Manley and Sally-Beth MacLean, ibid., p. 55.

241 Robert Greene, Greenes Groats-Worth of Wit, 1592.

242 Gary Taylor and Rory Loughnane, "The Canon and Chronology", op. cit. (2017), p 547.

243 L.H. Newcomb, "Greene, Robert (bap. 1558, d. 1592)". Oxford Dictionary of National Biography, (2004) (online ed.). Oxford University Press.

244 A. D. Wraight, Christopher Marlowe and Edward Alleyn, Adam Hart, Chichester, 1965, p. 187.

245 Greene, ibid.

246 Robert Greene, Francescos Fortunes, (1590).

247 Ibid.

248 Thomas Nashe, Pierce Pennilesse, (1592).

249 Cicero, Pro Archia Poeta

250 Gary Taylor and Rory Loughnane, The New Oxford Shakespeare Authorship Companion, Oxford University Press, 2017, p. 496.

251 Thomas Nashe, "Preface", in Menaphon, by Robert Greene, (1589)

252 John P. Collier, Memoirs of Edward Alleyn, Shakespeare Society, 1841, p. 59-60.

253 Ben Jonson, Discoveries Made Upon Men and Matter, Cassel & Company, Limited, London (1892), note 10.

254 W. W. Greg, Two Elizabethan Stage Abridgements, Oxford, The Clarendon Press, (1923). p. 138.

255 Wraight, ibid., p. 236.

256 Robert Greene, The Defence of Conney-Catching, by Cuthbert Cunny-Catcher, (1592).

257 Francis Meres, Palladis Tamia, 1598.

258 Bernard Beckerman, Shakespeare at the Globe, 1599-1609, New York, Macmillan, 1962, p. 9.

259 Henry Chettle, Kinde Hart's Dream, William Wright, (1592)

260 David Riggs, op. cit., p. 294

261 Harold Jenkins, The Life and Work of Henry Chettle, Sidgwick and Jackson, London, 1934.

262 John Jowett, "Notes on Henry Chettle", Review of English Studies, 45.179 (1994): 384-8, 517-22.

263 Warren B. Austin, A Computer-Aided Technique for Stylistic Discrimination: The Authorship of "Greene's Groats-Worth of Wit",

Washington D.C.: U.S. Department of Health, Education and Welfare, 1969.

264 Peter Bull, "Tired with a Peacock's Tail: All Eyes on the Upstart Crow", in English Studies, Routledge, Taylor and Francis Group, 2020, DOI: 10.1080/0013838X.2020.1717829, p. 25.

265 Gary Taylor and Rory Loughnane, The New Oxford Shakespeare Authorship Companion, Oxford, 2017, p. 498.

266 Barber, ibid.,

267 Howard S. Babb, "Policy in Marlowe's The Jew of Malta", ELH Vol. 24, No. 2 (Jun., 1957), pp. 85-94

268 Calvin Hoffman, The Murder of the Man Who was "Shakespeare", Julian Messner, New York, 1955, pp. 203 - 232.

Jew of Malta	Parallels
come all the world To rescue thee, so will we guard us now, As sooner shall they drink the ocean dry, Than conquer Malta, or endanger us. [Act V., end of play]	Come the three corners of the world in arms, An we will shock them. Nought shall make us rue, If England to itself do rest but true. [King John, Act V, end of play]
These arms of mine shall be thy Sepulchure [Act V]	These arms of mine shall be thyy winding sheet; My heart, sweet boy, shall. be thy sephulchure. [King Henry VI, Part 3, Act II, sc. 5]
I drank of poppy and cold Mandrake juice, [Act V]	Not poppy, nor mandragora Nor all the drowsy syups of the world. [Othello]
I count religion but a childish toy And hold there is no sin but ignorance [Prologue]	I say there is no darkness but ignorance. [Twelfth Night]

Die, life! Fly, soul!
Tongue, curse thy fill and die!
[Act V]
	Here lies a wretched corpse,
	   of wretched soul bereft;
	Seek not my name; a plague
	   consume you wicked caitiffs left.
	Here lie I, Timon, who, alive
	   all living men did hate.
	Pass by, and curse thy fill;
	   but pass and stay not here thy gait.
	[Timon of Athens]

Now, gentle Ithamore, lie in my lap. [Act IV]	Lady, shall I lie in your lap? [Hamlet]
What? Bring you Scripture to confirm your wrongs? [Act I]	The devil can cite Scripture for his purpose. [Merchant of Venice]
And every moon made some or other mad. [Act II]	It is the very error of the moon; She comes more nearer than she was wont And makes men mad. [Othello]
O my girl, my fortune, my felicity; O girl, O gold, O beauty, O my bliss! [Act II]	My daughter! O my ducats! My daughter! Fled with a Christian! O my Christian ducats! Justice! The law! My ducats and my daughter! [Merchant of Venice]
You have my goods, my money, and my wealth, My ships, my store, and all that I enjoy'd; And, having all, you can request no more, Unless your unrelenting flinty hearts Suppress all pity in your stony breasts, And now shall move you to bereave my life.	Nay, take my life and all; pardon not that. You take my house when you do take the prop That doth sustain my house; you take my life When you do take the means whereby I live. [Merchant of Venice]

[Act I]

He that denies to pay shall straight become a Christian. [Act I]	.... that for this favour, He presently become a Christian. [Merchant of Venice]
Infinite riches in a little room. [Act I]	A great reckoning in a little room. [As You Like It]
I learned in Florence how to kiss thy hand, Heave up my shoulders when they call me dog, And duck as low as any barefoot friar. [Act II]	Still have I borne it with patient shrug; For sufferance is the badge of all our tribe. You call me disbeliever, cut-throat, dog . . . [Merchant of Venice]
But stay: What star shines yonder in the East? The lodestar of my life, if Abigale. [Act II]	But soft! What light through yonder window breaks? It is the East, and Juliet is the sun! [Romeo and Juliet]
A fair young maid, scarce fourteen years of age, The sweetest flower in Cytherea's field. [Act I]	Death lies on her lips like an untimely frost, Upon the sweetest flower of all the field. [Romeo and Juliet (also fourteen)]
For when their hideous force environed Rhodes [Act II]	Environed with all those hideous fears. [Romeo and Juliet]
As sooner shall they drink the ocean dry [Act V, end of play]	The task he undertakes . . . . Is numbering sands and drinking oceans dry. [Richard II]
And Barabas, now search this secret out: Summon thy senses; call thy wits together. [Act I]	Stiffen the sinews, summon up the blood. [Henry V]

402

269 Thomas Corwin Mendenhall, "The Characteristic Curves of Composition", Science, 9 (1887), (214, supplement), pp 237-49, reprinted: "A Mechanical Solution of a Literary Problem", Popular Science Monthly, 9, (1901), pp. 97-105.

270 Calvin Hoffman, The Murder of the Man Who Was "Shakespeare", Julian Messner, NY, 1955, p. 139.

271 Mendenhall, ibid.

272 Hugh Craig and Arthur F. Kinney, Shakespeare, Computers and the Mystery of Authorship, Cambridge University Press, 2009, p. xvi.

273 Ibid., p. 64.

274 Ibid., p. 68.

275 Ibid., p. 76.

276 John Burrows and Hugh Craig, "A collaboration about a collaboration: The authorship of King Henry VI, part three", Marilyn Deegan and Willard McCarty (eds.), Collaborative Research in the Digital Humanities, (Farnham and Burlington VT, 2012), pp. 28–65. https://www.researchgate.net/publication/286942715_A_collaboratio n_about_a_collaboration_The_authorship_of_King_Henry_VI_part_t hree

277 Brian Vickers, "The Misuse of Function Words in Shakespeare Authorship Studies", www.etrap.eu > 2016-11-30-vickers-misuse

278 Vickers, ibid.,

279 David L. Hoover, "Authorship Attribution Variables and Victorian Drama: Words, Word-Ngrams, and Character-Ngrams", https://dh2018.adho.org/en/authorship-attribution-variables-and-victorian-drama-words-word-ngrams-and-character-ngrams/

280 Maciej Eder, "Does size matter? Authorship attribution, small samples, big problem", Digital Scholarship in the Humanities, 30(2) (2015a): 167-182.

281 Rosalind Barber, "Marlowe and overreaching: A misuse of stylometry", Digital Scholarship in the Humanities, Vol. 34, No. 1, 2019, Oxford University Press on behalf of EADH, p. 1.

282 Hugh Craig, "Contrast and Change in the Idiolects of Ben Jonson Characters", in Computers and the Humanities 33(3):221-240, May 1999.

283 David Hoover, "Stylometry, Chronology and the Styles of Henry James", in Digital Humanities, 06/05/2006, p. 79.

284 David Hoover, "The microanalysis of style variation", VL - 32, 10.1093/llc/fqx022, <u>Digital Scholarship in the Humanities</u>, 2017/04/28.

285 John Bakeless, <u>The Tragicall History of Christopher Marlowe</u>, Greenwood Press, CT, 1942, vol. 2., p. 289.

286 Ibid., p. 286.

287 "Among the echoes of a more familiar sort are such lines as

    The rancourous venome of thy mis-swolne hart

"In <u>Arden of Faversham</u>, which might well be an imitation of

    Swolne with the venome of ambitious pride

"from <u>Edward the Second</u>; while the line

    With mightye furrowes in his stormye browes

"resembles passages in <u>Tamburlaine</u> like "the folded furrowes of his browes" or "the furrowes of his frowning browes"; in <u>Edward the Second</u>, like "the furrowes of thy browes"; in <u>The Contention</u>, like "deep-trenched furrowes in his frowning browes" or in <u>Soliman and Perseda</u>, like "furrowes of her clowding brow."

"The words of the Queen in <u>Edward the Second</u>:

    Nay, to my death, for too long have I lived,

"find an echo in Mistress Alice Arden's repentant:

    But beare me hence, for I have lived too long.

"The lines are uttered in similar situations - in each case by an adultress who has connived at murder and is being led to punishment. Almost the same line appears in <u>The Contention</u>:

    Even to my death, for I have lived too long

"As another set of parallels, we have

    He weares a lords revenewe on his back
                    <u>Edward II</u>, II:704

    She beares a duke's whole revenues on her back
                    <u>Contention</u> (3rd 4to), I:iii

    She bears a duke's revenues on her back
                    <u>2 Henry VI</u>, I:iii. 83

    She'll lay her husband's benefice on her back
                    <u>Leir</u>, sc. 6

> I have my wish, in that I joy thy sight.
> Edward II, 151

> I have my wish in that I joy thy sight.
> Arden, V. i. 349

> Is this the love you beare your soveraigne?
> Is this the fruite your reconcilement beares?
> Edward II, 832-833

> Is this the end of all thy solemne oathes?
> Is this the frute thy reconcilement buds?
> Arden, I. i. 186-187

> Look up my lord. Baldock, this drowsiness
> Betides no good, here even we are betraied.
> Edward II, 1911-1912

> This drowsiness in me bodes little good.
> Arden, III. ii. 17

> Or like the snakie wreathe of Tisiphon
> Engirt the temples of his hateful head
> Edward II, 2031-2032

> That lyke the snakes of blacke Tisiphone
> Sting me with their embraceings.
> Arden, V. i. 156-157

> . . . a shaggy totter'd staring slave,
> That when he speakes, drawes out his grisly beard,
> And winds it twice or thrice about his eare.
> JofM, 1858-1860

> A lean faced writehn knave,
> Hawk-nosed and very hollow eyed. . . .
> A mustacio, which he wound about his ear.
> Arden, II. i. 51-56

> And witnesse heaven how deere thou art to me.
> Edward II, 463

> Heavens can witnesse, I love none but you.
> Edward II, 1112

> The heavens can witnes.
> Arden, I. i. 195

Bakeless, ibid., pp. 287-88.

288 Ibid.
289 Brian Vickers, ibid.,

290 Bakeless, ibid., p 70.

291 Note the similarity and proximity of this quote to the allegation in the Baines Note "That all they that love not Tobacco and Boies were fooles". It begs the possibility that Marlowe was either misquoted or misunderstood by Baines if/when he quoted Ovid in his presence. Also, the possibility that Nashe knew all about it.

292 M. L. Stapleton, "Marlowe's First Ovid: Certaine of Ovids Elegies", : https://works.bepress.com/mlstapleton/9/, p. 219.

293 Rev. Ronald Bayne, "Preface", Arden of Faversham, J. M. Dent and Co., Aldine House: London, 1897.

294 Rosalind Barber, "2 Henry VI and the Ashford Cage", Notes and Queries, September 2019, Oxford University Press, pp. 409-10.

295 Ibid.

296 Craig and Kinney, ibid., p. 76.

297 Kinney, ibid., p. 99.

298 Ibid., p. 97.

299 Jack Elliott and Brett Greatley-Hirsch, "Arden of Faversham, Shakespearean Authorship, and "The Print of Many," in The New Oxford Shakespeare Authorship Companion, ibid., pp. 139 - 181.

300 Mendenhall, ibid.,

301 Eder, ibid.,

302 E. H. C. Oliphant, "Marlowe's Hand in Arden Of Feversham, a Problem for Critics", The New Criterion A Quarterly Review Vol, Iv., No. I. January, 1926 P. 88-89.

303 Craig and Kinney, ibid., p. 39.

304 Ibid., p. 207.

305 Letters of Philip Gawdy of West Harling, Norfolk, and of London to various members of his family, 1579-1616; ed. from the originals in the British Museum with an introduction and notes, by Isaac Herbert Jeayes, London, J. B. Nichols and sons, 1906.

306 John Baker, letter to Notes and Queries 44.3 (1997), pp. 367–8

307 Rosalind Barber, The Marlowe Papers, St. Martin's Press, 2012, p. 416.

308 Peter Farey, "Arbella Stuart and Christopher Marlowe", The Marlowe-Shakespeare Connection, December, 2012, http://marlowe-shakespeare.blogspot.com/2012/12/peter-farey-is-co-winner-of-hoffman.html

309 William Bradley, quoted verbatim in the Coroner's Inquisition on William Bradley, Patent Rolls, 32 Elizabeth, part 4, C66/1340.

310 A. D. Wraight, In Search of Christopher Marlowe, Adam Hart, Chichester, Sussex, England, 1965, p. 118.

311 Baines Note, ibid.

312 Lawrence Manley and Sally-Beth MacLean, Lord Strange's Men and Their Plays, New Haven, Yale University Press, 2014, p. 47.

313 John Alleyn, quoted in Lord Strange's Men, ibid.

314 Albert Chatterley, ed., Thomas Watson, Italian Madrigals Englished, "Introduction", London, Stainer and Bell, 1999, p. xxxii,

315 Francis Meres, Palladis Tamia, 1598.

316 Nina Green, THE NATIONAL ARCHIVES PROB 11/118/441, 2010, p. 9, http://www.oxford-shakespeare.com/

317 Albert Chatterley, "Introduction", to Amyntas & Phyllis, the Pastorals of Thomas Watson, Marion Hopkins, Norwich, 2012, p. vi.

318 Mark Eccles, Christopher Marlowe in London, Octagon Books, Inc., New York, 1967, p. 64, citing K.B. 27/1335, m. 588.

319 Green, ibid.,

320 Dalya Alberge, "Shakespeare's Secret Co-writer Finally Takes a Bow … 430 Years Late", The Guardian, April 5, 2020, https://www.theguardian.com/stage/2020/apr/05/shakespeares-secret-co-writer-finally-takes-a-bow-430-years-late

321 https://en.wikipedia.org/wiki/1580_Dover_Straits_earthquake

322 Geoffrey Bullough, Narrative and Dramatic Sources of Shakespeare, Volume I, Routledge and Kegan Paul, 1966, p. 274.

323 Richard Paul Roe, The Shakespeare Guide to Italy, Harper Perennial, 2011, p, 8.

> "Benvolio: Madame, an houre before the worshipt sunne
> Peept through the golden window of the East,
> A troubled thought drew me from companie:
> Where vnderneath the groue Sicamoure,
> That Westward rooteth from the Citties side,
> So early walking might I see your sonne."

"Alone in the playwright's Romeo and Juliet - there and nowhere else, not in any other Italian or French or English version - has it been set down that at Verona, just outside its western walls, was a grove of sycamore trees."

324 Catherine Hatinguais, "The Sycamore Grove, Revisited" https://shakespeareoxfordfellowship.org/wp-content/uploads/TOX18_Catherine_Hatinguais_Sycamore.pdf, p. 95.

325 Roe, Ibid.

326 Thomas Watson, in Mark Eccles, Christopher Marlowe in London, Harvard, 1934, p. 130.

327 Mark Eccles, Christopher Marlowe in London, Octagon Books, Inc., New York, 1967, p. 134.

328 Ibid., p. 134-5,

329 "Prince: Come Capulet come you along with me,
    and Montague, come you this after noone,
    To know our farther pleasure in this case,
    To old free Towne our common iudgement place,
    Once more on paine of death each man depart."
    Q1, I: 1.97-101

330 Ibid.

331 Roe, ibid., p. 14.

332 Ibid., p. 18.

333 Ibid., p. 33.

334 Geoffrey Bullough, Narrative and Dramatic Sources of Shakespeare, Vol I, London: Routledge and Keegan Paul, 1966, p. 203.

335 Thomas Watson, Hekatompathia, 1584, "Introduction", Sonnet LXXI

336 Bullough, ibid., p. 205.

337 Ibid., p. 206.

338 Roe, ibid, pp. 35 - 61.

339 Ibid., p. 84.

340 "Some have opined that a traveler to the east wouldn't be using a north gate, that he should go out of an east gate, and straight east across the intervening flat lands to get to Mantua. These ideas stem from an unfamiliarity with the terrain and the long established route to Mantua or Venice, which first went northward for a time, before swinging east."
Ibid., p. 78.

341 "In examining the playwright's use of "wilderness," both here and in his other works, nowhere has he used that word as a synonym for "forest" or "woods," yet editors have done just that. Is this important? It most assuredly is, if the issue of the author's exact knowledge of Italy matters."
Ibid., p. 79.

342 "The accuracy of the playwright continues. In fact, the intervening distance in the sixteenth century from the north wall of Milan to the forest was about seven or eight meandering miles."

Ibid., p. 82

343 F. S. Boas, M.A., Ed., <u>The Taming Of A Shrew, Being The Original Of Shakes Peare's "Taming Of The Shrew"</u>, London: Chatto And Wlndus Duffield And Company: New York, 1908, p. ix.

344 Bullough, ibid., p. 61.

345 The play quotes, echoes and misquotes Tamburlaine and Faust twenty times. the following excerpts belong to Ferando:

1. ACT II., i., 131-2.

Fer. As was the Massie Robe that late adornd
   The stately legate of the Persian King.

(a) l Tamburlaine, III., i., 43-4.

Bass. And show your pleasure to the Persean
   As fits the Legate of the stately Turk.

(b) 2 Tamburlaine III., ii., 123-4.

Tamb.   And I sat downe cloth'd with the massie robe
   That late adorn'd the Affrike Potentate.

2. ACT II., i., 148-9.

Fer. Sweete Kate, the lovelier then Diana's purple robe,
   Whiter then are the snowie Apenis.

(a) 1 Tamburlaine, I., ii., 87-9.

Tamb.   Zenocrate, lovelier than the Love of Jove,
   Brighter than is the silver Rhodolfe,
   Fairer than whitest snow on Scythian hils.

3. ACT II., i., 151.

Fer. Father, I sweare by Ibis golden beake.

1 Tamburlaine, IV., iii., 35-6.

Soldan of Egypt. A sacred vow to heaven and him I make,
   Confirming it with Ibis holy name.

4. ACT II., 5., 156-9.

Fer. Thou shalt have garments wrought of Median silke,
   Enchast with pretious Jewells fecht from far,

By Italian Marchants that with Russian stemes
Pious up huge forrowes in the Terrcn Maine.

(a) 1 Tamburlaine, I., ii., 95-6.

Tamb.   Thy Garments shall be made of Medean silke,
Enchast with precious jewels of mine owne.

(b) 1 Tamburlaine, I., ii., 192-93.

Tamb.   And Christian Merchants, that with Russian stems
Plow up huge furrowes in the Caspian sea.

(c) 2 Tamburlaine, I., i., 37.

Orc. The Terrene Main wherin Danublus falls.

5. Act III., i., 49-51.

Fer. Were she as stuborne or as full of strength
As were the Thracian horse Abides tamde,
That King Egeus fed with flesh of men.

2 Tamburlaine, IV., iv., 12-14.

Tamb.   The headstrong Jades of Thrace Akldes tam'd,
That King Egeus fed with humaine flesh
And made so wanton that they knew their strengths.

346 Rev. Alexander Dyce, "Introduction", The works of Christopher Marlowe: With Some Account of the Author, and Notes, London, Routledge, 1876, p. liii.

347 Albert T. Tolman in "Taming of A Shrew", in <u>Publications of the Modern Language Association of America, Volume 5</u>, The Association of Baltimore, 1890, p. 245

348 Boas, ibid., p. xii.

349   Roe, ibid. p. 182
" . . . Vespasianio Gonzaga's guest's . . . gave it a second name, La Piccolo Atena - "Little Athens" - not because of its architecture but because of its immediate reputation as a hospitable gathering place for scholars and intellectuals."

350 Roe, ibid. p. 182-3

352 Roe, ibid."

352   https://en.wikipedia.org/wiki/Luca_Marenzio

353   The National Archives: Public Records Office, PC 2/16 f. 389.

354 David Riggs, The World of Christopher Marlowe, Henry Holt and Company, New York, 2004, p. 260-1.

355 Thomas Kyd, letter to Lord Puckering, CA June, 1593, BL Harlan MSS 6848, F. 154.

356 Burghley, William Cecil, Baron, The Execution of Iustice in England, for maintenance of publique and Christian peace, &c., Imprinted at London. 1583.

357 Riggs, ibid., p. 129.

358 Thomas Phelippes, letter dated October, 1591, quoted in Riggs, ibid., p. 277.

359 Ibid.

360 Charles Nicholl, The Reckoning, Harcourt, Brace & Company, New York, 1992, p. 230,

361 Riggs, ibid., p. 277.

362 Percy Simpson, "Unprinted Epigrams Of Sir John Davies", The Review of English Studies, Volume III, Issue 9, January 1952, Pages 49–62, 01 January 1952

363 Jenny C. Mann, "Marlowe's 'Slack Muse'", Modern Philology, Volume 113, No. 1, The University of Chicago, 2015

364 M. L. Stapleton, "Marlowe's First Ovid: Certaine of Ovids Elegies", https://users.pfw.edu/stapletm/MLSCMC.html

365 Riggs, ibid., p. 278.

366 Robert Sidney to Lord Treasurer Burghley, January 26, 1591/92, PRO SP 84/44.

367 Richard Baines, "recantation", reprinted in Christopher Marlowe and Richard Baines, by Roy Kendall, Madison, Fairleigh Dickenson University Press, 2003, pp. 25 - 28.

368 Philip Henslowe, Diary, Dulwich College Archive, MS VII, f. 4ff.

369 Lawrence Manley and Sally-Beth MacLean, Lord Strange's Men and Their Plays, New Haven, Yale University Press, 2014, p. 59.

370 Bryan Ellam, quoted by Charles William Wallace in The First London Theater, University Studies OF The University of Nebraska, Volume XIII, Lincoln Published by the University, 1913, p. 75.

371 Manley and MacLean, ibid., p. 62.

372 Burghley, ibid.

373 Riggs, ibid., p. 281.

374 Thomas Nash, Pierce Penilesse, His Supplication to the Devil, London, Imprinted by Richard Jones, 1592.

375 GLRO, Middlesex Sessions Roll 309, No. 13.
376 Eccles, ibid., p. 113.
377 Riggs, ibid., p. 297.
378 Honan, ibid., p. 288.
379 Katherine Duncan-Jones, ed., Shakespeare's Sonnets, The Arden Shakespeare, Bloomsbury, 1997, p. 152.
380 John Kerrigan, ed., The Sonnets and A Lover's Complaint, Penguin Classics, London, 1999, p. 22.
381 George North, A Brief Discourse of Rebellion and Rebels by George North, McCarthy & Schlueter, ed., D.S. Brewer, Cambridge, in association with the British Library (2018), p. 35.
382 The First Part of the Contention Betwixt the Two Famous Houses of York and Lancaster, Thomas Millington, London, (1600).
383 Dennis McCarthy, and June Schlueter, A Brief Discourse of Rebellion and Rebels by George North, McCarthy & Schlueter, ed., D.S. Brewer, Cambridge, in association with the British Library (2018), p. 32
384 Ibid., p. 1.
385 Ibid., p. 8.
386 David Riggs, The World of Christopher Marlowe, John Macrae, Henry Holt and Company (2004), p. 73.
387 Gabriel Harvey, quoted in A Brief Discourse of Rebellion and Rebels, op. cit., note 3., p. 4.
388 McCarthy and Schlueter, ibid., p. 87.
389 Ibid., p. 15.
390 Ibid., p. 27.
391 Constance Brown Kuriyama, Christopher Marlowe, A Renaissance Life, Cornell University Press, Ithaca, 2010, p. 116.
392 Riggs, ibid., p. 297.
393 Cynthia Morgan, "RECONSIDERING CORKYN v. MARLOWE", Oxford Journals, October 2012.
https://www.themarlowestudies.org/essay-morgan%20corkyn.html

   1. COURT OF PLEAS 1591-1592: William Corkyn v. Christopher Marlowe in placito transgressions.
   2. Quarter Sessions papers, Sep 1592: William Corkyn, Canterbury, tailor: assaulting Christopher Marlowe, gent in St Andrew's parish, Westgate ward 10 Dec 1591. Endorsed: ignoramus.

3. COURT OF PLEAS 1591-1592: Indictment of William Corkyn, Canterbury, tailor for assaulting Reginald Digges, gent in St Mary Breadman parish, Westgate ward 30 June 1592. Placed himself at the mercy of the court by pledge of Giles Wynston and evidently amerced 3s 4d

4. COURT OF PLEAS 1592-93: William Corkyn v. Thomas Elham.

5. COURT OF PLEAS 1592-93: Thomas Beane v. William Corkyn.

6. COURT OF PLEAS 1592-93: John Callowe v. William Corkyn.

7. COURT OF PLEAS, 30 Sept., 1594 - 25 Sept. 1595: William Corkyn v. Laurence Johnson.

8. COURT OF PLEAS 1594-95: Rowland v. William Corkyn.

9. COURT OF PLEAS 1597-98: William Corkyn, tailor, v. Henry Bromebrick, gentleman.

10. COURT OF PLEAS 1597-98: William Corkyn v. John Dunkyn.

11. COURT OF PLEAS 1597-98: Willelmus Corkyn quer. v. Nicholaum Colbrand.

12. COURT OF PLEAS 1597-98: Willelmus Corkyn quer. v. Willelmus Corkyn quer. v. Ambrosium Kynge.

13. COURT OF PLEAS 1597-98: Giles Golding v. Wm. Corkyn.

14. COURT OF PLEAS 1599-1600: William Corkyn as plaintiff. John Searing as defendant.

15. COURT OF PLEAS 1599-1600: William Corkyn v. Henry Rigden.

394 Morgan, ibid.

395 Gary Taylor, "Shakespeare and Others: The Authorship of Henry the Sixth, Part One", Medieval and Renaissance Drama, 7 (1995), 152.

396 R. B. McKerrow, "A Note on Henry VI, Part 2 and The Contention of York and Lancaster", The Review of English Studies, 9 (1933), 161.

397 Roslyn L. Knutson, "Pembroke's Men in 1592-3, Their Repertory and Touring Schedule", Early Theatre, Vol. 4 (2001), p. 132.

398 Philip Henslowe to Edward Alleyn, September 28, 1593, Dulwich College.

399 Manley and MacLean, ibid., p. 321.

400 William Camden, The Historie Of The Most Renowned And Victorious Princesse Elizabeth, Late Queen Of England. Contayning All The Important And Remarkeable Passages Of State Both At Home And Abroad, During Her Long And Prosperous Raigne. Composed By Way Of Annals. Neuer Heretofore So Faithfully And Fully Published In English, London Printed for B. Fisher, 1630.

401 Shakespeare's Christian name as written in his marriage bond, November 28, 1582, The Diocese of Worcester, Worcester, UK, x 797 BA 2783

402 Entry for Shakespeare's baptism on April 26, 1564: "Guilielmus filius Johannes Shakspere", Shakespeare Birthplace Trust, DR243/1: Baptismal register, folio 5 recto.

403 Shakespeare marriage bond, November 28, 1582, The Diocese of Worcester, Worcester, UK, x 797 BA 2783.

404 Marriage bond, November 28, 1582, ibid.

405 Catherine Duncan-Jones, Ungentle Shakespeare, Arden Shakespeare, London, 2001, p. 115.

406 Charles Nicholl, The Lodger, Viking, New York, 2008, p. 177.

407 Christopher Marlowe, All Ovid's Elegies: 3 Bookes. By C. M. Epigrams by I. D. At Middleborugh, n.d. (ca. 1592).

408 https://en.wikipedia.org/wiki/Marprelate_Controversy

409 William Pierce, An Historical Introduction to the Marprelate Tracts, Burt Franklin, New York, 1908, p. 220.

410 https://en.wikipedia.org/wiki/Richard_Harvey_(astrologer)

411 Gabriel Harvey, GORGON, or the wonderfull yeare, September, 1593

412 R. B. McKerrow, The Works of Thomas Nashe, Oxford, B. Blackwell, (1958a) V5, p. 102.

413 Charles Nicholl, The Reckoning, Harcourt Brace & Company, New York, 1992, p. 63.

414 Nicholl, ibid., p. 64.

415 A. D. Wraight, The Story the Sonnets Tell, Adam Hart, London, 1993, p. 137.

416 Rosalind Barber, "Shakespeare Authorship Doubt in 1593", Critical Survey, Vol. 21, Number 2, 2009, p. 89.

417 F. G. Hubbard, "Possible Evidence for the Date of Tamburlaine", PMLA, 33, (1918), 436-443.

418 A. D. Wraight provides the following gloss for lines 2 through 5 in The Story the Sonnets Tell, p. 135:

Parma hath kist: De-Maine entreates the rodd:

"The Duke of Parma, the Spanish Governor-General of the Netherlands, had recently died. The Duke of Mayenne contested for the vacant governorship, but failed to gain it."

Warre wondreth, Peace in Spain and Fraunce to see.

"Spain and France made peace to everyone's amazement, with the concession of a French port to Spain as part of the deal."

Brave Eckenberg, the dowty Bassa shames:

The Christian Neptune, Turkish Vulcane tames.

"Prince Eggenberg of Austria defeated the Turks with his united Christian forces against the Infidel, winning victories at sea."

Navarre wooes Roome: Charlmaine gives Guise the Phy:

"Henry of Navarre, now Henry IV of France, formerly the leader of the Protestants against the Catholic part of the Duke of Guise, had embraced Catholicism to bring reconciliation between France's warring factions. Charlemagne falls out with his kinsmen of the House of Guise."

419 V. F. Stern, Gabriel Harvey: His Life, Marginalia and Library, Oxford, Clarendon Press, (1979), p. 116:

420 Barber, ibid.

421 Ibid., p. 90, and note 23, p. 108.

422 L. Hopkins, A Christopher Marlowe Chronology, Springer, 2005, p. 122.

423 https://en.wikipedia.org/wiki/John_Wolfe_(printer)

424 Abraham Faunce, THE Third part of the Countesse of Pembrokes Yuychurch. Entituled, Amintas Dale. Wherein are the most conceited tales of the Pagan Gods in English Hexameters together with their auncient descriptions and Philosophicall explications, At LVNDON Printed, for Thomas Woodcocke, dwelling in Paules Church-yeard, at the signe of the blacke Beare. 1592, p. 1.

425 David Riggs, The World of Christopher Marlowe, Henry Holt and Company, New York, 2004, p. 299.

426 Wraight, ibid.

427 John Bakeless, The Tragicall History of Christopher Marlowe, Greenwood Press, Westport, Connecticut, 1942, p. 43

428 Edmund Malone, quoted in Bakeless, ibid., p. 44.

429 Katherine Duncan Jones, "Nashe and Sidney: the Tournament in 'The Unfortunate Traveller'", The Modern Language Review, Modern Humanities Research Association, Vol. 63, No. 1 (Jan., 1968), p. 3.

430 Ibid., pp. 3-4.

431 Edmund Goss, "The Life and Writings of Thomas Nash", Introduction to The Unfortunate Traveller or The Life of Jack Wilton, Charles Wittingham & Co., London, 1892.

432 L.S.Wheeler, "The Development of an Englishman: Thomas Nashe's The Unfortunate Traveller" In: Hawley J.C. (eds) Historicizing Christian Encounters with the Other. Palgrave Macmillan, London. (1998) https://doi.org/10.1007/978-1-349-14421-1_5

433 Nicholl, ibid., p. 58.

434 Akrigg, ibid., p. 38.

435 J. J. Jusserand The English Novel In The Time Of Shakespeare, Elizabeth Lee Trans., London, T. Fisher Unwin, Paternoster Square, 1899, P. 322,

436 Anna Whitelock, Elizabeth's Bedfellows: An Intimate History of the Queen's Court, Sarah Crichton Books, (2013), p. 279.

437 Terence G. Schoone-Jongen, Shakespeare's Companies, Routledge, Taylor and Francis Group, London and New York, 2008, p. 150.

438 Jonathan Bate, ed., "Introduction", Titus Andronicus, The Arden Shakespeare, London, 1995, p. 71.

439 Ibid., p. 76.

440 Jina Politi, "The Gibbet-Maker", Notes & Queries, 236, 1991, pp. 54-5

441 Constance Brown Kuriyama relates the interesting tale of Marlowe's generosity to Greenwood:

"The Corpus Christi Buttery Books, which record the amounts students paid for food and drink in addition to their regular commons, contain two unusual notations by Marlowe's name during the vacation term of 1581. The first accompanies a charge of 16 pence: "he left peetrs in commons being absent." On rare occasions, students might yield their places in commons to needy fellow students as a favor, and this first entry records one of these acts of accommodation by Marlowe. However, Marlowe yielded his place a second time only two weeks later, when another charge of 16 pence was added to his account with the notation "for putting Sr Grenewood in commons.""

Constance B. Kuriyama, Christopher Marlowe, A Renaissance Life, Cornell University Press, Ithaca, 2010, p. 57.

442 https://en.wikipedia.org/wiki/Henry_Barrowe

443 Ibid.

444 https://en.wikipedia.org/wiki/John_Penry

445 David A More, "Over Whose Dead Body--Drunken Sailor or Imprisoned Writer?", Marlowe Lives, 1996, http://www.marlovian.com/essays/penry.html

446 Bate, ibid., p. 91.

447 John M. Robertson, Did Shakespeare Write "Titus Andronicus?", Leopold Classic Library, 1905, p. 58.

448 T. S. Eliot, "Seneca in Elizabethan Translation," in Selected Essays, 1917 - 1932, New York: Harcourt Brace, 1932, p. 67.

449 Harold Bloom, Shakespeare, The Invention of the Human, Riverhead Books, Penguin Putnam, Inc., New York, 1998, p. 77.

450 Robertson, ibid., p. 58.

451 Bate, ibid., p. 85.

452 Leon Grek, "Performing Ovid's Metamorphoses in Titus Andronicus and a Midsummer Night's Dream", https://www.mcgill.ca/classics/files/classics/2008-9-04.pdf, p. 18.

453 Thomas Nashe, in Have With You To Saffron Walden, 1596, asserted that Gabriel Harvey wrote A New Letter of Notable Contents, 1593, an attack on Nashe, in part because he owed the printer John Wolfe "amounting to (with his diet) to 36 pounds" for publishing Pierce's Supererogation, 1593, an earlier attack on Nashe. Nashe does not split out the printing expense from the "diet", but according to Dr Robert Bearman, former Head of Archives and Local Studies at The Shakespeare Birthplace Trust, "a schoolmaster's annual salary was £20." https://www.bloggingshakespeare.com/shakespeares-money-come. Harvey was a "schoolmaster" of sorts; he was a junior proctor at Cambridge, a sometime lawyer and pamphleteer and if he was borrowing from Wolfe then twenty pounds would have been a lot of money for him and no less a consequential sum for Shakspere who, up to 1593, has no known means of support or saving money for printing costs.

454 Barbara L. Parker, Plato's Republic and Shakespeare's Rome: A Political Study of the Roman Works, Newark, University of Delaware Press, 2004, p. 51.

455 Feisal G. Mohamed, "Raison d'etat, Religion, and the Body in The Rape of Lucrece", Religions, 2019, 10, 426; doi:10.3390/rel10070426, p. 5

456 Annabel Patterson, Reading Between the Lines, Madison, University of Wisconsin Press, 1993, pp. 297 - 311.

457 Michael Platt, "the Rape of Lucrece and the Republic for which It Stands," The Centennial Review, 19, p. 76.

458 Mohamed, ibid.

459 Ibid., p. 6.

460 Robert S. Miola, Shakespeare's Rome, Cambridge, Cambridge University Press, 1983, pp. 24-25.

461 Penny Garnsworthy, Ibid., p. 8.

462 Christy Desmet, "Revenge, Rhetoric, and Recognition in The Rape of Lucrece," Multicultural Shakespeare: Translation, Appropriation and Performance, vol. 12 (27), 2015; DOI: 10.1515/mstap-2015-0003, p. 27.

463 Parker, ibid., p. 33.

464 Ibid., p. 48.

465 Penny Garnsworthy, summarizing Parker (note 20) in "Friend and Foe: Monarchism, Republicanism, and Civil Conflict in Rape of Lucrece," Working in English, University of Nottingham, 7 (2011): p. 4.

466 Parker, ibid., p. 51.

467 "The second edition of Venus and Adonis was published in 1594, only one year after the first edition. The speed with which it was republished suggests that the poem was popular enough to have already sold out or nearly sold out." https://shakespearedocumented.folger.edu/resource/document/venus-and-adonis-second-edition

468 https://dictionary.cambridge.org/us/dictionary/english/warrant

469 B. J. Sokol and Mary Sokol, Shakespeare's Legal Language, London, Continuum, 2004, p. 403.

470 https://en.wikipedia.org/wiki/Moiety

471 https://www.dictionary.com/browse/superfluous

472 NA, E 351/542, membrane 207d

473 Andrew Gurr, "Henry Carey's Peculiar Letter," in Shakespeare Quarterly, Johns Hopkins University Press, Vol. 56, No. 1, 2005, p. 52.

474 Andrew Gurr, The Shakespeare Company 1594-1643, Cambridge University Press, 2004, p. 2.

475 Mark Anderson, Shakespeare by Another Name, Gotham Books, 2005, p. 285.

476 Gary Taylor and Rory Loughnane, "The Canon and Chronology", The Oxford Shakespeare Authorship Companion, Oxford, 2017, p. 509.

477 Thomas, Sidney. "The Date of The Comedy of Errors", Shakespeare Quarterly, (Autumn 1956) 7 (4): 377–84.

478 Charles Whitworth, ed., The Comedy of Errors. The Oxford Shakespeare, Oxford University Press, (2003), pp. 1–10.

479 Gesta Grayorum, London, (1688).

480 https://erenow.net/biographies/shakespeares-theatre-history/22.php
481 Ibid.
482 Robert Greene, Perimedes The Blacksmith, printed by John Wolfe for Edward White, 1588.
483 Neil Rhodes, Common, The Development of Literary Culture in Sixteenth Century England, Oxford, 2018, p. 273.
484 The Comedy of Errors, Kent Cartwright ed. The Arden Shakespeare, Bloomsbury, New York, p. 261, n. 44.
485 Ibid., p. 240, n. 32-40.
486 Kent Cartwright, ed., The Arden Shakespeare: The Comedy of Errors, London, 2016, p. 353.
487 "According to J.J. M Tobin, Errors echoes further terms and phrases from Nashe; the character of Doctor Pinch in particular may allude satirically to Nashe's antagonist Gabriel Harvey." Ibid., p. 320.
488 Diary of the Rev. John Ward, A. M., Vicar of Stratford-upon-Avon, Extending from 1648 to 1679, Charles Severn, ed. (1839), p. 183.
489 https://discovery.nationalarchives.gov.uk/details/r/C32231
490 Lisa Hopkins, A Christopher Marlowe Chronology, Palgrave MaCMillan, Hampshire, 2005, pp. 139 - 146.
491 Geoffrey Bullough, Narrative Sources of Shakespeare, Vol. I, London: Routledge and Keegan Paul, 1966, p. 3.
492 Constance Brown Kuriyama, Christopher Marlowe, A Renaissance Life, Cornell University Press, 2010, p. 57.
493 March 15, 1595, The National Archives, Kew, UK, E 351/542, membr. 207d
494 F. E. Halliday, Shakespeare and His World, Thames and Hudson (1956), p. 22.
495 "Literacy" Internet Shakespeare Editions, University of Victoria, Friends of the ISE, SSHRC, (2014), http://internetshakespeare.uvic.ca/Library/SLT/ideas/education/literacy.html
496 Bill Bryson, Shakespeare: The World as Stage, HarperCollins (2007)
497 J. M. Pressley, SRC Editor Shakespeare's Source Material,1997–2018, The Shakespeare Resource Center, http://www.bardweb.net/content/ac/sources.html
498 Ameila Soth, "Her Majesty's Kidnappers", JStor Daily, December 17, 2020, https://daily.jstor.org/kidnapping-for-the-queens-choir/
499 Steve Mentz, Romance for Sale in Early Modern England: the Rise of Prose Fiction, Aldershot, Ashgate, 2006, p. 8.

500 Lukas Erne, <u>Shakespeare and the Book Trade</u>, Cambridge, 2013, p. 247, table 8.12.

501 Leonard R. N. Ashley, <u>Authorship and Evidence</u>, Genéve, Librairie Droz, 1968, p. 79.

502 Frederick Gard Fleay, <u>A Chronicle History Of The Life And Work Of William Shakespeare Player, Poet, And Playmaker</u>, London, John C. Nimmo, 1886, Pp. 328-9.
Https://Www.Gutenberg.Org/Files/46756/46756-H/46756-H.Htm#Page_327

1590	July 31	Richard Jones	A comedy of the pleasant and stately moral of the three Lords of London.
	Aug. 14	Richard Jones	The two comical discourses of "Tomberlein the Cithian shepparde."
1591	July 26	Richard Jones	The Hunting of Cupid, by G. Peele, M.A. of Oxford. "Provided always that, if it be hurtful to any other copy before licensed, then this to be void."
	Oct. 4	Mrs. Broome, widow of William Broome	Endimion, Galathea, Midas: three comedies played before her Majesty by the children of Paul's.
1592	April 3	Edward White	The tragedy of "Arden of Faversham and Blackwall."
	Oct. 6	Abel Jeffes	The Spanish Tragedy of "Don Horatio and Bellmipeia."
	Nov. 20	Edward White	The tragedy of "Salamon and Perceda."
1593	July 6	William Jones	The troublesome reign and lamentable death of Edward II. King of England, with the tragical fall of proud Mortimer.
	Oct. 8	Abel Jeffes	The Chronicle of K. Edward I. Longshank, with his return out of the Holy Land: with the life of "Leublen," rebel in Wales, with

		the sinking of Queen Elinour. An enterlude.
Oct. 19	Symond Waterson	The tragedy of Cleopatra.
Oct. 23	John Danter	The life and death of Jack Straw. An enterlude.
Dec. 7	John Danter	The history of Orlando Furioso, one of the 12 peers of France. A playbook.

503 Christine McCall Probes, "Senses, signs, symbols and theological allusion in Marlowe's The Massacre at Paris". In Deats, Sara Munson; Logan, Robert A. (eds.). <u>Placing the plays of Christopher Marlowe: Fresh Cultural Contexts</u>, Aldershot, England: Ashgate. (2008), p. 149.

504 Sonia Massai, <u>Shakespeare and the Rise of the Editor</u>, (Cambridge University Press, 2007), p. 82. Kirk Melnikoff gives detailed attention to Jones's career in two important essays: "Richard Jones (fl. 1564–1613): Elizabethan Printer, Bookseller and Publisher", Analytical & Enumerative Bibliography, 12 (2001): 153–84; "Jones's Pen and Marlowe's Socks: Richard Jones, Print Culture, and the Beginnings of English Dramatic Literature", Studies in Philology, 102 (2005): 184–209.

505 Melnikoff, "Richard Jones", 158.

506 Lukas Erne and Tamsin Badcoe, "Shakespeare and the Popularity of Poetry Books in Print, 1583–1622", Review of English Studies, 65 (2011): 45–6.

507
https://en.wikipedia.org/wiki/Doctor_Faustus_(play)

First entered as: 3914 The History of the damnable Life and deserved Death of Doctor John Faustus. Trs. [from the German by] P.F. 1592 A. E. White. I. O. - John Oxenbridge, dwelling at the Parrot in St. Paul's Churchyard.

508 (Simon Trussler, Dr Faustus - RSC Programme, 1989)

509 https://warwick.ac.uk/fac/arts/ren/archive-research/elizabethan_jacobean_drama/christopher_marlowe/dr_faustus/

510 https://public.wsu.edu/~delahoyd/shakespeare/locrine1.html

511 Baldwin Maxwell, Studies in the Shakespeare Apocrypha, New York, King's Crown Press, 1956, pp. 39 - 63.

512 Ronald McKerrow ed., The Tragedy of Locrine, Wentworth Smith, Supposed Author, Oxford, Printed for the Malone society by H. Hart, M. A., at the Oxford university press, 1908,

513 https://en.wikipedia.org/wiki/Wentworth_Smith

514 https://en.wikipedia.org/wiki/William_Smith_(poet)

515 Katherine Duncan Jones, Ungentile Shakespeare, Arden Shakespeare, 2001, p. 43.

516 Lukas Erne, Shakespeare and the Book Trade, Cambridge University Press, 2013, p. 69.

517 W. R. Streitberger, "On Edmund Tyllney's Biography", Review of English Studies, n.s. xxix (1978), 11-35.

518 https://en.wikipedia.org/wiki/George_Buck

519 W.W. Greg, "Three Manuscript Notes by Sir George Buc", Library, 4th series, xii (1931), 307-21.
Buc's note is quoted, including those parts obscured by the damage to the binding:
Char. Tiiney wrote <a>
Tragedy of this mattr <[w.sup.ch]>
hee named Estrild:<&[w.sup.ch]>
I think is this. it was l<ost?>
by his death. & now [?]
s<ome> fellow hath published <it>
I made dumbe shewes for it [w.sup.ch]
I yet have. G.B<.>

520 Benjamin Griffin, "English play 'The Lamentable Tragedie of Locrine' and Englishman Anthony Babington", Notes and Queries, March 1, 1997

521 Duncan-Jones, Ibid., p. 42.

522 Ibid., p. 43.

523 A. D. Wraight, Christopher Marlowe and Edward Alleyn, Adam Hart, Ltd., Chichester, 1965, pp. 65-108.

524 Robert A. J. Matthews and Thomas V. N. Merriam, "Neural Computation in Stylometry II: An Application to the Works of Shakespeare and Marlowe" in Literary and Linguistic Computing, Vol. 9, No. 1, 1994.

525 Thomas Merriam, "Edward III", in Literary and Linguistic Computing 15 (2000), 157–80.

526 Richard Proudfoot and Nicola Bennett, ed., "Introduction", in King Edward III, The Arden Shakespeare Third Series. London, Bloomsbury, 2017, p. 82.

527 by that sale
Price, Diana. Shakespeare's Unorthodox Biography, shakespeare-authorship.com, 2012, p. 305

528 Catherine Duncan-Jones, Philip Sidney, Courtier Poet, Yale University Press, New Haven, 1991, p. 148.

529 The Lady of May (1598), Note in original text, Samuel Johnson, Samuel Johnson on Shakespeare, J. and R. Tonson, London, 1765, p. 274.

530 Johnson, ibid.

531 H. R. Woudhuysen, ed., "Introduction", The Arden Shakespeare: Love's Labour's Lost, London, Bloomsbury, 1998, p. 3.

532 Richard Proudfoot, '"Love's Labour's Lost": sweet understanding and the Five Worthies', Essays and Studies, 34, 1984, 16 - 30.

533 Horace Howard Furness, New Variorum Shakespeare: Love's Labour's Lost, Vol 2., Philadelphia, 1904, p. 343.

534 Samuel Coleridge, Literary Remains, Collected and Edited By Henry Nelson Coleridge, Esq. M.A. Vol II, London, William Pickering, 1836, p. 107.

535 Woudhuysen, ibid., p. 6.

536 Glynne Wickham, "Love's Labor's Lost and The Four Foster Children of Desire, 1581", Shakespeare Quarterly, Spring 1985, Vol. 36, Number 1, Folger Shakespeare Library, p. 52.

537 A. C. HAMILTON, "Abstract", "Problems in Reconstructing an Elizabethan Text: The Example of Sir Philip Sidney's 'Triumph'", English Literary Renaissance, Vol. 26, No. 3, Monarchs (Autumn 1996), , The University of Chicago Press pp. 451 - 481.

538 Wickham, ibid.

539
   https://en.wikipedia.org/wiki/Penelope_Blount,_Countess_of_Devonshire

540 Fulke Greville, "Dedication", The Prose Works of Fulke Greville, Lord Brooke, ed. John Gouws, Oxford, Clarendon Press, 1986, pp. 37 - 41.

541 Love's Labour's Lost, Act 5, Scene 2, lines 315 - 16.

542 Duncan-Jones, ibid., p. 149.

543 Sophie Chiari, "Law, Discipline and Punishment in Love's Labour's Lost", Cycnos, Revel, 2015, p. 113-129, hal-01720076.

544 Chiari, ibid.

545 John Nichols, The Progresses and Public Processions of Queen Elizabeth, vol. 3, 1579-1595, eds. Elizabeth Goldring, Jayne Elisabeth Archer, Elizabeth Clarke, Oxford: Clarendon Press, 2014, p. 262.

546 Woudhuysen, ibid., p. 64.

547 "Be spite a sprite, a termagant, a bug,
Truth fears no ruth, and can the great devil tug."

Gabriel Harvey, Pierce's Supererogation, London, Imprinted by John Wolfe, 1593

548 Andrew Gurr, The Shakespeare Company, Cambridge, 2004, p. 302.

549 Woudhuysen, ibid., p. 71.

550 Ibid.

551 Robert Wilson, A. C. Wood, ed., The Cobler's Prophecy (1594), Malone Society Reprints, 1914.

552 Woudhuysen, ibid., p. 66.

553 Ibid., p. 46.

554 https://www.britannica.com/place/Warwickshire

555 Woudhuysen, ibid., p. 169, n. 138.

556 https://en.wikipedia.org/wiki/Antonio_Pérez_(statesman)

557 Felicia Hardison Londré, "Elizabethan Views of the Other", in Love's Labour's Lost: Critical Essays, Routledger, 2001, p. 333.

558 A. L. Rowse, "The Personality of Shakespeare." Huntington Library Quarterly, vol. 27, no. 3, 1964, pp. 193–209. JSTOR, www.jstor.org/stable/3816792.

559 Stephen Greenblatt, Will in the World, W. W. Norton & Company, New York, 2004, p. 13.

560 C. F. McClumpha, "Parallels between Shakespeare's Sonnets and Love's Labour's Lost", Modern Language Notes, June, 1900, Vol. 15, no. 6., p. 169.

561 Sidney Lee, A Life of William Shakespeare, London, Smith, Elder, & Co., 15 Waterloo Place, 1899, p. 88.

562 Geoffrey Bullough, "Introduction: Love's Labor's Lost", Narrative and Dramatic Sources of Shakespeare, Vol. I, Routledge and Keegan Paul, 1966, p. 427.

563 Jeffrey Brown, "Did Shakespeare Have Syphilis?", PBS Arts, Jan 25, 2013, https://www.pbs.org/newshour/arts/did-shakespeare-have-syphilis

564 Duncan-Jones, ibid., p. 224.

565 https://www.bartleby.com/213/1205.html

566 Sidney Lee, "The Elizabethan Sonnet", in The Cambridge History of English Literature, Vol. 3, ed. Sir Adolphus William Ward and Alfred Rayney Waller, G. P. Putnam's Sons, 1909, p. 288.

567 Daniel Cook, https://www.secondary-authorship.com/single-post/2016/06/12/shakespeare-vs-thomas-watson, School of Humanities, University of Dundee, Dundee, DD1 4HN

568 John Kerrigan, ed., The Sonnets and A Lover's Complaint, Penguin Books, London, 1999, p.24.

569 https://en.wikipedia.org/wiki/Audrey_Walsingham

570 Alastair Bellany and Andrew McRae, Ed., Early Stuart Libels: an edition of poetry from manuscript sources, Early Modern Literary Studies Text Series I (2005). <http://purl.oclc.org/emls/texts/libels/>

571 Bodleian MS Tanner 299, fols. 11v-12r

572 A. D. Wraight and Virginia F. Stern, In Search of Christopher Marlowe, Adam Hart, Chichester, 1993, p. 259.

573 https://en.wikipedia.org/wiki/The_Masque_of_Blackness

574 Memorials of Affairs of State from the papers of Ralph Winwood, vol. 2 (London, 1725), p. 44.

575 https://shakespeareoxfordfellowship.org/wp-content/uploads/John-Hamills-essay-on-Penelope-Rich.pdf

576 Kerrigan, ibid., p. 439.

577 Katherine Duncan-Jones, ed., Shakespeare's Sonnets, The Arden Shakespeare, Bloomsbury, London, p. 408.

578 http://www.tudorplace.com.ar/Bios/ThomasWalsingham.htm

579 Ibid.

580 A. D. Wraight and Virginia F. Stern, In Search of Christopher Marlowe, Adam Hart Ltd., Chichester, 1993, p. 250.

581 Lisa Hopkins, A Christopher Marlowe Chronology, Palgrave MacMillan, 2005, p. 146.

582 Ibid., p. 140.

583 Andrew Thrush, The History of Parliament Online, https://www.historyofparliamentonline.org/volume/1604-1629/member/walsingham-sir-thomas-1589-1669

584 Ibid., note 34.

585 Chan. Inq. P.M. Ser. 2, Vol. 226, no. 181 in the Public Record Office.

586 Thrush, ibid.

587 Ibid.

588 Kerrigan, Ibid., p. 343.

589 Katherine Duncan-Jones, ed., Shakespeare's Sonnets, The Arden Shakespeare, Bloomsbury, 1997, p. 366.

590 Park Honan, Christopher Marlowe, Poet & Spy, Oxford, 2005, p. 138.

591 Ibid.

592 Thomas Watson, Meliboeus, 1590.

593 http://www.tudorplace.com.ar/Bios/ThomasWalsingham.htm

594 Edward Blount, "Dedication", Hero and Leander. By Christopher Marloe. London, Printed by Adam Islip, 1598.

595 John Kerrigan, ed., The Sonnets and A Lover's Complaint, Penguin Books, 1986, p. 389.

596 Katherine Duncan-Jones, "Introduction", Shakespeare's Sonnets, Bloomsbury, 1997, p. 91.

597 As discussed in Chapter One, starting in early 1589 or thereabouts "one Morley ... attended on Arbell and read to her", as reported in a dispatch from Bess of Hardwick to Lord Burghley, dated 21 September 1592 (Blanche C. Hardy, Arbella Stuart: A Biography, Dutton, 1913, pp.64–67). Bess recounts Morley's service to Arbella over "the space of three years and a half". She also notes he had hoped for an annuity of £40 a year (equivalent to £11,100 in 2019) from Arbella based on the fact that he had "been so much damnified [i.e. that much out of pocket] by leaving the University". This has led to speculation that Morley was Christopher Marlowe, whose name was sometimes spelled that way (Charles Nicholl, The Reckoning: The Murder of Christopher Marlowe, 1992, pp.340–342).

See: https://en.wikipedia.org/wiki/Lady_Arbella_Stuart#cite_note-AS-7, Also Chapter Three: A Marriage Proposal.

598 Ian Donaldson, Ben Jonson, A Life, Oxford, 2011, p. 213.

599 https://www.poetryfoundation.org/poets/george-chapman

600 Auchter, Dorothy. Dictionary of Literary and Dramatic Censorship in Tudor and Stuart England. Westport, CT, Greenwood Press, 2001, p. 65.

601 Chapman, George, Al fooles: a comedy, presented at the Black Fryers, and lately before his Maiestie. Publisher At London: printed for Thomas Thorpe

602 J. W. Mackail, Essays and studies by members of the English Association Vol: 3 1912, pp. 51 - 70.

603 J. M. Robertson, Shakespeare and Chapman; a Thesis of Chapman's Authorship of "A Lover's Complaint", T. Fisher Unwin Ltd., London, 1917, p. 10.

604 A. D. Wraight & Virginia F. Stern, In Search of Christopher Marlowe, Adam Hart, Chichester, 1993, p. 259.

605 Sidney Lee, Dictionary of National Biography, 1885-1900, Volume 56, Smith, Elder & Co. (1900), p. 323.

606 Gary Taylor and Stanley Wells, William Shakespeare: A Textual Companion, W. W. Norton & Company (1997), p. 444.

607 Patrick H. Martin and John Finnis, "Thomas Thorpe, "W.S.," and the Catholic Intelligencers" in English Literary Renaissance, Blackwell Publishing, vol. 33, issue 1 (2003), p. 3.

608 E. K. Chambers, William Shakespeare, Oxford University Press (1930), p. 566.

609 Donald Foster, "Master W. H., R.I.P.", in Publications of the Modern Language Association of America, 102 (1987), p.44.

610 https://www.thefreedictionary.com/begetter

611 It was probably Audrey who Inserted the two Passionate Pilgrim sonnets, written before 1598, as numbers 138 and 144 which included sonnets from the 1605 period. It is almost as if she intended to point out that Marlowe had been making the same complaints about her for over ten years. Marlowe would notice the shift and understand her purpose.

612 https://archive.org/details/knightsofengland02shawuoft/page/n163/mode/2up?view=theater

613 Henry Ellis, Original Letters, 2nd series vol. 3 (London, 1827), p. 247.

614 Edward Alleyn, Letter from Thomas Bowker to Edward Alleyn, June 19, 1609, Dulwich College, London, UK, MSS 2 fol. 44v

615 Richard Knowles, "The Evolution of the Texts of Lear," in "King Lear": New Critical Essays, ed. Jeffrey Kahan, New York, Routledge, 2008, 124 - 54, 138.

616 Dennis McCarthy and June Schlueter, eds., A Brief Discourse on Rebellion and Rebels, by George North, D. S. Brewer, Cambridge, 2018, p. 52.

617 Howard Dobin, Merlin's Disciples: Prophecy, Poetry, and Power in Renaissance England, Stanford University Press, 1990, p. 195.

618 "lately two gentlemen poets made two madmen of Rome beat it out of their paper bucklers, & had it is derision for that I could not make my verses jet upon the stage in tragical buskins, every word filling the mouth like the fabunden of Bow-bell, daring God out of heaven with that atheist Tamburlaine, or blaspheming with the mad priest of the sun. But let me rather openly pocket up the ass at Diogenes' hand than wantonly set out such impious instances of intolerable poetry, such mad and scoffing poets that have prophetical spirits, as bred of Merlin's race."

Robert Greene, "To the gentlemen readers, health", Permides, the Blacksmith, John Wolfe, London, 1588.

619 Gary Taylor and Doug Duhaime, "Who Wrote the Fly Scene (3.2) in Titus Andronicus?", in The New Oxford Shakespeare Authorship Companion, Oxford, 2017, p. 67.

620 Ibid., p. 74

621 Ibid., p. 76.

622 Ibid., p. 75.

623 Ibid., p. 80.

624 Ibid., p. 89.

625 John Chamberlain, and Norman Egbert McClure. The Letters of John Chamberlain, Philadelphia: The American Philosophical Society, 1939, July 7, 1614.

626 Anthony B. Dawson and Gretchen E. Minton, eds., "Introduction", Timon of Athens, The Arden Shakespeare, 2008, p. 14.

627 Una Ellis-Fermor, "Timon of Athens: An Unfinished Play", Review of English Studies, vol. 18 (1942), 270 - 83.

628 E. K. Chambers, William Shakespeare: A Study of Facts and Problems, Vol. 1, Oxford, 1930, p. 483.

629 Dawson and Minton, ibid., p. 8.

Lightning Source UK Ltd.
Milton Keynes UK
UKHW010003201121
394181UK00003B/92